# Discrete Event Modeling
# and Simulation Technologies

T0212109

# Springer

*New York*
*Berlin*
*Heidelberg*
*Barcelona*
*Hong Kong*
*London*
*Milan*
*Paris*
*Singapore*
*Tokyo*

Hessam S. Sarjoughian
François E. Cellier
Editors

# Discrete Event Modeling and Simulation Technologies

A Tapestry of Systems and
AI-Based Theories and Methodologies

A Tribute to the 60th Birthday of Bernard P. Zeigler

With 169 Illustrations

 Springer

Hessam S. Sarjoughian
François E. Cellier
Electrical and Computer Engineering
University of Arizona
P.O. Box 210104
Tucson, AZ 85721-0104
USA
hessam@ece.arizona.edu
cellier@ece.arizona.edu

ISBN 978-1-4419-2868-9

Library of Congress Cataloging-in-Publication Data
Discrete event modeling and simulation technologies : a tapestry of systems and
AI-based theories and methodologies / editors, Hessam S. Sarjoughian, François E. Cellier.
    p.  cm.
    Papers presented at a conference in March 2000, Tucson, Ariz.
    Includes bibliographical references and index.

    1. Computer simulation—Congresses.  2. Mathematical models—Congresses.
    I. Sarjoughian, Hessam S.  II. Cellier, François E.
QA76.9.C65D54   2001
003′.3—dc21                                    00-69257

Printed on acid-free paper.

Production managed by Lesley Poliner; manufacturing supervised by Jacqui Ashri.
Camera-ready copy produced from the authors' Microsoft Word files.

Printed in the United States of America.

9 8 7 6 5 4 3 2 1

Springer-Verlag   New York  Berlin  Heidelberg
*A member of BertelsmannSpringer Science+Business Media GmbH*

# Foreword

The initial ideas behind this edited volume started in spring of 1998 — some two years before the sixtieth birthday of Bernard P. Zeigler. The idea was to bring together distinguished researchers, colleagues, and former students of Professor Zeigler to present their latest findings at the AIS' 2000 conference. During the spring of 1999, the initial ideas evolved into creating a volume of articles surrounding seminal concepts pertaining to modeling and simulation as proposed, developed, and advocated by Professor Zeigler throughout his scientific career. Also included would be articles describing progress covering related aspects of software engineering and artificial intelligence. As this volume is emphasizing concepts and ideas spawned by the work of Bernard P. Zeigler, it is most appropriate to offer a biographical sketch of his scientific life, thus putting into a historical perspective the contributions presented in this volume as well as new research directions that may lie ahead!

Bernard P. Zeigler was born March 5, 1940, in Montreal, Quebec, Canada, where he obtained his bachelor's degree in engineering physics in 1962 from McGill University. Two years later, having completed his MS degree in electrical engineering at the Massachusetts Institute of Technology, he spent a year at the National Research Council in Ottawa. Returning to academia, he became a Ph.D. student in computer and communication sciences at the University of Michigan, Ann Arbor. Upon graduation in 1969, he was offered a job as assistant professor within the same department, where he was promoted to associate professor four years later. From 1975 to 1980, wishing to expand his horizons, Dr. Zeigler joined the Department of Applied Mathematics at the Weizman Institute of Science, Rehovot, Israel. In 1980 he returned to his alma mater in Ann Arbor as a visiting professor, and a year later, he joined the faculty of the Computer Science Department at Wayne State University, Detroit, as full professor. During his last year at Wayne State University, he served as acting department head. Since 1985 Professor Zeigler has been with the Department of Electrical and Computer Engineering at the University of Arizona.

At the University of Arizona, Dr. Zeigler established himself as a cornerstone of the computer engineering program. He founded the AI & Simulation Research Group, which soon became one of the most active and best-funded research facilities within the department. Year after year, the research laboratory put out fresh Ph.D.s who were highly sought after by academia and industry alike. Since 1996 Dr. Zeigler had championed the establishment of a center for integrative modeling and simulation, which was officially approved by the Arizona Board of Regents in 2001.

Dr. Zeigler has been a pioneer, visionary, and promoter of research in discrete event modeling and simulation. Indeed, Dr. Zeigler's seminal contributions to the field, as manifest in the Discrete Event System Specification (DEVS), have fundamentally shaped the existence and evolution of system-theoretic, formal discrete-event modeling, as well as its application to a wide spectrum of areas in engineering and the sciences. His research contributions have been recognized by a number of professional societies including IEEE, The Society for Modeling and Simulation (SCS), and the Institute of Management Science (TIMS). Dr. Zeigler received Fellow recognition from IEEE in 1995, the SCS Founders Award — the most prestigious tribute to a simulation professional — in 2000 and, in 1984, the Best Book Award in simulation from TIMS for his book *Multifaceted Modeling and Discrete Event Simulation.*

Dr. Zeigler has authored four books on the foundations of modeling and simulation and on novel approaches in the area of intelligent systems and software engineering, which were published by John Wiley, Academic Press, and Springer-Verlag. In 2000, Zeigler, along with H. Praehofer and T.G. Kim, coauthored the second edition of his classic book entitled *Theory of Modeling and Simulation,* which was first published in 1976 by John Wiley and reissued in 1984 by the R.E. Krieger publishing company. The second edition, *Theory of Modeling and Simulation: Integrating Discrete Event and Continuous Complex Systems* is already seeing widespread acceptance as a pivotal publication serving the advancement of the fast-growing field of modeling and simulation. In addition to these books, Dr. Zeigler has coedited eight books including the highly influential series on modeling and simulation methodology published by North Holland and Elsevier. The longevity of use of Dr. Zeigler's publications speaks to the visionary and seminal nature of his scientific contributions.

Professor Zeigler's research continues to expand the frontiers of modeling and simulation theory and concepts. He steadfastly has been extending the frontiers and application of modeling and simulation to ever more challenging domains. The best measure of recognition for Dr. Zeigler's scientific work is the wide range of advances in discrete event modeling and simulation made by researchers in academic, government, and industrial institutions in the Americas, Europe, Asia, and the Pacific Rim, as documented in this book, where every contribution, in one way or other, has been influenced by Dr. Zeigler's research.

Professor Zeigler has been relentless in promoting and advancing modeling and simulation theory and methodology. Together with some of his colleagues, including most prominently T.I. Ören and M.S. Elzas, he has organized symposia around the world and cofounded the AI, Simulation, and Planning in High Autonomy conference. He has served as editor-in-chief of the *Transactions of SCS,* and was recently named vice president of SCS Publications, a position he was asked to fill in order to completely restructure the society's print and electronic publication offerings. To further advance modeling and simulation, he has served, and continues to serve, on numerous editorial boards of highly recognized journals in the field. He has been serving on National Research Council committees tasked with advising on the future role of modeling and simulation in the U.S. Department of Defense and the U.S. government in general. Agencies such as NSF, DARPA, and the U.S. Air Force, as well as various industries including Lockheed Martin, Raytheon, and Siemens, have supported Professor Zeigler's research.

With great enthusiasm, we, on the behalf of his many colleagues and students, look forward to many more years of outstanding contributions by Bernard Zeigler to the fields of modeling and simulation methodology in general, and DEVS theory and its extensions in particular. We eagerly anticipate continued deeper understanding of our world through the tapestry of modeling and simulation advances woven by Professor Zeigler, his colleagues, and students. We expect these advances to play a major role in the works of many other scientists and engineers engaged in the ever more pervasive expanse of information and knowledge-based science and technology.

Hessam S. Sarjoughian
François E. Cellier
Tucson, Arizona
April 2001

# Preface

This volume contains a collection of invited articles that were presented at AIS'2000, a conference held in March 2000 in Tucson, Arizona, organized in celebration of the sixtieth birthday of our colleague and friend Bernard P. Zeigler. Yet, this book is quite different from the ordinary set of conference proceedings. Every one of the invited speakers had been asked to write an article that would describe a piece of his or her research that was strongly influenced by the work of Bernie Zeigler. Hence, although the individual chapters have been written in isolation, they all follow a common thread, as the scientific work of Bernie Zeigler, during more than 30 years now, has focused on a single goal: the advancement of a theory of modeling and simulation that would bring us to a deeper understanding of the world surrounding us, that would allow us to communicate our knowledge of this world to one another in clear and unambiguous terms, and that would enable us to make predictions about the future, hopefully with the aim of preventing havoc before it would ever occur.

The volume thence represents a milestone on the way to developing such a universal theory, the *ieri-oggi-domani* of this adventurous route to mentally conquering a world that was physically conquered half a millennium ago; a milestone, not intended for rest, but for reflection, in order to refocus our efforts before moving ahead at undiminished speed.

Many of the articles have strong artificial intelligence components. The reason for this is twofold. First, intelligence is needed to understand the world, and hence, artificial intelligence is needed to make sense of its models. The models themselves encode the knowledge about the system under study, but artificial intelligence is used to organize that knowledge in a systematic and meaningful way. Second, as the world evolves, so should its models. Therefore, knowledge is not static, and artificial intelligence is thus needed to guide the evolution of models.

Managing computer models of complex systems is a difficult enterprise. It requires strict and rigorous adherence to sound principles of software engineering. While only few of the articles in this volume address directly and explicitly such software engineering related issues, principles, practices, and research, the observant reader will recognize that many of the approaches and frameworks discussed in this book are founded on well-known concepts, methodologies, computing frameworks, and practices born out of software engineering research.

In reverse, modeling and simulation concepts, techniques, and use have a strong influence on advances in both artificial intelligence and software engineering research.    Consequently, the articles presented in this volume, although centered on modeling & simulation, should be of interest and use also to researchers and practitioners of artificial intelligence and software engineering.

We truly hope that you, the readers, will enjoy this compilation of current knowledge about modeling in general, and discrete-event modeling in particular, and that you join us in our thank-you to Bernie for his dedication to the worthwhile undertaking of making sense of this confusing world.

Last but not least, we sincerely thank Xiaolin Hu for his assistance in typesetting some of the articles. We also wish to acknowledge our appreciation to Wayne Yuhasz and Wayne Wheeler of Springer-Verlag, New York for their encouragement and sometimes overstressed patience throughout the duration of this undertaking.

Hessam S. Sarjoughian
François E. Cellier
Tucson, Arizona
November 2000

# Contributors

**Chapter 1.** *Toward a Unified Foundation for Simulation-Based Acquisition*
Hessam Sarjoughian and François Cellier
Department of Electrical & Computer Engineering
The University of Arizona
Tucson, Arizona, 85721-0104, USA
Email: {hessam|cellier}@ece.arizona.edu

**Chapter 2.** *Why Engineering Models Do Not Have A Frame Problem*
Norman Foo
School of Computer Science & Engineering
University of New South Wales
NSW 2052, Sydney, Australia
Email: norman@cse.unsw.edu.au

**Chapter 3.** *Adaptive Designs for Multiresolution, Multiperspective Modeling (MRMPM)*
Paul Davis
RAND Corporation,
Santa Monica, Ca, 90407-2138, USA
Email: pdavis@rand.org

**Chapter 4.** *The Role of Uncertainty in Systems Modeling*
George Klir[a, b]
[a] 401 Manchester Road,
Vestal, NY 13850, USA
[b] Systems Science and Industrial Engineering
State University of New York at Binghamton
Email: gklir@binghamton.edu

**Chapter 5.** *Linguistic Dynamic Systems and Computing with Words for Modeling, Simulation, and Analysis of Complex Systems*
Feiyue Wang, Yuetong Lin, and James Pu
Department of Systems & Industrial Engineering
The University of Arizona,
Tucson, Arizona, 85721-0020, USA
Email: feiyue@sie.arizona.edu, ylin@u.arizona.edu

**Chapter 6.** *Towards a Modeling Formalism for Conflict*
*Management*
Tuncer Ören
TUBITAK-Marmara Research Center (MAM)
Informatics Institute (BTAE)
1 Hannibal Street
41470 Gebze-Kocaeli, Turkey
Email: tuncer@btae.mam.gov.tr

**Chapter 7.** *Systems Design: A Simulation Modeling Framework*
Jerzy Rozenblit
The University of Arizona,
Tucson, Arizona, 85721-0104, USA
Email: jr@ece.arizona.edu

**Chapter 8.** *DEVS Framework for Systems Development: Unified*
*Specification for Logical Analysis, Performance*
*Evaluation and Implementation*
Tag Gon Kim, Sung Myun Cho and Wan Bok Lee
Department of Electrical Engineering & Computer Science
KAIST
Taejon 305-701, Korea
Emails: tkim@ee.kaist.ac.kr, smcho@smslab.kaist.ac.kr,
wblee@atom.kaist.ac.kr

**Chapter 9.** *Representation of Dynamic Structure Discrete Event*
*Models: A Systems Theory Approach*
Fernando Barros
Universidade de Coimbra
Dept. Eng. Informatics
P-3030 Coimbram, Portugal
Email: barros@eden.dei.uc.pt

**Chapter 10.** *Timed Cell-DEVS: Modeling and Simulation of Cell*
*Spaces*
Gabriel Wainer[a] and Norbert Giambiasi[b]
[a] Department of Systems and Computer engineering
Carleton University
4456 Mackenzie Building
1125 Colonel By Drive
Ottawa, Ontario, K1S 5B6, Canada
Email: gwainer@sce.carleton.ca
[b] DIAM-IUSPIM 13397
Marseille Cedex 20, France
Email: norbert.giambiasi@iuspim.u-3mrs.fr

Email: {sujata|marefat}@ece.arizona.edu

**Chapter 17.** *Towards a Systems Methodology for Object-Oriented Software Analysis*
Herbert Praehofer
Institute of Systems Science
Systems Theory and Information Technology
Johannes Kepler University
Altenbergesstrasse 69
A-4040 Linz, Austria
Email: hp@cast.uni-linz.ac.at

# Contents

# List of Figures

# List of Tables

# Chapter 1

# Toward a Unified Foundation for Simulation-Based Acquisition

H.S. Sarjoughian and F.E. Cellier

*Simulation-Based Acquisition (SBA) has become an important framework for the development of engineering systems of high complexity. It offers a rapid prototyping capability for the design and/or evaluation of engineering systems, the components of which are by themselves complex systems that may be manufactured by different vendors. Using SBA, the designers of such Systems of Systems can verify that the interplay between the component systems functions correctly and reliably. The paper stipulates that SBA is enabled by the synergism of three technologies, namely Modeling & Simulation (M&S), Artificial Intelligence (AI), and Software Engineering (SE).*

## 1.1   Introduction

The average complexity of engineered systems has grown over the years at a phenomenal rate. Let us consider advances in the car industry. Modern cars are full of electronics that control everything, from the behavior of the brakes to the operation of the windshield wiper that turns automatically on and off depending on the current weather conditions. Even the servicing of the car is partly automated. When the car is brought to the garage, its on-board computers communicate via the Internet with the master computer of the car manufacturer to check whether the car operates as intended.

Engineered systems must be produced on an increasingly tight schedule. Let us consider advances in the building industry. A modern mobile home is delivered to the customer within weeks from the day it was ordered. Yet the house cannot truly be prefabricated. No two houses are ordered exactly the same way. There are lots of options, including the color of the carpets, the specs of the bathrooms, and the location of the electrical outlets. Depending on the state the house is to be delivered to and also the altitude where the house is to be used, building codes change, requiring a modification in the insulation, the inclination of the roof, and the length of the stacks. Furthermore, in line with modern just-in-time delivery, manufacturers no longer carry any spare parts. They no longer have warehouses to store them. Thus, even the parts are ordered exactly when they are needed, and it is expected that they will be delivered within days if not hours.

Such demands could not be met by the manufacturing industry if it were not for Simulation-Based Acquisition (SBA). There simply is no margin for trial and error in this process. When a manufacturer orders a part, he must know in advance that the part will function as desired, and that it will arrive at the time when he needs it. To this end, all facets of the manufacturing process are being simulated ahead of time, using models of parts that are provided by the part manufacturer, that can be downloaded across the Internet from the website of the part manufacturer, and that can be readily plugged into the overall models simulating the manufacturing process.

The scenario described in the previous paragraph is taken from a futuristic world. In the current reality, part manufacturers rarely offer models of their products, and if they do, these models are rarely in a form that they could be integrated easily and rapidly into the simulation model of a manufacturing process. Exact simulation results must more often than not be replaced by rough estimates that are based on engineering experience; overly optimistic assessments often lead to unforeseen delays and cost overruns; and many a company has already folded due to such errors.

It is the purpose of this chapter to outline some of the requirements for a successful application of SBA. It is the conviction of the authors that only a seamless synergy between three technologies: Modeling & Simulation (M&S), Artificial Intelligence (AI), and Software Engineering (SE) can create an environment in which SBA can be successfully employed.

Advances in areas such as Artificial Intelligence (AI), Modeling & Simulation (M&S), and Software Engineering (SE), have been instrumental in creating the technological era we live in. Significant recent developments in the theories and practices of AI (e.g., [15]), M&S (e.g., [6,14,32]), and SE ([13,22,26]) have already supported the development of numerous engineered systems such as distributed training simulators and multi-agent systems. Unprecedented technological advances necessitated by economic and geo-political globalization attest to the fact that systems will continue to grow in their complexities and interdependencies on one another. Let us consider training simulators in such diverse fields as medicine and warfare, where simulators demand realistic models for the engineered systems themselves, their environment, as well as interactions with the human users of these systems [3,27]. Sophistication of such systems, in part, can be attributed to two fundamentally distinct yet interdependent demands. First, systems are expected to interoperate, in a heterogeneous setting, in order to achieve shared objectives. Second, systems are required to exhibit sophisticated degrees of autonomy (or more realistically modest degrees of semi-autonomy). The capability of systems to behave collectively and autonomously in distributed heterogeneous settings promises to be one of the most difficult challenges posed to the scientific and engineering communities at large.

It is the purpose of this book to offer a kaleidoscopic view of the set of tools that will be needed to bring SBA to maturity. The vantages of the collection of articles included in this volume are manifold. Indeed this is to be expected given the breadth and depth of AI, M&S, SE, and in particular their interactions. Examinations of the articles reveal the essential roles that AI, M&S, and SE play not only individually, but also more importantly, synergistically. We note that perspectives portrayed by each article may be borne out of the reader's own interpretations or due to the authors' proclaimed perceptions and beliefs. These perspectives may, as matter of course and in their own unique ways, reveal some historical views, suggest the current state of knowledge, and/or foretell some elements of a near-term, and in some cases longer-term, futuristic information age landscape. These articles offer novel approaches –knowledge representation, reasoning, and/or simulation to name a few– suitable for addressing the needs of "Systems of Systems" based on the foundations and applications of AI, M&S, and SE.

We describe, in an abstract setting, the tapestry of the contributed articles from two specific, complementary viewpoints. The first presents a view of the landscape that has evolved from AI, M&S, and Software Engineering[1]. This treatment is centered on the discrete event worldview for reasons described in Section 1.2.1. The second suggests an approach toward systematic use of concepts, theories, and practices –rooted in a variety of disciplines and most notably AI, M&S, and SE– in building advanced systems as mentioned earlier. The approach has been called Concurrent Engineering (e.g., [8]), and more recently, Simulation-Based Acquisition [25].

## 1.2    AI, M&S, and SE: A Unified Perspective

From a conceptual point of view, the realization of distributed systems hinges on appropriate knowledge representation schemes, reasoning mechanisms, computational techniques, and evaluation strategies. A particularly elusive enigma for realization of engineered systems is their ability to evolve/adapt in dynamic environments. Challenges in modeling (e.g., model abstraction and validation), efficient computational techniques (e.g., parallel/distributed simulation), and realization of such systems (e.g., software design methodologies) are generally well known within AI, M&S, and SE. There are numerous overlaps in the research inquiries that are being pursued in each of these fields independently. In spite of these overlaps, the inquiries are not generally redundant, as they are based on the individual viewpoints and

---

[1]Our discussion is not founded on a rigorous treatment of a shared worldview on AI, M&S, and SE, as this is an open research inquiry.

idiosyncrasies characteristic of the three research areas. Yet, it is our conviction that these developments alone are insufficient to tackle the complex demands of SBA, and that only a consequent collaboration between researchers in these three areas, exploiting their synergism to the fullest extent, can bring SBA technologies to maturity. Stated differently, a unified approach is necessary to deal with the multitude of challenging issues such as model (software) composability, distributed execution, and elevating existing technologies to future higher grounds. Even under the best of circumstances, tackling the SBA problem will be a formidable undertaking!

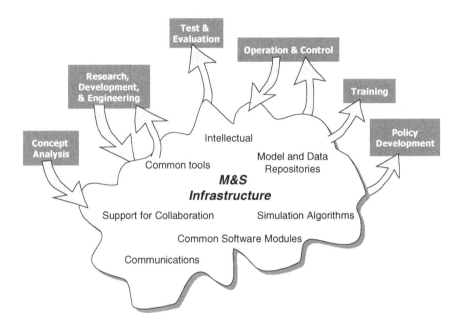

Figure 1.1: M&S infrastructure in support of SBA

Figure 1 illustrates various facets of modeling and simulation. It is easy to observe the need for capabilities offered by AI and SE in addition to those of M&S. Consider training systems where artificial intelligence techniques must be employed to represent a "virtual" patient being operated on in a synthetic operating room. During surgery, unforeseen events may happen, such as when the trainee accidentally perforates a blood vessel. The AI controlling the patient model needs to react to this situation, and drive the simulation such that it responds realistically to the incident by changing the patient's blood pressure and heart rate. Clearly, advanced Software Engineering practices are required to develop such extraordinary virtual training environments.

To bring together AI, M&S, and SE, it is imperative to adopt a general architectural framework and methodology. A candidate high-level architecture has been suggested in [31,24]. This architecture consists of seven layers (1) Network (the lowest layer), (2) middleware, (3) simulation, (4) modeling, (5) search, (6) decision, and (7) collaboration (the highest layer). Lower layers provide services for the upper layers, and higher layers can use and possibly subsume the roles of the lower layers. This architecture can be used for both simulation and system development. Adoption of a common architectural framework enables designers to study competing/alternative designs by employing a mixture of "simulated" and "performing" systems and therefore support migration from simulation design to operational design.

Based on the viability of such a layered architecture, the claim is put forth that AI, M&S, and SE are three distinct pillars upon which Systems of Systems can be built[2]. Indeed, our view stems from the fact that it is increasingly crucial for research in these areas and others (e.g., psychology and natural language) to unify in such a way that the whole is significantly more than the sum of its parts. In particular, a *modular*, *layered*, and *hierarchical* architectural framework is adopted as the scaffolding to unify the elements of these pillars. Clearly, each field must be valued and recognized in its own right, yet it is equally crucial to recognize that it is only through the strength of collective advances of the trio that there is any hope of developing systems that may withstand the demands described earlier.

The articles contained in this book offer a sample of initial, suggestive building blocks towards erecting the pillars of a unified framework and its associated technologies to support creation of Systems of Systems. The contributed articles are organized primarily from the point of view of their generality *vs.* specificity. Chapters 2 through 5 discuss concepts and theories primarily from the point of view of modeling and simulation. Chapters 6-8 present modeling and simulation frameworks and methodologies founded on a variety of system-theoretic, software engineering, and artificial intelligence principles. The remaining chapters present modeling and simulation approaches and techniques, such as discrete-event cellular automata, intelligent systems (e.g., agent modeling and planning, and neuron-based learning), and systems-based software analysis.

## 1.2.1   Discrete-Event Worldview and Distributed Computation

Distributed interoperability and autonomy are key attributes of Systems of Systems. The bottleneck in performance of a simulation of such a complex environment is the ability of the systems to communicate effectively and efficiently with each other across multiple hardware and software platforms.

---

[2] This view is reminiscent of the interplay of art, music, and mathematics described so eloquently by Hofstadter [17].

The demand for efficient interoperability can only be met by minimizing the need for communication between different systems. This can only be accomplished if different systems communicate with each other by means of discrete events. To this end, the authors postulate that the *Discrete-Event System Specification (DEVS)* [30,32] is the only meaningful approach to designing Systems of Systems.

Evidently, this does not preclude individual systems to embrace different M&S methodologies for internal communication. For example, one such tightly coupled system might represent a physical plant that, by itself, is composed of many different parts. It may be appropriate to represent that plant using a differential equation model, whereby each part is encoded as a separate software object. At compile time, the hierarchy of software objects representing the plant will be flattened, leading to a monolithic simulation code representing the entire plant. This system, which is loosely coupled with the other systems of the environment, will communicate with those other systems using a discrete-event protocol.

## 1.2.2   A Brief Account of Artificial Intelligence & Software Engineering

It is important to inquire about the role of AI in the proposed framework, and particularly its relationship with the discrete-event worldview. For example, are the knowledge representation schemes sought by the AI community fundamentally distinct from those of the M&S or SE communities? Does SE pose any constraints on AI and M&S, and vice-versa? Such questions, perhaps philosophical, are plentiful with expectedly a variety of different opinions and answers.

A major branch of AI research has focused on the knowledge representation problem in general, and the qualification and frame problems in particular. In addition to the wide interest and research activities focused on concepts and theories of intelligence and knowledge representation, the AI community has also had a keen appetite to address distributed computation and intelligence modeling. Yet, topics such as scalability, performance, and heterogeneity have not received as much attention. These and other closely related topics – openness, resource sharing, fault-tolerance, and architectural frameworks – have been under investigation primarily from the software engineering community. Indeed, software engineering has introduced a plethora of techniques and paradigms in support of software development (e.g., [1,4,9,19,21,26]) benefiting the AI and M&S communities.

Not surprisingly, the discoveries/inventions made in one area are generally founded on advances achieved in others. For example, advances in automated reasoning, genetic algorithms, fuzzy logic, and neural networks are incorporated into a variety of advanced modeling and simulation environments. Similarly, software engineering principles, practices, and environments have become indispensable in the development of M&S environments. On the other hand, software engineering tools employ a repertoire of modeling paradigms (Unified Modeling Language [28]) and AI-based techniques to support analysis, design, and realization of distributed heterogeneous systems.

## 1.2.3   Interoperability, Composability, and Distributed Computing

Many different modeling and simulation theories, methodologies, and practices exist for a variety of purposes and domains (cf. [7] for a sample of approaches and application areas). A simple way to differentiate among various approaches is to consider whether a system's structure is characterized as continuous or discrete. From a system-theoretic view, systems can be modeled using continuous-time, discrete-time, or discrete-event formalisms. Each approach offers features that are most suitable for addressing a set of demands. Discrete-event approaches are essential for a variety of systems that are event-oriented (e.g., enterprise resource planning, e-commerce, and semi-autonomous systems). Continuous approaches are most appropriate for the description of many physical plants, such as distillation columns or vehicles, the behavior of which changes continuously over time.

Use of these different modeling approaches, often in isolation, has served the needs of the M&S community well, as long as researchers were content to model and simulate homogeneous systems separately and in isolation. Only recently, the demand has risen for simulating heterogeneous complex Systems of Systems, often using a distributed computing environment. Surely, the previously developed modeling paradigms will continue to serve their domain-specific purposes. However, concentration on specific modeling methodologies has had a tendency to influence the modelers' mind, preventing them from considering facets of their systems that did not lend themselves to being described conveniently using the envisaged modeling approach. Consequently, these approaches often limited the scope of an M&S effort, and thereby created obstacles to dealing with Systems of Systems. It is important to note that, while each of these modeling approaches can be *augmented/extended* to enable heterogeneous, scaleable, composable simulation, the resulting tools will likely be ad hoc and unable to provide the broad encompassing foundation required for SBA.

With the emergence of large-scale simulations demanding a speed-up of several orders of magnitude, distributed computational techniques have become a necessity. Moreover, in recent years it has been realized that there are other motivations demanding distributed simulations. Specifically, due to anytime/anyplace access to (simulation-based) information, enterprise system modeling, knowledge (model) proprietary issues, and increasing need for combined logical and real-time simulations, the discrete-event M&S paradigm has become an attractive candidate for SBA [25].

Based on current and envisaged future simulation needs, the discrete-event framework promises to be the primary choice for unifying continuous and discrete modeling and simulation needs. Among the many approaches to discrete-event modeling and simulation, only the DEVS framework has been shown to embed all classes of dynamic systems. The DEVS framework lends itself naturally to computational efficiency, distributed computing, and component-based software realization such as DEVSJAVA, DEVS/HLA, and DEVS/CORBA) [2, 32].

The ability to support efficient distributed computation based on system-theoretic mathematical underpinnings is particularly promising in achieving model validation, simulation verification, and accreditation (VV&A). Due to the increasing complexity and time-critical nature of systems to be simulated, support for VV&A has become indispensable to modeling and simulation and more generally to SBA.

## 1.2.4   Continuous and Discrete-Event Modeling and Simulation

Since the 1970s, many approaches to combined continuous and discrete modeling and simulation frameworks have been proposed and developed (e.g., [5,11,12,14,16,17,23,29,30,33]). DEV&DESS [23] provides a uniform framework to model continuous and discrete-event models. With the discrete-event system specification, the dynamics of a system can be represented in terms of atomic and/or hierarchical coupled models. Input, output, and state sets as well as functions operating on these sets constitute atomic models. Functions are used to account for how the models are to respond to inputs, change states, and generate outputs. Hierarchical coupled models are used to synthesize complex models from simpler ones. These models communicate with one another through their input/output couplings. Both atomic and coupled models must have their input, output, and state trajectories being piecewise constant. To support larger classes of trajectories, two extensions of the DEVS formalism (Quantized DEVS and GDEVS) have recently been introduced.

These approaches further extend hybrid modeling and simulation of continuous and discrete-event systems. With the Quantized DEVS approach [33], continuous models, mapped into discrete-event descriptions at any chosen level of granularity, can be composed with ordinary discrete-event models. The Generalized Discrete Event Specification [16] has been developed to support the characterization of hybrid dynamical systems having piecewise linear input/output segments. With this approach, input, output, and state trajectories can be represented as piecewise polynomial segments.

Yet, in spite of the sheer generality of the DEVS approach to modeling, also the DEVS modeler is not immune to watching the world through a tinted pair of glasses, and interpreting what he or she observes using a limited, namely DEVS-indoctrinated, world view. The fact that a DEVS model can embed a subsystem that is described by differential equations does not adequately account for the needs of a modeler asked to provide such a differential equation model. The derivation of a set of differential equations describing a large electronic circuit or a complex multi-body system is a formidable task in its own right, a task that is not addressed by the DEVS formalism.

To this end, an object-oriented continuous system modeling methodology based on system theory was developed [11] and recently standardized [20]. Modelica [20] embraces many of the same principles that govern the design of DEVS. It also distinguishes between atomic and coupled models. Just like DEVS models, Modelica models are homomorphic, i.e., the interface of a coupled model is indistinguishable from that of an atomic model.

The most important difference between the two modeling methodologies is in the handling of inputs and outputs. Whereas DEVS models clearly distinguish between the two types of terminal variables, Modelica models do not. Terminal (interface) variables of a Modelica model are declared as terminal variables, not as either inputs or outputs. For example, an electrical resistor model may have two terminal variables: voltage and current. However, whether the current is input ($U = R \cdot I$) or output ($I = U/R$) depends on the environment in which the model is embedded, and therefore, the modeler should not be forced to make this choice ahead of time. The same model should be usable in both situations. DEVS models are based on the principle of cause and effect. An input event causes an output event to happen either immediately or later. Modelica models are based on the essentially acausal nature of physics (there is no physical experiment that can distinguish between a drunk driver driving his car into a tree and a tree driving itself into the car of the drunk driver). All variables are simultaneously dependent on each other.

Few M&S methodologies make a clear distinction between the underlying principles of *modeling* and *simulation*. Both DEVS and Modelica make this distinction. The purpose of the *modeling methodology* is to support the modeler in organizing his or her knowledge about the system to be described. The purpose of the *simulation methodology* is to apply input behavior to a given model for the purpose of generating output behavior.

Modelica is a pure *modeling methodology*. There is nothing in the Modelica specification that indicates how the model, once specified, is to be used in a simulation, or even, how the model ought to be translated into (interpreted by) a simulation code. Consequently, there is nothing in the Modelica specification that would prevent a Modelica model from being translated into a DEVS atomic model to be used as one monolithic node within a discrete-event simulation.

# 1.3    Simulation Based Acquisition

Simulation Based Acquisition (SBA) [25] is a relatively new and evolving initiative that has gained considerable attention within various United States federal agencies and business communities since its announcement in 1995 [10]. SBA was defined and adopted in 1997 by the Acquisition Council of the DoD EXCIMS as "an acquisition process in which U.S. Department of Defense and industry are enabled by robust, collaborative use of simulation technology that is integrated across acquisition phases and programs". Other initiatives similar to SBA have been promoting processes capable of minimizing cost, just-in-time delivery, supporting system evolution through reuse, and adhering to the principles of system engineering (e.g., [8]).

The expectations for SBA are to substantially improve the acquisition process through making early informed decisions, reducing risk, optimizing system performance *vs.* ownership cost, timely delivery, improving modularity/reuse, and supporting unprecedented information sharing among its stakeholders. It is important to note that the need for anytime/anyplace access to information is, arguably, the most significant driving force behind SBA. Based on this premise, SBA may be viewed as a means to seek a new breed of *what-to, why-to, know-to,* and *how-to* knowledge supporting the creation of Systems of Systems. Indeed, based on the need for anytime/anyplace information, a suitable SBA framework must explicitly enable creation, use, and transformation of *heterogeneous layered knowledge.*

Therefore, the success of SBA, similar to that of its earlier contemporaries, will hinge upon its ability to promote scalability, heterogeneity, openness, resource sharing, and fault-tolerance. Whereas such traits in their abstract forms are meanwhile universally accepted [4,13], there does not exist any accepted architectural framework to enable their realizations for SBA. Hence, based on the proposed unified approach and the suggested seven-layer architecture (cf. Section 1.2), a partial candidate architecture can be outlined as specified in Figure 1.2.

Obviously, it is beyond the scope of this article to undertake a complete exposition of SBA specification and architecture, and to provide a blue print for its realization. Nonetheless, the authors find it instructive to exemplify the proposed unified approach to SBA within the periphery of three layers of the seven-layer architecture (see Section 1.2). In the following paragraphs, a collective set of elements is identified and discussed for each of the three layers and their relationships among each other.

To describe Figure 2, let us begin with the modeling layer. In the previous section, the needs/requirements for continuous and discrete-event modeling were discussed. The application of SBA across the information technology spectrum demands modeling from the enterprise level (e.g., engineering resource planning) down to the elementary level (e.g., energy transportation). The simulation layer responsibility is to bring about seamlessly the overall behavior of a suite of models that may be characterized in different forms (continuous, discrete-event, and discrete-time). The simulation layer is to support execution of candidate composition of continuous and discrete models in suitable alternative modes using a variety of simulation protocols (e.g., message passing *vs.* publish and subscribe). Behavioral manifestations of models can be achieved via specialized simulation techniques executing in possibly both centralized and distributed modes. Adopting distinct layering of modeling and simulation promotes separation of knowledge incorporation from the demands of software engineering. Such separation plays a central role in achieving SBA, since it provides choice and flexibility in the selection of the elements of the modeling and simulation layers.

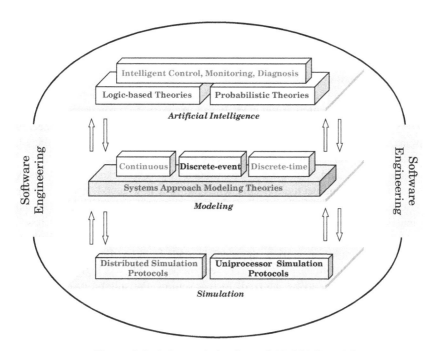

Figure 1.2: A Synergistic view of AI, M&S, and SE

The layer designated as Artificial Intelligence accounts for separation of modeling concerns. Rather than directly incorporating "intelligence" into the models represented at the modeling layer, intelligence features are to be represented distinctly. Intelligence behavior, such as monitoring, is modeled in a modular fashion in such a way as to be composed with the models from the modeling layer. It should be noted that the advocated separation of concerns, while seemingly rather simple, is difficult to accomplish in practice. The only known promising approach to facilitate the realization of separation of concerns is through the principles of software engineering.

The role of software engineering is emphasized through the ring that surrounds the three layers. The ring suggests the essential role that software engineering plays in the specification of the SBA architectural framework and its realization. As suggested earlier, scalability, heterogeneity, openness, resource sharing, and fault-tolerance traits are to be achieved by adhering closely to sound software engineering principles. Indeed, without exercising software engineering principles systematically and vigorously, the realization of SBA is likely to remain an unfulfilled dream.

It is our hope that the proposed unified approach and the seven-layer architecture lives up to its expectation and advances a united, broader, planned use of simulation assets (e.g., models, technologies, and methodologies) in accordance with the SBA vision.

## 1.4   Conclusions

Scientific and engineering communities alike are facing unprecedented challenges to bring about systems capable of supporting globalization of economies, cultures, etc. Simulation Based Acquisition promises to be the primary framework for realization of a wide range of futuristic engineered systems. Indeed, SBA is expected to be the catalyst in realization of distributed, complex, highly information rich systems by fostering integration of similar and disparate science and engineering technologies. However, existence of totally simulation-based engineered systems will require a new breed of engineering and scientific paradigms governed under an extensible, resilient scientific and engineering framework. Technologies developed in a synergistic fashion based on a unified framework will bring about a "world without borders". The authors argued that without a unified approach founded on artificial intelligence, modeling & simulation, and software engineering, SBA's highly regarded promises are unlikely to be realized. In this setting, the suitability of systems theory was discussed as the unifying approach to represent dynamical systems. Furthermore, the paper illustrates how Discrete Event System Specification and Modelica can support model interoperability and composability while supporting distributed modeling (different model entities can be created and maintained easily by different modelers) and distributed simulation (distributed computing across multiple heterogeneous platforms). Both modeling approaches also lend themselves naturally to the incorporation of a controlling artificial intelligence layer.

## References

[1] Andrews, G.R., *Concurrent Programming: Principles and Practices*, 1991, Redwood City, CA, Benjamin/Cummings, xvii+637.
[2] Arizona Center for Integrative Modeling and Simulation, Software Tools, http://www.acims.arizona.edu/SOFTWARE/software.html, 2000.
[3] Braham, R. and R. Comerford, *Sharing Virtual Wolds*. IEEE Spectrum, 1997, **34**(3), p. 18-19.

[4]  Booch, G., *Object-Oriented Design with Applications*, 1994, Redwood City, CA, Benjamin/Cummings.

[5]  Cellier, F.E., *Combined Continuous/Discrete System Simulation by Use of Digital Computers: Techniques and Tools*, 1979, ETH Zurich.

[6]  Cellier, F.E., *Continuous System Modeling*, 1991, Springer Verlag, xxvii + 755.

[7]  Cloud, D.J. and L.B. Rainey, *Applied Modeling and Simulation: An Integrated Approach to Development and Operation*, Space Technology Series, 1998, McGraw Hill. xviii+712.

[8]  Cutkosky, M.R., et al., *PACT: An Experiment in Integrating Concurrent Engineering Systems,* IEEE Computer, 1993, **26**(1), p. 28-37.

[9]  DMSO, *Runtime Infrastructure*, http://hla.dmso.mil/hla/rti, 1997.

[10]  DoD-5000.1, *DoD 5000.1, Defense Acquisition*, 1996, U.S. Department of Defense

[11]  Elmqvist, H., *Structured Model Language for Large Continuous Systems*, 1978, Lund Institute of Technology.

[12]  Elmqvist, H., F.E. Cellier, and M. Otter. *Object-oriented modeling of hybrid systems*, in *Proceedings of European Simulation Symposium*, 1993, Society for Computer Simulation.

[13]  Emmerich, W., *Engineering Distributed Objects*, 2000, John Wiley & Sons. xv+371.

[14]  Fishwick, P.A., *Simulation Model Design and Execution: Building Digital Worlds*, 1995, Prentice Hall.

[15]  Genesereth, M., N.J., Nilsson, *Logical Foundation of Artificial Intelligence*, 1987, San Mateo, CA, Morgan Kufmann, xviii+405.

[16]  Giambiasi, N., B. Escude, and S. Ghosh, *GDEVS: A Generalized Discrete Event Specification for Accurate Modeling of Dynamic Systems,* SCS Transactions, 2000.

[17]  Ho, Y.C., *Special Issue on Discrete Event Dynamic System,* IEEE Proceedings, 1989.

[18]  Hofstadter, D.R., *Godel, Escher, Bach: An Ethernal Golden Braid*, 1979, Vintage Books Edition, May 1989, xxi+777.

[19]  Javasoft, *Java Technology*, http://java.sun.com, 2000.

[20]  Modelica, http://www.modelica.org/, 2000.

[21]  OMG, *CORBA/IIOP 2.2 Specification*, http://www.omg.org/corba/corbaiiop.html, 1998.

[22]  Orfali, R., et al., *The Essential Distributed Objects Survival Guide*, 1995, John Wiley & Sons.

[23]  Praehofer, *Systems Theoretic Foundations for Combined Discrete Continuous System Simulation*, in *Institute of Systems Science, Department of Systems Theory and Information Engineering*, 1991, Johannes Kepler University.

[24]  Sarjoughian, H.S. and B.P. Zeigler, *DEVS and HLA: Complementary Paradigms for M&S.* Transactions of Society for Computer Simulation, vol. 17, no. 4, pp. 187-197, 2000.

[25]  SBA, *Simulation Based Acquisition: A New Approach*, 1998, Defense Systems Management College, Report of the Military Research Fellows DSMC.

[26]  SEI, *Software Engineering Institute*, http://www.sei.cmu.edu, 2000.

[27]  Sorid, D. and S.K. Moore, *The Virtual Surgeon,* IEEE Spectrum, 2000, **37**(7), p. 26-31.

[28]  UML, *Unified Modeling Language,* http://www.rational.com/uml/index.jtmpl, 2000.

[29] Wymore, W., *Model-based Systems Engineering: An Introduction to the Mathematical Theory of Discrete Systems and to the Tricotyledon Theory of System Design*, 1993, Boca Raton, CRC.

[30] Zeigler, B.P., *Toward A Formal Theory of Modeling and Simulation: Structure Preserving Morphisms*, Communications of the ACM, 1972, **19**(4), p. 742-746.

[31] Zeigler, B.P., H.S. Sarjoughian, and S. Vahie, *An Architecture For Collaborative Modeling and Simulation*, in *11th European Simulation Multiconference*, 1997, Istanbul, Turkey.

[32] Zeigler, B.P., H. Praehofer, and T.G. Kim, *Theory of Modeling and Simulation*. Second Edition, 2000, Academic Press.

[33] Zeigler, B.P., H.S. Sarjoughian, and H. Praehofer, *Theory of Quantized Systems: DEVS Simulation of Perceiving Agents,* Cybernetics and Systems, 2000, **31**(6), p. 611-647.

# Chapter 2

# Why Engineering Models Do Not Have A Frame Problem

N.Y. Foo

*The frame problem has occupied the attention of AI researchers in the logic of action in the last decade. To engineers who have had to cope with the modeling of dynamic systems, this sometimes seems to be a quaint obsession, and possibly an artifact of logic. This paper attempts to clarify the main issues so that engineers can understand why the frame problem is not contrived, but it also points out to AI scientists that as they search for efficient ways to deal with the frame problem, their solutions begin to look suspiciously like what the more sophisticated engineers have been doing.*

## 2.1   The Frame Problem

A central concern in logistic approaches to artificial intelligence (AI) in general and knowledge representation (KR) in particular is the *Frame Problem*. Its origin is a classic paper by McCarthy and Hayes [2] in which they alerted the AI and KR community to the potential difficulty of designing systems that automate reasoning about *change*. This can be illustrated, at the risk of some over-simplification, by a blocks world scenario in which we can specify the locations of uniformly sized blocks, their colors, weights, etc. Suppose we model the action of moving a particular block from location 1 to location 2 by retracting something like *on (A, loc1)* and then asserting *on (A, loc2)* from the logical facts that describe the state of the world prior to and after the action. On querying the system after the action there is no problem in getting an answer to where block A now sits --- if it is a logic based system in, say, Prolog, this is just a one-step resolution. However, such a system would also have to correctly answer queries of the form "What is now the color of block A?". In order to do so, it has to have some encoding of a state change rule that says intuitively "unless the action mentions color, all colors persist through the change". The apparent necessity to formally say such things is the essence of the Frame Problem. It is perceived to be a problem for a variety of reasons. First, most actions only have *local* effects, i.e., they affect only a small number of objects and their attributes. So, if one has to explicit mention all the things that are unaffected, the list will usually be unmanageably large (sometimes bordering on the ridiculous). Second, if soundness and completeness are desired for the reasoning system, not a single frame-like statement can be omitted. This can be an impractical requirement – the penalty for unawareness is very high. Third, part of the Frame Problem that is often isolated as a sub-problem called the *Qualification Problem* appears to be in principle unsolvable in the framework of a given ontology. As the details of this would divert attention from the central issues to be discussed, it is perhaps only necessary to describe it as the attempt to formalize the conditions for the success of actions, e.g., a block can be lifted if it is not too heavy. One can intuitively see how this is related to the "large list" difficulty as there can be an infinite number of reasons why a block cannot be lifted.

## 2.2   Models in Engineering

Engineering systems that have a notion of "state change" are modelled with no consideration for the Frame Problem. Moreover, even in discrete event simulation systems that are evidently close to the kinds of systems that AI engages, there appears to be no acknowledgement of the Frame Problem. Why is this so? Are engineers missing something, or is the AI community creating for itself a non-problem? I will try to identify the reasons for this apparent divergence and explain why there is really no conflict. As a preview, it suffices to say that engineering models have an implicit built-in solution to the Frame Problem and that this works because the principal role of such models is to predict and control, whereas AI models are designed to answer hypothetical queries for which the models might be used to interpolate, reason counter-factually, and explain.

For reference, the traditional state-space and discrete event models are now described in summary form.

The discrete time form of the linear state-space model is traditionally written as

$$q(t+1) = A\ q(t) + B\ u(t)$$

$$y(t) = C\ q(t)$$

where q, u and y are time-dependent vectors representing the state, input, and output respectively, t is an integer representing time, and A, B and C are matrices which convert the vectors into other vectors. If the system is time-varying, then A, B and C will also be time-dependent. The features to be noted about this model are the following: (i) it is Markov, (ii) each component of, say, the q(t+1) vector, is dependent on *some* components of q(t) and u(t), and most important (iii) the components of q(t+1) that are not affected by any prior state q(t) nor input u(t) components essentially have this non-dependence reflected in the elements of the A and B matrices. In the more general DEVS model below, these notions are brought to the fore in the definition of that class.

The discrete event model DEVS, whose formal specification reproduced below from the pioneering work of Zeigler [5,6,7] is a tuple $\{X, S, Y, \delta, \lambda, \tau\}$ where

i.      X is the external event set

ii.     S is the set of sequential states

iii.    Y is the output value set

iv.     $\delta$ is a quasi-transition function

v.      $\lambda$ is the output function

vi.     $\tau$ is the time advance function;

*with*

$\tau: S \rightarrow R+$

$Q = \{(s, e) \mid s \in S, 0 \leq e \leq \tau(s)\},$

$\delta: Q \times (X \cup \{\#\}) \rightarrow S, and$

$\lambda: Q \rightarrow Y.$

The intended meanings of the mappings are as follows. $\tau(s)$ is the "idle time" that the system is allowed to persist in state s. The pair (s, e) specifies that the system has been in state s for time e, called the *elapsed time* (so the remaining time is $(\tau(s) - e)$. In the definition of the quasi-transition function $\delta$, the symbol # may be regarded as signaling that no external event has occurred. Thus, $\delta(s, e, \#) = \delta_\#(s, e)$ where $\delta_\#$ is an *autonomous* transition function which essentially runs the system in state s until the elapsed time e reaches its "trigger time" $\tau(s)$, at which time a transition is made to another sequential state $(s_1, 0)$ with its elapsed time reset to 0. This sequential state $(s_1, 0)$ will have its own $\tau(s_1)$ that marks how far into the future another autonomous transition will be made if no external inputs are received. The "end" of a cascade of such transitions can be signified by letting $\tau(s_1)$ be infinity (hence the extended reals in the definition), meaning that the system state is at rest in s until an external input arrives. However, if the system is in sequential state (s, e) and a new (external) input x arrives, the system moves to a new sequential state $(s', 0)$ defined by $\delta(s, e, x)$. The new state $(s', 0)$ may be quite complex, depending on the system structure.

A classic visualization of a system that is easily captured by DEVS is that of a tap that can fill the top basin of a tower of basins, each of which can overflow into the one below. The action of opening or closing the tap are external inputs. The overflow of one basin starts a new state s, and it immediately (its $\tau$ (s) is 0) triggers another state $s_1$ that is the beginning of the filling of basin below it, with its $\tau$ ($s_1$) value determined by its volumetric capacity and filling rate. Once the bottom basin overflows onto the ground, the system stability with infinite $\tau$ value until the tap is turned off.

It is important that we understand the intuitions behind the DEVS model as I intend to relate it to approaches to the Frame and Qualification Problems. Zeigler's seminal contributions to these intuitions are four-fold. The first is essentially formalized as above, and involves the insight that in order to model the dynamics of discrete event systems one has to draw a *system boundary* that clearly separates the external from the internal changes. The external ones are the "true inputs" that are encoded as the space X. An internal one may be regarded as natural flow of a process that was triggered off earlier, which is why it is represented as an autonomous transition. Further, these autonomous transitions can "cascade", each one triggering another in succession, and they can even model a cascade that is *instantaneous* by the device of letting the $\tau$ (s) be 0. The second is his notion of *pre-emption*. Suppose the system is currently undergoing an internal (autonomous) transition, and an external input x arrives. The possibility that this input can interrupt the on-going internal transition, reshape its course, etc., is modelled as the new $\delta$ (s, e, x). The new input *pre-empts* the autonomous transition that would otherwise proceed to its conclusion as determined by the time $\tau$ (s). The third insight is that all state, input and output descriptions that are intelligible to humans are *co-ordinatized*, giving rise to the entities engineers call "state variables", "input lines", etc., and the AI community calls "fluents". In the standard state-space specification of dynamics above, the co-ordinates are already encoded as the indices of the state vectors. In AI, knowledge-base fluents are exactly the entities or properties of objects, beliefs of agents, occurrence of events, etc., that take either Boolean or set values. Zeigler had an elegant abstraction for these --- he defined a coordinatization as an *injection* of spaces into a Cartesian product. Each component of the Cartesian product is a state-variable, a fluent, etc., and can be as complex as one wishes. For instance, a fluent f can be a map from an object O into a set of colors {red, blue, white}. Likewise, a state variable $q_i$ can be a map from a wire i to a voltage. His fourth insight is a system-theoretic descendent of the notion of *causality*. It is that system components may have both *influencers* and *effects*, and these are specifiable using the co-ordinates described above. In AI, the representation of influence is by explicit causal rules, typically encoded as a directional connective between fluents. Actions trigger off initial effects called *post-conditions*, and these in turn may have *ramifications* that are often computed by using the causal rules to propagate further changes.

## 2.3    Models in AI

In the previous section some comparisons and analogies between engineering and AI models were made. In this section we will sharpen the discussion to the point where the differences will emerge. There is perhaps no better way to do this initially than by considering a popular AI "scenario", outlining how AI models it, and then considering what an engineering model might look like.

A system that has vexed AI theorists and yet stimulated a fair bit of research is the *Yale Shooting Problem* (YSP). In this scenario, there are three actions (events), *load, wait and shoot* executed in that sequence which refer to what is being done to a gun. In the *shoot* action the gun is supposed to be aimed at a turkey. The action rules specified in the style of dynamic *[load]$\rightarrow$ loaded*, and *loaded$\rightarrow$ [shoot]¯alive* Recall that dynamic logic formulas of the forms [A]p and p$\rightarrow$ [A]q mean respectively "after action A, p holds" and "if p holds now, then after action A, q will hold". The initial state is *{alive,¯loaded}*. There are two trajectories or state sequences that are consistent with the rules, viz.,

(a)    *{( alive,¯loaded), (alive, loaded), (alive,¯loaded), (alive)}*

(b)    *{( alive, ¯loaded), (alive, loaded), (alive, loaded), (¯alive)}*

The trajectories have four states because there is an initial state and three subsequent actions. In (a) the "no-op" *wait* seems to have resulted in the unloading of the gun, contrary to the notion that since no effects were specified for *wait*, nothing should have changed --- as in the case of the trajectory (b) which is therefore the more intuitive one. In AI, the reason why (a) is even considered is because the role of *logic* is taken very seriously. If a dynamic system is specified in a logic, then the behavior of the system should ideally be deducible in a calculus for that logic, or at least accountable by the *model theory* of the logic. Thus, every model of the specification is a viable one, unless ruled out by some other consideration. It can be verified that in fact both trajectories (a) and (b) satisfy the action specification, and moreover, each has the minimal (measured by set inclusion) number of fluent changes. The YSP was a scenario invented by Hanks and McDermott [1] to illustrate that even in a logic with the added requirement that the number of changes should be minimized (this policy is called "circumscription" [3]) there may be unintuitive models like (a) that survive.

It is a fair question, certain to be raised by engineers, as to why we should bother with logic when algebra in some form, as in state variable or DEVS specifications seem to suffice. There are a number of answers to this that I will elaborate in the following subsections.

## 2.3.1  Prediction, Abduction and Interpolation

Engineering specifications are primarily directed toward *prediction* --- i.e., given an initial state and some inputs what are resultant state trajectories. Moreover, they are typically *deterministic* and *completely specified*. Even in the case of stochastic systems, the calculation of probability vectors is a deterministic process. In the YSP, the *wait* action is apparently *non-deterministic*, and some states are incompletely specified, e.g., the last one where the logical value of *loaded* is a "don't care" condition. However the non-determinism arises not because any model is actually non-deterministic (none are, as can be seen from trajectories (a) and (b) above), but because we may choose a family of models as the "answer" to queries, hence have subsets of states as possibilities after a given action sequence. Incomplete specification is another consequence of the logic --- some queries may not have a definite answer because competing models yield contradictory answers. While it is not explicit in our discussion, the YSP specification is amenable to two other forms of queries other than prediction. It is possible to make *abductions* and *interpolations*. Abduction is a kind of backward prediction, sometimes also called post-diction, and is informally understood as *explanation*. Suppose you are told that at the end of the action sequence that the turkey is still alive. Then you can deduce that the *wait* action must have caused the gun to be unloaded. This is an abduction from an observation. An interpolation is a "filling in" of a partial trajectory. Again, we can use the YSP to illustrate it. Suppose the partial trajectory is *{(alive, ⁻loaded), (?), (alive, loaded), (⁻alive)}* where you are told that the missing state marked by *(?)* is to be inferred. Then from the models of the logical specification you can deduce that *(?)* is in fact *(alive, loaded)*. Similarly, if you are told that the fourth state is *(alive)*, then by consulting the admissible models you can infer that in the third state after the *wait* action, the gun had been mysteriously unloaded. This latter inference is the essence of a *diagnosis* to explain something that is unexpected, in other words an explanation or abduction. Ostensibly, therefore, it would seem that logic-based AI models are more versatile. To look ahead, I would say "yes", but this comes at a price. In an engineering encoding of the YSP, the non-determinism of *wait* will force a stochastic specification in which the outcome *loaded* or ¬*loaded* will be equally likely. Faced with the observation as before that the turkey is alive at the end, there are two alternatives. One, we could repeatedly *simulate* the stochastic system to identify or isolate those runs (trajectories) that result in the observation. Or two, we could *reason about or analyze* the stochastic specification to arrive at the same conclusion. It turns out that alternative two is in effect using *logic*, albeit informally, and the AI logic approach is a formalization of it without recourse to probability.

## 2.3.2 Inertia

Re-consider the hypothetical stochastic engineering specification of the YSP. How does one assign the probabilities to the two outcomes of the *wait* action? One may choose to reason informally thus: "Unless something very strange happens, just waiting will have no effect on the values of fluents". On this basis one may then bias heavily one probabilistic transition against the other. This bias is justified by an *inertia* rule, which is really a meta-rule that says unless an action is known to have some effect on fluent, we may assume it does not. Since the *wait* action has no rule associated with it, the inertia of *loaded* or *unloaded* with respect to it can be assumed. What logic does is to make this assumption explicit by the introduction of a frame axiom.

In engineering systems, the inertia rule is *encoded* into the state-transition definitions and calculations. To see how effective this encoding is, I will outline a very new approach due to Thielscher [4] in the logics of action that avoids many of the difficulties of the frame problem. What is remarkable is that this approach actually parallels that in DEVS, and to what extent it merely re-expresses the same ideas and procedures is something you may evaluate after the similarities below. Perhaps the best way to describe Thielscher's approach is by an example. Consider the following scenario, simplified from his paper. There are two people Arthur and Neville, and there are two kinds of drink, Soy and Milk. Neville is the drink mixer. Arthur is lactose-intolerant, so he can safely drink Soy, but not Milk. If he drinks Milk, he becomes -*Well*, i.e., unwell or sick. Otherwise he is Well. The action of interest is Neville mixing the Soy and the Milk in some state s, denoted by *Do (Mix(Neville, Soy, Milk),s)* and the mixed (contaminated) Milk is denoted by *Mixed(Milk)*. If a state of this system is *state(s)*, the key idea is to represent it as a *term* of a semigroup, e.g., *Well(Arthur) ∘ Well(Neville) ∘ -Mixed(Milk)*, meaning that both Arthur and Neville are Well, and the Milk is not mixed with Soy. This implies that an atomic term such as *Well(Neville)* can be regarded as a function from the space of Names to a *Term* space. A term like -*Mixed(Milk)* is considered atomic in its own right. Moreover, the term composition operator ∘ is an associative, commutative binary map from *Term×Term* to *Term*. The cleverness in this representation evidently resides in some key features that alleviate the frame problem. The first is that state information need only be partial, and achieved by the device of introducing some logic: $\exists z.\ state(s) = f{\circ}z$ to mean that in state s, the atomic term f is true. The "trailing" z is supposed to permit arbitrary extra state information. The second, to be elaborated below, is its avoidance of the need to compute which things remain unchanged. Officially, state(s) is just another term defined to be equal to (or in a computational sense, re-writable as) $f{\circ}\ z$. The term *Do(Mix(Neville, Soy, Milk),s)* is a nested term with *Mix* being the inner function and *Do* the outer one. The effect of this mixing operation on the initial state *Well(Arthur) ∘Well(Neville , -Mixed(Milk)* is intuitively to cause the Milk to be Mixed, i.e., change -*Mixed(Milk)* to *Mixed(Milk)*, and *all else is to be unchanged.* The italicised part is the inertial requirement. How this change is handled in Thielscher's approach is via general state-update axioms, the specific instance of which is

$state(s)= Well(Arthur) \circ Well(Neville) \circ -Mixed(Milk) \circ z \; ^\wedge$
$state(s1) \circ -Mixed(Milk)= state(s) \; ^\wedge$
$state(Do(Mix(Neville, Soy, Milk), s))= state(s1) \circ Mixed \,(Milk)$

The second of these conjuncts is just a neat way of saying "remove – *Mixed(Milk)* from state s to give state s1", since an axiom in the system enforces at most one occurrence of any atomic term in any expression. The *inertia* is therefore handled merely by "carrying forward" the unaffected terms *Well(Arthur) $\circ$ Well(Neville)* and the trailing z in the *term re-writing* from state to state. The identification of which terms an action *affect* is encoded in the above state-update formula, as well as which are the *influencing* terms.

From the state after s1, if an action *Do (Drink (Arthur, Milk), s1)* is performed, let us assume that another state-update axiom instance will result in *Well(Arthur)* to be removed and replaced by *-Well(Arthur)*. Assume then that the next step *automatically* follows whenever someone is unwell, that he/she will rest, and that further the effect of resting is to recover. In Thielscher's approach these are achieved by *causal rules*, instances of which are:

$Causes\,(state,\,effects,\,new\text{-}state,\,new\text{-}effects) \equiv$
$\exists z\; effects = -Well(Arthur) \circ z \wedge$
$new\text{-}state = state \circ Rest(Arthur) \wedge$
$new\text{-}effects = effects \circ Recover(Arthur)$

$Causes\,(state,\,effects,\,new\text{-}state,\,new\text{-}effects) \equiv$
$\exists z\; effects = Recover(Arthur) \circ z \wedge$
$new\text{-}state \circ -Well(Arthur) = state \wedge$
$new\text{-}effects = effects \circ Well(Arthur)$

Technically, these automatic state-updates are called *ramifications*. The consistency of states depends entirely on the constraint that for no fluent f is it the case that both f and -f are part of any state term. This can be guaranteed in either of two ways. One is by ensuring that the both the state-update axioms and the causal rules preserve consistency, e.g., by deleting f before adding -f. The other is more subtle, and depends on removing the need for negated fluents like -f to be atomic. Instead, we may define -t to be the "absence" of t in state s, i.e. we just negate the earlier "true-if-present" definition $\exists z. state(s) = f \circ z$ to obtain the "false-if-absent" definition of -f via $\forall z. state(s) \neq f \circ z$. Computationally, the latter is realized efficiently in logic programming as a negation-as-failure.

Now we are ready to display the parallels between this logic of actions and DEVS.

## 2.3.3  Parallels

Perhaps the easiest way to indicate the parallels is to show how one might translate the Thielscher system (abbreviate it to TS) into DEVS. I will do this informally, postponing the details to a future paper in which the notion of inertia will be properly formalized, and the translation below is made rigorous.

A typical TS state is a complex term consisting of fluents joined together by the composition operator $\circ$, followed by a "don't know" portion represented by the variable $z$. Since the DEVS formalism is traditionally associated with a sequential state set that is a cartesian product, the easiest way to translate a TS state of the form $f_i \circ f_j \circ z$ into a vector in the cartesian product is to have that vector take a value 1 in the $i$-th and $j$-th position and the value $u$ (for unknown) in the other positions. If it is desired to say that the fluent $f_k$ is not present in the vector, the DEVS formalism permits the use of tests on projections of vectors to do this, i.e., $project(vector, k) \neq 1$.

We now have to show how to translate the state update and automatic state-updates in TS into DEVS. But these are almost immediate. The updates in TS are the results of actions, and these correspond to *external events* in X in DEVS, from which we see that the TS state updates correspond to sequential state-transitions in DEVS. The components resulting from the DEVS transitions are expressed as logic functions of the various projections of the previous sequential state vector. There are some subtleties concerning how these functions work on the unknown value $u$, but they are determined by the implied equational algebraic semantics of TS. The fact that DEVS a state-transition is *inertial* in the sense above follows directly from its definition.

The automatic state-updates in TS will correspond to *quasi-transitions* in DEVS that are precisely the autonomous transitions in which there are no external inputs (formally the input #). As indicated earlier, even instantaneous transitions can be accommodated. In this way, any intermediate "ramification" state of TS is directly translatable. Each of these changes is again inertial by virtue of DEVS definitions.

Implicit in the above translation is the assumption that each action and causal rule in TS has an equivalent in DEVS. But this is again almost trivial. DEVS arose because of a need to specify simulation models succinctly and formally, and the necessity to identify which fluents (state variables!) influenced which others via an action was immediately obvious from the beginning. Hence Zeigler worked out a compact algebraic theory of *influencers* and *influencees*, on which the transition functions were based. Each fluent (co-ordinate in the vector of sequential states) is a function of its influencers. This is exactly the case in TS. Likewise, each TS causal rule has a DEVS transition function counterpart based on influencers and influencees.

In his paper Thielscher highlights two key points in his solution. The first is that in all his update axioms, the variable denoting the state appears only once per formula. The next is that his method focuses on the action, and not on the fluents, i.e. the update and causal formulas are action-based, and say what happens to the fluents for each action. *In DEVS these perspectives are taken for granted*, and indeed are central to its definition and philosophy.

## 2.4    So, Do We Need Frame Axioms?

The previous section might have given the impression that the most recent solution to the frame problem has been reduced to engineering in the sense that it has all the characteristics of an engineering formalism like DEVS and is embeddable into the latter. So, is the frame problem an artifact of logic? Is it not the case that the Thielscher solution has revealed that it is *algebra*, specifically abelian monoid semigroups, that is responsible for an efficient solution to the frame problem?

For an answer, I refer back to section 3.1. If we do not care about knowledge-based queries or hypotheticals ("what if?"), and are only concerned with forward runs in time, i.e., prediction, then a DEVS solution is fine. DEVS "solves" the frame problem exactly as in TS, by only worrying about influenced fluents (variables) and "carrying forward" the balance. However, observe that if we are interested in abductive or interpolative queries as in section 3.1, and wish to use TS to answer them, *logic is inescapable*. Correspondingly, in DEVS, if we are not prepared to exhaustively simulate and observe exhaustively, we will have to wrap a logic around the DEVS algebra in order to answer specific queries. The basic reason why both TS and DEVS need logic to handle such queries is that connecting across many time points in either directions requires logical operations like *unification* and logical rules like *term re-writing*, not to mention the role of logical *disjunction* in non-deterministic actions and logical *conditionals* in choosing or favoring an action outcome. Once logic is introduced, frame axioms either have to be  "hard-coded" into the logical procedures and operations or as explicit frame axioms.

Further evidence of the necessity of logic in explanatory or hypothetical use of system theories is the *symbolic extension of DEVS* [7] (let me call it SYM-DEVS for short) in which DEVS can handle a kind of on-line reasoning about alternative futures based on the specific instantiations of time values during simulation. However, an interesting feature of SYM-DEVS is that it requires only a small meta-reasoning component for it to be used as a hypothetical reasoner that can answer queries of the abductive or interpolative kind. This power is derived from constraint solving and propagation, which are central to logic as manifested in constraint logic programming. SYM-DEVS is expressive enough to encode alternative state-transition traces for the YSP, and in the presence of a meta-reasoner can account for, say, why the turkey is alive at the end of the action sequence. But it seems that DEVS, which began as an algebraic specification, begins to assume logical features in SYM-DEVS when the objectives are extended to such hypothetical model executions.

It should be a source of comfort to both AI scientists and engineers that their respective approaches seem to have converged when the objective is the same. Zeigler's insights from over two decades ago have been vindicated. The role of logic appears to be one that fulfills his insights and embellishes them.

## 2.5    Future Directions and Conclusion

We have outlined a demarcation of the respective roles of engineering-inspired and AI-inspired formalizations of dynamic systems. Can this be made rigorous? The conjecture is that it can be. An outline of how this can be achieved is as follows. As we have to specify dynamic systems in some formal sense in order to prove anything about them and their specifications, it is necessary to say how we can translate between one specification and another. Not all specifications are equal in terms of granularity, so to be fair, the *ontology of observables* has to be fixed. This much is familiar to systems theorists --- it is the input-output view of systems. Then we have to say what it means for one specification to be computationally more efficient than another. This cannot ignore the kinds of problems we wish to solve using the specification. If we can define a notion of what it means for specification A to be computationally reducible to specification B modulo a class of problems P, then we are on the way to validating the conjecture. This is an enterprise that I invite you to join with us to complete. It would "solve" the frame problem by literally putting it in its proper place.

## Acknowledgements

My understanding of the frame problem has been sharpenned by discussion over the years with members of the Knowledge Systems Group (KSG), particularly Yan Zhang, Maurice Pagnucco, Pavlos Peppas, Dongmo Zhang and Abhaya Nayak. Visitors to KSG who have critiqued our ongoing work in the logic of actions include Hector Levesque, Patrick Doherty, John McCarthy and Michael Thielscher.

# References

[1]   Hanks, S. and McDermott, D., "Non-monotonic Logic and Temporal Projection", Artificial Intelligence, 33, pp. 379-412, 1987.

[2]   McCarthy, J. and P.J. Hayes, "Some Philosophical Problems from the Standpoint of Artificial Intelligence", in Machine Intelligence 4, ed. B. Meltzer and D. Michie, pp. 463-502, Edinburgh University Press, Edingurgh, 1969.

[3]   McCarthy, J., "Applications of Circumscription to Formalizing Common-Sense Knowledge", Artificial Intelligence, 28, pp. 86-116, 1986.

[4]   Thielscher, M. "From Situation Calculus to Fluent Calculus: State Update Axioms as a Solution to the Inferential Frame Problem", Artificial Intelligence, 111, pp. 277-299, 1999.

[5]   Zeigler, B.P. "Theory of Modelling and Simulation", Wiley-Interscience, New York, 1976.

[6]   Zeigler, B.P. "Multifaceted Modelling and Discrete Event Simulation", Academic Press, Orlando, Florida 1984.

[7]   Zeigler, B.P. and S. Chi, "Symbolic Discrete Event System Specification", IEEE Trans. Systems, Man and Cybernetics, 22, no.6, Nov/Dec 1428-1443, 1992.

# Chapter 3

# Adaptive Designs for Multiresolution, Multiperspective Modeling (MRMPM)

P.K. Davis

*This paper describes and illustrates certain principles for designing adaptive multi-resolution, multi-perspective models (MRMPM). It also demonstrates that modern interactive visual-modeling environments can be key enablers of MRMPM. The benefits are not just for the original model builder, but also for collaborators and subsequent users, who will typically need to adapt the model to their own special circumstances. The design-it-right-the-first-time ideal is a false god. The final purpose is to identify challenges for research on modeling and analysis environments.*

## 3.1    Introduction

### 3.1.1    Prefacing Comments

The subject of this paper is a kind of modeling that cuts across levels of detail and perspectives—covering complex, detailed, in-the-trees work and simpler depictions that are often useful for big-picture "forest" work. It is a frontier subject for research.

I am delighted to observe that the honoree of this festschrift, Bernard (Bernie) Zeigler, has spent many years teaching and practicing modeling and simulation with the quaint notion that it is important to understand *both* the forest and the trees, and to have concrete ideas and tools to help in doing so. This has been evident since his first text [19], which introduced the concept of experimental frames and emphasized the need to understand problem context when deciding on issues such as level of detail. It became even more evident later, when he introduced the method of system-entity diagrams [18] to highlight the differing perspectives or aspects, and levels of detail, that characterize an overall problem. And, in recent years, it has been evident in his research on the challenges of hierarchical system modeling [20,16]. In parallel, he and his collaborators have worked on modeling and simulation environments, with tools implementing the theoretical concepts [17]. Zeigler and I have discussed such issues off and on for many years, and have sometimes been able to collaborate directly (e.g., National Research Council, 1997). It is a pleasure to be able to summarize for this volume some of my own work on subjects of mutual interest.[1] Perhaps doing so will hasten Zeigler's efforts to solve some of the residual problems I find so difficult.

### 3.1.2  Objective

With this preface, the primary purpose of this paper is to describe and illustrate certain principles for designing adaptive multi-resolution, multi-perspective models (MRMPM). A second purpose is to demonstrate that modern interactive visual-modeling environments can be key enablers of MRMPM. The benefits are not just for the original model builder, but also for collaborators and subsequent users, who will typically need to adapt the model to their own special circumstances. The design-it-right-the-first-time ideal is a false god. The final purpose is to identify challenges for research.

## 3.2    Background

### 3.2.1  Definitions

Multiresolution, multiperspective modeling (MRMPM) is building models, model families, or both so as to permit users to think *and input* data at different levels of resolution and from different perspectives of the problem being modeled. [2]  Different perspectives focus on different aspects of the model. Note that a highly detailed model is not an example of MRMPM as I define it—even if it can generate output displays with varied resolutions and perspectives—if it demands the specific, detailed inputs.

---

[1] The principal reference for this paper is [3], which summarizes and extends the conclusions of earlier papers [6, 4, 7]. See also [13]. For a recent application see [2] and [11].

[2] In earlier work I used the terms variable-resolution and cross-resolution modeling for what is now more commonly called multiresolution modeling. For literature-search purposes, other useful terms include model abstraction, model aggregation and disaggregation, lumped models, multi modeling, and hierarchical modeling.

## 3.2.2   Motivations

There are many reasons for wanting MRMPM, but the most basic is cognitive: our need to *describe and reason about* systems at different levels of detail and from different perspectives. That is, we need models with cause-effect relationships expressed in the natural variables of a particular resolution or perspective. A second basic reason includes the need to use empirical data that come in varied detail and forms. Yet a third reason is that we are in fact incapable of building detailed models and data bases adequate to correctly generate the behaviors of many complex systems: we need to work at more aggregate levels. For related reasons, aggregate-level data is sometimes more reliable than the data available for more detailed models.

Models of different types also have different virtues [8]. Simple, low-resolution models may be ideal for quick, agile analysis of many cases (e.g., "exploratory analysis" of how a strategy fares across a broad scenario space, as discussed in [5] ). In contrast, detailed models may be superior for clarifying the underlying phenomenology and for identifying specific and concrete places to reflect particular options such as a new subsystem. So also, different aspects of a problem are best viewed with models representing different perspectives, much as physicists find that changes of representation can simplify and clarify issues.

Despite frequent claims to the contrary, then, our choice of resolution and perspective is not simply a matter of economics or time. *Even with infinite computer speed, we would still need models with different aggregations and choices of variables!*

This said, several questions remain: (1) to what extent is MRMPM feasible; (2) what design principles apply; (3) what tools help, or would help if they existed; and (4) how do we assess the adequacy of various approximations? These are all questions for both fundamental and applied research.

## 3.2.3   Feasibility of MRM and MRMPM

### 3.2.3.1    The Ideal

The ideal of MRMPM is that one should be able to decide, at the time of use, what resolution and perspective one wants, enter the data, exercise the model, and manipulate results usefully. In this ideal, one would get roughly the same answer to aggregate-level questions using simpler or more detailed models, or models with differing perspectives. That is, the MRMPM ideal is one with reasonable *consistency* among models in a family. Obviously, one cannot usually ask detailed questions with a simple model, but one might hope to be able to predict many important aggregate behaviors of a system using an aggregate version of the model, rather than being burdened by an enormous computer program with a voracious appetite for unavailable data. The hope is that the answer would be the same—at least approximately—for the principal purpose to which the model is being put, as if one had indeed found all the relevant data and used the large program.

### 3.2.3.2    The Reality

The reality, of course, is that we seldom have such models or model families to work with. All too often, we either have a model that is too simplistic for some of the questions of interest, or a model that is too complicated and expensive for quick and agile calculations. Similarly, one often finds that the data available simply doesn't "work" for the model one has: it is either too detailed or too aggregated, or it somehow represents a different perspective of the problem. This is the *normal* situation.

Some of the causes of this problem relate to the widespread pathology of modelers believing that their level of resolution is "correct," that those working at more aggregate levels are being simplistic, and that those working in more detail are lost in the weeds. Another cause is organizational dynamics generating "requirements" for increasingly complex models that are then given more credit than they deserve, and which become very burdensome to use. Some causes, then, are anti-intellectual. However, many of the causes are inherent in the nature of the problems we seek to address with models. That is, problems often *are* complex at their root. And yet, they can often be "understood" much more simply. This paradox is resolved only if we accept the fundamental role of approximations in our everyday lives and in good modeling. I shall return to this issue later in the paper.

## 3.2.4    The Challenge: Enabling the Ideal

This, then, is the subject of what follows—understanding something of the complexity that makes MRMPM modeling difficult, and suggesting ways to deal with that complexity. Because the subject is too large for a comprehensive summary here, this paper focuses on some particular issues. For more details, see the papers cited earlier [footnote 1] and their references. See also [1], a dissertation that includes citations too much of the older literature on the related issue of model abstraction. Although Axtell's conclusions are much more pessimistic than mine, there is something of the half-full half-empty phenomenon at work.

More generally, there is a rapidly growing literature on multiresolution modeling, although much of it is focused on visualization, computational methods, robotics, and other subjects different from those of interest here. Good web sites can be found at the California Institute of Technology (Paul Schröder), Carnegie-Mellon University (Paul Heckbert), and the University of Florida (Paul Fishwick). Many of Fishwick's papers are relevant here. [15] describes an interesting concept for MRM within distributed simulation. Another source of papers, with abstracts on the web, is the series of "enabling techology" sessions of the yearly SPIE conference in April, chaired by Alex Sisti of the Air Force Research Laboratory.

## 3.3   Understanding the Problem with a Parable

### 3.3.1   Illustrative Problem

In this paper I shall avoid general theoretical discussion and instead sketch a notional problem that illustrates many of the practical issues, work it through, and infer some more general principles. This approach is less elegant than others, but it has the advantage of understandability.

### 3.3.2   A Parable Begins: Boss's Image of a Solution

The boss of a small software company is speaking to his chief modeler: "Joe, I want to describe my problem so that you can model it. It shouldn't take you long, since I've pretty well thought it through, but having a computerized model will be convenient. Here's the problem. We are now in the programming business and we are often asked by clients to estimate how fast progress will be made in building programs for them. Further, I have to price the job and hire people for it. In the past, this has sometimes been a seat-of-the-pants matter, but we really can't afford to do it that way. So, here's the way I see it (referring to Figure 3.1)."

Continuing, he says "We can estimate pretty well the size of the programming job in lines of code, because we've done a lot of work in recent years. We also know how much programmers can get done per day. So, why don't you build me the model I've sketched out? I will then be able to estimate progress versus time by simply using the equation

$$remaining\ code(t) = initial\ code - \int_0^t N(s)P(s)ds \qquad (1)$$

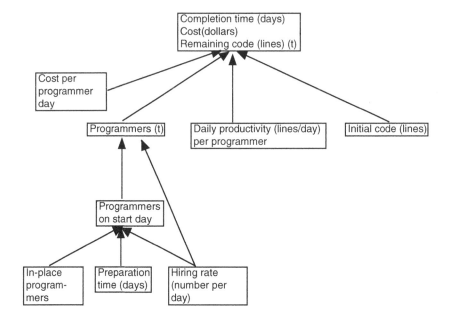

Figure 3.1: Initial Model Concept

where N(s) and P(s) represent, for day s, the number of programmers and the number of lines of code they write per day, respectively.

You see, it's just a matter of knowing how fast we can hire programmers and how efficient they are. And, by the way, note the variable resolution: unless I need more detail, I can lop off the bottom part of this tree and work just with Programmers (an average value over the duration of the job), daily productivity of programmers, daily per-programmer costs, and initial code. That's only four inputs instead of 6!" The cost of the job, of course, is just the daily cost of a programmer C, times the number of programmers, times the days to do the job, which is $T_{total}$, which comes from seeing what t is when remaining code is 0 in Eq (1):

$$\int_0^{T_{total}} N(s)P(s)ds = initialcode \tag{2}$$

$$Cost = C\int_0^{T_{total}} N(s)ds \tag{3}$$

This first act of our parable ends with Joe leaving, after having said "O.k., I hear what you have in mind. I'll see and get back to you."

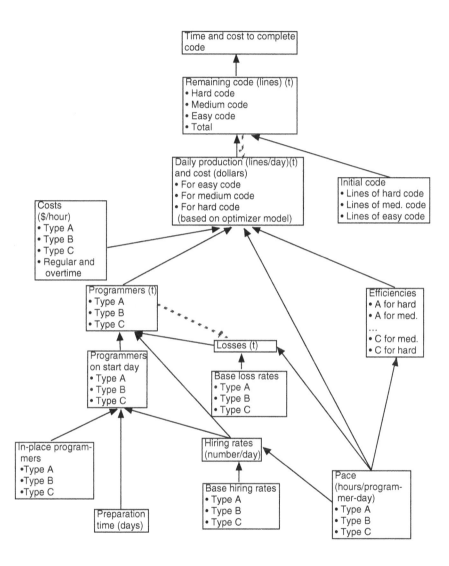

Figure 3.2: The Modeler's Model

### 3.3.3    The Second Act

In the second act of our parable, the boss meets with Joe a few days later and eagerly asks about the model. Joe says that there is now a working model, but he's evasive about details. Instead, he shows a graph of remaining code versus time. The boss asks, "Yes, this is terrific, but let me see the interface." After hemming and hawing, Joe admits that things did not go the way the boss had intended. He says, with a whine: "Well, you see, when you get into things, it turns out they are more complicated that you thought. There are more variables. It's always this way. He pulls out a diagram of the actual model (Figure 3.2)."

Joe goes on to say "As you can see, I had to make a distinction between kinds of code. Because you wanted things simple, I only have three types of code—easy, medium, and hard—but without this distinction we could get into serious trouble estimating. And, you know, there are big differences between programmers. Again, I have tried to be super-simple, so I've just identified three types. Type A are the superstars, who are efficient but expensive, Type B are the journeymen, and Type C are a bit subpar. To make things more complicated, Type A programmers aren't all that much better than Type B and Type C programmers for easy stuff (at least on a dollar basis), but they are night-and-day better for hard things."

"Anyway, to go on, you see I put costs into the model explicitly, because you had mentioned pricing, and I include pace—how many hours per day we make the programmers work. We need an optimizer submodel and more data—to keep track of the efficiencies of the several types of programmers for the different types of code. There's a feedback loop because the losses depend on the number of programmers and how long they have worked. And, of course, if we push the programmers too hard, some will drop out. They will get sick, burned out, or disgusted. But even that's not straightforward because some programmers will be *more* likely to hire on with us if they see the chance for overtime. And so on. I know you wanted something simpler, but this seems to be about as simple as I can make it."

Quickly scanning the two figures, the boss says, incredulously, "Do you mean to tell me that instead of 4 or 6 inputs we now need more like thirty?" Joe pauses, grimaces, and says, "Well, actually, it's worse than that, because there are a bunch of parameters in the submodels estimating losses and predicting the optimal mix and allocation. I didn't have the courage to show those, but they are parameters—we don't know their correct values. Oh, by the way, I don't see any way to do multiple-resolution work."

### 3.3.4   The Apparent Conclusion—Perhaps Unsatisfactory

The boss mumbles about the need to keep things simple, but he doesn't immediately see anything wrong with Joe's design. He takes Joe's point that distinguishing among types of programmer and code is often important. He thanks Joe and ends the meeting, but he's still very frustrated. It "ought" to be possible to do back-of-the-envelope calculations that are pretty good. "Heck," he thinks, "In the old days, when I estimated the price to charge clients while sitting in their offices, I just did things in my head. To be sure, I sometimes messed up, but on the other hand, sometimes I overestimated the expense and ended up with a windfall. There *must* be a simpler model—if not the one I sketched, then something like it."

Perhaps the moral of the parable is that one can't have what one wants; or that things are more complex than they seem. But perhaps not. Is this really the end of the story?

### 3.3.5   Observations

Arguably, the most striking thing in this parable is that both the boss and Joe are "right." The situation, which includes a cognitive disconnect, is not merely one of attitude or background, but also a reflection of the real underlying complexity of even this simple problem. The boss believes intuitively in a reductionist approach that involves little more than figuring that the number of programmers times the numbers of lines per day that an average programmer can write should be pretty good as an estimate of daily productivity. That may very well be true, but it is not obvious from the more careful treatment that this approach "works.

This problem manifests itself more generally in efforts to design models to have convenient multiple levels of resolution. It worsens when we consider alternative perspectives (and Figures 3.1 and 3.2 certainly represent different perspectives, not just differences in detail).

## 3.4   Interlude for Key Principles

### 3.4.1   Need for hierarchical trees

Before continuing with the illustrative problem, let us digress for a time into more general discussion, to recall some principles of MRM design. The first principle is that in MRM design one would like to end up with clean hierarchical trees analogous to Figure 3.1. That is, we seek designs in which the branches are distinct. Why? In part because it modularizes the work and makes it possible to calibrate a simpler, more aggregate version of the model from results of the more detailed version.[3] For example, looking to Figure 3.1, it is immediately obvious that if we want to work at the more aggregate level in which Programmers(t) is an input, then we should choose values of that parameter (or the form of a stochastic input variable) that are consistent with the more detailed calculation, averaged over the range of cases of interest with due account of relative frequencies.[4] Or, conversely, if we have macroscopic information based on experience—e.g., that it "always" takes about 2-4 weeks to get a programming team together and operating, then anyone attempting to work bottom-up from estimates of hiring rate, etc. must be able to reproduce that experience. This may mean, for example, having to reduce estimates of hiring rate or increase estimates of preparation time to tune the lower-level (higher-resolution) data so as to get proper answers.

The point here is that—despite myths to the contrary—calibration is not simply bottom-up, but rather a matter of using all available information, whether macroscopic and microscopic, and working back and forth in the hierarchy until the model as a whole fits all the known data. If the design generates clean trees, this can be done for each main branch separately, within each subordinate branch, and so on. Again, the model is decomposable into modules. In contrast, if some of the branches are connected—if we have some "brushiness"—then things are more difficult.

### 3.4.2   Need to account for branches

These difficulties can be appreciated by imagining how to truncate the tree to provide a simpler version of the model. Unfortunately, because of all the "crosstalk" between branches, there is little modularity. To better understand implications, suppose that we went ahead and *did* some "snipping" to isolate the leftmost part of the tree as shown in Figure 3.3.

---

[3] Several authors discuss this to greater or lesser degree, sometimes under the rubric of representing the input-output "behavior" of a module without maintaining all the details within. See, for example, [9] and [14].

[4] This calibration is not straightforward if some of the variables at the tree's leaves are correlated. See [5].

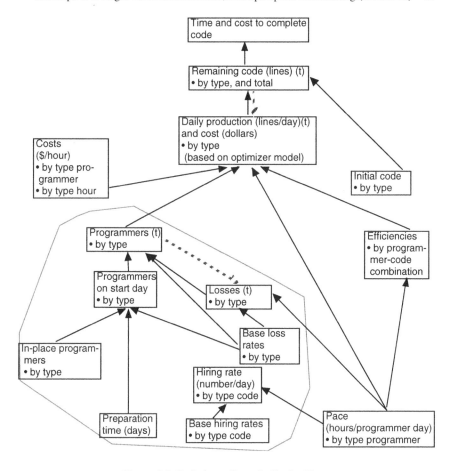

Figure 3.3: Isolating a Part of a Bushy Tree

We could again think of calibrating up and down our subtree on the left—or use a stochastic variable with appropriate statistics. We would try to assure that inputs for Programmers (t), of types A,B, and C, are consistent with *averages* of the lower-level (higher-resolution) depiction over the range of interesting cases. However, if we then try to use the result in the larger model, we see some inconsistencies because pace is still an explicit variable. Thus, the values we should use for estimating Programmers (t) should not be averages over all interesting cases, but rather averages over only the variables other than pace. The problem is not fully modular. Calibration will also be complicated because of the feedback loop involving losses. A little thought will convince the reader that matters have become complex. Again, then, MRMPM is about developing designs with clean hierarchical trees. Brushiness and feedback loops cause difficulties.

### 3.4.3    Approximations Are Fine but Must Be Context Dependent

As our illustrative problem demonstrates, but as is much more generally the case, *real* problems do not lend themselves to clean-tree designs: that's not the way systems work.

It follows that salvation must lie in the use of *approximations.* Although this may seem to be an obvious and unexceptionable observation, it is actually more profound if we realize that a great deal (and perhaps most) of the discussion about why model abstraction and the related multiresolution modeling are infeasible has revolved around arguments dealing with *exact* relationships. This has been true not only at the hand-waving level, but also in more careful theoretical work (e.g., [1] ). What has been even worse is that some theoretical work has concluded (based on exact relationships) that various abstractions are valid only in manifestly unphysical cases (i.e., essentially never). An example of this occurred in one of my own projects, where colleagues did some very interesting work to derive the circumstances under which the matrix version of Lanchester equations of combat generate the same aggregate-level results as a scalar version [10]. They solved the problem, but the conditions for exact consistency turned out to be unphysical. Many readers incorrectly concluded that the authors had proven, once and for all, that the aggregate equation was "wrong." In fact, the authors did not intend this and noted that subsequent work should assess the quality of approximations. Unfortunately, there was no easy way to explore that issue at the time.

### 3.4.4    The Issue of Consistency

To sharpen discussion of what we should mean when talking about the quality of approximations, we need to discuss the concept of reasonable consistency between models. The issue of model consistency is often discussed in university coursework and research papers, but the role of approximation is seldom clear.

Figure 3.4 shows a consistency diagram [3] that is quite different from that normally shown. The diagram compares results from two procedures. The first starts with a high-resolution state (1), aggregates (1 to 2), and then uses a lower-resolution, aggregate, model (model B), to simulate behavior until a final aggregate state is reached (6). That state is used to generate aggregate-level results of the analysis (6b), which may involve further averaging, rounding off, embedding the result in a more complicated function, etc. Sometimes, one can take the final aggregate state (6) and apply some rule to estimate the likely final detailed state (7) and the final high-resolution results (7b) of the problem. The second approach also starts with an initial high-resolution state (1), but proceeds with the high-resolution model A to determine the final high-resolution state (3), the aggregation of that state (4), and the final high-resolution and aggregate results of the problem (3b and 4b). Exact consistency in the aggregate of models A and B would mean that (4) and (6) are equal; exact consistency in detail would mean that (3) and (7) are identical. More relevant, however, are the results for the analysis problem being worked.

The funnel-like objects between 6 and 6b, 4 and 4b, 7 and 7b, and 3 and 3b indicate that what matters is not the identity of final states, as computed with exact and approximate models, but rather whether the "projection" of those states into the problem-solving context is "close." This is worth elaborating. Often, in policy work, what matters is whether a graph displayed to a large audience, if calculated from the approximate model, is "pretty much the same" as if it were generated from the more nearly exact model: does it have the right shape, roughly the right intercepts, roughly the right values, etc.? Often, even the better model is distinctly imperfect, so the most one can hope for is the "roughly right" situation. In that case, modest differences between the two curves are of no significance! It is also worth emphasizing that there are *many* problems in which (3b)[mislabeled as 3 in the original figure of [3] ] and (7b) will be effectively the same—because the information discarded in the aggregation (1 to 2) turns out not to have been very important or because the final analytic result is simply not sensitive to the precision of the final states generated by the models.

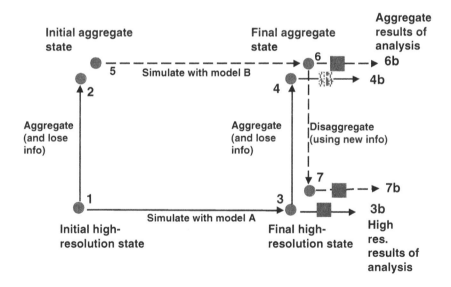

Figure 3.4: Assessing Consistency of Higher- and Lower-Resolution Models

It is worth noting that although this discussion of consistency is distinctly different from the usual one, it fits nicely within the conceptual structure that Bernie Zeigler uses more generally—in particular, his discussion of "experimental frame." He has also used the concept of morphisms to discuss model abstraction, which can be quite helpful—especially when the abstraction is truly consistent with the original model (a homomorphic relationship). This occurs, for example, when the detailed model uses inputs a, b and c only through the factor d = (a)(b)/(c). A more abstract model could be created by substituting the parameter d everywhere so that the model does not depend explicitly on a,b, and c. However, there would be straightforward one-to-one relationships between states of the two models. The more general case of approximate consistency and approximate morphism, however, is not well developed. See discussion in Appendices G and H of [13].

Let us now suppose that many people would cheerfully agree that, in principle, there might be aggregate models that would sometimes be reasonably good representations of detailed models for predicting the more aggregate behaviors of a system well enough to generate the results they are looking for. Such acceptance, regrettably, would not take us far because it too abstract. Without knowing *what* approximation, and in what context, approximations would be good enough, we have only abstractions. To make things worse, there is no simple theory of how to go about approximations. Nonetheless, much can be done if one persists—and is willing to exploit specifics of the particular problem being worked rather than pursuing the holy grail of generality. Let us now return to our illustrative problem to see this.

## 3.5    Milking Our Example for More Insights

### 3.5.1    A First Simplification

Reviewing our illustrative problem, there are some obvious possibilities. First, we could ignore losses and assume that hiring rate is unaffected by pace. Chances are, however, that this assumption—however convenient—is just plain wrong and would introduce systematic bias, perhaps causing serious pricing problems. A better approach would be: (1) to replace the losses function by a fractional-loss parameter estimated with some side calculations (e.g., if one has hired N programmers as of time t, then perhaps experience indicates that only about 0.95N will show up that day); and (2) to limit the use of the model to a range of paces for which it is reasonable to assume that hiring rates and efficiencies are not sensitive to changes in pace. This better approach, then, would attempt to avoid an obvious bias and accept some constraints of applicability. It would be easy enough to test results for sensitivity to the assumed value of fractional losses. With those assumptions, the model collapses to a simple MRM design (Figure 3.5).

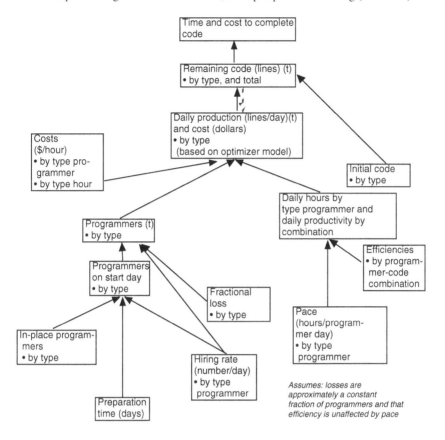

Figure 3.5: An Approximate MRM Design, but in "Wrong" Perspective

Unfortunately, the design of Figure 3.5 would not meet the goal expressed by our fictional boss. The key variables are vectors (one-dimensional arrays) and some of the key parameters are matrices (two-dimensional arrays). There is no way to correctly compute daily productivity as simply programmers times per-programmer productivity. Instead, one must at least compute a scalar product (Equation 4, where DP represents daily productivity in lines of code, $N_{ij}$ is the number of programmers of type i allocated to code of type j, and $P_{ij}$ is the productivity of those programmers for that task). As indicated, DP is not generally equal to some simple-minded product of the total number of programmers times some average productivity, independent of the nature of the job. In a more general example, instead of three categories of code (easy, medium, and hard), there might be a half-dozen, dozen, or even more.

$$DP = \sum_{i}^{3} \sum_{j}^{3} N_{ij} P_{ij} \qquad (4)$$

### 3.5.2   An Alternative Perspective of the Same Problem

But suppose we do not choose to give up so easily. Suppose, we anticipate that sometimes, like the boss in the example, we will have a strong desire to think in terms of programmers times productivity—because we "know" it often works, or because it makes explanation so convenient. We then need to make our model more adaptive by introducing the concepts of "equivalent" code and "equivalent programmers," so that if we have a mix of easy, medium, and hard code, we characterize it by some number of lines of "equivalent code."

This approach is, of course, quite similar in spirit to what we routinely do in a great many modeling problems—sometimes explicitly, and sometimes with a sleight of hand. We turn a collection of distinguishable entities or groups into a larger quantity of "average" entities.

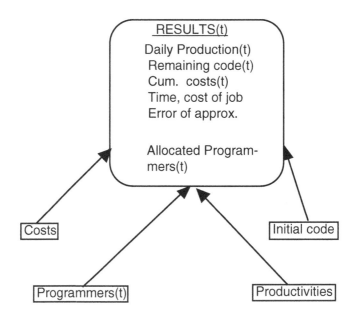

Figure 3.6: An Alternative Design

If we know we will sometimes want this kind of model perspective (as suggested by the form of Figure 3.1), then we can restructure to obtain something like Figure 3.6. As in Figure 3.1, we see results being generated from costs, supply of programmers, productivities, and the size of the job. However, a lot is going on within the module labeled "RESULTS." It *is* possible to mirror the form of Figure 3.1, but the complexity is preserved: it merely appears in different places.

If, now, we wish to introduce the equivalent-programmer concept, then we should replace the variables Programmers(t), Productivities, and Initial code with modules that contain both the original variables and the variables that are natural in an equivalent-programmer construct. Figures 3.7-3.9 show the contents of three of the modules. Some of the modularity is conceptual only. Italic letters indicate variables that are actually defined in another module. Note that, at this point, the number of equivalent programmers is an output, not an input. So is the initial lines of equivalent code. Neither of them is used as yet to compute anything, but we are laying the groundwork for adaptations and approximations by building in the concepts.

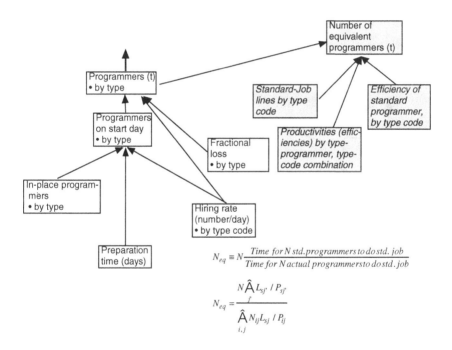

Figure 3.7: Programmers (t) Module

### 3.5.3   The Equivalent-Programmer Approximation

So fare, we've merely defined some extra variables that are not "doing anything." Now let us use them for an approximations. The equivalent-programmer approximation estimates the time to complete the job (or the price of the job) by converting programmers to equivalent programmers and code to equivalent code, and then setting time equal to the quotient of equivalent code and the product of equivalent programmers times standard-programmer productivity. That approximate model can be built in from the start as well, as shown in Figure 3.10, which represents merely a portion of the results module in Figure 3.6. Note that in this design we build in the measurement of error (error in estimating completion time) from the outset. That is, we are adding building-blocks as we go along.

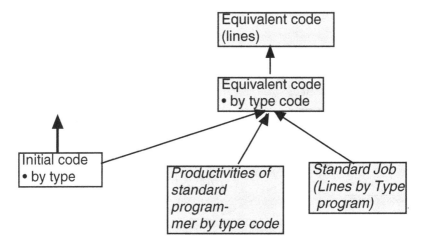

$$Equivalent\, code = L_{total}\, \frac{Time\, for\, std.\, programmer}{Time\, for\, std.\, programmer\, for\, std.\, job}$$

$$L_{eq} = L_{total}\, \frac{\hat{A}_{j}\, L_{j}\, /\, P_{sj}}{\hat{A}_{j'}\, L_{sj'}\, /\, P_{sj'}}$$

Figure 3.8: Initial Code Module

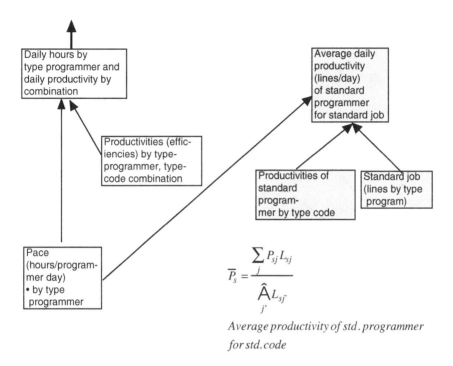

$$\overline{P}_s = \frac{\sum_j P_{sj} L_{sj}}{\hat{A}_{j'} L_{sj'}}$$

*Average productivity of std. programmer*
*for std. code*

Figure 3.9: The Productivity Module

Having generated this design, it is only natural to assess the magnitude of the error over the case space of interest. That is, how big are errors likely to be over a wide range of jobs and circumstances? Not long ago, it would have been very tedious to generate such estimates except for extreme cases. However, with new technology, we can do this readily even with a personal computer.

For the sake of illustration, I built the corresponding model on a Macintosh personal computer, assuming that all programmers were hired as of the starting time. I then calculated the distribution of errors assuming "probability distributions" for the percentages of hard code, Type-A, and Type-C programmers in jobs. I had no firm basis for the distributions, so they should not really be thought of as probabilities, but rather this is like estimating error for a test set of cases over a broad and "reasonably chosen" domain of possibilities. The results, of course, depend on the inputs I assumed, but using those inputs, Figure 3.11 shows the results of 80 Monte Carlo samples from a subset of the test set in which 20 % of the programmers are of Type A. We see that the error is on the order of 30 or 40 % (meaning that the true completion time much exceeded the equivalent-programmer model's estimate) when the per cent of

Type-C programmers is large (75 %) and the per cent of hard code is large. In contrast, if the percent of Type-C programmers is kept small, then the error will be to overestimate the time to complete the job and that error will more typically be on the order of 5%.

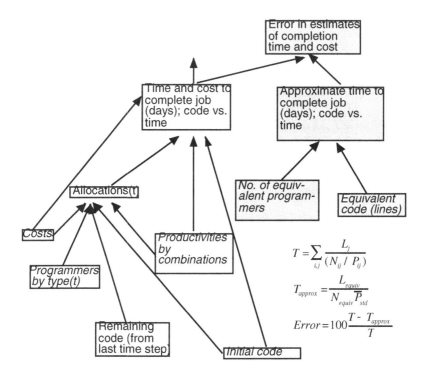

$$T = \sum_{i,j} \frac{L_j}{(N_{ij} / P_{ij})}$$

$$T_{approx} = \frac{L_{equiv}}{N_{equiv} \overline{P}_{std}}$$

$$Error = 100 \frac{T - T_{approx}}{T}$$

Figure 3.10: Carrying Along "Exact" and Approximate Models

Much more extensive error analysis would be possible. For example, if one studied the consequences of hiring only sub-par (Type-C) programmers to save money, one would quickly see that there would be a significant chance of seriously underbidding a job and even failing completely. The point here, however, is merely that it is possible to do such error analysis rather straightforwardly with modern tools—and do so within a single model or family of models.

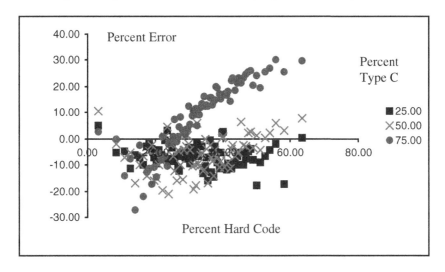

Figure 3.11: Illustrative Depiction of Error Across a Case Space

Significantly, the design of Figure 3.10 is actually superior in many respects, despite the additional complications. It particular, it is adaptive: it permits thinking at different levels of detail, including the back-of-the-envelope level in which one merely works with equivalent programmers and equivalent lines of code. That makes it easy for the boss to explain—which may be valuable in justifying the price to the client, in discussing the bid price with his partner who must also approve, and in explaining to the programming team just what has to be accomplished. Furthermore, it modularizes the problem, so that the task of hiring programmers is a separate back-of-the-envelope calculations from the task of estimating the magnitude of the job and the time it will take to complete it. And, finally, one may have a good deal of experience providing estimates of the aggregate quantities such as lines of average code per day by average programmers. Rather than deriving these from below, one may want to use experienced-based data at that level of detail.

At this point, some readers may wish to conclude that the moral of the story is always to do the modeling "right." Then, if necessary, one could always cut some corners and know how bad the error was. That is not really the point I would prefer to make, however, because doing things "right" in this sense—and then maintaining all the machinery, documentation, and data bases for the "right" way—has a high price in the general case. How far down does one go (molecules?). And do we *really* want the complex version of our model to be the baseline? Perhaps a better notion might be to focus on the simpler and more flexible model from the outset and to develop a sufficiently good approximation of a "good" model so as to understand the issues and be able to estimate the error in using the simple model. A rule of thumb I like on this is that if we want to use a model at level n of resolution, then we really need to understand the problem well at level n+1, which requires having a model at that level also—at least until such time as we are convinced that we know when and how to use the simple model. After that, it is not obviously necessary to maintain the n+1 model and its data. If it's useful to do so (e.g., for occasional finely tuned proposals, or because one will frequently be working with questions or data at the different levels of detail), fine; but not just for the sake of apparent precision. Recall again also that in the real world, that detailed data—especially when maintained inexpensively over long periods of time—will often be wrong, misunderstood, or entered incorrectly. Thus, the predictions of the more detailed model may also be wrong—and it may be difficult to catch the errors. Thus, the results may not truly be more precise, and they may actually be worse. Finally, from a pragmatic perspective, we should always remember that the more serious blunders of a simpler model can often be avoided by some auxiliary rules developed by doing some initial error analysis such as that above. The rules migh be of the form "don't bid on jobs with really hard code," or "always have at least 20% first-rate programmers, and never use sub-par programmers."

If one *does* maintain a multresolution family, which is sometimes quite valuable, then a big advantage of the design approach taken is that one can, from time to time, do the calibrations both up and down the hierarchy until the *family* of models represents all the information. At that point, one can use simpler or more complex versions of the model depending on the context. Similarly, one can connect building-block modules in different ways to represent different perspectives.

# 3.6   Inferences and Conclusions

## 3.6.1   What We Now Understand Better

The first conclusion from our simple example—and more complicated realistic ones with which I am familiar—is that there is strong reason for a family-of-models approach. Multiple levels of detail and alternative perspectives are very helpful and can enable an organization to be agile and nimble sometimes, and careful and in-depth on other occasions.

A second conclusion is that multi-resolution, multi-perspective design methods are needed if one is going to be able to compare across levels of detail or between alternative perspectives. The goal in such designs should be hierarchical trees with respect to the processes (hierarchical design with respect to objects is much easier and not worth discussing here).

A third conclusion is that, regrettably, such designs will only seldom be rigorous. Thus, approximations must be a focus of attention from the outset, rather than something to be added with apologies late in the game. This means that it is helpful, from the start, to build in alternative building blocks modules that can be hooked up as needed.

A fourth conclusion is that any particular set of approximations will likely be valid—that is such as to keep errors reasonably small for the purposes intended—only in certain domains of the input variables. In other domains, the approximations needed may differ not only in parameter values, but even in functional form. In our example, the equivalent programmer approximation failed for particularly difficult jobs (or, not shown, if one hires only sub-par programmers). Another familiar example may be the drag on a body in flight, which may vary with the speed V, with $1/V$, or even with $1/V^2$ depending on the speed regime. Thus, no single design will necessarily be useful for a good MRMPM model or model family. Variants may be needed for different regimes.

## 3.6.2   The Role of the Modeling Environment

It follows that successful multiresolution, multiperspective modeling needs to be done in a modeling environment that facilitates model adaptations—not merely lopping off some detailed modules, but also "seeing structures," moving functions around, introducing new concepts (e.g., equivalent programmers), and measuring the consequences of approximations. This "facilitation" should include making self-documentation easy and natural, making it possible to keep track of relationships readily without, for example, having the same name mean mysteriously different things in different versions of the model or without having overlapping but seriously inconsistent data bases. Moreover, when I use the adjectives easy and natural, I have in mind the boss's perspective (or the chief analyst's), not just the perspective of the superb C programmer who understands everything and can figure out how to make adaptations promptly. Such programmers—even if superhuman—will sometimes not be present, will often not be able to explain simple, will often be busy, may move on to other jobs and lose the intimate sense of the code, and so on.

In my own work over the last few years, I have moved increasingly to the use of personal-computer environments with at least some of these attributes. Spreadsheet systems like Microsoft's *EXCEL*® are quite powerful now. Even more attractive, in some respects, is the approach taken in Lumina's *Analytica*,® an outgrowth of the Demos program developed at Carnegie Mellon University (see also [12] ). Analytica, and several other modern systems such as iThink® and Extend,® have visual-modeling; some are highly interactive; some have excellent statistical functions built in, which permits stochastic modeling; some are well designed for self-documentation. Unfortunately, all have limitations as well. Nonetheless:

- The advent of personal-computer modeling environments with features of visual-programming, interactiveness, high-level languages, and self documentation now facilitates multiresolution, multiperspective designs.

Given the determination to build models with such designs, familiarity with a relatively few principles, and the right environment, much can be done that was simply not feasible even a few years ago—except for a few individuals working in developmental environments, usually with traditional languages such as C.

Although this paper has been tutorial and down-to-earth, in nature, my colleagues and I now have considerable experience in this domain—including practical applications to real-world analysis problems of considerable interest to the Department of Defense and other organizations. As a result, I am bullish about possibilities.

### 3.6.3   Opportunities for the Future

This said, there remain profound problems. In particular, finding and assessing good approximations remains an ad hoc procedure. We have nothing comparable to "standard methodology" such as the Taylor's series of calculus (except, arguably, when the more abstract models of a family are to be generated by mere statistical analysis of lower-level behaviors rather than phenomenological considerations). Much less do we have adequate at-your fingertip tools to help apply and test such approximations. Because so many modeling problems involve complex, nonlinear systems, it seems likely that the tools needed will have to be computational rather than analytical. One example would be tools to help assure "optimal" or "realistic" use of higher-resolution processes that contribute to an lower-resolution abstraction. Without such tools, people often make naive assumptions involving uniformity or some such.

At the same time, modeling and simulation theory needs to address these approximation-related matters cogently at a more abstract level, so that students and practitioners will have deeper principles to guide them.

Although even currently available personal-computer modeling environments are quite powerful, there is much more to be sought. Today, they tend either to be strong analytically but mediocre for simulation, or vice versa; others tend to be excellent for object-oriented modeling, but poor for more general modeling; and so on. Moreover, one of the principal reasons for modeling is to explore the consequences to decisions of massive uncertainty, but current modeling systems—although greatly superior to those from a few years ago—do not yet incorporate adequate tools for exploratory analysis and visualization [5].

In conclusion, this paper is unabashedly upbeat about conceptual and technological progress in modeling and simulation. At the same time, it can end with the proverbial demand for more research—because, in truth, more research is needed and will prove fruitful.

# References

[1] Axtell, Robert Lee, *Theory of Model Aggregation for Dynamical Systems with Applications to Problems of Global Change*, Dissertation, Carnegie-Mellon University, UMI Dissertation Services, Ann Arbor, MI, 1992.

[2] Davis, Bigelow, and McEver, Jimmie, Effects of Terrain, Maneuver, Tactics, and C4ISR on the Effectiveness of Long Range Precision Fires: a Stochastic Multiresolution Model (PEM) Calibrated to High-Resolution Simulation, RAND, Santa Monica, CA, 2000.

[3] Davis, Paul K. and Bigelow, James, *Experiments in Multiresolution Modeling*, RAND, Santa Monica, CA, 1998.

[4] Davis, Paul K. and Hillestad, Richard "Families of Models that Cross Levels of Resolution: Issues for Design, Calibration, and Management, *Proceedings, 1993 Winter Simulation Conference*, 1993.

[5] Davis, Paul K. and Hillestad, Richard, *Exploratory Analysis for Strategy Problems with Massive Uncertainty*, RAND, Santa Monica, CA, 2000.

[6] Davis, Paul K. and Reiner Huber, *Variable Resolution Modeling: Issues, Principles, and Challenges*, RAND, N-3500-DARPA, Santa Monica, CA, 1992.

[7] Davis, Paul K., *An Introduction to Variable-Resolution Modeling and Cross-Resolution Model Connection*, RAND, Santa Monica, CA, 1993. Also, *J. of Naval Logistics*, **42**. No.2, 1995.

[8] Davis, Paul K., Bigelow, James and McEver, Jimmie, *Analytical Methods for Studies and Experiments on Transforming the Force*, RAND, Santa Monica, CA, 1999.

[9] Fishwick, Paul and Lee, Kangsung, "Dynamic Model Abstraction," *Proceedings of the 1996 Winter Simulation Conference*, pp 764-771, San Diego, CA, 1996.

[10] Hillestad, Richard and Juncosa, Mario, *Cutting Some Trees to Save the Forest: on Aggregation and Disaggregation in Combat Models*, RAND, Santa Monica, CA, 1993.

[11] McEver, Jimmie, Davis, Paul K., and Bigelow, James, *EXHALT: an Interdiction Model for the Halt Phase of Armored Invasions*, RAND, Santa Monica, CA, 2000.

[12] Morgan, M. Granger and Henrion, Max, *Uncertainty: A Guide to Dealing with Uncertainty in Quantitative Risk and Policy Analysis*, Cambridge University Press, Cambridge, 1990; reprinted in 1998.

[13] National Research Council, *Modeling and Simulation, Volume 9 of Tactics and Technology for the United States Navy and Marine Corps: 2000-2035*, National Academy Press, Washington, 1997.

[14] Popken, Doublas, "Application of System Identification Techniques to Simulation Model Abstraction," a paper presented at the April, 1999 SPIE conference, *Proceedings of SPIE*, Enabling Technology for Simulation Science III. Volume 3696. 1999.

[15] Reynolds, P., Natrajan, N. and Srinivasan, S., "Consistency Maintenance in Multiresolution Simulation," *ACM Transactions in Modeling and Computer Simulation*," Vol. 7, No. 3, 368, 1997.

[16] Zeigler, Bernard P., "A Framework for Modeling and Simulation," Ch. 3 of David J. Cloud and Larry B. Rainey (editors), *Applied Modeling and Simulation: An Integrated Approach to Development and Operation*, McGraw Hill, New York, 1998.

[17] Zeigler, Bernard P., "DEVS Representation of Dynamical Systems: Event-Based Intelligent Control," *Proceedings of IEEE*, Vol. 77, No. 1, 1989, pp. 72 ff.

[18] Zeigler, Bernard P., *Multifaceted Modelling and Discrete Event Simulation,* Academic Press, New York, 1984.

[19] Zeigler, Bernard P., *Theory of Modeling and Simulation*, Wiley, New York, 1976. The second edition is Zeigler, Bernard P., Kim, Tag Gon, and Praehofer, Herbert, *Theory of Modeling and Design*, Academic Press, 2000.

[20] Zeigler, Bernard P., Object-Oriented Simulation with Hierarchical, Modular Models: Intelligent Agents and Endomorphic Systems, Academic Press, San Diego, 1990.

# Chapter 4

# The Role of Uncertainty in Systems Modeling

G.J. Klir

*A personal account of the emergence and development of generalized information theory (GIT) in the context of data-driven (inductive) systems modeling. In GIT, information is defined in terms of relevant uncertainty reduction. Main results regarding measures of uncertainty and uncertainty-based information in Dempster-Shafer theory of evidence and in generalized possibility theory are overviewed, and their role in three basic uncertainty principles is discussed: the principles of maximum uncertainty, minimum uncertainty, and uncertainty invariance. Finally, some open problems and undeveloped areas in GIT are examined.*

## 4.1 Introduction

Writing this paper for a book dedicated to Bernard P. Zeigler brings forth many pleasant memories of our interactions, primarily in the 1970s and 1980s. During this period, we both were interested in developing a broad conceptual framework for systems modeling. Although we approached systems modeling differently, our motivations and ways of thinking were surprisingly similar. As a consequence, we developed quite similar frameworks for conceptualizing and classifying all conceivable systems [14, 15, 16, 18, 37, 38].

In the 1980s, Bernie developed a broad-based methodology for systems modeling and simulation [39, 40]. I, on the other hand, focused on the various issues of inductive systems modeling [17, 18, 19]. It is interesting that many aspects of inductive modeling are relevant to the recently emerging area of knowledge discovery.

In inductive modeling, I found it inevitable to deal with nondeterministic systems. This required, in turn, to deal with relevant uncertainty (predictive, retrodictive, prescriptive, diagnostic, etc.) and the associated uncertainty-based information [21]. The more I dealt with uncertainty, the more I realized that it is a valuable commodity, which can be traded for complexity reduction or credibility increase in the process of systems modeling.

Initially, I considered two classical mathematical frameworks for dealing with uncertainty in nondeterministic systems, both based on classical set theory. One of them was probability theory and the associated classical information theory; the other one was classical (crisp) possibility theory. Since the late 1970s, I increasingly felt that these frameworks were not sufficient for capturing the full scope of uncertainty. This uneasiness motivated me to explore more general mathematical frameworks. These were based upon various nonadditive measures [35] with the  underlying structure of either classical set theory or, more generally, fuzzy set theory [26].

First, I considered generalized possibility theory [6,8], particularly its fuzzy-set interpretation [23], and the Dempster-Shafer theory of evidence [32]. Later, I also considered the various emerging theories of imprecise probabilities [34]. Unfortunately, none of the novel theories of uncertainty was developed at the level comparable with classical information theory, which is needed for system modeling. Extensive research into the information aspects of these theories was thus needed. This area, for which I coined the name "generalized information theory" [22], has been one of my principal research foci since the early 1980s [25]. Writing this paper is an opportunity to overview the spirit, aim, and current results of this research.


# 4.2    Generalized Information Theory

*Classical information theory* has two distinct bases. One of them is probability theory and the well-known Shannon measure of probabilistic uncertainty, usually referred to as the *Shannon entropy* [33]. The other one is classical (crisp) possibility theory and the associated measure of uncertainty introduced by Hartley [10]. The term *generalized information theory* (GIT) was introduced to describe a research program whose objective is to develop a broader concept of information, not restricted to these classical notions of uncertainty [22].

In GIT, as in classical information theory, the primary concept is *uncertainty*, and information is defined in terms of uncertainty reduction. To reduce uncertainty (predictive, retrodictive, prescriptive, diagnostic, etc.) in a situation formalized within a mathematical theory (e.g., probability theory in the case of classical information theory) requires that some relevant action be taken by a cognitive agent, such as performing a relevant experiment, searching for a relevant fact, or accepting and interpreting a relevant message. If results of the action taken (an experimental outcome, a discovered fact, etc.) reduce uncertainty involved in the situation, then the amount of information obtained by the action is measured by the amount of uncertainty reduced — the difference between *a priori* uncertainty and *a posteriori* uncertainty.

Measuring information in this way is clearly contingent upon our capability to measure uncertainty within the various mathematical frameworks. The primary focus of GIT is thus on developing this capability for all conceivable types of uncertainty. Information measured solely by uncertainty reduction is an important, even though restricted, notion of information. To distinguish it from the various other conceptions of information, it is common to refer to it as *uncertainty-based information* [25].

To develop a fully operational theory for dealing with uncertainty and uncertainty-based information of some conceived type requires that a host of issues be addressed at four distinct levels:

* LEVEL 1 — we need to find an appropriate *mathematical representation* of the conceived type of uncertainty.
* LEVEL 2 — we need to develop a *calculus* by which this type of uncertainty can be properly manipulated.
* LEVEL 3 — we need to find a meaningful way of *measuring* relevant uncertainty in any situation formalizable in the theory.
* LEVEL 4 — we need to develop methodological aspects of the theory, including procedures for making the various *uncertainty principles* operational within the theory.

The two branches of classical information theory are well developed at all these levels. Although an appreciable number of new information theories now exist that are fairly well developed at levels 1 and 2, only a few of them are developed, at least partially, at level 3; and they are even less developed at level 4. These are the levels to which current research in GIT is primarily oriented.

## 4.3    New Uncertainty Theories: Relevant Concepts and Notation

Dempster-Shafer theory (DST) and generalized possibility theory (GPT) are the only new (nonclassical) uncertainty theories that are at this time adequately developed at levels 1-3, even though further research in these theories is still pursued at these levels. This paper focuses thus on these two theories. Other uncertainty theories, none of which is fully developed at level 3 as yet, are mentioned only casually.

The purpose of this section is to introduce some basic concepts and notation pertaining to level 1 and 2 of DST and GPT. Only those concepts of these theories are introduced that are needed for dealing with issues at level 3 — the issues of measuring uncertainty and uncertainty-based information.

### 4.3.1    Dempster-Shafer Theory (DST)

DST is based on two dual nonadditive measures: belief measures and plausibility measures. Given a universal set X (usually referred to in DST as the *frame of discernment*), assumed here to be finite, a *belief measure* is a function

$$\text{Bel:}\ \mathsf{P}(X) \to [0,1]$$

such that $\text{Bel}(\varnothing) = 0$, $\text{Bel}(X) = 1$, and

$$\text{Bel}(A_1 \cup A_2 \cup \Lambda \cup A_n) \geq \sum_j \text{Bel}(A_j) - \sum_{j<k} \text{Bel}(A_j \cap A_k)$$
$$+ \Lambda + (-1)^{n+1} \text{Bel}(A_1 \cap A_2 \cap \Lambda \cap A_n) \tag{1}$$

for all possible families of subsets of X, where $\mathsf{P}(X)$ denotes the power set of X. Due to (1), belief measures are mathematically *monotone capacities of order* $\infty$ [2], which implies that they are also *superadditive*. When X is infinite, function Bel is also required to be *semicontinuous from above* [35].

A *plausibility measure* is a function

$$\text{Pl:}\ \mathsf{P}(X) \to [0,1]$$

such that $\text{Pl}(\varnothing) = 0$, $\text{Pl}(X) = 1$, and

$$\text{Pl}(A_1 \cap A_2 \cap \Lambda \cap A_n) \leq \sum_j \text{Pl}(A_j) - \sum_{j<k} \text{Pl}(A_j \cup A_k)$$
$$+ \Lambda + (-1)^{n+1} \text{Pl}(A_1 \cup A_2 \cup \Lambda \cup A_n) \tag{2}$$

for all possible families of subsets of X. Due to (2), plausibility measures are *alternating of order* $\infty$ [2], which implies that they are also *subadditive*. When X is infinite, function Pl is also required to be *semicontinuous from below* [35].

It is well known that either of the two measures is uniquely determined from the other by the equation

$$\text{Pl}(A) = 1 - \text{Bel}(\overline{A}) \tag{3}$$

for all $A \in \mathsf{P}(X)$. It is also known that

$$\text{Pl}(A) \geq \text{Bel}(A) \tag{4}$$

for each $A \in P(X)$. In the special case of equality in (4) for all $A \in P(X)$, we obtain a classical (additive) probability measure.

DST, which has become an important tool for dealing with uncertainty, is best covered in a book by Shafer [32]. Its position in fuzzy measure theory is described by Wang & Klir [35].

Belief and plausibility measures can conveniently be characterized by a function

$$m : P(X) \to [0, 1],$$

which is required to satisfy two conditions:

$$(i) \quad m(\varnothing) = 0;$$
$$(ii) \sum_{A \in P(X)} m(A) = 1.$$

This function is called a *basic probability assignment*. For each set $A \in P(X)$, the value $m(A)$ expresses the proportion to which all available and relevant evidence supports the claim that a particular element of $X$, whose characterization in terms of relevant attributes is deficient, belongs to the set $A$. This value, $m(A)$, pertains solely to one set, set $A$; it does not imply any additional claims regarding subsets of $A$. If there is some additional evidence supporting the claim that the element belongs to a subset of $A$, say $B \subset A$, it must be expressed by another value $m(B)$.

Given a basic probability assignment $m$, the corresponding belief and plausibility measures are determined for all sets $A \in P(X)$ by the formulas

$$Bel(A) = \sum_{B|B \subseteq A} m(B), \tag{5}$$

$$Pl(A) = \sum_{B|A \cap B \neq \varnothing} m(B). \tag{6}$$

Inverse procedure is also possible. Given, for example, a belief measure Bel, the corresponding basic probability assignment $m$ is determined for all $A \in P(X)$ by the formula

$$m(A) = \sum_{B|B \subseteq A} (-1)^{|A-B|} Bel(B), \tag{7}$$

as proven by Shafer [32]. Hence, each of the three functions, $m$, Bel, and Pl, is sufficient to determine the other two.

Given a basic probability assignment, every set $A \in P(X)$ for which $m(A) \neq 0$ is called a *focal element*. The pair $(F, m)$, where $F$ denotes the set of all focal elements induced by m is called a *body of evidence*.

Total ignorance is expressed in evidence theory by $m(X) = 1$ and $m(A) = 0$ for all $A \neq X$. Full certainty is expressed by $m(\{x\}) = 1$ for one particular element of X and $m(A) = 0$ for all $A \neq \{x\}$.

To investigate ways of measuring the amount of uncertainty represented by each body of evidence, it is essential to understand properties of bodies of evidence whose focal elements are subsets of the Cartesian product of two sets. That is, we need to examine basic probability assignment of the form

$$m : P(X \times Y) \to [0, 1],$$

where X and Y denote universal sets pertaining to two distinct domains of inquiry (e. g., two investigated variables), which may be connected in some fashion. Let m of this form be called a *joint basic probability assignment*. In this case, each focal element induced by m is a binary relation R on $X \times Y$. When R is projected on set X and on set Y, we obtain, respectively, the sets

$$R_X = \{x \in X \mid (x, y) \in R \text{ for some } y \in Y\}$$

and

$$R_Y = \{y \in Y \mid (x, y) \in R \text{ for some } x \in X\}.$$

These sets are instrumental in calculating *marginal basic probability assignments* $m_X$ and $m_Y$ from the given joint assignment m:

$$m_X(A) = \sum_{R \mid A = R_X} m(R) \quad \text{for all } A \in P(X),$$

$$m_Y(B) = \sum_{R \mid B = R_Y} m(R) \quad \text{for all } B \in P(Y).$$

Let bodies of evidence associated with $m_X$ and $m_Y$ , $(F_X, m_X)$ and $(F_Y, m_Y)$, be called *marginal bodies of evidence*. These bodies are said to be *noninteractive* if and only if for all $A \in F_X$ and all $B \in F_Y$

$$m(A \times B) = m_X(A) \cdot m_Y(B)$$

and

$$m(R) = 0 \text{ for all } R \neq A \times B.$$

## 4.3.2    Generalized Possibility Theory (GPT)

GPT is based on two dual semicontinuous fuzzy measures, called possibility measures and necessity measures. A *possibility measure* is a function

$$\text{Pos: } \mathsf{P}\,(X) \to [0,1]$$

such that $\text{Pos}\,(\varnothing) = 0$, $\text{Pos}\,(X) = 1$, and

$$\text{Pos}\left(\underset{i \in I}{Y}\,A_i\right) = \underset{i \in I}{\sup}\,\text{Pos}\,(A_i) \tag{8}$$

for any family of subsets of X defined by an arbitrary index set I; it is semicontinuous from below. A *necessity measure* is a function

$$\text{Nec: } \mathsf{P}\,(X) \to [0,1]$$

such that $\text{Nec}\,(\varnothing) = 0$, $\text{Nec}\,(X) = 1$, and

$$\text{Nec}\left(\underset{i \in I}{I}\,A_i\right) = \underset{i \in I}{\inf}\,\text{Nec}\,(A_i) \tag{9}$$

for any family of subsets of X; it is semicontinuous from above.

Given a possibility measure Pos, a function r on X defined by the equation

$$r(x) = \text{Pos}\,(\{x\})$$

for all $x \in X$ is called a *possibility distribution function*. This function uniquely characterizes the possibility measure via the formula

$$\text{Pos}(A) = \underset{x \in A}{\sup}\,r(x), \tag{10}$$

for all $A \in \mathsf{P}(X)$. Since possibility and necessity measures are, respectively, special plausibility and belief measures, the counterpart of (3) in possibility theory is the equation

$$\text{Nec}(A) = 1 - \text{Pos}(\overline{A}) \tag{11}$$

and the counterpart of (4) in possibility theory is the inequality

$$\text{Pos}(A) \geq \text{Nec}(A). \tag{12}$$

Several other important properties of possibility and necessity measures can readily be derived [8] :

$$\text{Pos}\,(A \cap B) \leq \min\,[\text{Pos}\,(A), \text{Pos}\,(B)], \tag{13}$$
$$\text{Nec}\,(A \cup B) \geq \max\,[\text{Nec}\,(A), \text{Nec}(B)], \tag{14}$$
$$\text{Pos}\,(A) < 1 \Rightarrow \text{Nec}\,(A) = 0 \tag{15}$$

$$\text{Nec}(A) > 0 \Rightarrow \text{Pos}(A) = 1 \qquad (16)$$

for all A, B $\in$ P(X).

For the sake of simplicity, let us assume that X is a finite set and let $X = \{x_1, x_2, \cdots, x_n\}$. Assume further (without any loss of generality) that $r(x_i) \geq r(x_{i+1})$ for all i= 1, 2, $\cdots$, n−1. Using this notation, it is easy to show that the basic probability assignment function m associated with r is given by the formula

$$m(A) = \begin{cases} r(x_i) - r(x_{i+1}) & \text{for } A = E_i, i \in \mathbf{N}_n = \{1,2,...,n\} \\ 0 & \text{for } A \neq E_i \text{ for all } i \in \mathbf{N}_n \end{cases} \qquad (17)$$

for all A $\in$ P(X), where $E_i = \{x_1, x_2, \cdots, x_i\}$ for all i $\in$ $\mathbf{N}_n$, and $r(x_{n+1}) = 0$ by convention. The inverse formula is

$$r(x_i) = \sum_{k=i}^{n} m(E_k) \qquad (18)$$

for all i $\in$ $\mathbf{N}_n$.

When r is a joint *possibility distribution function* defined on a finite Cartesian product X × Y, *marginal possibility distribution functions*, $r_X$ and $r_Y$, are determined by the formulas

$$r_X(x) = \max_{y \in Y} r(x, y) \qquad (19)$$

for each x $\in$ X and

$$r_Y(y) = \max_{x \in X} r(x, y) \qquad (19')$$

for each y $\in$ Y. The marginal bodies of evidence are viewed as *noniteractive* in GPT when

$$r(x,y) = \min[r_X(x), r_Y(y)] \qquad (20)$$

for all x $\in$ X and y $\in$ Y.

At the level 1 (representation), GPT may be viewed as a special branch of DST, in which focal elements are always nested. However, at level 2 (calculus), the two theories are not comparable. Via its fuzzy-set interpretation [23], GPT is important for representing and manipulating linguistic information [36].

## 4.4   Uncertainty Measures: Key Requirements

A measure of uncertainty of some conceived type represented within a given mathematical theory (probability theory, GPS, DST, etc.) is a function that assigns to each representation of evidence in the theory ( a probability distribution, a possibility distribution, a body of evidence, etc.) a nonnegative real number. Intuitively, numbers obtained by this function should be inversely proportional to the strength and consistency in evidence, as expressed in the theory employed: the stronger and more consistent the evidence, the smaller the amount of uncertainty.

Uncertainty measures are distinguished from one another by the mathematical representation employed and by the type of uncertainty involved. Although each uncertainty measure should make sense on intuitive grounds, it is even more important that it satisfies certain axiomatic requirements. In the rest of this section the most fundamental requirements are described. Since the mathematical form of each of these requirements depends on the uncertainty theory employed, they are described in generic terms, independent of the various uncertainty calculi.

The following requirements are essential in the sense that they apply to all uncertainty theories:

1.  *Subadditivity* — the amount of uncertainty in a joint representation of evidence (defined on a Cartesian product) cannot be greater than the sum of the amounts of uncertainty in the associated marginal representations of evidence.
2.  *Additivity* — the two amounts of uncertainty considered under subadditivity become equal if and only if the marginal representations of evidence are noninteractive according to the rules of the uncertainty calculus involved.
3.  *Range* — the range of uncertainty is [0, M], where M depends on the cardinality of the universal set involved and on the chosen unit of measurement.
4.  *Continuity* — any measure of uncertainty must be a continuous function.
5.  *Expansibility* — expanding the universal set by alternatives that are not supported by evidence must not affect the amount of uncertainty.
6.  *Branching/Consistency* — when uncertainty can be computed in more ways, all intuitively acceptable, the results must be the same (consistent).

The remaining two requirements are applicable only to some theories of uncertainty:

7.  *Monotonocity* — when evidence can be ordered in the uncertainty theory employed (as in possibility theory), the relevant uncertainty measure must preserve this ordering.

8.  *Coordinate invariance* — when evidence is described within the n-dimensional Euclidean space ($n \geq 1$), the relevant uncertainty measure must not change under isometric transformation of coordinates.

## 4.5    Uncertainty Measures in DST and GPT

It is recognized that two types of uncertainty coexist in DST. They are usually referred to as nonspecificity and entropy-like uncertainty. The various issues regarding their measurement are covered in Sec. 5.1 and 5.2, respectively. Sec. 5.3 is devoted to the measurement of aggregate uncertainty in DST, which subsumes uncertainties of both types.

### 4.5.1   Nonspecificity

Perhaps the most fundamental type of uncertainty is expressed in terms of a finite set of possible alternatives. To describe this uncertainty, let X denote the set of all alternatives under consideration (predictions, retrodictions, diagnoses, etc.), and let it  be called a *universal set*. In each situation, only one of the alternatives is correct, but we do not necessarily know which one. Assume that we only know, on the basis of all available evidence, that the true alternative is in a subset A of X. This means that only the alternatives in A are considered as *possible* candidates for the true alternative.

It is well established that the only sensible way to measure the amount of uncertainty associated with any finite set A of possible alternatives is to use function H defined by the simple formula

$$H(A) = \log_2 | A | , \qquad (21)$$

provided that the measurement unit is a *bit*. This formula was originally derived by Hartley [10], and it is thus usually referred to as the *Hartley measure of uncertainty*. Its uniqueness was later proven in several different ways on axiomatic grounds [25].

The type of uncertainty quantified by the Hartley measure is well captured by the term *nonspecificity*. Indeed, this uncertainty results from the lack of specificity in characterizing the true alternative. The larger the set of possible alternatives, the less specific is the characterization. Full specificity is obtained when only one alternative is possible.

Viewed from the standpoint of DST, the nonspecificity quantified by the Hartley measure is expressed by simple bodies of evidence, each with one focal element. To measure nonspecificity of arbitrary bodies of evidence in DST, we need a function by which values of the Hartley measure for all focal elements can be properly aggregated. The most natural way of aggregation in this case is to take the average of these values, weighted by the associated values of the basic probability assignment function m. The general measure of nonspecificity in DST, N, is then defined for each given m by the formula

$$N(m) = \sum_{A \in P(X)} m(A) \log_2 |A|. \tag{22}$$

If all focal elements are singletons, which means that the body of evidence represents a probability measure, then N(m) = 0. If all focal elements are nested, then it is convenient to replace function N with a special function, which is usually denoted in the literature by U. Assuming, as in Sec. 3.2., that $X = \{x_1, x_2, \ldots, x_n\}$ and $r(x_i) \geq r(x_{i+1})$ for all $i \in N_{n-1}$, the possibilistic measure of nonspecificity U is defined by the formula

$$U(r) = \sum_{i=2}^{n} [r(x_i) - r(x_{i+1})] \log_2 i. \tag{23}$$

The connection between N and U is facilitated by Eq.(17).

When employing the fuzzy-set interpretation of GPT [23], U(r) measures the amount of nonspecificity in evidence expressed by the proposition "$X$ is F," where $X$ is a variable whose values are in X and F is a fuzzy set. Then,

$$U(r_F) = \sum_{i=2}^{n-1} [F(x_i) - F(x_{i+1})] \log_2 i + [F(x_n) + 1 - h_F] \log_2 n, \tag{24}$$

where $h_F$ denotes the height of F.

In the historical context, function U was proposed by Higashi & Klir [11], and its uniqueness under a set of well-justified axiomatic requirements was proven by Klir & Mariano [24]. Function N was proposed, as a generalization of U, by Dubois & Prade [7], and its axiomatic characterization was investigated by Ramer [31]. As us well known [25], both these functions satisfy all the requirements stated in general terms in Sec.4, except coordinate invariance, which is not applicable when we deal with finite sets.

The Hartley measure is applicable only to finite sets. A *Hartley-like measure*, HL, for convex subsets of the n-dimensional Euclidean space $R^n (n \geq 1)$ was proposed by Klir & Yuan [27]. For any convex subset A of $R^n (n \geq 1)$, HL is defined by the formula

$$HL(A) = \min_{t \in T} \ln \left[ \prod_{i=1}^{n} [1 + \mu(A_{i_t})] + \mu(A) - \prod_{i=1}^{n} \mu(A_{i_t}) \right], \tag{25}$$

where $\mu$ denotes the Lebesgue measure, T denotes the set of all transformations from one orthogonal coordinate system to another, and $A_{i_t}$ denotes the i-th one-dimensional projection of A in coordinate system t.

The Hartley-like measure HL was proven to satisfy all properties that such a measure is expected to satisfy (monotonicity, continuity, subadditivity, additivity, coordinate invariance, and appropriate range), but its uniqueness has not been established as yet. The measure can be extended to fuzzy sets via the fuzzy-set interpretation of possibility theory [23]. This results in a new function, UL, a counterpart of function U, which for each convex fuzzy set F is defined by the formula

$$UL(F) = \int_0^{h_F} HL(^\alpha F)d\alpha + (1 - h_F)HL(X), \tag{26}$$

where $^\alpha F$ denotes the $\alpha$-cut of F ($\alpha \in [0, 1]$) [26]. When the set of focal elements is finite, we can also use the formula

$$NL(m) = \sum_{A \in P(X)} m(A)HL(A), \tag{27}$$

as a counterpart of (22), provided that all focal elements are convex sets.

## 4.5.2  Entropy-Like Uncertainty

Nonspecificity is not the only type of uncertainty in DST and GPT. This follows directly from the fact that nonspecificity is not applicable to probability measures at all. Shannon entropy, which is a well-established measure of uncertainty in probability theory, measures thus uncertainty of a different type. This means that two types of uncertainty coexist in DST.

The Shannon entropy, S, which is applicable only to probability measures, is expressed within DST by the formula

$$S(m) = -\sum_{x \in X} m(\{x\}) \log_2 m(\{x\}).$$

This function, which forms the basis for *classical information theory*, has been proven in numerous ways as the only sensible measure of the average uncertainty in predicting outcomes of a random experiment.

Attempts to find a well-justified generalization of the Shannon entropy in DST have not been successful thus far. Although several functions have been proposed in the literature for this purpose on intuitive grounds, none of them satisfies all mathematical properties expected of such a function. In most cases, the proposed functions do not satisfy the property of subadditivity. An historical overview of these various attempts, primarily in the 1980s and the early 1990s, is given in [25].

### 4.5.3   Aggregate Uncertainty

In the early 1990s, the unsuccessful attempts to find a generalized Shannon entropy in DST were replaced with attempts to find an aggregate uncertainty measure. Such a measure should capture the total amount of uncertainty for each given body of evidence in DST. After some initial failures, these attempts were eventually successful. An aggregate measure of uncertainty in DST that satisfies all required properties was found independently by several authors [25]. This aggregate uncertainty measure is a function AU that for each given body of evidence based on belief measure Bel is defined as follows:

$$AU(Bel) = \max_{P_{Bel}} \left[ -\sum_{x \in X} p_x \log_2 p_x \right], \qquad (28)$$

where the maximum is taken over all probability distributions that are consistent with the given belief measure. That is, $P_{Bel}$ in (28) consists of all probability distributions $\langle p_x \mid x \in X \rangle$ that satisfy the following constraints:

(i)   $p_x \in [0,1]$ for all $x \in X$ and $\sum_{x \in X} p_x = 1$;

(ii)  $Bel(A) \le \sum_{x \in A} p_x$ for all $A \subseteq X$.

Since the common defect of all other functions proposed in the literature to measure entropy-like uncertainty or aggregate uncertainty in DST is the lack of subadditivity, it is significant that function AU satisfies all required mathematical properties, including subadditivity.

Since function AU is defined in terms of the solution to a nonlinear optimization problem, its practical utility was initially questioned. Fortunately, the following relatively simple and fully general algorithm for computing the measure was soon discovered [25].

## 4.6   Principles of Uncertainty

Once measures of uncertainty and uncertainty-based information are well justified in a mathematical theory of uncertainty, they can be effectively utilized for dealing with systems formalized in this theory. In inductive modeling, for example, they can be utilized for extrapolating evidence, assessing the strength of relationship between given groups of variables, measuring the loss of information when a system is simplified, and the like. As shown by Ashby [1] and Conant [5], there are even some laws of information that govern systems. Since systems of various types may be viewed as knowledge structures, these laws are fundamental to knowledge management as well.

The role of well-justified uncertainty measures is particularly significant in three fundamental principles of uncertainty, each of which is operationally contingent upon such measures. Two of these principles are optimization principles referred to as the *principles of minimum and maximum uncertainty*; the third is a principle of preserving uncertainty (and information), often referred to as the *principle of uncertainty invariance*. Since types and measures of uncertainty substantially differ in different uncertainty theories, the principles result in considerably different mathematical problems when we move from one theory to another.

## 4.6.1    Principle of Minimum Uncertainty

The *principle of minimum uncertainty* is an arbitration principle. It facilitates the selection of meaningful solutions from a solution set obtained by solving any problem in which some initial information is inevitably lost. By this principle, we should accept only such solutions for which the amount of lost information is minimal. This is equivalent to accepting solutions with the minimum relevant uncertainty (predictive, prescriptive, etc.). Well-justified measures of uncertainty are essential for ordering the obtained solutions in terms of their information values, which makes the principle operational.

A major class of problems for which the principle of minimum uncertainty is applicable are *simplification problems*. When a system is simplified, it is usually unavoidable to lose some information contained in the system. The amount of information that is lost in this process results in the increase of an equal amount of relevant uncertainty. Examples of relevant uncertainties are predictive, retrodictive, or prescriptive uncertainty. A sound simplification of a given system should minimize the loss of relevant information (or increase in relevant uncertainty) while achieving the required reduction of complexity. That is, we should accept only such simplifications of a given system at any desirable level of complexity for which the loss of relevant information (or the increase in relevant uncertainty) is minimal. When properly applied, the principle of minimum uncertainty guarantees that no information is wasted in the process of simplifications.

Given a system formulated within a particular experimental frame, there are many distinct ways of simplifying it. Three main strategies of simplification can readily be recognized.

- simplifications made by eliminating some entities from the system (variables, subsystems, etc.)
- simplifications made by aggregating some entities of the system (variables, states, etc.)
- simplifications made by breaking overall systems into appropriate subsystems.

Regardless of the strategy employed, the principle of minimum uncertainty is utilized in the same way. It is an arbiter which decides which simplifications to choose at any given level of complexity.

Another application of the principle of minimum uncertainty is the area of *conflict-resolution problems*. For example, when we integrate several overlapping partial models into one larger model, the models may be locally inconsistent. It is reasonable then to require that each of the models be appropriately adjusted in such a way that the overall model become consistent. To guarantee that no fictitious (biasing) information be introduced, the adjustments must not decrease the uncertainty of any of the partial models involved, but may increase it. That is, to achieve local consistency of the overall model, we are likely to loose some information contained in the partial model. This is not desirable. Hence, we should minimize this loss of information. That is, we should accept only those adjustments for which the total loss of information (or total increase of uncertainty) is minimal. The total loss of information may be expressed, for example, by the sum of all individual losses or by a weighted sum, if the partial models are valued differently.

## 4.6.2   Principle of Maximum Uncertainty

The second principle, *the principle of maximum uncertainty*, is essential for any problem that involves *ampliative reasoning*. This is reasoning in which conclusions are not entailed in the given premises. Using common sense, the principle may be expressed by the following requirement: in any ampliative inference, use all information available but make sure that no additional information is unwittingly added. That is, the principle requires that conclusions resulting from any ampliative inference maximize the relevant uncertainty within the constraints representing the premises. This principle guarantees that our ignorance be fully recognized when we try to enlarge our claims beyond the given premises and, at the same time, that all information contained in the premises be fully utilized. In other words, the principle guarantees that our conclusions are maximally noncommittal with regards to information not contained in the premises.

Ampliative reasoning is indispensable to science and engineering in a variety of ways. For example, whenever we utilize a scientific model for predictions, we employ ampliative reasoning. Similarly, when we want to estimate microstates form the knowledge of relevant macrostates and partial information regarding the microstates (as in image processing and many other problems), we must resort to ampliative reasoning. The problem of the identification of an overall system from some of its subsystems is another example that involves ampliative reasoning.

The principle of maximum uncertainty is well developed and tested within the classical information theory based upon the Shannon entropy, where it is called the *maximum entropy principle*. Perhaps the greatest skill in using this principle in a broad spectrum of applications, often in combination with the complementary minimum entropy principle, has been demonstrated by Christensen [3, 4].

The maximum entropy principle was founded, presumably, by Jaynes [12]. Literature concerned with the principle is extensive. An excellent overview is a book by Kapur [13], which contains an extensive bibliography.

A general formulation of the principle of maximum entropy is: determine a probability distribution ( $p(x)|x \in X$ ) that maximizes the Shannon entropy subject to constraints $c_1$, $c_2$, ..., which express partial information about the unknown probabilities $p(x)$, as well as general constraints (axioms) of probability theory. The most typical constraints employed in practical applications are the mean (expected) values of random variables under investigation or various marginal probability distributions of an unknown joint distribution.

Although we have now well-justified measures of uncertainty in DST and GPT, the optimization problems that emerge in these theories from the maximum uncertainty principle for various constraints have yet to be properly investigated and tested in praxis. These problems will undoubtedly involve some formidable technical problems.

Since two types of uncertainty coexist in DST and GPT, we may focus on maximizing uncertainty of one of the types or, alternatively, using measures of both types as objective functions. Which of the three possible applications of the maximum uncertainty principle is appropriate depends, of course, on the context of each application. Maximizing nonspecificity (as illustrated in [25]) is advantageous from the computational point of view since the measure of nonspecificity (22) is a linear function. Examples of some typical constraints are: belief functions for some subsets of the frame of discernment, marginal bodies of evidence, upper and lower estimates of the basic probability assignment function.

### 4.6.3   Principle of Uncertainty Invariance

The third principle, the *principle of uncertainty invariance*, facilitates connections among representations of uncertainty and information in alternative mathematical theories. The principle requires that the amount of uncertainty (and information) be preserved when a representation of uncertainty in one mathematical theory is transformed into its counterpart in another theory. That is, the principle guarantees that no information is unwittingly added or eliminated solely by changing the mathematical framework by which a particular phenomenon is formalized. As a rule, uncertainty invariant transformations are not unique. To make them unique, appropriate additional requirements must be imposed.

In comparison with the principles of minimum and maximum uncertainty, which have been investigated and applied within probability theory for at least 40 years, the principle of uncertainty invariance was introduced only in the early 1990s [20]. It is based upon the following epistemological and methodological position: every real-world decision or problem situation involving uncertainty can be formalized in all the theories of uncertainty. Each formalization is a mathematical model of the situation. When we commit ourselves to a particular mathematical theory, our modeling becomes necessarily limited by the constraints of the theory. For example, probability theory can model decision situations only in terms of conflicting degrees of belief in mutually exclusive alternatives. These degrees are derived in some ways from the evidence on hand. GPT, on the other hand, can model a decision situation only in terms of degrees of belief that are allocated to consonant (nested) subsets of alternatives; these are almost conflict-free, but involve large nonspecificity.

Clearly, a more general theory (such as DST) is capable of capturing uncertainties of some decision situations more faithfully than its less general competitors (such as probability theory and GPT). Nevertheless, every uncertainty theory, even the least general one, is capable of characterizing (or approximating, if you like) the uncertainty of every situation. This characterization may not be, due to constraints of the theory, as natural as its counterparts in other, more adequate theories. However, such a characterization does always exist. If the theory is not capable of capturing some type of uncertainty directly, it may capture it indirectly in some fashion, through whatever other type of uncertainty is available.

To transform the representation of a problem-solving situation in one theory, $T_1$, into an equivalent representation in another theory, $T_2$, we should require that:

    (i)   the amount of uncertainty associated with the situation be preserved when we move form $T_1$ into $T_2$; and

    (ii)  the degrees of belief in $T_1$ be converted to their counterparts in $T_2$ by an appropriate scale, at least ordinal.

These two requirements express the *principle of uncertainty invariance.*

Requirement (i) guarantees that no uncertainty is unwittingly added or eliminated solely by changing the mathematical theory by which a particular phenomenon is formalized. If the amount of uncertainty were not preserved then either some information not supported by the evidence would unwittingly be added by the transformation (information bias) or some useful information contained in the evidence would unwittingly be eliminated (information waste). In either case, the model obtained by the transformation could hardly be viewed as equivalent to its original.

Requirement (ii) guarantees that certain properties, which are considered essential in a given context (such as ordering or proportionality of relevant values), be preserved under the transformation. Transformations under which certain properties of a numerical variable remain invariant are known in the theory of measurement as scales.

Due to unique connection between uncertainty and information, the principle of uncertainty can also be conceived as a *principle of information invariance or information preservation.* Indeed, each model of a problem-solving situation, formalized in some mathematical theory, contains information of some type and some amount. The amount is expressed by the difference between the maximum possible uncertainty associated with the set of alternatives postulated in the situation and the actual uncertainty of the model. When we approximate one model with another one, formalized in terms of a different mathematical theory, this basically means that we want to replace one type of information with an equal amount of information of another type. That is, we want to convert information from one type to another while, at the same time, preserving its amount. This expresses the spirit of the principle of information invariance of preservation: no information should be added or eliminated solely by converting one type of information to another. It seems reasonable to compare this principle, in a metaphoric way, with the principle of energy preservation in physics.

Examples of generic applications of the principle include problems that involve transformations from probabilities to possibilities and vice versa, approximations of fuzzy sets by crisp sets (defuzzification), and approximations of bodies of evidence in DST by their probabilistic or possibilistic counterparts.

## 4.7   Open Problems and Undeveloped Areas

While the Hartley-like measures of nonspecificity in DST and GPT are well established and their uniqueness proven, acceptable entropy-like measures in these theories are yet to be found. As described in [25], none of the hitherto considered candidates for these measures satisfies the essential requirement of subadditivity. Finding counterparts of the Shannon entropy in DST and GPT are thus open problems. Fortunately, the aggregate uncertainty measure AU allows us to define Shannon-like measure (on strictly mathematical grounds) as $AU - N$.

One promising direction of research on these open problems is motivated by the following idea. Given a body of evidence in DST or GPT, the union of all focal elements can always be uniquely partitioned in such a way that each resulting block of partition consists of elements that are covered by the same set of focal elements. Elements in each block of this partition are equivalent in the sense that they have the same value of plausibility (or possibility) measure. Hence, the situation is analogous to probability theory: we have a set of disjoint alternatives, each characterized by a single number in [0, 1], which expresses the given evidence. It is thus reasonable to define the Shannon-like measure, SL, in the form

$$SL = -\sum_{B \in \mathsf{B}} w(B) \log_2 f(Pl(B)),$$

where $\mathsf{B}$ denotes the partition and f, w are appropriate functions that have to be yet determined.

Although the aggregate uncertainty measure AU is acceptable on mathematical grounds in DST as well as GPT, it is rather insensitive to changes that seem significant on intuitive grounds. This undesirable feature of measure AU is well illustrated by the following very simple example. Let $X = \{x_1, x_2\}$ and let $m(\{x_1\}) = a$, $m(\{x_2\}) = b$, and $m(\{x_1, x_2\}) = 1 - a - b$. Then, Bel $(\{x_1\}) = a$,

$Bel(\{x_2\}) = b$, and $Bel(\{x_1, x_2\}) = 1$. It is clear that $AU = 1$ for each combination of values a and b when $a \leq 0.5$ and $b \leq 0.5$. In this example, changes in evidence within a fairly large space are thus not distinguished by measure AU at all.

Another undesirable feature of the aggregate measure AU should be mentioned. The measure does not take into account differences in convex sets of probability distributions that are consistent with the various bodies of evidence. Thus, for example, the situation of total ignorance, when $m(X) = 1$, has the same value of AU as the situation characterized by the uniform probability distribution $m(\{x\}) = 1/|X|$ for all $x \in X$. However these two situations are associated with very different sets of probability distribution. In the first situation, the set consists of all probability distributions that can be defined on X; in the second situation, the set consists of a single probability distribution, the uniform one. This is an important difference, at least from the behavioral point of view. While the second situation contains information for rational betting, no such information is available in the first situation.

One way to overcome both these shortcomings of measure AU is to define a total uncertainty in DST, TU, as a linear combination of measure AU and the Hartley-like measure N of nonspecificity defined by Eq. (22). That is,

$$TU = (1-\delta)U + \delta AU, \tag{29}$$

where $\delta \in [0,1]$ is here viewed as discounting factor of the measure AU. Since AU is a measure of aggregate uncertainty as opposed to strictly a generalization of the Shannon entropy, such a discounting factor is appropriate when combining it with U. This linear combination of U and AU has several very desirable properties as a measure of total uncertainty in DST. Most notably, both U and AU are well established mathematically. They satisfy all of the desired requirements of an uncertainty measure, including required range and subadditivity. Thus, a linear combination of the two measures does also satisfy the essential requirements.

An open problem associated with the total uncertainty TU is the choice of the discounting factor $\delta$. Its appropriate value may be justified on mathematical grounds or, alternatively, it may be derived from the context of each particular application.

Further research is still needed to investigate the Hartley-like measure of nonspecificity for the n-dimensional Euclidean space ($n \geq a$). Although the measure defined by Eq.(25) is well justified, it is confined to convex subsets of the space, and this is often too restrictive in practical applications.

Since research regarding measures of uncertainty in DST and GPT is still ongoing, there is little motivation to pursue research in these theories at level 4. Nevertheless, some important results based on the aggregate measure AU and the Hartley-like measure of nonspecificity N have already been obtained for information-preserving transformations between probabilities and possibilities and for probabilistic and possibilistic approximations of arbitrary bodies of evidence in DST [9].

Several nonclassical theories of uncertainty, in addition to DST and GPT, are now well developed at levels 1 and 2. Some of these theories are based on interval-valued probability distributions [29], fuzzy probability distributions [30], Sugeno $\lambda$ -measures [35], and closed convex sets of probability distributions [28]. However, none of these theories is developed at level 3 as yet.

## 4.8    Conclusions

One of the basic characteristics of inductive modeling is that it is conceivable only in terms of nondeterministic systems. It is in the nature of nondeterministic systems that the mathematical framework within which they are formalized must be capable of describing uncertainty. One of the advantages of inductive modeling is that uncertainty enters into each model naturally in the modeling process itself. It is one of the essential characteristics of each model, together with descriptive complexity and credibility, by which models can be compared.

Each model is developed for some purpose. The aim of modeling is to construct a model that is as useful as possible for the given purpose. This means, in turn, to determine a model with a proper blend of the three essential characteristics -- complexity, credibility and uncertainty. The search for this desirable model is greatly facilitated by the three principles of uncertainty, provided that they are properly developed within the mathematical theory in which the models of concern are formalized.

Classical formalisms for describing uncertainty (probability theory and crisp possibility theory), notwithstanding their useful role in inductive modeling, are not adequate to capture uncertainty inherent in some applications. Broader, nonclassical formalisms has been emerging since 1950s. Research on these formalisms has been concerned predominantly with levels 1 and 2. However, to use these formalisms in systems modeling, we need to develop them at levels 3 and 4 as well. To pursue this development, which is the aim of generalized information theory [22], is a formidable task, as illustrated by the brief discussion of the pertinent issues in this paper.

## References

[1]  Ashby, W. R. [1972], "Systems and their informational measures." In: Klir, G. J., ed., *Trends in General Systems Theory*. Wiley-Interscience, New York, pp. pp. 78-97.

[2]  Choquet, G. [1953-54], "Theory of capacities." *Annales de L'Institut Fourier*, **5**, pp. 131-295.

[3]  Christensen, R. [1985], "Entropy minimax multivariate statistical modeling - I: Theory." *Intern. J. of General Systems*, **11**(3), pp. 231-277.

[4]  Christensen, R. [1986], "Entropy minimax multivariate statistical modeling -

II: Applications." *Intern. J. of General Systems*, **12**(3), pp. 227-305.

[5]  Conant, R. [1976], "Laws of information which govern systems." *IEEE Trans. on Systems, Man, and Cybernetics*, **SMC-6**(4), pp. 240-255.

[6]  De Cooman, G. [1997], "Possibility theory." *Intern. J. of General Systems*, **25**(4), pp. 291-371.

[7]  Dubois, D. and Prade, H. [1985], "A note on measures of specificity for fuzzy sets." *Int. J. of General Systems*, **10**(4), pp. 279-283.

[8]  Dubois, D. and Prade, H. [1988], *Possibility Theory*. Plenum Press, New York.

[9]  Harmanec, D. and Klir G.J. [1997], "On information-preserving transformations." *Intern. J. of General Systems*, **26**(3), pp. 265-290.

[10] Hartley, R. V. L. [1928], "Transmission of information." *The Bell System Technical J.*, **7**(3), pp. 535-563.

[11] Higashi, M. and Klir, G. J. [1983], "Measures of uncertainty and information based on possibility distributions." *Intern. J. of General Systems*, **9**(1), pp. 43-58.

[12] Jaynes, E. T. [1979], "Where do we stand on maximum entropy?" In: R.L.Levine and M.Tribus, (eds.), *The Maximum Entropy Formalism*. MIT Press, Cambridge, Mass., pp. 15-118.

[13] Kapur, J. N. [1989], *Maximum Entropy Models in Science and Engineering*. John Wiley, New York.

[14] Klir, G. J. [1969], *An Approach to General Systems Theory*. Van Nostrand Reinhold, New York.

[15] Klir, G. J. [1975], "On the representation of activity arrays." *Intern. J. of General Systems*, **2**(3), pp. 149-168.

[16] Klir, G. J. [1976], "Identification of generative structures in empirical data." *Intern. J. of General Systems* , **3**(2), pp. 89-104.

[17] Klir, G. J. [1983], "General systems framework for inductive modelling." In: Oren, T. et al., eds., *Simulation and Model-based Methodologies*. Springer-Verlag, New York, pp. 69-90.

[18] Klir G. J. [1985], *Architecture of Systems Problem Solving*. Plenum Press, New York.

[19] Klir, G. J. [1989], "Inductive systems modelling: An overview." In: Zeigler, B. P. et al., eds., *Modelling and Simulation Methodology*. North-Holland, New York, pp. 55-75.

[20] Klir, G. J. [1990], "A principle of uncertainty and information invariance." *Intern. J. of General Systems*, **17**(2-3), pp. 249-275.

[21] Klir, G. J. [1991], "Aspects of uncertainty in qualitative systems modeling." In: P.A. Fishwick and P.A. Luker, (eds.), *Qualitative Simulation Modeling and Analysis*. Springer-Verlag, New York, pp. 24-50.

[22] Klir, G. J. [1991], "Generalized information theory." *Fuzzy Sets and Systems*, **40**(1), pp. 127-142.

[23] Klir, G. J. [1998], "On fuzzy-set interpretation of possibility theory." *Fuzzy Sets and Systems*, **108**(3)

[24] Klir, G. J. and Mariano, M. [1987], "On the uniqueness of possibilistic measure of uncertainty and information." *Fuzzy Sets and Systems*, **24**(2), pp. 197-219.

[25] Klir, G. J. and Wierman M.J. [1998], *Uncertainty-Based Information: Elements of Generalized Information Theory*. Physica-Verlag/Springer-Verlag, Heidelberg and New York.

[26] Klir, G. J. and Yuan, B. [1995], *Fuzzy Sets and Fuzzy Logic: Theory and Applications*. Prentice Hall, PTR, Upper Saddle River, NJ.

[27] Klir, G. J. and Yuan, B. [1995], "On nonspecificity of fuzzy sets with continuous membership functions." *Proc. 1995 Intern. Conf. on Systems, Man, and Cybernetics*, Vancouver.

[28] Kyburg, H. E. [1987], "Bayesian and non-Bayesian evidential updating." *Artifical Intelligence*, **31**, pp. pp.271-293.

[29] Pan, Y. and Klir, G.J. [1997], "Bayesian inference based on interval probabilities." *J. of Intelligent and Fuzzy Systems*, **5**(3), pp. 193-203.

[30] Pan, Y. and B.Yuan [1997], "Bayesian inference of fuzzy probabilites." *Intern.l J. of General Systems*, **26**(1-2), pp. 73-90.

[31] Ramer, A. [1987], "Uniqueness of information measure in the theory of evidence." *Fuzzy Sets and Systems*, **24**(2), pp. 183-196.

[32] Shafer G. [1976], *A Mathematical Theory of Evidence*. Princeton Univ. Press, Princeton, NJ.

[33] Shannon, C. E. [1948], "The mathematical theory of communication." *The Bell System Technical J.*, **27**(3&4), pp. 379-423, 623-656.

[34] Walley, P. [1991], *Statistical Reasoning With Imprecise Probabilities*. Chapman and Hall, London.

[35] Wang, Z. and Klir, G. J. [1992], *Fuzzy Measure Theory*. Plenum Press, New York.

[36] Zadeh, L. A. [1975], "The concept of a linguistic variable and its application to approximate reasoning." *Information Sciences*, **8&9**, pp. 8, pp.199-249, 301-357, 9, pp.43-80.

[37] Zeigler, B. P. [1974], "A conceptual basis for modelling and simulation." *Intern. J. of General Systems*, **1**(4), pp. 213-228.

[38] Zeigler, B. P. [1976], *Theory of Modelling and Simulation*. John Wiley, New York.

[39] Zeigler, B. P. [1984], *Multifaceted Modelling and Discrete Event Simulation*. Academic Press, New York.

[40] Zeigler, B. P. [1990], *Object-Oriented Simulation with Hierarchical Models*. Academic Press, San Diego.

# Chapter 5

# Linguistic Dynamic Systems and Computing with Words for Modeling, Simulation, and Analysis of Complex Systems

F-Y Wang, Y. Lin, and J.B. Pu

*This paper outlines a computational theory of linguistic dynamic systems for computing with words by fusing procedures and concepts from several different areas: Kosko's geometric interpretation of fuzzy sets, Hsu's cell-to-cell mappings in nonlinear analysis, equi-distribution lattices in number theory, and dynamic programming in optimalcontrol theory. The proposed framework enables us to conduct a global dynamic analysis, system design and synthesis for linguistic dynamic systems that use words or linguistic terms in computation, based on concepts and methods well developed for conventional dynamic systems. This theory has significant potential for modeling and analysis of systems where model, goal, control and feedback are primarily specified in words or linguistic terms.*

## 5.1 Introduction

The pioneering work and significant contributions by B.P. Zeigler and his colleagues [17-20] are the foundation of modern theory of modeling and simulation, especially in the area of integrated discrete event and continuous complex dynamic systems. Through modeling and simulation, one is able to reproduce and/or generate events, situations, and processes under specified rules, relationships, and operating conditions for a system before it is built or without disturbing its operation. Its results are extremely valuable for decision-making and evaluation in complex systems for various fields. In its traditional sense, modeling and simulation are based on computing involves manipulation of numbers and symbols. By contrast, humans employ mostly words in computing and reasoning, arriving at conclusions expressed as words from premises expressed in a natural language. Therefore, incorporating computing with words into Zeigler's framework of modeling and simulation will be an interesting and important direction for future research. This is true especially when one is dealing with social or economical, rather than engineering or physical systems. In this chapter, we outline an approach along this direction based on the theory of linguistic dynamic systems by Wang [12-13].

For conventional dynamic systems modeled by differential/difference equations, various concepts and methods for both system analysis and synthesis have been well developed and widely used. For many large complex systems, however, due to the complexity involved and the intrinsic nature of information incompleteness, developing a conventional mathematical model to describe system behavior in a meaningful way is either infeasible or impracticable. Even in the case that a mathematical description has been established for a large complex system, in many situations it is still extremely difficult to convert collected data into forms appropriate to the model and then interpret obtained analysis and synthesis results in human understandable terms.

Fortunately, humans have accumulated working knowledge for many large complex systems from experience and practice. Generally, this kind of knowledge is expressed in natural language, i.e., words or linguistic terms. Using this knowledge, we are able to describe, predict, control and evaluate behaviors of large complex systems. For example, operations of many large complex industrial processes cannot be modeled analytically, yet human operators are capable of monitoring the state of a given task process, and take appropriate control actions in response to the process state. And in the financial area, although mathematical market forecasting has been studied for many decades, experts usually assess market behaviors and specify actions to be taken in linguistic terms. In order to make the analysis and synthesis of such systems systematic, consistent, and formal, we need to consider a special class of dynamic systems, i.e., linguistic dynamic systems (LDS). In LDS problems (plants), situations (states), policies (controllers), observations (feedback), goal and evaluation (performance indices) are specified in linguistic terms. To deal with large complex systems effectively with linguistic human knowledge, especially when human and computers are integrated, a theory for modeling, analysis, and synthesis of linguistic dynamic systems must be developed.

Clearly, many efforts have already been taken toward this objective in the past [1, 2, 10, 11, 15]. For example, knowledge based systems, expert systems, linguistic structures, multi-valued logic, fuzzy logic, and so on. Although these methodologies have been successfully used to solve many problems in large complex systems, none of them has been able to establish a theoretical framework upon which concepts and methods for system analysis and synthesis parallel to those well known for conventional dynamic systems, such as stability analysis and control design, can be developed. Consider the problem of evaluating the stability of or designing a controller for a system described by a set of fuzzy IF-THEN rules, there has been no systematic approach to achieve it.

The objective of this paper is to propose a theory of linguistic dynamic systems that is computationally feasible and can utilize the concepts and methods developed for the analysis and synthesis of conventional dynamic systems, especially stability concepts, global analysis, and design methods for optimal controllers [13]. Figure 5.1 illustrates a block diagram representation of linguistic dynamic systems. Considering the process of making a policy or regulation to address certain problems. In this process, words are used to present the problems, describe the situation, state the goal of the policy, specify the policy, and finally define and implement the evaluation procedures. Correspondingly, a linguistic dynamic model for this process can be constructed as follows:

- *Problems and Situation described in Words:*
    Linguistic Plant Description

- *Goal Statement in Words:*
    Linguistic Objective Function

- *Policy Specification in Words:*
    Linguistic Control Design

- *Evaluation Procedures in Words:*
    Linguistic Feedback

This model will enable us to conduct dynamic simulation for different policies at a high level (word level).

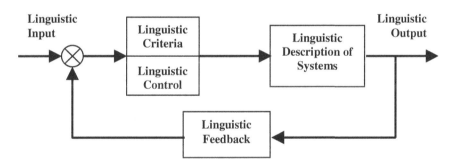

Figure 5.1: Block Diagram Representation of Linguistic Dynamic Systems

The development of microprocessor technology has made digital signal processing essential for interacting with most physical systems. When communicating analog signals in physical systems to digital computers and digital numbers in computers to analog signals physical systems, one needs to use analog/digital (A/D) and digital/analog (D/A) converters (Figure 5.2). We believe the development of intelligent computers will make linguistic information processing essential for analyzing and interacting with most man-made systems. When this becomes reality, structured and domain-specific sets of linguistic terms will be used as words/numbers (W/N) and numbers/words

(N/W) converters for interface between human and computers (Figure 5.3). While D/A and A/D converters are implemented through hardware where accuracy is the key, N/W and W/N converters are carried out through software where vocabulary is the key.

A/D

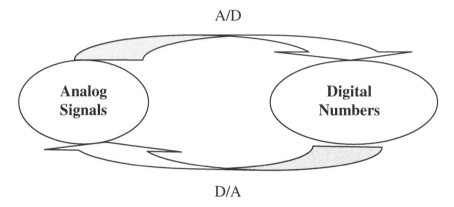

D/A

Figure 5.2: Communication between Physical Systems and Computers: From Analog Signals to Digital Numbers

W/N

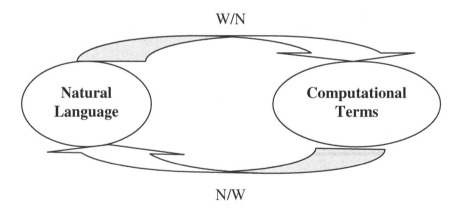

N/W

Figure 5.3: Interface between Human and Computers: From Word to Numbers

Our basic idea here is to represent a LDS as a fuzzy dynamic system. Then, using Kosko's interpretation [9], we can consider LDS as mappings on fuzzy hypercubes. By introducing cellular structures on hypercubes using equi-distribution lattices developed in number theory [8], these mappings can be approximated by cell-to-cell mappings in a cell space [5, 6], in which each cell represents a linguistic term (a word) defined by a family of membership functions of fuzzy sets. In this way, LDS can be studied in the cell state space, and thus, methods and concepts of analysis and synthesis developed for conventional nonlinear systems, such as stability analysis and design synthesis, can be modified and applied for LDS. Especially, linguistic controllers for LDS can now be obtained using the dynamic programming method.

## 5.2   Fuzzy Sets as Points

Zadeh [16] first used a membership function to describe a fuzzy relationship between an entity and a set. Since then fuzzy sets have provided us an ideal tool to express the vagueness in human language. But further research on methods to analyze and design fuzzy systems has difficulties based on this sets-as-functions representation. Kosko proposed an interpretation of fuzzy sets from a geometric point of view: *fuzzy sets as points*, which has been overlooked by most fuzzy theorists [9]. As we will see, this interpretation enables us to carry out the stability analysis and system synthesis for linguistic dynamical systems.

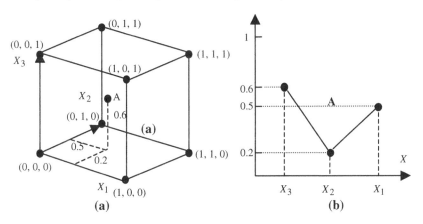

Figure 5.4: Fuzzy Hypercube and Membership Function

Let $V_d = \{v_1, v_2, ... v_n\}$ denote the discretized universe of discourse. Mapping $\mu_A : V_d \rightarrow [0,1]$ is a membership function for fuzzy set $A$. Traditionally, $\mu_A$ is only visualized as a two dimensional graph with domain $V_d$ being on a one-dimensional axis. The new interpretation of a fuzzy set is based on the fuzzy power set $F\left(2^{V_d}\right)$, which consists of all fuzzy subsets on $V_d$ and is a unit $N$-dimensional *fuzzy hypercube* $I^N = [0,1]^N$. Using $F\left(2^{V_d}\right)$, a fuzzy set is considered as a point or vector

$X = (x_1,...,x_N)^T \in F(2^{V_d})$, where $x_i = \mu_A(v_i)$. According to this interpretation, the vertices of the cube $I^N$ define the Boolean ordinary power set $2^{V_d}$ that consists of all $2^N$ nonfuzzy sets of $V_d$. So fuzzy sets fill in the lattice $2^{V_d}$ to produce a solid fuzzy hypercube $F(2^{V_d}) = I^N$. Figure 5.4 presents an example of fuzzy hypercube when $N = 3$, where a point $A$ (Figure 5.4(a)) in the hypercube actually represents a membership function (Figure 5.4(b)).

Clearly, a fuzzy mapping can now be considered as a conventional mapping on fuzzy hypercubes. This provides us a basis for studying linguistic dynamic systems on fuzzy hypercubes.

Based on fuzzy hypercubes, concepts such as the distance between two fuzzy sets and a neighborhood of a fuzzy set can be introduced easily. For example, the distance between two fuzzy sets, represented as points $X_1$ and $X_2$ in a fuzzy hypercube, can be defined as,

$$d_W(X_1, X_2) = \|X_1 - X_2\|_W , \ \|X\|_W = \sqrt{X^T W X} \qquad (1)$$

where $W$ is a metric, i.e., positive and definitive matrix. $W$ can be used to reflect the subjectiveness of a person's view of membership functions. Correspondingly, a quantitative measure of vicinity of a fuzzy set $X_0$ can be defined as,

$$N(X_0, \delta) = \{X \mid d_W(X, X_0) \le \delta, X \in I^N\}, \ \delta > 0 \qquad (2)$$

where $N(X_0, \delta)$ denotes the neighborhood of $X_0$ with radius $\delta$.

## 5.3   Formulation of Linguistic Dynamic Systems

Based on the discussion in the previous section, we can consider a conventional numerical dynamical system as a time dependent mapping from $R^n$ to $R^n$, and a linguistically dynamical system as a time dependent mapping from $I^N$ to $I^N$, where $N$ is much larger than $n$ (see Figure 5.5). Furthermore, using fuzzy sets as linguistic terms, we can model a linguistic dynamic system as a fuzzy dynamic system on fuzzy hypercubes. Generally, a LDS can be described as,

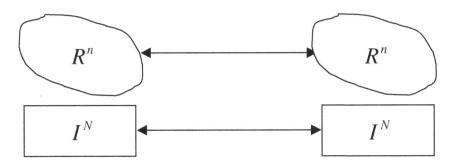

Figure 5.5: Numerical vs. Linguistic Dynamic Systems

*State Equation:*

$$X_{k+1} = F(X_k, U_k, k),$$ (3)

where $F : I^n \times I^m \times Z^+ \to I^n$

*Output Equation:*

$$Y_k = H(X_k, k)$$ (4)

where $F : I^n \times I^m \times Z^+ \to I^n$

*Feedback Control:*

$$U_k = R(Y_k, V_k, k)$$ (5)

where $R : I^p \times I^q \times Z^+ \to I^m$

Note that $Z^+ = \{0, 1, \mathrm{K}\}$, $X_k \in I^n$ is a vector representing a term for the state of the system, $Y_k \in I^p$ the output term, $V_k \in I^q$ the input term, $U_k \in I^m$ the control term, $k$ a discrete time instance, and $F$, $H$, $R$ are fuzzy logic operators which define the system, output, and control mappings of the LDS, respectively.

The universe of discourse of each variable of the above system is defined as,

$$D_X = \{x_1, \mathrm{K}, x_n\},$$
$$D_Y = \{y_1, \mathrm{K}, y_p\},$$

$$D_U = \{u_1, \text{K}, u_m\},$$
$$D_V = \{v_1, \Lambda\ v_q\}.$$

The corresponding terms or fuzzy sets are defined as

$$X = \sum_{x_i \in D_X} \mu_X(x_i)/x_i,$$
$$Y = \sum_{y_i \in D_Y} \mu_Y(y_i)/y_i,$$
$$U = \sum_{u_i \in D_U} \mu_U(u_i)/u_i,$$
$$V = \sum_{v_i \in D_V} \mu_V(v_i)/v_i.$$

clearly, various fuzzy rule-based systems are special cases of our formulation.

Incorporating the output equation and feedback control into the state equation, we can write a LDS in the form of,

$$X_{k+1} = F(X_k, V_k, k),\ k = 0,1,2,\text{K K} \tag{6}$$

When there is no input, i.e., $V_k = 0$, the LDS is called an *autonomous LDS*.

## 5.4   Stability Definitions of Linguistic Dynamic Systems

Using fuzzy hypercubes, we can directly generalize almost all the concepts developed for conventional dynamic systems to a LDS. The following are some examples for a time-invariant autonomous LDS $X_{k+1} = F(X_k)$.

**Trajectory of a LDS**: Let $F^k$ denote mapping $F$ applied $k$ times with $F^0$ as the identity mapping. Starting with an initial term $X_0$, LDS $X_{k+1} = F(X_k)$ generates a sequence of terms $X_k = F^k(X_0)$, $k = 0,1,2,\text{K}$. This sequence of terms is called a *term trajectory* or simply *trajectory* of the LDS with initial term $X_0$.

**Limit Term of a Term**: Consider a trajectory $X_k = F^k(X)$, $k = 0,1,2,\text{K}$. A term $X^*$ is said to be a *limit term* of $X$ under $F$ if there exists a sequence of non-negative integers $n_k$ such that $n_k \to \infty$ and $F^{n_k}(X) \to X^*$ as $k \to \infty$. The set of all limit terms of $X$ is denoted by $\Omega(X)$.

**Positively (Negatively) Invariant Term Set**: For a set of terms, $\Theta \subset I^N$, $F(\Theta)$ denotes the one-step image terms of $\Theta$ under mapping $F$. A term set $\Psi$ is said to be *positively (negatively) invariant* under mapping $F$ if $F(\Psi) \subset \Psi (\Psi \subset F(\Psi))$. $\Psi$ is called *invariant* under $F$ if $F(\Psi) = \Psi$.

**Equilibrium Term**: A term $X$ is said to be an *equilibrium term* if $X = F(X)$.

**P-K Trajectory:** A periodic trajectory of the LDS with period $k$ is a sequence of $k$ distinct terms $X_i$, $i = 1, 2, \Lambda, k$, such that

$$X_{i+1} = F^i(X_1), \ i = 1, 2, \Lambda, k-1, \ X_1 = F^k(X_1)$$

any of the terms $X_i$, $i = 1, 2, \Lambda, k$, is called a periodic term of period $k$. We call term sequence $(X_1, \Lambda, X_k)$ a *P-K trajectory* and any of its elements a *P-K term*.

**Stability**: An equilibrium term $X^* \in I^N$ is *stable* if there is an $\varepsilon_0 > 0$ with the following property: for all $\varepsilon_1$, $0 < \varepsilon_1 < \varepsilon_0$, there is an $\varepsilon > 0$ such that whenever $\left\| X - X^* \right\|_W < \varepsilon$ and $X \in I^N$, then $\left\| F^k(X) - X^* \right\|_W < \varepsilon_1$ for all $k \geq 0$.

**Asymptotical Stability:** An equilibrium term $X^* \in I^N$ is *asymptotically stable* if it is stable and there is an $\varepsilon_0 > 0$ with the following property: for all $\varepsilon_1$, $0 < \varepsilon_1 < \varepsilon_0$, if $\left\| X - X^* \right\|_W < \varepsilon_1$ and $X \in I^N$, then $F^k(X) \to X^X$ as $k \to \infty$.

**Global Asymptotical Stability:** An equilibrium term $X^* \in I^N$ is *global asymptotically stable* if it is stable, and with arbitrary initial term $X_0 \in I^N$, $F^k(X_0) \to X^*$ as $k \to \infty$.

One may argue that our discussion so far works only for discrete universes of discourse while many fuzzy sets use continuous ones that would lead to hypercubes of infinite dimensions. In practice, this is not a problem since membership functions are subjective: we do not need to specify them with high accuracy; instead we only need to know their values at some typical sample points in a universe of discourse. Of course, fine discretization of a universe of discourse will result in an accurate approximation of membership functions and a hypercube of higher dimension.

In theory, the above definitions will enable us to conduct modeling and analysis of LDS by applying various methods established for conventional numerical dynamic systems. However, a direct extension from conventional dynamic systems to LDS would not work for most practical applications.

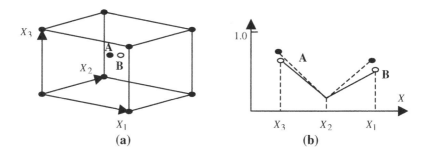

Figure 5.6: A Point and its Adjacent in Fuzzy Hypercube

The reason is simple. Two adjacent points in a fuzzy hypercube will be treated as two different points in the above definitions. Therefore, a LDS that oscillates between two adjacent points will be considered as unstable. However, in terms of the two words represented by the two points, these two points might be considered as the same in a practical sense and the system should be considered as stable. For example, Figure 5.6 shows a point $A$ and its adjacent point $B$ in a fuzzy hypercube. Although $A$ and $B$ are treated as two different points (Figure 5.6(a)), their corresponding membership functions are very close (Figure 5.6(b)), and should be normally treated as the same linguistic term due to the nature of the subjectiveness of membership functions. This consideration leads us to consider the possibility of treating points in a small neighborhood as a single point, i.e., taking the entire neighborhood as a single "linguistic term". Another argument for this consideration is the subjectiveness of fuzzy logic operators. It is well known that different operators can be used for the same logic operations, thus a fuzzy mapping can map a point on the domain hypercube to different points on the image hypercube under different logic operators. Since these image points should be close and within a small neighborhood, the whole neighborhood could be considered as a single image term. These observations have inspired us to introduce cellular structures to fuzzy hypercubes.

## 5.5   Cell Spaces on Fuzzy Hypercubes

The cellular structure of a cell space can be introduced in various ways. Figure 5.7 shows a general cellular structure. The simplest one is the uniform cell division of a fuzzy hypercube. The basic idea behind the fuzzy cell space is to consider a fuzzy hypercube space not as a continuum but as a collection of cells, with each cell being taken as an entity.

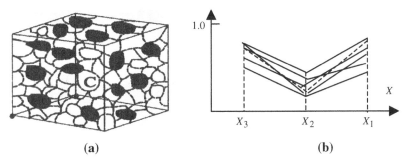

(a)                                    (b)

Figure 5.7: Cellular Structure over Fuzzy Hypercube

Let $x_i$, $i = 1,2,\Lambda ,N$, be $N$ components of a point in the fuzzy hypercube $I^N$, and let the coordinate axis of variable $x_i$ be divided into a large number of intervals of uniform interval size $h_i$. Interval $z_i$ along the $x_i$-axis is defined to be the one that contains all $x_i$ satisfying

$$z_i - h_i /2 \leq x_i < z_i + h_i /2, \ 0 \leq x_i \leq 1$$

such an $N$-tuple $(z_1, z_{2,} \Lambda , z_N )$ is then called a *fuzzy cell vector* (or *fuzzy cell, cell*) and is denoted by $Z$. The *fuzzy cell state space* $S_C$ is the collection of all such cell vectors. The cell center is a representative of the cell in the sense that all points in the cell have similar membership functions and are considered as a single linguistic term.

An essential question for cell space construction is that, for a specified number $N_t$ of terms to be used to describe a system, how can we create a cellular structure so that these $N_t$ terms or cells can be "optimally" distributed in a fuzzy hypercube? This question is especially important for dealing with high dimensional hypercubes, since we can only assign a limited number of cells. One way to define "optimality" is to distribute these terms as uniform as possible. This can be achieved by using the equi-distribution lattices developed in number theory for numerical integration in high dimensional space [4]. For example,

$$Z_i = \left( \left\{ \left[ \frac{i}{F_n} \right] \right\}, \left\{ \frac{iF_n(2)}{F_n} \right\}, \Lambda, \left\{ \frac{iF_n(N)}{F_n} \right\} \right),$$

where $1 \le i \le N_t = F_n$, $\{w\}$ is the decimal remainder of $w$, $F_0 = F_1 = \Lambda = F_{N-2} = 0$, $F_{N-1} = 1$, $F_k = F_{k-1} + \Lambda + F_{k-N+1} + F_{k-N}$, $k \ge N$, and $F_k(j) = F_{k+j-1} - F_{k+j-2} - \Lambda - F_k$, $2 \le j \le N$. Cell $Z_i$ includes all points $X$ such that $d_W(X, Z_i) = \min_{1 < j < N_t} d_W(X, Z_i)$. Many other equi-distribution lattices can be found in [8].

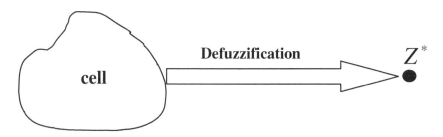

Figure 5.8: Defuzzification of a Fuzzy Cell

Based on the defuzzification of fuzzy sets, we can introduce the defuzzification of a fuzzy cell. For example, the *center of area* method can be generalized to defuzzify a cell $Z$ as,

$$Z^* = \sum_{i=1}^{N} \alpha_i v_i , \quad \alpha_i = \int_V \frac{x_i}{\sum_{j=1}^{N} x_j} \ dV / |V| \tag{7}$$

where $V$ is the domain occupied by $Z$ (see Figure 5.8). Obviously, $Z^*$ can be used to calculate the fuzzy cell vector for a fuzzy cell.

## 5.6   Analysis of LDS using Cell-to-Cell Mappings

Once cell spaces have been established on fuzzy hypercubes, we can use the methods developed by Hsu [5,6] for nonlinear differential dynamic systems to convert a LDS defined by Eqs. (3-5) to cell-to-cell mappings,

$$Z_{k+1} = C_F\left(Z_k, Q_k, t_k\right),$$
$$P_k = C_H\left(Z_k, t_k\right), \; Q_k = C_R\left(P_k, W_k, t_k\right) \tag{8}$$

where $t_k$ is the new time interval, $Z_k \in S_C^X$, $Q_k \in S_c^U$, $P_k \in S_C^Y$, $W_k \in S_C^V$ are cells defined in the fuzzy state, control, output, and input hypercubes, and $C_F$, $C_H$, and $C_R$ are cell-to-cell mappings constructed from $F$, $H$, and $R$. Combining the above equations into one, we get,

$$Z_{k+1} = C\left(Z_k, W_k, t_k\right), \tag{9}$$

$Z_k$ and $Z_{k+1}$ are called the *domain cell* and *image cell*, respectively.

All concepts introduced for a LDS in fuzzy hypercubes can directly be used in cell spaces. In cell spaces, however, the system analysis becomes computationally feasible. Once the cell mapping $C$ is known, we can systematically study the global dynamic properties of a LDS, i.e., equilibrium cells, P-K trajectories, and stability. For the purpose of numerical analysis, we introduce the following two additional definitions:

**R-Step Removable Cell**: A cell $Z$ is said to be *r-step removable* from a P-K trajectory if $r$ is the minimum integer such that $C^r(Z) = Z_j$, where $Z_j$ is any one of the P-K cells in a P-K trajectory.

**R-Step Domain of Attraction**: For a P-K trajectory, the set of cells that are removed from the trajectory in $r$ or less steps is called its *r-step domain of attraction*. When $r \to \infty$, we get the *total domain of attraction* or simply the *domain of attraction* for a P-K trajectory.

Since the number of cells is finite, a cell is a member of either a P-K trajectory or an r-step domain of attraction of a P-K trajectory. A global search algorithm for analysis of autonomous dynamic systems using cell mappings has been developed in [7]. This search algorithm will find the total number of different P-K trajectories of a dynamic system, denoted as $M$, and link each cell with one of P-K trajectories for an autonomous LDS $Z_{k+1} = C(Z_k)$. Assume we have enumerated all its P-K trajectories by $g = 1, \Lambda, M$. Let $S(Z)$ be the number of steps for cell $Z$ to reach a P-K trajectory $g$, $G(Z) = g$ the group number of the P-K trajectory reached, and $P(Z) = k$ the periodic number of the P-K trajectory. To start the search algorithm, we first set $M = 0$, and classify cells in the searching process into three types, i.e., *unprocessed cells, cells under processing*, and *processed cells*. The group number of unprocessed cells are set to be zero at the beginning of the algorithm. When an unprocessed cell is called upon to be processed, we change its group number to -1. After the process, a cell is assigned a group number and becomes a processed cell.

Consider an unprocessed cell $Z$, when it is called upon for processing and generates a sequence of image cells,

$$Z \to C(Z) \to C^2(Z) \to \Lambda \to C^j(Z)$$

then the search algorithm can be described as,

1. The newly generated image cell $C^j(Z)$ is an unprocessed cell. In this case, we change its group number to -1, which indicates it has become a cell under processing, and proceed to the next image cell $C^{j+1}(Z)$.

2. The newly generated cell $C^j(Z)$ is a processed cell with a positive group number. In this case, the current processing sequence is mapped into a cell with known properties, i.e., its group number, step number and periodic number have been found. Obviously, all cells in the sequence will have the same group and periodicity numbers with those of $C^j(Z)$. The step numbers of the other cells in the sequence can be calculated as,

$$S(C^i(Z)) = S(C^j(Z)) + j - i, \ 0 \le i \le j - 1 \quad (10)$$

   All these cells are then marked as processed and the search process continues with another unprocessed cell.

3. The newly generated cell $C^j(Z)$ is a cell under processing. In this case, a new periodic motion is discovered, therefore $M = M + 1$. All

the cells in the sequence are assigned a new group number $g = M$. Assume that the first reappearing cell to be the $(i-1)$th cell in the sequence, i.e., $C^{l(Z)} = C^j(Z)$ for the minimum $l > i$. Then the periodicity number is $(l-i)$ for this new periodic trajectory and it is assigned to every cell in the sequence. The step numbers of the cells be determined by

$$S\big(C^k(Z)\big) = i - k, \; k = 0,1,\Lambda \; i-1,$$
$$S\big(C^k(Z)\big) = 0, \; k \geq i, \tag{11}$$

When each of these three possible situations has been processed, the algorithm will call another unprocessed cell and begin a new search.

This process will be conducted repetitively until every cell in the cell space has been processed and the global dynamic behavior of the system is then completely determined. As a result, the cell space is divided into different P-K trajectories and their domains of attractions. Every cell in the cell space belongs to a certain group. The step number of a cell indicates the distance of the cell to its converging periodic trajectory.

## 5.7    Design of Optimal Control in Cell Spaces

The problem of optimal control design for a LDS is to find a linguistic feedback law that optimizes a linguistic performance index,

$$J(U; X_0) = \sum_{i=0}^{T} \Phi(X_k, U_k, V_k, k), \; X_T \in \Gamma \subset I^n$$

where $\Gamma$ is the linguistic target subset representing the terms to be reached in $T$ steps, $\Phi : I^n \times I^m \times I^q \times Z^+$ is the logic operator of the one-step linguistic cost function, $I^l$ is the fuzzy hypercube of the one-step cost universe $D_\Phi = \{\phi_1,...,\phi_l\}$. To make the fuzzy addition meaningful, we can assume that $\Phi$ always generates a fuzzy number [3]. However, as we can see, this is not important in our formulation. For the sake of simplicity, we assume $Y = X$, i.e. output terms are the same as state terms.

In cell spaces, a one-step cost function can be approximated by a cell-to-cell mapping,

$$\Phi_k = C_\Phi(Z_k, Q_k, W_k, t_k), \; Z_T \in S_\Gamma \subset S_C^X \tag{12}$$

where $S_\Gamma$ is the cell subspace of the target subspace, and $\Phi_k$ is a cell in $I^l$. Using the defuzzification method introduced in section 5, we can defuzzify $\Phi_k$ so that a numerical value $\gamma_k = DF(\Phi_k)$ is obtained for cell $\Phi_k$, i.e.,

$$\gamma_k = DF\big(C_\Phi(Z_k, Q_k, W_k, t_k)\big), \; Z_T \in S_\Gamma \subset S_C^X$$

Clearly, with cell-to-cell mappings (8) and (9), the design of optimal controller for a LDS becomes a standard dynamic programming problem with discrete state and control variables. Therefore, all the methods developed for dynamic programming can be used here.

A general search algorithm for optimal linguistic control has been proposed in [12]. In this method, the one-step cost is quantified into finite levels, $\beta_1\Delta < \beta_2\Delta < \Lambda < \beta_L\Delta$, where $\beta_i$ are integers and $\Delta$ is a quantifying unit. As a result, the accumulated cost can be expressed as,

$$J = \Delta \sum_{i=1}^{L} k_i \beta_i$$

where $k_i$ are integers. In this way, the accumulated cost is also quantified into finite levels.

The search procedure can be outlined simply as,

*Step 1*: Set $S_0 = S_\Gamma$ and $i = 1$. Mark all cells in $S_\Gamma$ as processed, and all other cells as unprocessed.

*Step 2*: Search through all unprocessed cells to find the cells that can be mapped into $S_{i-1}$ Y$\Lambda$ Y$S_0$ with the $i$ th accumulated cost level. Let $S_i$ be the collection of all newly founded cells. Mark all the cells in $S_i$ as processed.

*Step 3*: If all the cells of interest have been marked as processed, stop. Otherwise, set $i = i + 1$, and go back to Step 2.

After the search algorithm is complete, an optimal control table is established that gives the optimal control action at each cell to enter the specified target $S_\Gamma$. Note that the result of this search process is independent of the initial state. Discussions on parallel search algorithms have been given in [14].

## 5.8   Conclusions

A computational theory for linguistic dynamic systems (LDS) has been outlined in this paper. The proposed theory is a fusion of procedures and concepts from several different areas: geometric theory of fuzzy sets, cell-to-cell mappings in nonlinear analysis, equi-distribution lattices in number theory, and dynamic programming in optimal control theory. This theory enables us to numerically conduct the global dynamic analysis, system design and synthesis for linguistic dynamic systems based on concepts and methods developed for conventional dynamic systems.

## References

[1]   Braae, M. and D..A. Rutherford, Theoretical and Linguistic Aspects of the Fuzzy Logic Controller, *IFAC J. Automatica* vol.15, no.5, pp.553-577, 1979.

[2]   Cleveland, B. and A. Meystel, Dynamic Predictive Planning + Fuzzy Logic Control = intelligent Control, *Proc. of IEEE Symp. Intelligent Control*, Philadelphia, PA, 1990.

[3]   Bardossy, A. and L. Duckstein, *Fuzzy Rule-Based Modeling in Geophysical, economic, Biological, and Engineering Systems*, Boca Raton, FL: CRC Press, 1995.

[4]   Halton, J.H., On the Efficiency of Certain Quasi-random Sequences of Points in Evaluating Multi-Dimensional Integrals, *Numerical Mathematics*, vol 2., pp.84-90, 1960.

[5]   Hsu, C.S., *Cell-to-Cell Mapping*, New York, NY: Springer-Verlag, 1987.

[6]   Hsu, C.S., A Generalized Theory of Cell-to-cell Mapping for Nonlinear Dynamical Systems, *ASME J. Applied Mechanics*, vol.48, pp.634-842, 1981.

[7]   Hsu, C.S. and R.S. Guttalu, An Unravelling Algorithm for Global Analysis of Dynamic Systems: An Application of Cell-to-Cell Mapping, *ASME J. Appl. Mechanics*, vol. 47, pp.940-948, 1985.

[8]   Hua, L.K. and Y. Wang, *Applications of Number Theory to Numerical Analysis*, New York, NY: Springer-Verlag, 1981.

[9]   Kosko, B., Neural Networks and Fuzzy Systems: A Dynamical Systems Approach to Machine Intelligence, Englewood Cliffs, NJ: Prentice Hall, 1992.

[10]  Mamdani, E.H. and S. Assilian, Applications if Fuzzy Logic to Approximate Reasoning Using Linguistic Synthesis, *IEEE Trans. Computer*, vol. C-26, no.12, pp.1182-1191, 1977.

[11]  Procyk, T.J. and E.H. Mamdani, A Linguistic Self-Organizing Process Controller, *IFAC J. Automatica*, vol.14, pp.15-30, 1978.

[12]  Pu J.B., *A Cell-to-Cell Mapping Based Analysis and Design of Fuzzy Dynamic Systems and Its Applications*, Ph.D. Dissertation, Systems and Industrial Engineering Department, University of Arizona, 1995.

[13]  Wang F-Y., Modeling, Analysis and Synthesis of Linguistic Dynamic Systems: A Computational Theory, *Proc. of IEEE International Workshop on Architecture for Semiotic Modeling and Situation Control in Large Complex Systems*, Monterey, CA, August 1995.

[14] Wang, F-Y. and X.Y. Fan, Time-Optimal Trajectory Generation for Coordinated Robot Arms Handling a Common Object Using the Cell-to-Cell Mapping Method, *Journal of Optimization Theory and Applications*, vol.86, no.2, 1995.

[15] Wang, P.P. and C-Y. Tyan, Fuzzy Dynamic System and Fuzzy Linguistic Controller Classification, *IFAC J. Automatica*, vol.30, no.12, 1994.

[16] Zadeh, L.A. , Fuzzy Sets, *Information and Control*, vol.12, pp338-353, 1965.

[17] Zeigler, B.P., Multifaceted Modeling and Discrete Event Simulation, London: Academic Press, 1984.

[18] Zeigler, B.P., Toward A Simulation Methodology for Variable Structure Modeling, in *Modeling and Simulation Methodology in the Artificial Intelligence Era,* M. S. Elzas, and B.P. Zeigler, Eds, Amsterdam: Elsevier North Holland Press, 1986.

[19] Zeigler, B.P., A Framework for Modeling & Simulation, in *Applied Modeling & Simulation: An Integrated Approach to Development & operation,* D. Cloud and L. Rainy, Eds, New York, NY: McGraw-Hill, 1997.

[20] Zeigler, B. P., H. Praehoffer, and T.G. Kim, *Theory of Modeling and Simulation,* Academic Press, 1999.

# Chapter 6

# Towards a Modeling Formalism for Conflict Management

T.I. Ören

*The article starts with brief reviews of conflict management and limitations of classical Newtonian paradigm in the studies of human-related disciplines. A new modeling formalism and associated simulation formalism for conflict management simulation studies are presented. The modeling formalism is based on multimodels. A multimodel is a modular model where only one module (alternate model) is active at a certain time. Special cases of multimodels are introduced as metamorphic models and multi-aspect models. In a metamorphic model, there is a predefined sequence for the alternate models. A multi-aspect model is a special case of a multimodel where the condition of having only one alternate model active at a given time is relaxed; the resulting formalism can be useful in modeling (and simulating) several aspects of an entity simultaneously. Evolutionary models can also be conceived as special cases of multimodels. In a multistage modeling formalism, several aspects of the reality can be formulated by sets of component models. Under emerging conditions, one can add emerging successor models to existing models to explore behavior of alternative system models. In the article, multistage model formalism is suggested as a simulation modeling formalism for sociocybernetics systems in general and for conflict management such as conflict avoidance and conflict resolution in particular.*

## 6.1   Introduction

Conflicts are worth studying because they affect quality of life everywhere. They have been common throughout the human history. National and international conflicts are ubiquitous [2]. They have been common during the 20th century [11] and they are at least as worthy of study as during the cold war [1][15]. Even more important, perhaps, is the study of conflict management, i.e., conflict avoidance, and conflict resolution [36]. For example, Davis and Arquilla

[6], based on behavioral science's prospect theory, assert that "possible opponents are likely to become increasingly and unreasonably risk-accepting as they become emotionally more dissatisfied with current situation and trends." Game theory has been applied to social problems [39]. Schelling's pioneering work of analytical game theory recommends identification and consideration of focal points which are the perceived mutual expectations, obsessions, sensitivities, appreciation, and the like for conflict resolution in search of win-win conditions [38].

Several aspects of conflict management are already studied. Searches in RAND Corporation's Web site reveal over 800 documents on conflict [31] and 70 RAND documents on the same subject [32]. A search in amazon.com reveals that nearly 10000 books related with several types of conflict exist.

The aim in this paper is to explore whether or not a modeling formalism – such as multistage modeling formalism– and associated simulation formalism, i.e., multisimulation, can be developed for the simulation of conflict avoidance and conflict resolution. Such modeling and simulation formalisms might also be useful in modeling other social phenomena and hence may be useful for sociocybernetics studies.

We need appropriate paradigms and modeling methodologies to perceive, conceive, and foresee conflicting situations to ideally avoid them and –if they are inevitable– to resolve them. Regardless of their type and origin, conflicts, are parts of social systems; similar to other social phenomena, they are difficult to model. Social systems are sometimes labeled in the literature as soft systems or ill-defined systems where the usefulness of traditional mathematical representations is questioned [48, p. 42].

A major effort [5] used the structure of war gaming, and included artificial intelligence models (rule-based systems) to represent national and international leaders and commanders. This and other works were described by Zeigler [47] as an example of the more general approach of variable-structure agent-based simulation. The studies of a special type of conflict, namely war gaming has been numerous. In war gaming, military decision-makers (i.e., commanders at different levels) can get "war experience" basically at peacetime. Nowadays, war gaming studies use computers extensively although such studies predate computers. For example, in a bibliography on professional war gaming, early studies date back the second half of the 1880s [33]. There are two types of war games, for professionals and for hobbyists. In war gaming, it is much easier to model equipment than humans. Recently, there are studies to remedy the situation [27].

It is argued that conflict avoidance and conflict resolution deserve levels of efforts similar to war gaming. Similar to war gaming experience, military and civilian decision-makers can enhance their conflict management skills through conflict management simulation studies.

Conflict systems are complex social systems. Some already available modeling approaches based, for example, on different types of game theories (e.g., sequential games, differential games, evolutionary games, and hyper games) as well as several other approaches such as bounded rationality, deterrence theory, and crisis destabilization are used for their solutions. Some novel simulation modeling formalisms, not conflicting with already proven theories and approaches may be useful for the proper formulations and resolutions of conflicts.

Some references on complexity are Waldrop [43] and Kaufmann [15]. There are examples in conceiving complexity in elegant ways. For example, by using fractals [3], a complex system can be generated based on simple initial knowledge. An L-system [30][42] can be used to model the growth of a plant at different stages (or steps). A catastrophic manifold [4] can represent interesting (sometimes contradictory) patterns of behavior.

Cybernetics has been considered as a source of paradigm for simulation of complex systems including social systems [17][20]. For a bibliography on contemporary sociocybernetics studies see Geyer and van der Zouven [9].

In developing a modeling formalism for conflict management, one should take into account the bias and limitations of classical scientific thinking toward Newtonian way of perceiving reality which is well documented in the literature (e.g., [29][19]). Toffler even expresses this in more vigor: "Most phenomena of interest to us are, in fact, *open* systems, exchanging energy or matter (and, one might add, information) with their environment. Surely, biological and social systems are open, which means that the attempt to understand them in mechanistic terms is doomed to failure" [41, p. XV]. Newtonian paradigm is indeed very powerful and useful, in engineering and most of the scientific studies (except of course in quantum physics and the domain of relativity). However, Newtonian paradigm is not well suited to complex human-related disciplines. The suggested modeling and associated simulation formalisms, i.e., multistage modeling, and multisimulation formalisms, respectively, would allow experimenting with different –even contradictory– aspects of reality simultaneously. For computational convenience, they can also be executed sequentially, in depth-first search mode. Results of the experiments with multistage models can be simultaneously displayed by taking advantage of the possibilities offered by virtual and augmented realities.

## 6.2   Towards a Modeling Formalism and an Associated Simulation Formalism

It is a philosophical issue whether or not as humans we can deal with reality directly. It is paramount that we develop aids to perceive and to conceive reality properly. The question is whether we can develop a modeling formalism to conceive and to perceive such soft systems in a more systematic way. When properly developed, such a modeling formalism could be useful to model conflicts and associated events. It could be used to develop appropriate models to be used in simulation gaming to provide simulation-based experience for future decision-makers. Such models could be used in getting experience to develop and sharpen abilities to steer the events to achieve desired states to achieve and maintain desirable social order. Since all the details of such a modeling formalism are not yet ready, the term "towards" is used in the title of this article where the concepts are discussed for the first time.

The simulation modeling formalism can benefit from the synergies of conventional simulation and artificial intelligence techniques. For war gaming, use of artificial intelligence, more specifically, rule-based knowledge processing techniques was advocated by [5]. However, a systematic treatment of the subject reveals also other possibilities of application of artificial intelligence in simulation studies [24]. Zeigler elaborated on the use of intelligent software agents to represent high autonomy systems [47]. The relevance of this and another important concept, called endomorphy by Zeigler will be discussed in Section 2.5.

### 6.2.1   Background for Multistage Modeling Formalism

In this section, two modeling formalisms are reviewed to provide background knowledge for multistage models. They are multimodel and evolutionary models.

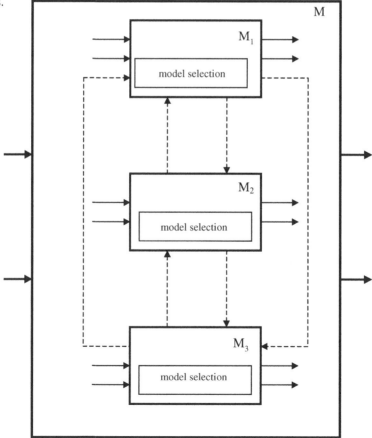

Figure 6.1: A multimodel.

## 6.2.1.1 Multimodels

A multimodel is a modular model where only one model module is active at a certain time. Each model module is an *alternate model*. The "multimodel" formalism was introduced as a generalization of discontinuity in piece-wise continuous systems [21][22]. However, the concept is applicable to continuous, discrete, and memoryless models, as well as to other modeling formalisms such as rule-based models and software agents, including intelligent agents and mobile agents. The models can be atomic or coupled [23]. An extension of the multimodel formalism to combined discrete event and differential equation specified systems (DEV & DESS) as well as coupled multi-formalism system formalism is developed by Praehofer [28].

Figure 6.1 depicts a multimodel M composed of three component models $M_i$, i = 1, 2, and 3. At the beginning, one of the $M_i$ is the initial model to represent M. The inputs of M are connected to the inputs of the initial model. The outputs of the initial model are connected to the outputs of the initial model. While the initial model is running, its behavior is generated through its state transition function and output function. There is a monitoring done at the same time. Model selection (or model transition) conditions are checked to decide whether another module model will represent the multimodel M.

In general, the dynamics of each alternate model is represented by three distinct sections to represent state transition function, output function, and model selection or model transition specifications. Some special cases are as follows: Memoryless models do not have a state transition function. In some other special cases, some/all state variables can be outputted directly. This corresponds to the situation where output function(s) are reduced to identity function(s). If a model transition section does not exist, instead of a multimodel, there is only a conventional model, which can be represented by any appropriate modeling formalism. Two essential characteristics of multimodels are: (1) before the beginning of the behavior generation phase of a simulation study, all the alternate models are known; and (2) only one alternate model is active at a given time.

As an example, the simulation study may start with model $M_1$, then at a model selection instant, model $M_3$ can be selected. Then model $M_2$ can represent the model M; afterwards model $M_1$ can be used again. In all these transitions, all the alternate models are known a priori as well as the transition conditions. During the behavior generation of a simulation study, the model selection conditions have to be monitored to cause interrupts for model selections. In systems with learning abilities, rules for model selection can be learned, hence can be time varying. In the latter case, consistency checks should be done at appropriate times; to assure acceptability of learned knowledge.

With multimodels, similar to any conventional simulation study, only one aspect of reality can be simulated at a given time.

## 6.2.1.2 Special Cases of Multimodels

Two special cases of multimodels are metamorphic models and multi-aspect models. A metamorphosis can be represented by a *metamorphic model* which, in turn, can be represented as a special case of a multimodel. For example, alternate models can represent egg, larva, pupa, and butterfly; alternate models can be selected, under well-defined conditions. However, in this case, there is a predefined sequence for the alternate models; i.e., transitions from alternate models would be rather limited.

A *multi-aspect model* is another special case of a multimodel where the condition of having only one alternate model active at a given time is relaxed. An example usage might be representation of solid, fluid, and vapor phases of the same mass of material (e.g., ice, water, and vapor) and the transitions from one phase to another. The transitions can include sublimation, i.e., passing from solid to vapor state and vice versa. In the example, alternate models representing both water and vapor can exist concurrently with a mass transfer from one to another alternate model. The direction of the transfer of an entity, in the example, water, or vapor, depends whether or not energy is given to, or taken from the multimodel itself.

## 6.2.1.3 Evolutionary Models

Evolution is irreversible change in an open system [37]. At each phase of its evolution, an open system can be represented by a different model. Hence, *evolutionary models* would start with an initial model and a mechanism would alter the current model based on some external and internal conditions.

An evolutionary model is represented by the series of variant models $m_i$ where i is not repeated. Evolutionary models –or *mutational models*– consist of *variant models*. Not all variant models are known a priori. In an evolutionary model, an initial model and the mechanism to generate variant models are known a priori. In *a simulation with evolutionary models,* only one variant model is active at a given time. Furthermore, only one aspect of reality is simulated at a given time.

## 6.2.2   Multistage Models and Multisimulation

The multistage model formalism is suggested as a simulation modeling formalism for sociocybernetics systems in general and for conflict management such as conflict avoidance and conflict resolution in particular. Figure 6.2 is given as an example of multistage models where component models are $M_i$, i = 1, …, 8. For example, the following multistage models are identified: $M_1$, $M_1M_2$, $M_1M_2M_5$, $M_1M_2M_6$, $M_1M_3$, $M_1M_3M_7$, $M_1M_3M_8$, $M_1M_4$, and $M_1M_4M_8$. A model, which can be used after another one in a multistage model, is a successor model.

In a multistage modeling formalism, several aspects of the reality can be formulated by sets of components models. Normally all the multistage models may not be known a priori. For example, only the initial model $M_1$ may be known. In this case, one can attempt to model alternative models to get ready for contingencies. Supposing that $M_2$ and $M_3$ are also modelled, one can have two multistage models: $M_1M_2$ and $M_1M_3$. One can perform a simulation study with each multistage model to find out for example, the outcomes of having $M_2$ or $M_3$. Accordingly, one can try to control the conditions to facilitate transition to a specific model module and/or to make it difficult the transition to another one. If the status of a module of a multistage model is not acceptable or desirable, one has to generate successor model(s) and facilitate transition to that module model.

If all or some of the component models of the multistage models are known a priori, one can use only relevant component models and several simulations can be performed. Multistage model formalism can allow *multisimulation,* or multisim, in short. A multisimulation can be in parallel, to experiment with several aspects of reality simultaneously. For computational convenience, it can also be executed sequentially, in depth-first search mode. When some previously unforeseen conditions arise, i.e., under *emerging conditions*, one can add *emerging* successor *models* to existing models to explore behavior of alternative system models.

Multisim may be the simulation paradigm to experiment with Schrödinger's cat –which can be alive *and* dead at the same time [19]. In non-quantum theoretic realm, it is argued that ability to experiment with several –even contradictory aspects of reality may bring new vistas in conflict management.

Similar to war gaming (or business gaming) one can have experience in conflict avoidance and/or resolution by using appropriate computerized simulation systems. As it is the case with  war gaming systems, knowledge about several types of conflict avoidance and conflict resolution can be made available to the user of computerized simulation system.

## 6.2.3   State Machines

State machine formalism (SM) can be used as an example to develop model modules for multistage models. However, the concept of multistage model is not bound with SM formalism.

Let us start our discussion by reviewing the basic finite-state machine formalism. In a Moore or Mealy machine [10][13] there are three sets and two functions. These sets define finite number of state, input, and output values. A state transition function defines how next state value can be obtained based on current state and current input. The two types of the finite state machine formalisms differ in their output functions. In Moore machine, current output depend on current state; in Mealy machine, current output depends on the current state and current input. The transition and output functions of finite state machines are specified in tabular and/or in graphic notations. In the later, circles depict states, arrows between circles, depict transition between states. Outputs are represented as associated with states or as the labels of the arrows. In Moore machines, current output depend on current state; hence, outputs are associated with corresponding states. In Mealy machines, current output depend on current state and current input; hence, outputs are associated with transitions.

Finite state machine formalism, as a classical modeling formalism, can be used in depicting well defined modules of systems where all the values of the state, input, and output variables as well as state transition and output functions are known a priori. Inputs and outputs may also include events. With the knowledge about the initial state and the values of the input variable, it is possible to generate the state and the output of the system at every update time.

## 6.2.4  Multistage State Machines

A *multistage state machine* is a multistage model that is based on state machine formalism. In a multistage state-machine formalism, each component model is a state-machine. With this generalization, it is possible to represent at any stage known states, inputs, and outputs as well as known transitions and output functions –by using the finite state machine formalism. More importantly, we can add new (emerging or desirable) states, inputs, and outputs. Given the current state, one can identify the possible next states and the needed inputs for each of them. Considering the inputs as the conditions for the associated transitions, one can nurture some conditions to avoid transitions associated with others and hence one can force transitions to desirable state(s). The transitions can involve several intermediary states, some of which can be induced to facilitate transition to desirable one.

In some social cases, the conditions are often very fluid and the equilibrium, if any, is very unstable. In these cases one needs a clear picture of the status, and systematic exploration of the possible states and the conditions to nurture (or the necessary inputs) to reach each one of them. According to the desired state, one would block some conditions to be satisfied or one would steer the conditions to realize the transition to a desirable state. Often, at every state, one would need to explore possible next states and the conditions to reach them. That means the system description is not know a priori but the system can evolve in a fluid way.

In a finite-state machine, there is only one state that is active at any time. In social systems, not only reality, but also the perceptions of the reality by different groups or individuals are also important. Therefore, a system can be perceived by different observers/players to be at different states at the same time. Hence, different images (models) of a real system may be active at the same time. This can be represented as a multistage model or as a multi-aspect model.

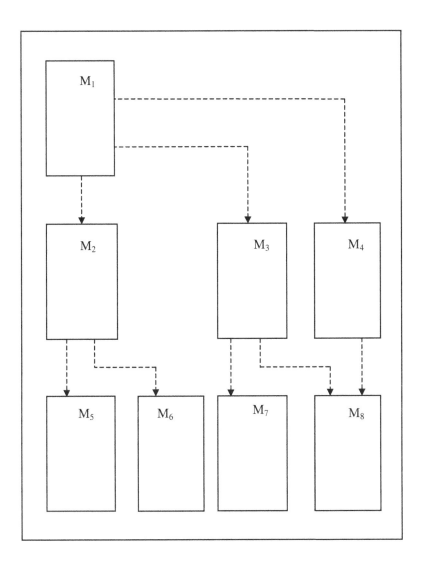

Figure 6.2: An example to multistage models.

Once a modeling formalism is developed, one can develop a high-level specification language and a computer-aided environment to model systems graphically and with the assistance of a knowledge-based system. Maintenance of the model base can be managed by system entity structure (SES) developed by Zeigler [46]. A program generator can translate the specifications given in this high-level specification language into a compilable simulation gaming program. The simulation gaming program can be used to enhance conflict management abilities of by current or future decision-makers

### 6.2.5   Some Other Multistage Modeling Formalisms

Multisimulation can be associated with several modeling formalisms. FSM formalism is used to illustrate the concept. Some other possibilities can be the use of Petri nets –especially to represent deadlocks and synchronization, or use of linguistic variables such as the case in fuzzy logic. The synergy of artificial intelligence techniques with simulation can be explored systematically [24].

The concept of endomorphic models introduced by Zeigler [47] is directly applicable. To take into account different perceptions of an opponent, model(s) of an opponent can be embedded in a model. In less technical terminology, the embedded models are also called ghost models. If an entity – represented by a model – has an internal model of itself, this embedded model can be called an introspective model.

In conflict situations, opponents are often autonomous (or quasi autonomous) under operating constraints. Software agents are the most natural computerization possibilities for autonomous or quasi-autonomous entities. Furthermore, they are also open to more powerful formalisms such as multi-agent formalism where an agent can be represented by several agents only one of them being active similar to a multimodel. Therefore, in simulation studies used for conflict management, one should explore possibilities offered by intelligent agents. Gelenbe [8] investigates and evaluates novel paradigms for simulation of intelligent behavior and learning in interacting autonomous agents. In his work, each agent's external control mechanism can be a FSM or a set of rules. FSM transitions or rules can change through learning which proceeds by observing the environment and of other agents. A systematization of the possibilities offered by the synergies of simulation, artificial intelligence, and software agents was discussed by Ören [25]. Furthermore, endomorphic models –both ghost models and introspective models– can be expressed as intelligent agents.

## 6.3   Conclusion and Challenges

It appears that appropriate formulation of complex social phenomena may improve our perception of reality and may provide a paradigm to conceive innovative solutions. Hence, we may learn ways, which might be useful in steering the course of the events in such a way as to achieve desirable or at least acceptable states. In the article, an attempt for such a challenging task is presented. Especially the concept of multisimulation is explored to experiment with different perceptions of reality simultaneously. Intelligent and knowledge-based conflict management simulation environments should be developed to provide extensive experience to decision makers for conflict avoidance and conflict resolution as well as peace keeping. Not taking advantage of the power of simulation in these vital issues would be similar to a hypothetical case where pilot training is not completed by using aircraft simulators.

## Acknowledgements

Invitations are often honorific and sometimes inspirational. I considered this invitation, in honor of my good friend and colleague Prof. Bernard P. Zeigler, to be both honorific and inspirational; hence, I wanted to introduce a new concept as we did so many times working together. The invitation reminisced the time when he was an invited speaker in a symposium I organized in Namur, Belgium, in 1976 [20]. Then in 1978, he invited me, to the Weizmann Institute, Rehovot, Israel, to conceive and write an article in one week – we delivered, and the editor took almost a year to comprehend and to accept it [26]. Thereafter, we worked together in our series of symposia and many other projects to advance the state of the art of modeling and simulation. It is a great pleasure to notice that after a quarter of a century, we still find each other's contributions inspirational for our own research.

I would also like to express my pleasure to return to Tucson, Arizona, the hometown of the University of Arizona, one of my alma maters. There I had the privilege to work in late 1960s, with Dr. A. Wayne Wymore on the synergy of system theories – and especially his own theory [45]– and modeling and simulation. Getting a Ph.D. degree for these pleasurable moments was a rewarding excuse.

An anonymous reviewer made very valuable observations on an interim version of this article. His/her contribution is gratefully acknowledged.

## References

[1] Arquilla, J. and Ronfeldt, D., *A New Epoch –and Spectrum– of Conflict* (RAND, Santa Monica, CA., 1997),
http://www.rand.org/publications/MR/MR880/

[2] Balencie, J–M. and de La Grange, A., *Monde rebelles – Guerres civiles et violences politiques –Encyclopedie des conflits–* (Editions Michalon, Paris, France, 1999).

[3]  Barnsley, M.F. et al., *The Science of Fractal Images* (Springer-Verlag, New York, 1988).

[4]  Casti, J.L., *Connectivity, Complexity, and Catastrophe in Large-Scale Systems* (Wiley–Interscience, Chichester, England, 1979).

[5]  Davis, P., *Applying Artificial Intelligence Techniques to Strategic-Level Gaming and Simulation*. In: M.S. Elzas, T.I. Ören, and B.P. Zeigler (eds.) Modelling and Simulation Methodology in the Artificial Intelligence Era. (North-Holland, Amsterdam, the Netherlands, 1986), pp. 315-338.

[6]  Davis, P.K. and Arquilla, J., *Thinking About Opponent Behavior in Crisis and Conflict: A Generic Model for Analysis and Group Discussion.* (RAND/R-4111-JS, RAND, Santa Monica, CA, 1991).

[7]  Davis, PK., Bankes, SC., and Weissler, R., *Formalization of Tradeoff Rules and Other Techniques for Comprehending Complex Rule-Based Models*. In: M.S. Elzas, T.I. Ören, and B.P. Zeigler (eds.) Modelling and Simulation Methodology –Knowledge Systems' Paradigms. (North-Holland, Amsterdam, 1989), pp. 231-240.

[8]  Gelenbe, E., *Interacting Assemblies of Goal-Based Learning Agents,* (Presentation at the Dagstuhl Conference on: Agent-Oriented Approaches in Distributed Modelling and Simulation: Challenges and Methodologies July 4-9, 1999, Schloss Dagstuhl, Germany).

[9]  Geyer, F. and van der Zouven, J., *Bibliography on Sociocybernetics* (3$^{rd}$ edition). (http://www.unizar.es/sociocybernetics/bibliografia.html, 1998).

[10] Gill, A., *Introduction to the Theory of Finite-State Machines*, (McGraw-Hill, New York, 1962).

[11] Grant, N., *Illustrated History of 20$^{th}$ Century Conflict,* (Reed Consumer Books, London, England, 1992).

[12] Hart, S.and Mas-Colell, A., (eds.) *Cooperation: Game-Theoretic Approaches*. NATO ASI Series. Series F, Computer and Systems Sciences, vol. 155, (Springer-Verlag, New York, 1997).

[13] Hartmanis, J. and Stearns, R.E., *Algebraic Structure Theory of Sequential Machines*. (Prentice-Hall, Englewood Cliffs, NJ, 1966).

[14] Holden, A.V., (ed.) *Chaos*. (Princeton University Press, Princeton, NJ, 1986).

[15] Kaufmann, S., *At Home in the Universe : The Search for Laws of Self-Organization and Complexity*, (Oxford Univ. Press, Oxford, England, 1996).

[16] Khalilzad, Z. and Lesser, I.O., *Sources of Conflict in the 21$^{st}$ Century – Regional Futures and U.S. Strategy*, (RAND, Santa Monica, CA, 1998).

[17] Knight, D.E., H.W. Curtis, and Fogel, L.J., (eds.) *Cybernetics, Simulation, and Conflict Resolution,* Proc. of the 3$^{rd}$ Annual Symposium of the American Society for Cybernetics (Spartan Books, New York, 1971).

[18] Lund, M., *Preventing and Mitigating Violent Conflict A Guide for Practitioners* (Creative Associates Inc., Washington, DC,1996).

[19] Marshall, I., and Zohar, D., *Who's Afraid of Schrödinger's Cat?* (Quill-William Morrow, New York, 1997).

[20] Ören, T.I., (ed.) *Cybernetics & Modelling & Simulation of Large-Scale Systems,* (International Association for Cybernetics, Namur, Belgium, 1978).

[21] Ören, T.I., *Model Update: A Model Specification Formalism with a Generalized View of Discontinuity,* (Proceedings of the Summer Computer Simulation Conference, Montreal, Quebec, Canada, 1987 July 27-30), pp. 689-694.

[22] Ören, T.I., *Dynamic Templates and Semantic Rules for Simulation Advisors and Certifiers,* In: P.A. Fishwick and R.B. Modjeski (eds). Knowledge-Based Simulation: Methodology and Application, (Springer-Verlag, New York, 1991), pp. 53-76.

[23] Ören, T.I., *Computer-Aided Systems Technology: Its Role in Advanced Computerization,* (In. F. Pichler and R.M. Diaz (eds.) Computer Aided Systems Theory –EUROCAST '93, Springer-Verlag, New York, 1993), pp. 11-20.

[24] Ören, T.I., *Artificial Intelligence and Simulation: A Typology.* (In: Proceedings of the 3rd Conference on Computer Simulation, S. Raczynski (ed.), Mexico City, Nov. 15-17, 1995), pp. 1-5.

[25] Ören, T.I., *Agent-Oriented Approaches in Distributed Modelling and Simulation: Challenges and Methodologies,* (Presentation at the Dagstuhl Conference on: Agent-Oriented Approaches in Distributed Modelling and Simulation: Challenges and Methodologies July 4-9, 1999, Schloss Dagstuhl, Germany).

[26] Ören, T.I., Zeigler, B.P., *Concepts for Advanced Simulation Methodologies,* (Simulation, 32:3, 1979), pp. 69-82.

[27] Pew, R.W. and Mavor, A.S., (eds.) *Modeling Human and Organizational Behavior –Application to Military Simulation* (National Academy Press, Washington DC, 1998).

[28] Praehofer H., *Modelling and Simulation.* (Chapter 3 of the book by F. Pichler and H. Schwaertzel, CAST Methods in Modelling, Springer-Verlag, New York, 1992), pp. 123-241.

[29] Prigogine, I. and Stengers, I., *Order out of Chaos –Man's New Dialog with Nature,* (Bantam Books, New York, 1984).

[30] Prusinkiewicz, P. and Hanan, J., *Lindenmayer Systems, Fractals, and Plants.* (Springer-Verlag, New York, 1980).

[31] RAND-1, *Over 800 Documents on Conflict,* (http://www.rand.org, 2000).

[32] RAND-2, *70 RAND Corp. Abstracts on Conflict - 1952-1999,* http://www.rand.org/cgi-bin/Abstracts/ordi/abnew.pl, 2000

[33] Riley, V.G. and Young, J.P., *Bibliography on War Gaming,* (Operations Research Office, The John Hopkins University, Chevy Chase, MD, 1957).

[34] Rubinstein, A., *Modeling Bounded Rationality,* (MIT Press, Cambridge, MA, 1998).

[35] Rupesinghe, K., (ed) *Conflict Transformation,* (Macmillan, Basingstoke, England, 1995).

[36] Rupesinghe, K. and Anderlini, S.N., *Civil Wars, Civil Peace – An Introduction to Conflict Resolution,* (Pluto Press, London, England, 1998).

[37] Salthe, S.N., *Evolving Hierarchical Systems,* (Columbia University Press, New York, 1985).

[38] Schelling, T., *The Strategy of Conflict,* (Harvard Univ Press, 1960 – reprint edition: 1980).

[39] Shubik, M., (ed.) *Game Theory and Related Approaches to Social Behavior.* Wiley, New York, 1964).

[40] Spriet, J.A., and Vansteenkiste, G.C., *Computer-Aided Modelling and Simulation.* Academic Press, London, England, 1982).

[41] Toffler, A., *Science and Change* –Forward to the Book: Order out of Chaos – Man's New Dialog with Nature by I. Prigogine and I. Stengers, (Bantam Books, New York, 1984).

[42] Vitanyi, P.M.B., *Lindenmayer Systems: Structure, Languages, and Growth Functions*, (Mathematical Center, Amsterdam, the Netherlands, 1980).

[43] Waldrop, M.M., *Complexity : The Emerging Science at the Edge of Order and Chaos*, (Touchstone Books, 1993).

[44] Wegrirzyn, S., Gille, J–C. and Vidal, P., *Developmental Systems – At the Crossroads of System Theory, Computer Science, and Genetic Engineering,* (Springer-Verlag, New York, 1990).

[45] Wymore, A.W., *A Mathematical Theory of Systems Engineering – The Elements*, (Wiley, New York, 1967).

[46] Zeigler, B.P., *Multifaceted Modelling and Discrete Event Simulation* (Academic Press, London, England, 1984).

[47] Zeigler, B.P., *Object-Oriented Simulation with Hierarchical, Modular Models –Intelligent Agents and Endomorphic Systems* (Academic Press, London, 1990).

# Chapter 7

# Systems Design: A Simulation Modeling Framework

J.W. Rozenblit

*This chapter surveys a model-based approach to the design of complex, multifaceted systems. The discussion is organized as follows: first, a brief introduction to the model-based design (MBD) methodology is given. Then, supporting concepts, knowledge representation and modeling techniques are discussed. Brief, illustrative examples are given to elucidate the theory-based notions. The chapter concludes with postulates for a computer-aided system that can automate the design of heterogeneous systems.*

## 7.1  Introduction and Motivation

Modern engineering design is a highly complex process. It involves a multiplicity of objectives, constraints, materials, and configurations. Despite great strides in computational tools such as high performance workstations, distributed and concurrent processing environments intended to help to cope with this rising complexity, the design process remains error prone. Given the often severe constraints imposed by cost, environmental impacts, safety regulations, etc., designers are forced to make compromises that would not be necessary in an ideal world

In the late nineteen eighties and early nineteen nineties, we had witnessed a proliferation of efforts to support the design process with computer aided tools and environments. Most successful in that undertaking was the electronic design automation community whose efforts led to the definition of "electronic design framework" and subsequent developments of design environments and tools such as Falcon and Synopsis.

The term framework in electronic design automation denotes a computer-based, integrated design environment that binds and supports design tools [2]. In their seminal paper, Harrison et al. [8] defined a framework as  "...all the underlying facilities provided to the CAD tool developer, the CAD system integrator, and the end user necessary to facilitate their tasks."

The CAD Framework Initiative (CFI) viewed a framework as a collection of extensible programs/modules used to develop a unified CAD system [2] For the sake of brevity, we do not discuss the history of electronic CAD here nor do we trace the evolution of the framework concept. (Excellent summaries are given in [3,8,23].

Another notable thrust in the efforts to support complex design was the Defense Advanced Research Projects Agency (DARPA) program in concurrent engineering. In 1987, DARPA had asked experts from industry, academia, and government to investigate the shortcomings in the defense-related product development process. Japanese product development techniques were studied in which the so-called "tiger approach" was applied. In this approach, all personnel involved in the project were assembled at its conception in order to find a solution which addresses the participants' individual concerns but also benefits the team as a whole. From this relatively general description, stemmed the term "concurrent engineering" (CE). The term was refined by Winner et al. in [27] as "...a systematic approach to the integrated, concurrent design of products and their related processes, including manufacture and support. [CE] is intended to cause the developer, from the outset, to consider all elements of the product life cycle from conception through disposal, including quality, cost, schedule, and user requirements."

To transplant the approach into the American research and development environment, DARPA concluded that an advanced computer technology was needed to create virtual teams who might be scattered all over the country. Thus came about the DICE program (DARPA Initiative in Concurrent Engineering) [24]. Special issues of archival journals had reported extensively on CE [9,10].

Simulation modeling had long been recognized as a useful tool in assessing the quality of sub-optimal design choices and arriving at acceptable trade-offs prior to the physical realization of the system being designed. Often termed "virtual prototyping", or "simulation-based design" (SBD), this approach was endorsed by the concurrent engineering community and applied primarily in the mechanical engineering domain [5]. Subsequent, efforts focused on the development of techniques that would integrate distributed simulation technologies, physics-based modeling, virtual and collaborative environments. The long-range goal of such an integration is the application of these, and other, technologies that permit integrated process and product development (IPPD). The perceived benefits of simulation-based design clearly justify the research and development expenditures. If successfully applied to complex engineering enterprises, SBD can facilitate assessment of products and process designs early in the lifecycle and eliminate the cost of physical prototyping.

Our position is that computer simulation and other advanced computational tools are of limited effectiveness without a methodology to induce a systematic handling of the multitude of goals and constraints impinging on the design process. Therefore, our work focuses on the development of techniques in which design models can be synthesized and tested by simulation within a number of objectives, taken individually or in trade-off combinations. We strive to provide a uniform treatment of the design process at different levels of system representation and abstraction. By providing a spectrum of performance evaluation methods, including trade-off measurements and evaluation of multilevel, multicomponent, hierarchically specified models, our approach facilitates description of designs through quantitative and, more generally, comparative measures.

Our approach, termed model-based design (MBD) [16,17,18,19], was initially strongly influenced by multifaceted modeling concepts developed by Zeigler [29] in the late seventies and mid-eighties. The approach is primarily intended to support the development of simulateable models of the system under design. It offers: a) representation methods to capture structural and behavioral design knowledge, b) heuristics for managing design space complexity, c) techniques for simulation-based design assessment and trade-offs, and d) methods for design partitioning [13].

This chapter surveys the fundamental tenets of the MBD framework. A high level example serves to illustrate the methodology and its various phases. For an comprehensive exposition of the formal concepts underlying the methodology and its phases, we refer the reader to [16,178,18,19].

## 7.1.1   System Design and Modeling: Synergies

As opposed to system analysis where models are typically derived from an existing real system, in design the model comes first as a set of "blueprints" from which the system will be built, implemented or deployed. The blueprints take several forms; they could be simple verbal descriptions, a set of equations, an architectural drawing, or a netlist file. The goal of such defined systems design is to study models of design before they are physically realized.

Here, a question arises: "How can modeling and simulation concepts support systems design?" To address this question, we enumerate some principal elements in the dynamics of the design process and relate them to simulation modeling.

1. Designs are created by individuals who use basic problem solving techniques such as problem definition, proposal of a solution, and test of the solution against the problem statement and requirements. Modeling, as a creative act, follows similar steps. To build a model, the modeler interprets requirements and objectives of the project, proposes a suite of simulateable models that serve as "design blueprints." Simulation is a means of executing the models and testing how well they meet the project's requirements.

2. Designs are often of a large scale. Thus, techniques are needed for decomposing the design problem into subproblems that are easily

comprehensible to the designers. Partial solutions could then be generated and integrated using proper aggregation techniques. Simulation modeling methodologies provide techniques for model decomposition, hierarchical specification and aggregation of model components.

3. The attributes of design are described in the form that allows comparative studies and trade-off analyses. Simulation-based design performance evaluation uses model generated data for such analyses.

4. Complex designs comprise heterogeneous components – techniques are needed to properly integrate them into a complete system. Recent advances in embedded systems modeling [1,4,6,11,13] and real-time systems modeling are a promising step in this direction.

In what follows, we survey the MBD framework and illustrate its elements on an example.

## 7.2    The MDB Methodology

Our approach to design is shown in Figure 7.1. The process depicted in the figure uses simulateable models as virtual prototypes of the system under design (SUD). The core activities in the framework are system specification, modeling, simulation, refinement, and partitioning (technology assignment).

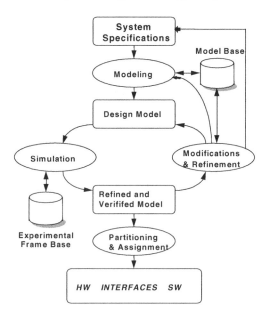

Figure 7.1: Simulation-Based Design Methodology

To build a simulateable design model, we first construct object models, ie. representations of components from which a system will be built, their relationships, and attributes. Such models are given behavioral specification so that they can be simulated.

Simulation is then used in a two-fold manner: a) as a means of verifying the functionality of the proposed solution, ie. the execution of the model's dynamics to ensure that the behaviors are consistent with those perceived for the system being designed, and b) as a way of assessing how well performance requirements are met by the proposed solution (for example, we can collect data on component utilization, system's throughput, etc.).

An assessment of simulation data leads to either further model refinement and design modifications, or to the system partitioning and technology assignment phase. During this phase, decisions as to which components are realized in hardware, software and interfaces are made. (This particular phase is pertinent to design of heterogeneous systems that contain such mixed elements).

Our overall design model combines various representations, simulation modeling, and heuristic techniques. They are now described in more detail.

## 7.3    MBD Process Elements

### 7.3.1    System Specifications

In the first phase, the designer converts the system's requirements and constraints into a formal specification. This specification defines the interface between the system and its environment and the system's functionality. Nonfunctional requirements such as size, weight, etc. are also documented. Since our approach strives for implementation independence, designers can refine the specification without modifying any physically realized components.

### 7.3.2    Modeling

This is the core activity that leads to virtual design prototypes. In our approach, we take a holistic view that aims at the development of the overall system's model rather than its individual components. A model is a set of instructions for generating data. Valid model-generated data is a subset of the system's behavioral data. A specification of the system and its environment forms the basis for building models that correspond to a set of questions about the design, including its objectives and reason for being [15,17]. The modeling phase of MBD is depicted in Figure 7.2.

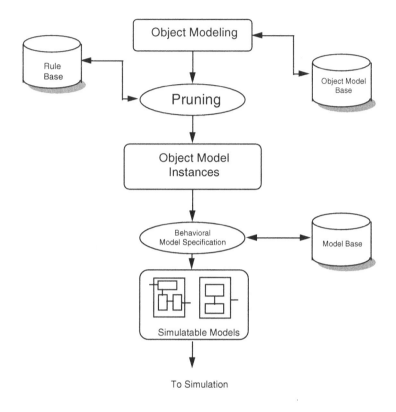

Figure 7.2: Generation of Simulateable Models

## 7.3.2.1 Object Modeling

The design model construction process begins with developing a representation of design components, their decompositions, variants, and attributes. As a step toward a complete knowledge representation scheme for design support, we combined the decomposition, taxonomic, and coupling relationships in a knowledge representation scheme called the *system entity structure* (SES). Previous work [16,17,18,19] identified the need for representing the structure and behavior of systems, in a declarative scheme related to frame-theoretic and object-based formalisms. The elements represented are motivated, on the one hand, by systems theory concepts of decomposition (ie. how a system is hierarchically broken down into components) and coupling (ie. how these components may be interconnected to reconstitute the original system). On the other hand, systems theory has not focused on taxonomic relations, as represented for example in frame-hierarchy knowledge representation schemes. In the SES scheme, such representation concerns the admissible variants of components in decompositions and the further specializations of such variants.

The interaction of decomposition, coupling and taxonomic relations in an SES affords a compact specification of a family of models for a given domain. In a system entity structure, entities refer to conceptual components of reality for which models may reside in a model base. Also associated with entities are slots for attribute knowledge representation. An entity may have several aspects, each denoting a decomposition, and therefore having several entities. An entity may also have several specializations, each representing a classification of possible variants of the entity.

Object modeling requires several types of decisions on the part of design project engineers. The classical object model development process advocated by Rumbaugh et. al. [20] involves a syntactic analysis of the requirements document. Through this analysis, noun, verb, and adjective phrases are identified. Classes are then constructed to reflect the nouns (objects that represent system components). Association links are derived from the verb phrases. For example, a "has part" phrase can be directly expressed through a decomposition link while an "is a kind of" phrase can be reflected through the generalization relation.

The syntactic analysis results in the initial object model. However, the model's refinement is a responsibility of the modelers who make the following decisions:

a)  further identify how components decompose into subcomponents in the project's domain and provide a set of alternative decompositions,
b)  identify sets of variants for components specified in various decompositions (for example, a computer display type could be an LCD or a CRT monochrome, or a CRT color display),
c)  identify attributes for the components that describe the components' properties and characteristics salient to the project at hand.

The system entity structure organizes possibilities for a variety of system decompositions and taxonomies and, consequently, a variety of model constructions. Its generative capability facilitates convenient definition and representation of models and their attributes at multiple levels of aggregation and abstraction. More complete discussions of the system entity structure and its associated structure transformations are presented in [16,17]. The SES representation can be rendered using the Object Modeling Technique (OMT) notation (a less complex precursor to the Unified Modeling Language). Here, we illustrate its expressive power using the basic concepts from an Air Traffic Display/Collision Warning (and Monitoring) System (ATD/CWS) system design example.

The ATD/CWM system is intended to monitor air traffic and issue warnings should a threat of collision between a host aircraft and other aircraft occur.

Figure 7.3 depicts the system entity structure of the ATD/CWS system rendered using the OMT notation. The ATD/CWS is a part of a larger distributed network. Through the aggregation symbol (diamond in Figure 7.3) we show its decomposition into a) location records library, b) collision warning monitor, c) external interfaces (in OMT, the filled circle denotes one or more elements; thus the plural interpretation of the class object "External Interface"), and d) CPUs. The external interface object is classified through the specialization relation (or, as termed in the OMT notation, through the generalization relation depicted by the triangle symbol) into *radar, communication system, user interface, alarm device,* and *navigation system.* Furthermore, the radar object is specialized into *simple,* and *complex* radar. The air traffic display has two variants: a) color display and b) monochrome display.

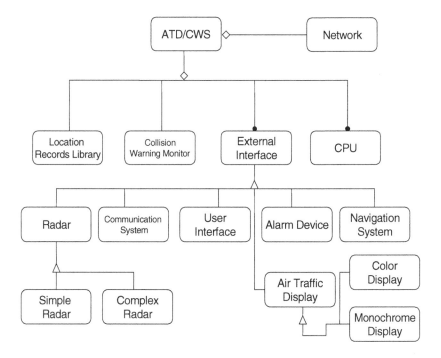

Figure 7.3: Object Model of the ATD/CWM System

The object model of Figure 7.3 can be refined further to show attributes of the system's components and their methods. In Figure 7.4, we refine the object instance of ATD/CWM to include the attribute *mode* (with a possible range *normal,* and *degraded*) and a method *detect collision.* This method would implement the collision detection algorithm. Similarly, we have refined the class object Location Records Library to show the structure of the Location Record object. Such an object has attributes that relay the flight information as shown in

Figure 7.5. In Figure 7.6, we illustrate a refinement of the Air Traffic Display and the Aircraft ID Icons.

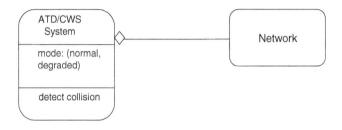

Figure 7.4: Refined Class Object ATD/CWM

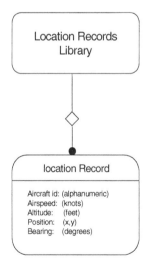

Figure 7.5: Refined Instance of Location Records Library Class

This high level representation, shown in the OMT diagrams, sets up an object model from which a specific design instance of system components (as well as their relationships) for the ATD/CWM system can be synthesized. We discuss this synthesis in the following section.

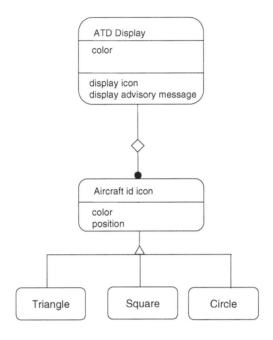

Figure 7.6: Refinement of the Air Traffic Display Object

## 7.3.2.2 Pruning

In our methodology, a model is synthesized from elements stored in the model base. More specifically, behaviors are associated with design components identified in the object models. This synthesis is the result of *pruning* a substructure from the system entity structure or an OMT diagram. Pruning can be viewed as a knowledge-based search through the space of candidate solutions to the design problem. This is consistent with a commonly taken view that design is a search process in which a satisfactory design solution is produced from a number of alternatives [17,19]. Those alternatives come from knowledge of the relevant domain. We use *production rules* [19] to represent design objectives, constraints, requirements and performance expectations. The aim of pruning is to recommend plausible object model instances for further design assessment using simulation.

The following steps are required to provide the rules that guide pruning of the system entity structure:

1.  for each specialization (ie. generalization relationship), specify a set of rules for selecting an object; that is select an instance of a system's component from possible variants,
2.  for an entity with several aspects, ie. decompositions (or in the OMT terminology aggregations), specify rules for generating a unique aspect;
3.  for each aspect, ie. aggregation,  specify rules that ensure that the objects selected from specializations are configurable, ie., the components they represent can be validly coupled.

Thus, to guide the search through the design space defined by the object models, we specify a) selection rules for choosing a component instance from a variety of elements offered by the generalization relations, b) synthesis rules for combining the selected instances.

To specify the pruning rules, the knowledge engineering team elicits domain expertise from subject matter experts (SMEs). The expertise is encoded in the form of if-then production rules that constrain the choices offered by specializations and provide a coupling recipe for aggregating components identified in decompositions. In addition to encoding the experts' domain knowledge, the rules may translate a requirements statement into an operational means of selecting the most adequate choice of object models for the system under design (SUD) (for example, when distributed processing is required, select a multiprocessor computing platform).

Several attributes play a role in this phase of the SBD process:

a)  in the elicitation process, subject matter experts provide knowledge that is biased by personal experiences and preference,
b)  communication skills of the elicitors, ie. knowledge engineers, as well as SMEs impact the confidence in information provided; thus, confidence factors are typically embedded in the rules (they are based on the assessment of how reliable the information provided by experts is),
c)  the pruning methodology may be driven by designers' preferences that stem from their experience and intuition.

We now illustrate the pruning concepts by using the ATD/CWM example. Recall the object model of Figure 7.3. Through the specialization relations (captured in OMT using the triangle symbol) we outline the choices for component selections. More specifically, a simple or a complex radar can be selected for the radar components. A choice of a color or  a monochrome display is given for the air traffic display device. Moreover, through the one-to-many relation (depicted in OMT by the filled circle), the ATD/CWM system may have more than one CPU.

The following production rules can be used in the selection and synthesis of a specific instance of the system.

### Rules for Radar Selection

```
If required aircraft_bearing is two-dimensional and
   range is <= 250 miles
   then radar_type is simple

If required aircraft_bearing is three-dimensional and
   range is > 250 miles
   then radar_type is complex
```

### Rules for Display Selection

```
If aircraft type classification based on color separation
   then display_type is color

If aircraft type classification based on brilliance and
shape separation
   then display_type is monochrome
```

### Synthesis Rule for ATD/CWM

```
If selected radar_type is simple and
   selected display_type is color and
   required emergency mode is degraded
   then the ATD/CWM system is configurable and
        it has at least 2 CPUs and
        it has a simple radar  and
        it has a color display and
        it has a location records library and
        it has a collision warning monitor and
        it has a communication system and
        it has an alarm device and
        it has an navigation system and
        it has a user interface.
```

In our methodology, the selection and synthesis rules (given in the form of production rules) are used by a reasoning engine that generates a specific design instance given specific values of design variables [19]. Such values instantiate design parameters which are associated as attributes with various entities (object classes). For example, a design requirement may impose a choice of two-dimensional

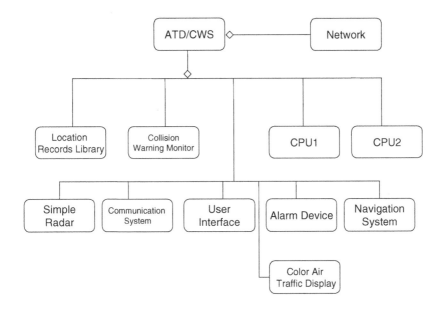

Figure 7.7: Pruned Instance of the ATD/CWM Object Model

aircraft bearing or a color-based identification of aircraft type on the air traffic display. Those values are entered by the designer during the pruning process. Their combinations result in a specific object model instance that results from the family of design configurations given by the overall system's object model. In Figure 7.7, we show a possible instance of the ATD/CWM that can be pruned from the system entity structure object model (Figure 7.3).

## 7.3.2.3 Behavioral Model Specification

Behaviors can be associated with object models instances selected through the pruning process using Petri nets, StateCharts [7], Discrete Event System Specification (DEVS) [29], other finite state machine based formalisms, or continuous system specifications. In MBD, we strive to use formal modeling methods that allow  the designer to construct a hierarchy of models using representations that are closed under coupling. The type of specification language used in modeling is very important. The specification must accommodate different levels of granularity so that the developer can map components at different levels of abstraction to corresponding hardware or software modules.

In our framework, we have worked extensively with the Discrete Event System Specification formalism [29]. DEVS is a general, formal specification language that allows the designers to specify a system as a mathematical object. The specification comprises a time base, inputs, states, and outputs and functions of determining next states and outputs. Designers make no decisions about how to build the components at this stage; they connect elementary blocks hierarchically until they arrive at a preliminary model that conforms to the project's requirements. We have used DEVS and its implementation environment DEVSJAVA to build models in a hierarchical and modular fashion [21]. This manner of model development permits a systems-oriented approach that has not been possible in the past with such simulation languages as Simscript or SIMAN. We must note, however, modularity and module composition features are now common in object-oriented simulation languages such as MODSIM or Modula.

### 7.3.3  Simulation

In this phase, execution of design models is carried out using the *experimental frame* paradigm [10,12,17]. Experimental frames define conditions under which models can be observed and experimented with. An experimental frame reflects modeling objectives. The statement of objectives is translated into specific performance measures. Necessary output, input and control variables are defined so that such measures can be obtained through simulation experiments. An experimental frame plays the following roles: a) it subjects a model to input stimuli (which represent potential interventions into the model's operation), b) it observes the model's reactions to the input stimuli and collects the data about such reactions (output data), and c) it controls the experimentation by placing relevant constraints on values of the designated model state variables and by monitoring these constraints.

Figure 7.8 illustrates the separation of a model and its experimental frame. A model can be executed in various experimental frames, each reflecting a specific

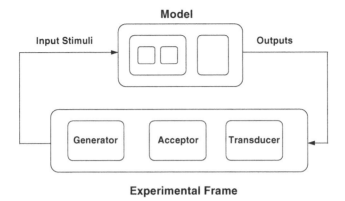

Figure 7.8: Model/Experimental Frame Coupling

objective of a simulation study. An experimental frame can be coupled to several design models (each reflecting an alternative, virtual design solution) so that trade-offs can be made and the best model can be selected with respect to the specific assessment objective that this frame represents.

Therefore, the experimental frames provide the design team with a quantifiable means of trading off design solutions (in the form of simulation models)  with respect to the set of design objectives. Such trade-off decisions can be made by team members using multiple criteria decision making (MCDM) techniques as depicted in Figure 7.9. In the scenario shown in the figure, alternative design solutions are given as models $M_1, \ldots, M_n$. The experimental frames, $EF_1$ and $EF_2$ reflect two performance objectives, eg. component utilization ($EF_1$) and task throughput ($EF_2$). The models can now be cross evaluated in both frames and the tradeoff solution (the model M*) can be selected.

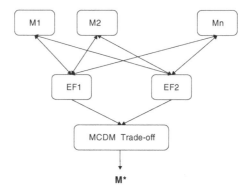

Figure 7.9: Trading-off Design Solutions using Experimental Frames and MCDM

Experimental frames are given concrete form – employing the concepts of automata theory, a frame can be defined as a composition of a *generator* which produces the input segments sent to a model, an *acceptor*, ie., a device that continually monitors the simulation run for satisfaction of constraints, and a *transducer* which collects the input/output data and computes summary performance measures. Experimental frame template specifications can be stored in the experimental frame base (recall Figure 7.1) for reuse and rapid simulation run setup.

We refer again to the ATD/CWM system example to illustrate the experimental frame concept. Assume that one of the objectives of the simulation based design process is to determine the optimal number of the CPUs in the system so that their utilization is maximized. Gaining introspection into this aspect of the system's performance would assist designers in selecting an appropriate number of processors in the air traffic detection system.

First, we translate the utilization objective into a specific performance measure. Utilization is measured by monitoring the busy/idle ratio of the CPUs' operation. In addition, we introduce a variable that computes the joint utilization of the system's processors so that we can determine the fraction of time that both processors are simultaneously busy (the "and" is a logical conjunction in the formula below that we use for computing the joint utilization). We now specify the requisite elements of an experimental frame derived from these desiderata.

## 7.3.4    Experimental Frame CPUs Utilization

### 7.3.4.1 Generator

Generate input segments:
- radar sweep once per one-quarter second
- communication messages (a sequence of randomly distributed events)
- operator messages (a sequence of randomly distributed events)

### 7.3.4.2 Transducer

Monitor model variables:
> CPU1.Status (with range: busy, idle, fail)
> CPU2.Status (with range: busy, idle, fail)
> Time (with range: non-negative reals)

Compute measures:
> CPU1.Utilization = Time.CPU1.Busy / Global.Observation.Time
> CPU2.Utilization = Time.CPU2.Busy / Global.Observation.Time

> CPU.Joint.Utilization = Time (CPU1.Busy and CPU2.Busy) / Global.Observation.Time

### 7.3.4.3 Acceptor

Monitor simulation run
> Run until CPU1.Status = Fail or CPU2.Status = Fail or Global.Observation.Time >= End.Time

Simulation (driven by a set of experimental frames) is followed by analysis of how well design functionality and performance are met. Based on this analysis, the design model at hand may be further refined and modified.

## 7.3.5    Design Modifications and Refinement

The ability to modify and refine designs in an iterative manner at the level of virtual prototypes is not well addressed in the systems engineering community. The development of design modification procedures and thereby the incorporation of simulation into a design feedback and iteration loop is an open, general research challenge.

A simple case would be to define methods to identify which elements and components of the design fail to meet the specification and provide this information to designers. The designers would then change the requirements or refine the design models including their behavior, and would repeat the assessment using simulation.

A complex approach would incorporate reasoning and heuristic procedures that would automatically iterate through the design space by changing various parameters and would arrive at the optimal solution. Such procedures are possible for well-defined domains (for instance see [22] for examples in the VLSI interconnect design domain). However, for projects that do not afford a high degree of design automation, the refinement heuristics would be driven by attributes such as the experience of design engineers, confidence in validity of simulation models, ability of team members to reach a consensus, and change risk tolerance.

## 7.3.6   Partitioning and Technology Assignment

After the system design is completed and evaluated at the virtual model level, a physical realization of the system must be carried out. The translation from the model to the actual implementation is typically done based on the available technology constraints and performance estimates for realizations of components in software or hardware. In traditional design, the partitioning scheme is often tied to the target architecture. In our approach, mapping model components to hardware and software is not as limited since the design is independent of the implementation until this phase, which is relatively late in the design.

There is a great body of partitioning work that is well documented in the literature [1,12,26]. [1] provides an excellent review of the major classes of partitioning algorithms that not only can be used for VLSI circuit design, but for any system in which components are grouped and whose inter-group communication must be kept to a minimum. Among these classes of partitioning algorithms are the following: (1) move-based approaches such as greedy and iterative exchange algorithms, (2) geometric approaches such as vector partitioning, (3) combinatorial approaches such as max-flow min-cut, and (4) clustering-based approaches [1,26]. In addition, other researchers have either augmented the general algorithms (for example, Vahid [26] modified the min-cut algorithm for functional partitioning), or introduced new types of algorithms (such as Wolf who employed an object-oriented approach [28]).

In the design of heterogeneous systems, the choice of how to implement the system architecture can make significant differences in performance and reliability. In the past, a hardware platform was often chosen and then software was written for correcting the inadequacies of the hardware. Currently, however, research has progressed from the idea of partitioning hardware elements, to that of partitioning a high level functional model of a system. Figure 7.10 shows an example partitioning into hardware and software, with the system model containing four functional components (A, B, C, D) that are partitioned into hardware (A, C, D) and software (B).

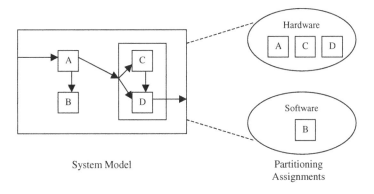

Figure 7.10: An illustration of the partitioning problem.

We have been exploring the application of Bayesian Belief Networks (BBN) [14] to the partitioning problem. The application of BBN to hardware/software partitioning was first introduced by Olson and Rozenblit [13]. Before classification into hardware or software can begin, a functional description of the model is created (in a manner similar to the Specification Level Intermediate Format (SLIF) [25]). Next, the BBN is generated with nodes representing functional components, and causal links corresponding to component couplings, function accesses, and functional independence of components. The choice of which values to place inside the conditional matrices associated with each link depends on the communication needs between the given pair of elements, and how tightly their performance is coupled. Once the BBN is created, it can be used to evaluate the current design by incorporating the simulation results as evidences.

Results are obtained from simulation and converted into evidence that is propagated throughout the BBN. The beliefs for each available type of classification are calculated at each component node and the system model (now possibly with some classified components) is altered to reflect the new classifications. Simulation is performed again, and the process is repeated until the components of the system model reach a level that requires the introduction of structural requirements for any further classification. The result of the refinement of the behavioral simulation is a functionally correct virtual prototype of the design. Each component is assigned to a general classification of a type of hardware or software.

# 7.4    Towards an Integrated Design Support Environment

Clearly, the efficacy of a design methodology can only be confirmed through its application in a design environment. Although much research has been done on codesign, only few successfully implemented environments have emerged that support heterogeneous embedded systems design. At the University of Arizona, we are developing a computer-aided design environment called SONORA [4]. This environment implements the theory-based tenets of the model-based codesign. We are striving to provide an integrated tool set that will support the design automation of complex, real-time embedded systems.

We are currently implementing SONORA on a network of UNIX workstations by integrating commercial and academic tools. We are planning to work with the graphical interfaces provided by commercial tools for design entry as well as informal text descriptions. Requirements can be entered prior to the modeling phase and updated during model refinement using the STATEMATE MAGNUM Requirements Tracer™. The requirements will be formatted in a semi-formal manner and extracted to allow custom tools to generate top level functional model structures and test cases for experimental frame construction. Various modeling formalisms will be used in combination to be able to accurately reflect the different modeling aspects: DEVS, SES, and StateCharts to build a complete model specification. The resulting model will then be simulated with the appropriate simulation engines. We currently use DEVS-Java, the most recent implementation of the DEVS formalism, to simulate models of a system. However, we are investigating the automatic generation of DEVS models from StateChart descriptions as well as the use of DEV and DESS (Difference Equation System Specification) to represent system components that are more appropriately modeled in the continuous time domain.

Research is being conducted on introducing simulation results into a BBN during the simulation cycle. When the model is refined to a synthesizable level, the information from the BBN is used by model-to-realization mapping algorithms to prepare the verified model for prototype synthesis. The use of the hardware and software language synthesis tools within STATEMATE [7] is finally considered for use in SONORA to provide the realization descriptions for functions (e.g., C and VHDL). Synthesis of control and communication descriptions requires further research in order to realize a fully automated prototype synthesis. The advantage of SONORA over other environments is that it will be able to heavily leverage from the benefits offered by model-based codesign.

# 7.5   Summary

To gather the strands up, we now summarize the steps and phases in the MBD process. The phases required to execute the methodology are:

- Decompositions, specializations, and attributes of components of the system being designed are conceptualized using the object modeling approach. We utilize the object model base as a repository of previous design modeling experience. Thus, we may retrieve an object model from this base that is applicable to the modeling domain at hand. Such a model is modified and enhanced with entities required in the new project.
- A rule base to be used in the pruning process is developed. Requirements and constraints are translated into production rules.
- Pruning is invoked which generates recommendations for candidate solutions to the design problem in the form of object model instances.
- Behaviors are associated with the object model instances.
- Relevant experimental frames that reflect design objectives are defined.
- Simulation is run and results are evaluated and design models are ranked. They are assessed and refined until a final design model is obtained. The above phases may be iterated in a feedback process.
- The final model (ie. virtual design prototype) is handed over to partitioning and technology assignment.

## Acknowledgements

The material presented here is based in part on a report to Systems World, Inc. I appreciate the assistance of Dr. Stephanie White for facilitating this publication. I am also grateful to my research team members: Tony Ewing, John Olson, Steve Cunning and Stephan Schulz for all their contributions to the development of the hardware/software codesign framework.

## References

[1]   C. J. Alpert and A. B. Kahng, "Recent Directions In Netlist Partitioning: a Survey," Integration, the VLSI Journal, Vol. 19, No. 1-2, August 1995, pp. 1-81.

[2]   J. Bhat and F. Taku. A seven-layer model of framework functionality. Electronic Engineering, September 1990, pp.67-73.

[3]   F. Bretschneider. A Process Model for Design Flow Management and Planning. PhD Dissertation. Department of Computer Science, University of Kaiserslautern, Germany, July 1992.

[4]  S. Cunning, T.C. Ewing, J.T. Olson, J.W. Rozenblit, and S. Schulz, Towards an Integrated, Model-Based Codesign Environment. *Proceedings of the 1998 IEEE Conference on Engineering of Computer-Based Systems,* 136-143, Nashville, March 1999.

[5]  M. Cutkosky et al. PACT: An Experiment in Integrating Concurrent Engineering Systems. IEEE Computer, January 1993, pp. 28-37.

[6]  D. Gajski, S. Narayan, F. Vahid, and J. Gong, *Specification and Design of Embedded Systems,* Englewood Cliffs, NJ: Prentice-Hall, 1994.

[7]  D. Harel et al. Statemate: A Working Environment for the Development of Complex Reactive Systems. IEEE Trans. on Software Engineering, 16(4), 403-414, April 1990.

[8]  D. S. Harrison et al. Electronic CAD Frameworks. *Proceedings of the IEEE,* v 78 n 2, FEB 1990, pp. 393-417.

[9]  IEEE Computer. January 1993.

[10] IEEE Spectrum. July 1991.

[11] S. Kumar, *A Unified Representation for Hardware/ Software Codesign,* Ph.D. Dissertation, University of Virginia, 1995.

[12] G. De Micheli and R.K. Gupta, "Hardware/Software Co-Design," *Proceedings of the IEEE,* 85(3), pp. 349-65, 1997.

[13] J.T. Olson and J.W. Rozenblit, A Framework for Hardware/Software Partitioning Utilizing Bayesian Belief Networks, *Proceedings of the 1998 IEEE Conference on Systems, Man and Cybernetics,* 3983-3988. San Diego, October, 1998.

[14] J. Pearl, *Probabilistic Reasoning in Intelligent Systems : Networks of Plausible Inference,* Morgan Kaufmann Publishers, San Mateo, CA, 1988.

[15] J.W. Rozenblit and K. Buchenrieder (Eds.), *Codesign: Computer-Aided Software/Hardware Engineering,* IEEE Press, 1994.

[16] J.W. Rozenblit and B.P. Zeigler, Design and Modeling Concepts, In *International Encyclopedia of Robotics.* (Ed. R. Dorf), 308-322, John Wiley and Sons, New York, 1988.

[17] J.W. Rozenblit and J.F. Hu, Integrated Knowledge Representation and Management in Simulation Based Design Generation, *IMACS Journal of Mathematics and Computers in Simulation,* 34(3-4), 262-282, 1992.

[18] J.W. Rozenblit, Experimental Frame Specification Methodology for Hierarchical Simulation Modeling, *International Journal of General Systems,* 19(3), 317-336, 1991.

[19] J.W. Rozenblit and Y.M. Huang, Rule-Based Generation of Model Structures in Multifaceted Modeling and System Design, *ORSA Journal on Computing,* 3(4), 330-344.

[20] J. Rumbaugh et al., Object Oriented Modeling and Analysis. Prentice Hall, 1991.

[21] S. Schulz, J.W. Rozenblit, M. Mrva, and K. Buchenrieder, "Model-Based Codesign: the Framework and its Application, *IEEE Computer,* August 1998.

[22] T. Simunic, J.W. Rozenblit, and J. Brews, VLSI Interconnect Design Automation Using Quantitative and Symbolic Techniques, *IEEE Transactions on Components, Packaging, and Manufacturing Technology,* 19(4), 803-812, Nov. 1996.

[23] Special Technology Area Review (STAR) on Computer Aided Design.Report of the Department of Defense Advisory Group on ElectronDevices, Washington, D.C., (open publication), Feb. 1993.

[24] R. A. Sprague, K. J. Singh, and R. T. Wood.  Concurrent Engineering in Product Development.  {\em Ieee design and test of computers}, MAR 01 1991 v 8 n 1, pp. 6-13.

[25] F. Vahid and D. Gajski, "SLIF:  A Specification-Level Intermediate Format for System Design," Proceedings. The European Design and Test Conference. ED&TC 1995, pp. 185-189.

[26] F. Vahid, "Modifying Min-Cut for Hardware and Software Functional Partitioning," Proceedings of the Fifth International Workshop on Hardware/Software Codesign. CODES/CASHE '97, pp. 43-48.

[27] R. Winner et al. The Role of Concurrent Engineering in Weapons Acquisition, IDA Report R388, Institute of Defense Analysis, Washington, D.C., 1988.

[28] W. Wolf, "Object-Oriented Cosynthesis of Distributed Embedded Systems, ACM Transactions on Design Automation of Electronic Systems, Vol. 1, No. 3, July 1996, pp. 301-31.

[29] B.P. Zeigler, Multifaceted Modeling and Discrete Event Simulation. Academic Press, 1984.

# Chapter 8

# DEVS Framework for Systems Development: Unified Specification for Logical Analysis, Performance Evaluation and Implementation

T.G. Kim, S.M. Cho and W.B Lee

*This paper presents a DEVS-based methodology for systems development. The methodology is a unified framework for developing real-time software systems in which logical analysis, performance evaluation, and implementation can be performed, all based on the DEVS formalism. Extended DEVS formalisms, namely Communicating DEVS for logical analysis and Real-time DEVS for implementation are given. Interpretation means associated with the formalisms are also given. An example of development of alternating bit protocol within the framework demonstrates effectiveness of the methodology.*

## 8.1    Introduction

Systems design is an iterative process which involves modeling, simulation and analysis of candidate systems. If sub-systems and algorithms within larger systems, such as communication networks, manufacturing systems, computer systems, and others, are to be developed a discrete event modeling and simulation method can be employed. Once a discrete event model for such a sub-system or an algorithm is developed logical/behavior analysis as well as performance evaluation of the model is performed before implementation. Thus, the design process transits among three phases, namely logical analysis, performance evaluation and implementation each of which often employs a different model. If transitioning between such different models is performed manually, it would be a major hurdle to a seamless design process. A unified modeling framework which provides a basis to specify models at different phases in common semantics would overcome such a hurdle.

A DEVS-based design methodology, shown in Figure 8.1, is such a unified framework for development of discrete event systems. The framework provides a basis for modeling of discrete event systems on which logical analysis, performance evaluation, and implementation can be performed - all with the DEVS (Discrete Event Systems Specification) formalism. The DEVS formalism provides a general, theoretical basis for solving various problems, but extended formalisms may address distinctive design issues in a more efficient manner. For example, a DEVS model developed for performance evaluation would typically contain timing with associated probability distributions. However, an untimed model, a model with time advance undefined, is more amenable to logical analysis. In general, models developed for logical analysis typically reside at higher levels of abstraction than their performance-oriented counterparts. Since logical analysis explores a state space constructed by a set of untimed models, required is a new semantics for communication between such models, which is not the case with performance-oriented models. Thus, means for extending the DEVS formalism within the framework are essential.

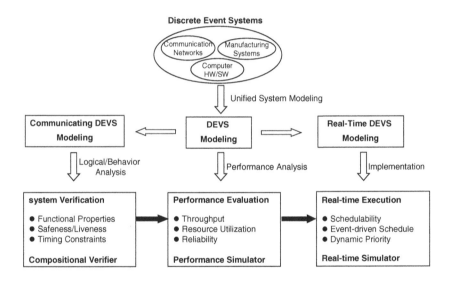

Figure 8.1: DEVS-Based Design Framework

Logical analysis within the proposed methodology occurs within the model verification phase. The phase not only verifies safeness and liveness of a designed model but checks operational correctness. The verification checks lower-level operational specification against higher-level assertional specification. Specifications for the two levels may employ either one formalism or different formalisms. The former is called a single specification approach; the latter a dual specification approach. A dual specification approach in which the operational specification expressed in DEVS formalism is checked against an assertional specification specified in temporal logic is previously developed [9]. This chapter shows a single specification approach in which both operational and assertional specifications are expressed in the extended DEVS formalism, called the Communicating DEVS(C-DEVS) formalism. Thus, verification is a process to check if a lower-level operational C-DEVS model behaves correctly as specified in a higher-level assertional C-DEVS model. Details of logical analysis based on a single specification approach will be presented in Section 3.

Performance evaluation within the framework employs object-oriented simulation of hierarchical DEVS models for which simulation environments running on different languages are developed. Such environments include DEVSim++ [13] of a C++ based environment and DEVSimjava of a java based environment. Such environments are successfully applied for performance evaluation of different application areas. More recently, the DEVSim-HLA [17] environment, based on the concepts of DEVS-BUS[16] running on RTI, has been developed for heterogeneous simulation of models developed in different environments.

Implementation within the framework is no longer an error-prone transformation of a DEVS model to executable program code. Instead, the DEVS model used in the designed phase itself is an implementation which runs in real-time on a real-time simulation engine. An executable DEVS model is specified by the real-time DEVS formalism [10] to be discussed in Section 2. Specification of a real-time DEVS requires an activity associated with each state. The activity is function which is executed during internal state transition. In this sense, each activity can be thought of as an implementation of the internal state transition, which may not require in logical analysis and performance evaluation phases. Thus, any function that is required in the real system is implemented as an abstract activity in the real-time DEVS formalism. Since each atomic model has a set of activities, an overall coupled model has a set of activities running concurrently. Sojourn time for a state within the real-time DEVS formalism defines actually computation time for an activity associated with the state. Such time may not defined as a single value against which a value of real-time clock is checked for real-time scheduling during execution. Thus, sojourn time for each state in the real-time DEVS formalism is defined as a time interval. Details of the real-time DEVS formalism and an associated real-time simulator will be presented in later sections.

This paper is organized as follows. Section 2 presents extensions of the DEVS formalism to be used for logical analysis and implementation phases. Section 3 shows a compositional verification as a logical analysis method. Section 4 briefly discusses simulation-based performance evaluation. Section 5 deals with implementation of a modeled system without transformation of the developed model into executable code. In Section 6, the proposed methodology is exemplified in a design and implementation problem of Alternating Bit Protocol. Section 7 concludes our discussion.

# 8.2    Extended DEVS Formalisms

As shown in Figure 8.1, the unified DEVS framework for systems development employs the DEVS formalism for logical analysis, performance evaluation, and implementation. However, DEVS models for logical analysis and implementation may not be the same as a performance-oriented DEVS model specified in the standard DEVS formalism. Table 8.1 summaries characteristics and differences of such models in specifications.

Table 8.1: Characteristics of Extended DEVS Formalism

|  | Performance Analysis | Logical/Behavior Analysis | Implementation |
|---|---|---|---|
| **Required Information** | Timed States/Events Sequence | Untimed States/Events Sequence | Timed States/Events/Activities Sequence |
| **Modeling Formalism** | DEVS | Communicating DEVS (C-DEVS) | Real-time DEVS (RT-DEVS) |
| **Semantics Different from DEVS** | Same as DEVS | No output/no time advance functions; Non-deterministic internal transition; No select function | Interval Time Advances; Activity Associated with Each State |
| **Time Used in Model Interpretation** | Virtual Time (Logical Clock) | Time Unused(No Clock) | Real Time (Wall Clock) |

## 8.2.1    DEVS Formalism

The DEVS (Discrete Event Systems Specification) formalism can specify a dynamic system at any of the behavior-structure specification levels [25]. Although models at different aspects can be expressed in the DEVS formalism a performance-oriented DEVS model is most commonly used one. The DEVS formalism defines two classes of models: atomic model and coupled model. Operationally, an atomic DEVS model is a timed state transition mechanism that operates over time base with two transition modes: an internal means of self scheduling of events and a means of responding to external events. Formally, an atomic DEVS model (AM) is defined as follows [23].

$$AM = \langle X, S, Y, \delta_{ext}, \delta_{int}, \lambda, ta \rangle, \text{ where}$$

$X$ : a set of input events;

$S$ : a set of sequential states;

$Y$ : a set of output events;

$\delta_{ext.} : Q \times X \rightarrow S$, an external transition function,

where $Q = \{(s,e) \mid s \in S \text{ and } 0 \le e \le ta(s)\}$, total state set of M;

$\delta_{int.} : S \rightarrow S$, an external transition function;

$\lambda : S \rightarrow Y$, an output function;

$ta : S \rightarrow R^{+}_{0,\infty}$ (non-negative real number), time advance function.

A coupled model is a composition of DEVS models, each of which can be either atomic or coupled ones, thus supporting hierarchical construction of a complex model. A well-known DEVS property of *closed under coupling* is a theoretical basis for such a hierarchical models construction, similar to a process of assembling a complex hardware from pieces of components. A formal definition of a coupled DEVS model (CM) is as following.

$CM = \langle X, Y, D, \{M_i\}, EIC, EOC, IC, Select \rangle$, where

$X, Y$ : same as in *AM*;

$D$ : an index set for components of *CM*,

for each $i \in D$,

$M_i$ :a component DEVS model, atomic or coupled;

$EIC \subseteq X \times \cup_i X_i$, external input coupling relation;

$EOC \subseteq \cup_i Y_i \times Y$, external output coupling relation;

$IC \subseteq \cup_i Y_i \times \cup_j X_j$, internal coupling relation;

$Select: 2^{\{Mi\}} - \varnothing \rightarrow \{M_i\}$, tie-breaking selector.

## 8.2.2    Communicating DEVS(C-DEVS) Formalism

The C-DEVS formalism is a modification of the DEVS formalism for logical/behavior analysis of a discrete event system. The analysis usually employs a set of component models with time advances unspecified (untimed). Interaction between such component models reveals more complex operational behavior than that of a time-specified (timed) discrete event model. Actually, analysis of an untimed discrete event model requires a generation of a set of all possible state trajectories induced by interactions between components, each having its own untimed state transitions. Such generation requires a sound semantics for communication and synchronization between untimed components. Since no time advance is specified for each state in an untimed component, behavior of a composite model may be non-deterministic.

There are two cases of such non-determinism: internal state transition and output generation. State transition non-determinism occurs when two components have an identical output with which different internal transitions are performed. Output generation non-determinism occurs when a state has more than two outputs to be generated. For the former, internal transition function of a standard atomic DEVS needs to be changed to internal transition relation. For the latter, select function of a standard coupled DEVS is left undefined. Introduction of such non-determinism is intentional to explore all possible state trajectories of a composite untimed model. In fact, state trajectories generated by a non-deterministic untimed model include all those generated by a deterministic timed model. Based on the above discussion we now defines the C-DEVS formalism for logical/behavior analysis, which again has two model classes: atomic and coupled. An atomic C-DEVS, C-AM, is defined as:

$$C\text{-}AM = <X, Y, Q, \delta_{ext}, T_{int}>, \text{ where}$$

$X$ : a set of input events;

$Y$ : a set of output events;

$Q$ : a set of states;

$\delta_{ext.} : Q \times X \to Q$, an external transition function;

$T_{int} \subseteq Q \times (Y \cup \{\tau\}) \times Q$, an internal transition relation,

where $\tau$ means no external output event is generated.

Note that there are differences between DEVS and C-DEVS definitions in an atomic model. First of all, the definition of C-AM has no time advance function to leave sojourn time at each state unspecified. Secondly, the definition has no explicit output function. Instead, output generation is included in the internal transition relation for simplicity in composition operation for logical analysis which we shall discuss later. Finally, internal transition function is modified into internal transition relation for modeling of non-determinism in the transitions.

Definition of a coupled model within the C-DEVS formalism, a C-CM, is similar to a coupled DEVS as:

$$C\text{-}CM = <X, Y, D, \{M_i\}, EIC, EOC, IC>, \text{ where}$$

$X, Y, D, EIC, EOC, IC$ : the same as DEVS formalism;

$M_i$ : an atomic C-DEVS model, $C\text{-}AM$.

Note that there are two differences between C-DEVS and DEVS formalisms in coupled model definition. One is that a component in C-CM can be only an atomic C-DEVS model. The other is that no select function is defined in C-CM as discussed earlier. The following section introduces composition and minimization operations defined on the C-DEVS models for logical verification.

Composition of two atomic C-DEVS models requires an accurate semantics for communication and synchronization between the two, which is not defined in coupled C-DEVS. The coupled C-DEVS only defines static couplings between the two. Heymann classified the interactions between two processes into three categories: strict synchronization, broadcast synchronization and prioritized synchronization [Heymann 1990].

Strict synchronization restricts the shared events to be either executed by both processes concurrently or by none. In broadcast synchronization each process can generate their events for execution and the other process will participate in their execution synchronously if it is ready to accept the events. Otherwise, only initiating process executes the event while the other process stays as it was. For prioritized synchronization, refer to [7]. From the above classification, the interaction between two C-DEVS models conforms to the broadcast synchronization.

## 8.2.3   Real-time DEVS (RT-DEVS) Formalism

The RT-DEVS formalism is an extension of the DEVS formalism for modeling real-time systems which can be executed in real-time. The formalism also defines two classes of RT-DEVS models. An atomic model in RT-DEVS formalism, *RT-AM*, is defined as follows [10]:

$RT\text{-}AM = <X, S, Y, \delta_{ext}, \delta_{int}, \lambda, ta, \psi, A>$, where

$X$ : a set of input events;

$S$ : a set of sequential states;

$Y$ : a set of output evetns;

$\delta_{ext.} : Q \times X \rightarrow S$, an external transition function,

where $Q = \{(s,e) \mid s \in S \text{ and } 0 \le e \le ta(s)\}$;

$\delta_{int.} : S \rightarrow S$, an internal transition function;

$\lambda : S \rightarrow Y$, an output function;

$ta : S \rightarrow I^{+}_{0,\infty} \times I^{+}_{0,\infty}$, a time interval function,

where $I^{+}_{0,\infty}$ is the non-negative integers with $\infty$ adjoined;

$\psi : S \rightarrow A$, an activity mapping function;

$A = \{a \mid t(a) \in I^{+}_{0,\infty} \text{ and } t(a) \le ta \mid_{max}\} \cup \emptyset$, a set of activities.

Note that the RT-DEVS formalism defines a set of activities associated with a state, which is not defined in the DEVS formalism. Each activity is an abstraction of a task in a real system to be modeled. Within the RT-DEVS formalism, execution time for the task is specified by the time advance function defined for the state. Note also that a time advance, *ta(s)*, for RT-DEVS is given by an interval $ta(s)|_{min} \le ta(s) \le ta(s)|_{max}$ of integers, which is a real number in DEVS. A reason for such interval time advance is that a RT-DEVS simulator checks a specified time advance of a RT-DEVS model against a real-time clock within the simulator during simulation. If the clock falls in the scheduled time interval correctness of the schedule would be verified. Integers in time advance specify computation time of an activity in terms of ticks generated by an underlying computing system. Such specification enables a modeler to specify the computation time adaptable to the implemented computing system.

Specification of a coupled model within the RT-DEVS formalism, a RT-CM, is the same as a coupled DEVS except that no *Select* function is defined in RT-DEVS. This is because an execution order of simultaneous events cannot be controllable by the simulation environment but by the underlying computing environment.

# 8.3 Logical Analysis: Verification

## 8.3.1 Verification Framework

Verification is a process of proving equivalence between system operation and system requirement. Generally, four elements are involved in verification process [20]: property specification, operational specification, conformation criteria, and checking algorithm.

- Property specification: this is a description of what the system should satisfy. This level of specification needs a means to express global system properties such as safeness, liveness, and fairness without considering details of system's operation. Formalisms such as Temporal Logic, Calculus of Communicating Systems (CCS), Assertion Calculi are widely employed for such specification

- Operational specification: this level describes how the system behaves. Such behavior is specified either in an event-based or in a state-based view point of system dynamics. Formalisms such as Automata, Petri net, StateChart, Discrete Event Specification (DEVS) are frequently used for such specification.

- Conformation criteria: conformation is to check whether behavior of a system, specified in operational specification, meets requirement of the system, specified in property specification. Sound mathematical methods are required to eliminate an error-prone process of a case-by-case test. Such methods include *satisfiability* 18], *bisimulation* [19], and *model checking* [3]. The application of which depends on formalisms used for the property and operational specifications.

- Checking algorithm: an answer for the above conformation criteria requires comprehensive computation to explore a state space of a system from its representation. Such exploration requires an efficient algorithm by which all possible state trajectories are automatically generated. The most important issue in automation is the state explosion problem. Some techniques, such as symbolic representation, partial order, and others, can overcome the problem.

This section presents a compositional verification method based on single specification approach which employs the C-DEVS formalism for both property and operational specification.

## 8.3.2 Compositional Verification

Figure 8.2 shows the overall procedure of the proposed compositional verification method. As shown in the Figure, the method is a single specification approach in which both property and operational specifications are modeled by the C-DEVS formalism. More specifically, property specification is modeled as an assertional C-DEVS model, and operational specification is modeled as an operational C-DEVS model. Thus, verification is to check if the operational model meets property specified in the assertional model. Since an operational C-DEVS model consists of component C-DEVS models an efficient means to compose them into an equivalent C-DEVS model is to be devised. Events extraction is an operation to extract all events in a given C-DEVS model. Such events constitute an interest events set (IES), which only related to interested properties to be verified. Thus, IES can be used to reduce a C-DEVS model to a simplified one that is equivalent to the original one from the viewpoint of interested properties.

Composition of two operational C-DEVS models into one employs communication semantics of broadcast synchronization between the two. Composition is followed by minimization. Minimization is to find observational equivalence relation, to be explained later, in conjunction with IES. Composition-minimization is performed for each pair of atomic C-DEVS models in an incremental manner until a composite operational C-DEVS model is obtained. Such a series of the composition-minimization operations prevents the verification process from the state space explosion problem. Once a final operational C-DEVS model is obtained, observational equivalence relation is used as a conformance criterion to check equivalence between the operational C-DEVS model and the assertional C-DEVS model. Finally, the checking algorithm in our method is an implementation of observational equivalence relation based on Paige and Tajan's partition algorithm [21]. We now explain composition, minimization, and observational equivalence relation in details.

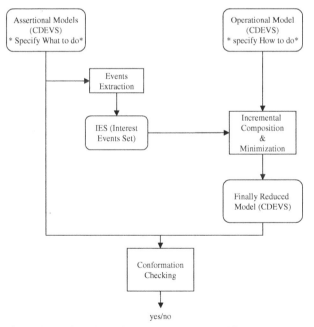

Figure 8.2: Overview of Proposed Compositional Verification

### 8.3.2.1 Composition

Consider a coupled C-DEVS model which consists of a set of atomic C-DEVS models and the Coupling Scheme (CS) of three coupling relations, EIC, EOC, and IC. Composition operation is applied to a pair of atomic C-DEVS models within a coupled C-DEVS model. That is, composition of two atomic models needs specification of each, along with coupling scheme between two. Formally, a composite model of two atomic C-DEVSs $M1$ and $M2$, denoted by $M1\|M2$, is an atomic C-DEVS defined as:

[Definition 3.1] Composition
Given a coupled C-DEVS model including two atomic C-DEVSs $M1$ and $M2$, composition of $M1$ and $M2$, denoted by $M1 \| M2$, is defined as:

$$M1 \| M2 = < X, Q, Y, \delta_{ext}, T_{int} >, \text{ where}$$
$$X \subseteq X1 \cup X2;$$
$$Y \subseteq Y1 \cup Y2;$$
$$Q \subseteq Q1 \times Q2;$$
$$\delta_{ext.} : Q \times X \to Q;$$
$$T_{int} \subseteq Q \times (Y \cup \{\tau\}) \times Q,,$$

with the following constraints:
$Xi$, $Yi$, $Qi$ are the input events set, output events set and states set of $Mi$, respectively.

$\delta_{ext}$ is defined as:

(1) $(s_1, s_2) \xrightarrow{?x} (s'_1, s'_2)$

if $(x, x_1) \in EIC \wedge (x, x_2) \in EIC \wedge s_1 \xrightarrow{?x_1} s'_1 \wedge s_2 \xrightarrow{?x_2} s'_2$

(2) $(s_1, s_2) \xrightarrow{?x} (s'_1, s_2)$

if $[(x, x_1) \in EIC \wedge (x, x_2) \in EIC \wedge s_1 \xrightarrow{?x_1} s'_1 \wedge s_2 \xrightarrow{?x_2} \setminus] \vee$

$[(x, x_1) \in EIC \wedge \forall x_2 (x, x_2) \notin EIC \wedge s_1 \xrightarrow{?x_1} s'_1]$

(2) $(s_1, s_2) \xrightarrow{?x} (s_1, s'_2)$

if $[(x, x_1) \in EIC \wedge (x, x_2) \in EIC^* \wedge s_1 \xrightarrow{?x_1} \setminus \wedge s_2 \xrightarrow{?x_2} s'_2] \vee$

$[(x, x_2) \in EIC \wedge \forall x_1 (x, x_1) \notin EIC \wedge s_2 \xrightarrow{?x_2} s'_2]$

$T_{int}$ is defined as:

(1-1-1)    $((s_1, s_2), y, (s'_{1i}, s'_2)) \in T_{int}$   if $\exists s'_{1i}$ such that

$$(y_1, y) \in EOC \land (y_1, x_2) \in IC \land s_1 \xrightarrow{!y_1} s'_{1i} \land s_2 \xrightarrow{?x_2} s'_2$$

(1-1-2)    $((s_1, s_2), y, (s'_{1i}, s_2)) \in T_{int}$   if $\exists s'_{1i}$ such that

$$[(y_1, y) \in EOC \land (y_1, x_2) \in IC \land s_1 \xrightarrow{!y_1} s'_{1i} \land s_2 \xrightarrow{?x_2} \backslash] \lor$$
$$[(y_1, y) \in EOC \land \forall x_2 (y_1, x_2) \notin IC \land s_1 \xrightarrow{!y_1} s'_{1i}]$$

(1-2-1)    $((s_1, s_2), \tau, (s'_{1i}, s'_2)) \in T_{int}$   if $\exists s'_{1i}$ such that

$$(y_1, y) \notin EOC \land (y_1, x_2) \in IC \land s_1 \xrightarrow{!y_1} s'_{1i} \land s_2 \xrightarrow{?x_2} s'_2$$

(1-2-2)    $((s_1, s_2), \tau, (s'_{1i}, s_2)) \in T_{int}$   if $\exists s'_{1i}$ such that

$$[(y_1, y) \notin EOC \land (y_1, x_2) \in IC \land s_1 \xrightarrow{!y_1} s'_{1i} \land s_2 \xrightarrow{?x_2} \backslash] \lor$$
$$[(y_1, y) \notin EOC \land \forall x_2 (y_1, x_2) \notin IC \land s_1 \xrightarrow{!y_1} s'_{1i}]$$

(1-3)    $((s_1, s_2), \tau, (s'_{1i}, s'_2)) \in T_{int}$   if $\exists s'_{1i}$ such that $s_1 \xrightarrow{\tau} s'_{1i}$

(2-1-1)    $((s_1, s_2), y, (s'_1, s'_{2i})) \in T_{int}$   if $\exists s'_{2i}$ such that

$$(y_2, y) \in EOC \land (y_2, x_1) \in IC \land s_1 \xrightarrow{?x_1} s'_1 \land s_2 \xrightarrow{!y_2} s'_{2i}$$

(2-1-2)    $((s_1, s_2), y, (s_1, s'_{2i})) \in T_{int}$   if $\exists s'_{2i}$ such that either

$$[(y_2, y) \in EOC \land (y_2, x_1) \in IC \land s_1 \xrightarrow{?x_1} \backslash \land s_2 \xrightarrow{!y_2} s'_{2i}] \lor$$
$$[(y_2, y) \in EOC \land \forall x_1 (y_2, x_1) \notin IC \land s_2 \xrightarrow{!y_2} s'_{2i}]$$

(2-2-1)    $((s_1, s_2), \tau, (s'_1, s'_{2i})) \in T_{int}$   if $\exists s'_{2i}$ such that

$$(y_2, y) \notin EOC \land (y_2, x_1) \in IC \land s_1 \xrightarrow{?x_1} s'_1 \land s_2 \xrightarrow{!y_2} s'_{2i}$$

(2-2-2)    $((s_1, s_2), \tau, (s'_1, s'_{2i})) \in T_{int}$   if $\exists s'_{2i}$ such that either

$$[(y_2, y) \notin EOC \land (y_2, x_1) \in IC \land s_1 \xrightarrow{?x_1} \backslash \land s_2 \xrightarrow{!y_2} s'_{2i}] \lor$$
$$[(y_2, y) \notin EOC \land \forall x_1 (y_2, x_1) \notin IC \land s_2 \xrightarrow{!y_2} s'_{2i}]$$

(2-3)    $((s_1, s_2), \tau, (s'_1, s'_{2i})) \in T_{int}$   if $\exists s'_{2i}$ such that $s_2 \xrightarrow{\tau} s'_{2i}$

In above definition, $s \xrightarrow{?x} s'$ is a transition relation, meaning that the state $s$ could accept an input event $x$ to transit into $s'$. $s \xrightarrow{\tau} s'$ represents an internal transition relation which changes the state from s to $s'$ with no output generated. $s \xrightarrow{!y} s'$ denotes a spontaneous transition relation from the state $s$ into $s'$ with an output event $y$ to be transmitted to the external environment. $s \xrightarrow{\tau} \backslash$, $s \xrightarrow{?x} \backslash$ or $s \xrightarrow{!y} \backslash$ means that there is no transition relation with respect to the corresponding event on state $s$.

[Example 3.1] Composition
$AB$ is a coupled C-DEVS , consisting of $A$ and $B$ as shown in Figure 8.3(a). $A\|B$ is obtained as shown in Figure 8.3(b).

Note that a composite state (0,0) has two output events to be generated. Since *time advance function* and *Select* are not defined in the C-DEVS formalism, the order of output generation at the state is non-deterministic.

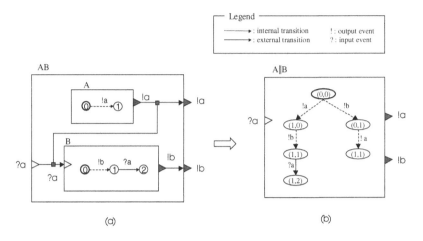

Figure 8.3: Composition of two atomic C-DEVSs
(a) Coupled Model *AB* consisting of *A* and *B*
(b) Composed Model *A* ∥ *B*

### 8.3.2.2 Minimization

Minimization is an operation to collapse the equivalent states into a representative state. The equivalent states exhibit observable behaviors equivalent to each other. Minimization operation consists of two steps. The first is an event internalization process. In the step, an output event of a component is renamed as an internal hidden event $\tau$ if it has no interaction with an external world. The second step is an aggregation of the observational equivalent states. Observational equivalent states are defined as follows.

[Definition 3.2] Observational Equivalence Relation
A binary relation $\rho$ on $Q = \{\, s_1, s_2, \ldots, s_n \,\}$ is said to be an observational equivalence relation if and only if the followings hold.

$$(1\text{-}1) \quad \forall y (s_1 \xrightarrow{\,!y\,} s_1' \Rightarrow \exists s_2' : (s_2 \xrightarrow{\,\tau\,}{}^* \xrightarrow{\,!y\,} s_2' \wedge (s_1', s_2') \in \rho))$$

$$(1\text{-}2) \quad \forall x (s_1 \xrightarrow{\,?x\,} s_1' \Rightarrow \exists s_2' : (s_2 \xrightarrow{\,?x\,} s_2' \wedge (s_1', s_2') \in \rho))$$

$$(1\text{-}3) \quad s_1 \xrightarrow{\,\tau\,} s_1' \Rightarrow \exists s_2' : (s_2 \xrightarrow{\,\tau\,}{}^* s_2' \wedge (s_1', s_2') \in \rho)$$

The notation $\xrightarrow{\,\tau\,}{}^*$ in above definition means zero or more internal transition might happen. The equivalence relation is reflexive, symmetric and transitive. The above definition is different from that of weak bisimulation relation defined in CCS [19]. This is because communication semantics in CCS is strict synchronization [7], but that in C-DEVS is broadcast synchronization.
[Definition 3.3] Observational Equivalence States

Two or more states are said to be equivalent if and only if they have equivalence relations to each other.

[Definition 3.4] Observational Equivalence
Two or more C-DEVSs are said to be equivalent if their initial states are equivalent to each other.

[Example 3.2] Minimization
Assume that a C-DEVS model *M* in Figure 8.4 was obtained by a series of composition-minimizations of a coupled C-DEVS model to be analyzed. Then, minimization of *M* can be performed by using concepts of observational equivalent states defined in [Definition 3.3].

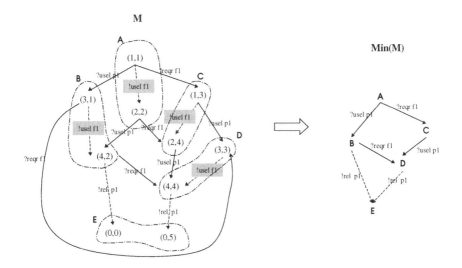

Figure 8.4: Minimization Using Equivalent States

In Figure 8.4, events in the gray box are internalized, each renamed as $\tau$. By using [Definition 3.3], nodes in a dotted line are equivalent states. For example, two states (3,3) and (4,4) are equivalent by applying (*1-1*) of [Defintion 3.2]. Merging of all such equivalent states into a representative state results in the minimized C-DEVS model, *Min(M)*.

# 8.4   Performance Evaluation

Performance evaluation can be done by simulation of DEVS models. To measure time related performance, such as delay time and throughput, requires sojourn time between states for each model which is not defined in C-DEVS models but well defined in DEVS models. Once such DEVS models are constructed, simulation is performed by using the abstract simulators algorithm explained in [23]. Different hierarchical simulation environments which realize the algorithm have been developed using different programming languages.

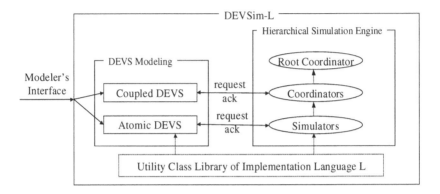

Figure 8.5: Generic Architecture for Hierarchical DEVS Simulator

A generic architecture for the hierarchical simulation environment is shown in Figure 8.5. In the Figure, DEVSim-L means a DEVS simulation environment developed with a programming language L. As shown in the Figure, it is natural to implement the abstract simulators algorithm in an object-oriented language such as C++. Representative implementations include DEVS-Scheme [12] in LISP and DEVSim++ [13] in C++. The main purpose of the OO implementation is to exploit reusability of DEVS models in models development. In fact, a well-designed environment would supports two-dimensional reusabilty as shown in Figure 8.6, one from the OO paradigm and the other from the DEVS methodology [15]. Proposal of reuse metrics for DEVS models developed in the DEVSim++ environment and measure of such reusability were reported in [5].

Speedup of simulation time can be obtained by distributed simulation of DEVS models [14], [22] or hybrid simulation of simulation models combined with analytic ones [1]. A heterogeneous simulation environment, called DEVSim-HLA 17], which supports interoperation of different simulators has been recently developed based on concepts of DEVS-BUS [16] implemented on HLA/RTI.

Simulation-based performance analysis requires careful design of experimental frame, the concepts of which has been proposed in [23]. An experimental frame basically consists of three models: a generator model for generating inputs to a model under evaluation, a transducer model for collecting output data, and an acceptor model for controlling simulation run. The three models are analogous, in their respective functions, to a signal generator, a spectrum analyzer, and an oscilloscope in an electronic circuit experiment. Figure 8.7 shows such analogy.

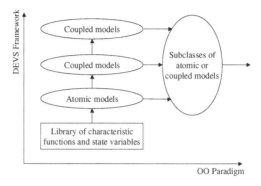

Figure 8.6: Two Dimensional Reusablity in DEVSim++

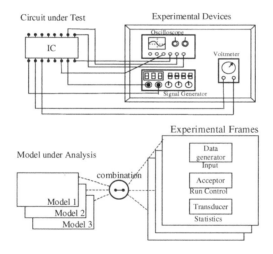

Figure 8.7: Analogy between Circuit Experiment and Simulation Experiment

Design of experimental frame is objective-driven, meaning that different design objectives require different experimental frames. More specifically, a set of design objectives is transformed into a set of performance indices. Then, an experimental frame is designed such that the desired performance indices are measured by simulation. Thus, simulation is done in a way that a model is simulated with a set of different experimental frames, or a set of candidate models are simulated with an experimental frame until a desired design is found (See

Figure 8.6). An efficient method to evaluate such combinations, called the SES/Model Base framework, was originated with [11] and [24].

# 8.5    Implementation: Real-time Simulation

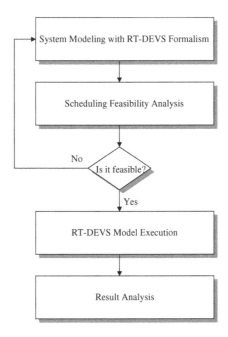

Figure 8.8: Real-time Simulation Procedure

## 8.5.1    Methodology Overview

As discussed earlier, implementation within our framework of Figure 8.1 is no longer an error-prone transformation of a model to executable program code. Instead, the RT-DEVS model itself is an implementation which runs in real-time under a real-time simulation engine. A typical simulation procedure within the framework is depicted in Figure 8.8. First of all, a target system is modeled with the RT-DEVS formalism discussed in section 2.3.

A modeler specifies atomic and coupled RT-DEVS models for the system under development. The modeling step is followed by the scheduling feasibility analysis phase. For the analysis, a schedulability test graph is first extracted from the model and corresponding transient graphs are generated. Then, checking of scheduling feasibility is performed on each transient graph. If the given

RT-DEVS models are not feasible for real-time execution in simulation, the modeler calibrates the models to satisfy the real-time scheduling. In this step, he/she often divides a time consuming activity function into smaller ones and modifies corresponding atomic models to make the proposed real-time scheduling to be feasible.

After the given simulation models pass the scheduling feasibility analysis, the real-time scheduler for real-time simulation now simulates them as follows. First, the scheduler flattens all coupled models to minimize communication delays between atomic models. Then, it spawns model threads for corresponding atomic models and establishes communication channels between them. When real-time simulation is done without any run-time exception due to timing violation, the modeler analyzes the simulation result. We now explain analysis of scheduling feasibility and a real-time simulation environment.

## 8.5.2   Event Driven Scheduling

To meet timing requirement under real-time simulation, the execution priority of a model should be determined by its time advance value. In the RT-DEVS formalism, the next scheduling time of a model is associated with $t_N$, time of a next event, which is given as time advance value at last scheduling time. One important observation is that $t_N$ associated with a RT-DEVS model is varying during execution. Therefore, the execution priority of a model should be given dynamically and an atomic model with a smaller $t_N$ must be given higher priority. Besides, atomic models are supposed to update their $t_N$ whenever they receive an internal or external event, thereby performing a state transition. When a model receives such an external event, the real-time model scheduler sets execution priority of that model to the highest one. This is because the received event immediately reschedules the model, thus updating $t_N$. Therefore, events, either external or internal ones, causes a priority reassignment. That is why we refer our scheduling algorithm as to *event driven scheduling* algorithm. Table 8.2 summarizes characteristics of the scheduling algorithm.

Table 8.2: Characteristics of Event Driven Scheduling

| | Event Driven Scheduling |
|---|---|
| Task Characteristic | $RT\text{-}AM = < X, S, Y, \delta_{ext}, \delta_{int}, \lambda, ta, \psi, A >$ Aperiodic event driven task |
| Goal of Scheduling | Preservation of Causality |
| Factor of Priority Assignment | Updated scheduling time due to either an external event or an internal event |
| Dependencies among tasks | Input/output dependencies affect on execution orders |

### 8.5.3    Scheduling Feasibility

There are often cases where a real-time simulation model is not simulated in real-time due to the limitation of CPU capacity. Therefore, a scheduling policy for such real-time simulation is required based on which a certain criterion for scheduling feasibility is to be analyzed. To give a scheduling feasibility criterion for a RT-DEVS model the following assumptions are made.

A1) Structure of an overall RT-DEVS model is not variable during simulation.

A2) Each atomic RT-DEVS model has a cyclic trajectory.

A3) Any overhead, including context switching time, during simulation is ignored.

The second assumption above is essential to analyze schedule feasibility for a given RT-DEVS model, which we define as follows.

[Definition 5.1] Cyclic Trajectory
Consider a RT-DEVS atomic model $m$ with a states set of $S = \{ s_1, s_2, ..., s_n \}$. Assume that for each state $s_i \in S$ in $m$, there is a maximum deadline $dt_{Ni}|_{max}$ which is specified in $ta(s_i)$ of $m$. Assume also that $m$ deterministically performs a sequence of state transitions $s_1 \rightarrow s_2 \rightarrow s_3 \rightarrow \cdots \rightarrow s_n$. Then , $m$ is said to have a cyclic trajectory if it repeats such a sequence in a cyclic manner

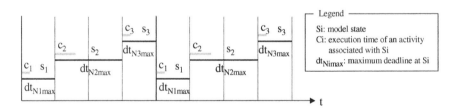

Figure 8.9: Cyclic Trajectory of $s_1 \rightarrow s_2 \rightarrow s_3 \rightarrow s_1 \rightarrow s_2 \rightarrow s_3 \cdots \rightarrow s_3$.

Figure 8.9 illustrates an example of a model with a cyclic trajectory, where $c_i$ denotes the execution time of the activity associated with $s_i$. A cyclic RT-DEVS model may not be executed alone. Instead, a set of such models is executed together with interaction between them. To analyze schedule feasibility of an overall RT-DEVS model, a means to represent a global state trajectory is to be devised. To explain such a global state trajectory consider two atomic RT-DEVS models $m_1$ and $m_2$ as shown in Figure 8.10, each having a cyclic trajectory.

Note that Figure 8.10 represents a sequence of state transitions for the two models on a synchronized discrete-time base the interval of which is $T$. Assume that $m_1$ and $m_2$ are executed concurrently. Then, concurrent behavior of the two can be represented by a sequence of transitions of ordered pairs of states each of which is represented by $(s_1, s_2)$, where $s_1$ is a state of $m_1$ and $s_2$ is a state of $m_2$.

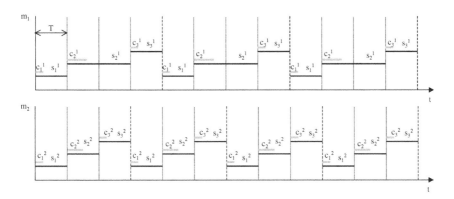

Figure 8.10: RT-DEVS Model $m_1$, $m_2$ with Cyclic Trajectory

Note that each transition occurs at the end of each time interval $T$. Since the sequence of transitions represent concurrent behavior of the two on the time base it can be used as a means to analyze schedulability. We call the transitions sequence a schedulability test graph, or a test graph in short. Figure 8.11 shows a test graph of a composite model consisting of $m_1$ and $m_2$ in Figure 8.9. Formally, a schedulability test graph is defined as follows.

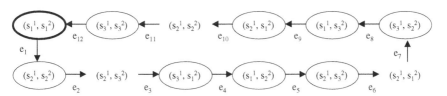

Figure 8.11: Schedulability Test Graph

[Definition 5.2] Schedulability Test Graph
A schedulability test graph $G$ is defined as $G = (N, E)$, where $N$ is a finite set of composite states and $E \subset N \times N$ is a set of edges. Each composite state is an ordered pair of single states and an edge between two nodes represents an expiration of the maximum deadline of a scheduled time denoted by $e_i$.

[Definition 5.3] Distinguished Node
A distinguished node of $G$ is a node that satisfies the following conditions.

1) The initial node is a distinguished node.
2) A node all of whose element states are different from those of the previous distinguished node.

[Definition 5.4] Transient Node
A node is a transient node if it is not a distinguished one.
[Example 5.1] Transient and Distinguished Nodes
In Figure 8.11, nodes in a circle mark are distinguished nodes and others are transient nodes.

[Definition 5.5] Transient Graph
A graph $g$ is a transient graph of a test graph $G$ if an initial and a final nodes are distinguished nodes and zero or more transient nodes exist between the two. Therefore, $G$ consists of one or more transient graphs.

[Example 5.2] Transient graph.
Figure 8.12 shows a general transient graph, where $e_i$ represents an elapse of time and $\underline{c_i}$ represents the total sum of the computation time of activity functions that must be performed during $e_1$

$$(s_0{}^1, s_0{}^2,..,s_0{}^M) \xrightarrow[\underline{c_1}]{e_1} (s_1{}^1, s_1{}^2,..,s_1{}^M) \xrightarrow[\underline{c_2}]{e_2} (s_2{}^1, s_2{}^2,..,s_2{}^M) \xrightarrow[\underline{c_3}]{e_3} \cdots \xrightarrow[\underline{c_N}]{e_N} (s_N{}^1, s_N{}^2,..,s_N{}^M)$$

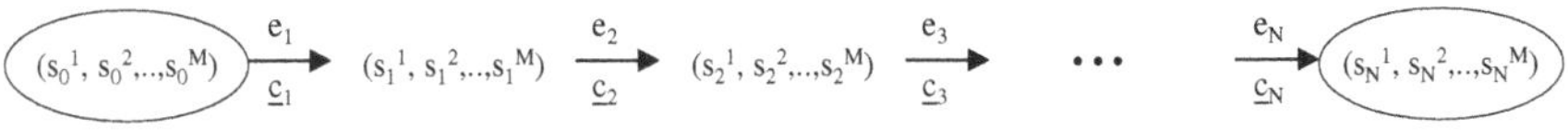

Figure 8.12: General Transient Graph

[Theorem 5.1] Scheduling Feasibility of a Transient Graph
A transient graph $g$ is schedulable iff $\forall i, e_i - \underline{c_i} \geq 0$, where $e_i$ is an elapse of time that the edge represents and $\underline{c_i}$ is the total sum of the computation time of activity functions that must be performed during $e_i$.

*Proof*:
(i) $g$ is schedulable $\Rightarrow \forall i, e_i - \underline{c_i} \geq 0$

We prove the above by contradiction. Suppose that $\exists i, e_i - \underline{c_i} < 0$. Then, the total computation time of activity functions exceeds the time available at the edge $i$. Therefore, $g$ is not schedulable.

(ii) $\forall i, e_i - \underline{c_i} \geq 0 \Rightarrow g$ is schedulable

We prove the above by contradiction. Suppose that $g$ is not schedulable. Then, at least one edge in the transient graph has a total computation time that exceeds an available time.

### 8.5.4    Real-time Simulation Environment

The architecture of RT-DEVS simulation environment is layered structure as shown in Figure 8.13. The RT-DEVS micro kernel provides basic functions based on which a set of model threads are executed concurrently. The lower layer in the micro kernel has a thread context-switch routine and a real-time alarm clock management routine. The real-time alarm clock routine supplies facilities which

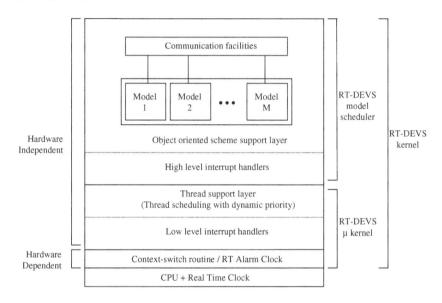

Figure 8.13: Architecture of RT-DEVS Simulation Environment

produce current time and support timer services. Thread support layer in the micro kernel enables CPU to switch between model threads and interrupt routines handles events from external environment.

The primary goal of our simulation framework is to run RT-DEVS models interacting with its environment in real-time. To achieve this goal, a real-time model scheduler is developed, which executes each RT-DEVS models as real-time tasks by using facilities provided by the thread support layer. The scheduler dynamically changes priorities of RT-DEVS models based on the proposed priority assignment policy. In this sense, the micro kernel can be viewed as a kernel-thread execution engine and the scheduler as a model execution engine. Recall that a real-time simulation of a hierarchical RT-DEVS model is performed after flattening the model into atomic ones to reduce communication delay. Figure 8.13 shows interaction between the scheduler and the micro kernel.

Each atomic model spawns its own thread to execute its characteristic functions concurrently with other model threads associated with corresponding atomic models. The real-time scheduler performs the Concurrent Model Execution algorithm to be explained later. The algorithm changes an execution priority of each model by using the priority function P with argument $t_N|_{max}$ of each model, which is notified to the micro kernel. Then, the kernel-thread execution engine of the micro kernel switches CPU to a model thread based on the priority. By this way, a model with the highest priority is executed the first.

As shown in Figure 8.14, each model has an associated independent program which concurrently executes internal transition and external transition of the model. Such an execution is different from that of conventional DEVS simulators in which the two transitions are executed in a sequential manner.

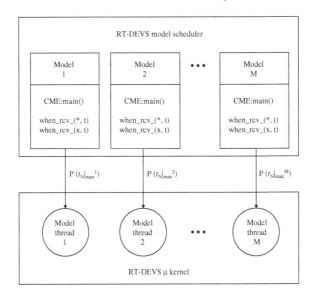

Figure 8.14: Relation between Model Scheduler and Micro Kernel

## 8.5.5    Real-time Simulator Algorithms

We now explain the program associated with each atomic RT-DEVS model, which consists of a main program **CME:main()** and two concurrent model execution algorithms, **CME:when_rcv_(*,t)** and **CME:when_rcv_(x,t)**, as abstract simulators.

1. **CME:when_rcv_(*, t):**
2. **if** $t_N|_{min} \leq t \leq t_N|_{max}$ **then**
3.    $y := \lambda(s)$;
4.    send message(y, t) to the associated port;

5.    $s := \delta_{int}(s)$;

6.    $t_L := t$;

7.    $t_N := [t_L + ta(s)|_{min}, t_L + ta(s)|_{max}]$;

8.    $P(t_N|_{max})$

9.    $\psi(s)$

10. **else**

11.    error;

12. **end if**

Figure 8.15: CME: when_rcv(*, t)

1. **CME:when_rcv_(x, t):**

2. **if** $t_L \leq t \leq t_N|_{max}$ **then**

3.    $e := t - t_L$;

4.    $s := \delta_{ext}(s,e,x)$;

5.    $t_L := t$;

6.    $t_N := [t_L + ta(s)|_{min}, t_L + ta(s)|_{max}]$;

7.    $P(t_N|_{max})$

8.    $\psi(s)$

9. **else**

10.    error;

11. **end if**

Figure 8.16: CME: when_rcv(x, t)

1. **CME:main():**

2. $s = s_0$        /* initialize */

3. $t_N := [ta(s_0)|_{min}, ta(s_0)|_{max}]$;

4. **concur_forever for each RT-DEVS model**
                     /* main loop */

5.    wait for an event

6.    **if** an external event **then**

7.      when_rcv_(x, t);

8.    **else if** an internal time out event **then**

9.      when_rcv_(*, t);

10.    **end if**

11. **end concur_forever**

Figure 8.17: CME: main()

The algorithm **when_rcv_(*, t)** is similar to that for a DEVS atomic model with the following differences. First, checks of validity of a scheduled time in

Line 2 of Figure 8.15 and a next schedule in Line 7 in Figure 8.15 are different from those for a DEVS model. Next, Line 8 in Figure 8.15 computes an execution priority of the associated model from which priorities of other models are updated. Finally, Line 9 in Figure 8.15 executes an activity function associated with the current state.

The algorithm **when_rcv_(x, t)** is similar to that for a DEVS model and discussion of differences is the same as the **when_rcv_(*, t)** case. Whenever the priority function $P(t_N|_{max})$ in Figure 8.15 and Figure 8.16 is called, the kernel-thread engine switches CPU to the model thread with highest priority. A context switching is also occurred, when a model performs output function (Line 4 in Figure 8.15). This is because a model with a pending external event is given to a highest priority, thus immediately getting CPU.

The above algorithm **main()** shows the main routine of the CME. Each atomic model waits for an external event until an internal timeout occurs. If an external event is occurred before an internal timeout expires, it proceeds **when_rcv_(x,t)**. If an internal time expires without external event, it proceeds **when_rcv_(*,t)** and sets new internal timeout. To synchronize time between atomic models and the environment, the model scheduler suspends an atomic model upon completing its activity. The suspension lasts until a scheduled time advance is completely elapsed. However, if an external event occurs during that interval, the scheduler wakes up the corresponding atomic model. The above scheduling approach is different from one reported in [10] where a round robin scheduling approach has been taken.

# 8.6    Example: Logical Analysis and Implementation

To show the DEVS-based design methodology within the proposed framework, design of Alternating Bit Protocol (ABP) is to be considered. ABP is a communication protocol for secure transmission of the messages from a source to a destination. Generally the existing communication media is not perfect. Thus, there always exists such possibility that messages generated from the sender might be lost, duplicated or corrupted before arriving to the destination. Thus a secure communication protocol is needed to ensure a correct transfer of the messages between the two entities. This section exemplifies logical analysis and implementation of ABP while leaving performance evaluation to readers.

## 8.6.1    System Description

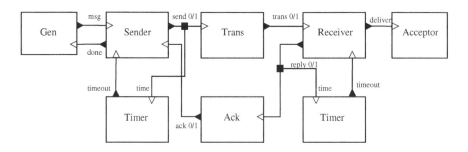

Figure 8.18: Overall System Model of ABP

Figure 8.18 shows an overall system model of ABP, which consists of eight atomic models. The *Sender* delivers a message through the media *Trans*, then the *Receiver* acknowledges through the media *Ack*. We shall assume that the Trans line may lose or duplicate messages (but not corrupt) and the *Ack* line may lose messages. To determine whether the message is lost or not, both the *Sender* and the *Receiver* are notified by a timeout event if no message is arrived in a specified time interval. Once a timeout event is notified, retransmission is made assuming that a message transmitted previously has been lost. Messages are sent tagged with a bit 0 and 1 alternatively, and also the acknowledgements are constituted of the bits. Details of such description can be found in [2][19][8].

## 8.6.2    Compositional Verification: Logical Analysis

Generally, properties to be verified are classified into two types: safeness property and liveness property [18]. Safeness says that something bad will never happen; liveness means that something good will eventually happens. Deadlock freedom is an example of safeness property. The following example will verify that the ABP system holds the liveness property by using the proposed verification method. Recall that the method employs a single language approach. Thus, both assertional model and operational model are C-DEVS models. We follows the steps shown in the proposed method of Figure 8.2.

### 8.6.2.1   Operational C-DEVS Modeling

Operational C-DEVS modeling requires details knowledge of ABP to be modeled. Here, we present all eight atomic C-DEVS models in Figures 8.19, 8.20 and 8.21 for operational specification of ABP without detail descriptions of operational behavior of each component model. Details of such description can be found in [19][2].

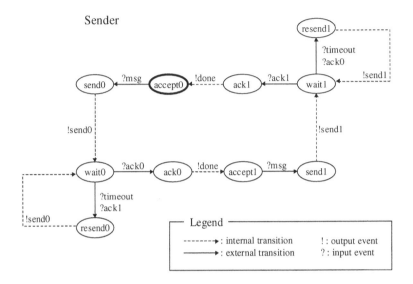

Figure 8.19: Atomic C-DEVS Model: Sender

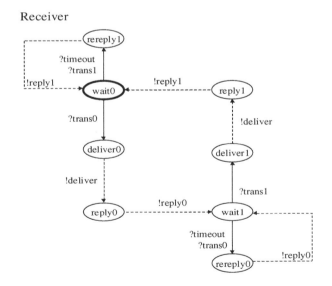

Figure 8.20: Atomic C-DEVS Model: Receiver

Trans

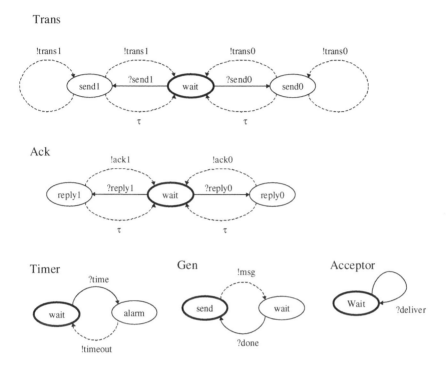

Figure 8.21: Atomic C-DEVS Models: Trans, Ack, Timer, Gen and Acceptor

## 8.6.2.2  Assertional C-DEVS Modeling

Figure 8.22: Desired Behavior and Assertional Model in C-DEVS.
(a) Desired High Level Behavior; (b) Assertional Model.

A desired behavior of ABP is represented by a high level conceptual C-DEVS model as shown in Figure 8.22(a) in which four actions are repeated in a cyclic manner. The message *!msg* means generation of a new message to be sent. "Transferring action" denotes the repetitive actions to safely transmit the message to the receiver. The message *!deliver* represents an acceptance of the message by *Receiver*. Finally, the *!done* message is to notify that all trials of *Sender* to transmit the previous message have been completed.

A property of the ABP system could be constructed from the high level conceptual model. One such system property may be liveness, "a message sent by a sender will be eventually delivered to a receiver". This property could be specified as an assertional C-DEVS model depicted in Figure 8.22(b). The set of events associated with the property in the C-DEVS model is called IES (Interest Events Set) which is {*!msg*, *!deliver*}in this example. IES is used in a series of composition-minimization processes to reduce an operational C-DEVS model into a simplified one by using observationally equivalent relation.

### 8.6.2.3 Incremental composition and minimization

In the process of a series of composition and minimization processes of an overall operational C-DEVS shown in Figure 8.19, 8.20, and 8.21, several composition orderings may be considered which determine the size of the composed models. Thus, an efficient ordering in such composition should be devised. It is note worthy that reduced models with different ordering are all observational equivalent.

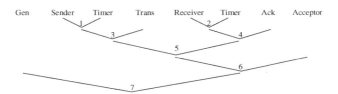

Figure 8.23: Composition Ordering

Consider a composition ordering in seven steps as shown in Figure 8.23. We explain a composition-minimization process in steps 2 and 4. At the step 2, composition of two C-DEVS models, Receiver and Timer, is perform. However, minimization of each C-DEVS models with respect to IES is performed before and within the composition. Before composition of the two, Receiver is minimized as shown in Figure 8.24 and Timer was not reduced. Figure 8.25(a) shows the result of composition of the minimized Receiver and Timer. Minimization within composition takes two phases: event internalization and states aggregation. The two phases is briefly explained. After composition, the *!timeout* event is no longer coupled with any other components. Moreover, the event does not have to be observed to prove the property specified in the assertional C-DEVS model in Figure 8.22(b). Thus the event/*timeout* is internalized. After event internalization, equivalent states in dot-lined circles are obtained and then aggregated into representative one. A resultant minimized C-DEVS model is obtained as shown in Figure 8.25(b).

A series of composition-minimization operations following the ordering shown in Figure 8.23 transforms the operational model into the smaller one shown in Figure 8.26. Note that the operational C-DEVS model of Figure 8.26 has an internalized event τ which is invisible outside, thus not being considered in verification using observationally equivalent relation.

Min(Receiver)

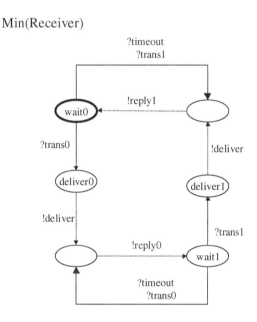

Figure 8.24: Minimized C-DEVS Model of Receiver

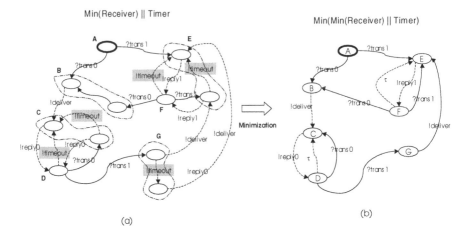

Figure 8.25: Composition and Minimization
(a) Composed Model. (b) Minimized Model.

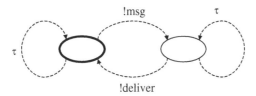

Figure 8.26: Finally Reduced Operational C-DEVS Model

Table 8.3 shows the size of the intermediate models during the seven composition-minimization steps of Figure 8.23. Note that each minimization reduces the size of states. Different orderings, however, would result in different sizes of states in composition-minimization steps.

Table 8.3: Number of States in Composition/Minimization

| Composition step | Size of the composed model | Size after minimization |
|:---:|:---:|:---:|
| 1 | 14 | 8 |
| 2 | 11 | 7 |
| 3 | 24 | 22 |
| 4 | 19 | 17 |
| 5 | 100 | 3 |
| 6 | 3 | 3 |
| 7 | 3 | 2 |

### 8.6.2.4   Conformation Checking

The proposed verification method employs observational equivalence relation as a conformation criterion. Thus, proof of a given property of a system is a claim that an assertional C-DEVS model is observationally equivalent to an operational C-DEVS model. In this example, the liveness property of ABP is verified since the assertional C-DEVS model of Figure 8.22 (b) is observationally equivalent to the reduced operational C-DEVS model of Figure 8.26.

From the above, it is guaranteed that whenever an event *!msg* happens, the event *!deliver* eventually happens in ABP. From the operational C-DEVS model of Figure 8.26 another property of deadlock-free can be easily verified, for each state of the model automatically transits a next state without an external event.

## 8.6.3   Implementation

We follow the steps shown in Figure 8.8. The ABP system model of Figure 8.18 consists of RT-DEVS models to be analyzed, a software process in remote host, and a LAN environment interacting with models. *Trans* and *Ack* models represent the LAN environment and *Receiver* and *Acceptor* models are considered as a software process in a remote host. *Gen, Sender* and *Timer* are models to be analyzed for feasibility of real-time execution. Although all components have been modeled in RT-DEVS, we only present RT-DEVS models of *Sender, Gen*, and *Timer* for schedulability analysis. The rest of RT-DEVS models are similar to C-DEVS models shown in section 6.2.1. Figure 8.27 shows RT-DEVS models, where a time interval $@(ta|_{min}, ta|_{max})$ in given in ticks, one tick in100 milliseconds

### 8.6.3.1   Scheduling Feasibility Analysis

Figure shows the state transition diagram of the given system in which time base is represented by discrete ticks, 100 miliseconds each. To check the scheduling feasibility of given simulation models using [Theorem 5.1], we build a schedulability test graph from Figure 8.28. We assume that each activity function takes 5 ticks at most. The test graph and transient graphs are depicted in Figure 8.29. By [Theorem 5.1] for scheduling feasibility the given simulation model can be simulated in real-time on our real-time simulation engine.

### 8.6.3.2   Real-time Execution and Result

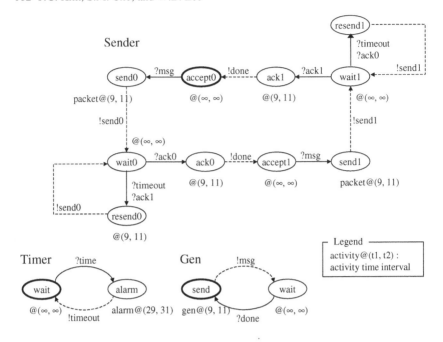

Figure 8.27: RT-DEVS Models: Sender, Timer, Gen

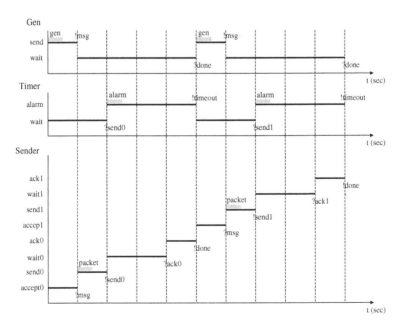

Figure 8.28: Timed State Transition of RT-DEVS Models in Figure 8.27

We demonstrate real-time execution of RT-DEVS models. *Receiver* model is considered as a software process in a remote host. *Trans* and *Ack* models originally represent a LAN environment. Therefore, the LAN environment is used as it is. *Gen*, *Sender* and *Timer* models are implemented as RT-DEVS model in our real-time simulation framework. We verified correctness of our real-time simulator by observing communication between *Sender* and *Receiver* in real Figure 8.30 shows the state trajectories of the target system in real-time simulation. The time at which event occurs is verified to be bounded within the time intervals specified in RT-DEVS models.

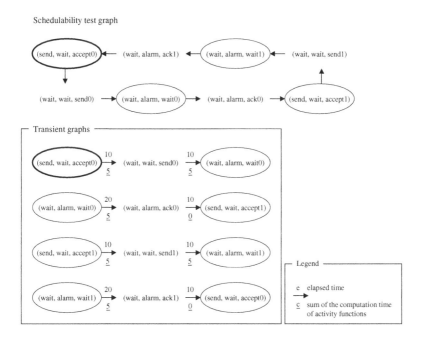

Figure 8.29: Schedulability Test Graph and Transient Graphs

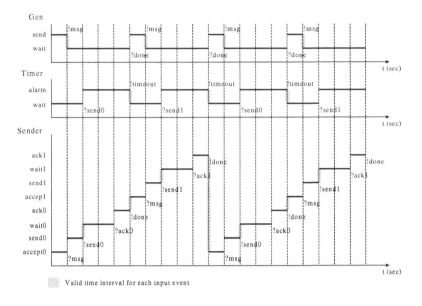

Figure 8.30: Simulation Result

## 8.7 Conclusions

A DEVS-based framework supports a unified specification for systems development. The DEVS formalism is a basis for modeling a system to be developed as a discrete event model based on which logical analysis, performance evaluation, and implementation can be performed, all in the DEVS formalism. Extensions of the DEVS formalism have been made to address distinctive design issues in a more efficient manner. Such extensions were the C-DEVS (Communicating DEVS) formalism and the RT-DEVS (Real-Time DEVS) formalism for logical analysis and implementation, respectively.

A compositional verification method has been proposed for logical analysis which verifies properties as well as operational correctness of a system to be designed. The method has employed a single formalism approach in which both assertional and operational specifications are modeled by the C-DEVS formalism. It has been shown that the proposed verification method is a solution for the state explosion problem faced in the state-based verification.

Implementation has been no longer an error-prone transformation of a analyzed model into executable code. Instead, a RT-DEVS model itself is an implementation, which has been executed in real-time on the developed real-time simulation environment. Thus, the proposed method has shown a new method of systems implementation, which we call the "modeling = implementation" paradigm.

To demonstrate the effectiveness of the proposed framework, a design example of logical analysis and implementation for ABP has been presented. The example has first verified such properties of ABP as liveness and deadlock-free. It then has verified that the RT-DEVS ABP model itself is executed in real-time on a developed real-time simulation environment.

# References

[1] Ahn, M.S. and T.G. Kim, "A Framework for Hybrid Modeling/Simulation of Discrete Event Systems," AIS'94, pp. 199-205, Dec., 1994, Gainesville, FL.

[2] Bartlett, K.A., R.A. Scantlebury and P.T. Wilkinson, "A note on reliable full-duplex transmission over half-duplex lines," *Comm. of the ACM*, 12(5):260-265. 1969.

[3] Clarke, E.M., E.A. Emerson and A.P. Sistla, "Automatic verification of finite state concurrent systems using temporal logic," *ACM Transactions on Programming Languages and Systems*, 8:244-263, 1986.

[4] Cho, S.M. and T.G. Kim, "Real-time DEVS Simulation: Concurrent Time-selective Execution of Combined RT-DEVS and Interactive Environment," SCSC-98, pp 410-415, Reno, Nevada, U.S.A., 1998.

[5] Choi, Y. and T.G. Kim, "Reusability Measure of DEVS Simulation Models in DEVSim++ Environment," Proc. of SPIE-97, pp. 244-255, Orlando, FL, U.S.A. 1997.

[6] Heymann, M., "Concurrency and discrete event control," *IEEE Control Systems Magazine*, 10(4):103-112, Jun. 1990.

[7] Holzmann, G.J., *Design and Validation of Computer Protocols*. Prentice Hall, 1991.

[8] Hong, G.P. and T.G. Kim, "A Framework for Verifying Discrete Event Models Within a DEVS-Based System Development Methodology," *Transactions of the Society for Computer Simulation*, Vol. 13, No. 1, 19 - 34, 1996.

[9] Hong. J.S., H.S. Song, T.G. Kim and K.H. Park, "A Real-time Discrete Event System Specification Formalism for Seamless Real-time Software Development," *Discrete Event Dynamic Systems*, vol. 7, pp. 355-375, 1997.

[10] Kim, T.G., et al, "System Entity Structuring and Model Base Management," *IEEE Tran SMC*, 20(5), pp. 1013-1024, 1990

[11] Kim, T.G. and B.P. Zeigler, "The DEVS-Scheme Modeling and Simulation Environment," *Knowledge-Based Simulation,* Chapter 3, pp. 20-35, 1991.

[12] Kim, T.G. and S.B. Park, "The DEVS Formalism: Hierarchical Modular Systems Specification in C++," 1992 European Simulation Multiconference, pp. 152-156, June, 1992, York, England.

[13] Kim, K.H., Y.R. Seong and T.G. Kim, "Distributed Simulation of Hierarchical DEVS Models: Hierarchical Scheduling Locally and Time Warp Globally," *Transactions for SCS*, vol. 13, no.3, pp. 135-154, 1996.

[14] Kim, T.G. and M.S. Ahn, "Reusable Simulation Models in an Object-Oriented Framework," Chapter 4, *Object-Oriented Simulation*, IEEE Press, 1996.

[15] Kim, Y.J. and T.G. Kim, "A Heterogeneous Distributed Simulation Framework Based on DEVS Formalism," AIS'96, pp. 116 - 121, San Diego, CA, 1996.

[16] Kim, Y.J., J.H. Cho, and T.G. Kim, "DEVS-HLA: Heterogeneous Simulation Framework Using DEVS Bus Implemented on RTI," In Proceedings of the 1999 Summer Computer Simulation Conference, pp 37-42, Chicago, IL, 1999.

[17] Manna, Z. and A. Pnueli, *The Temporal Logic of Reactive and Concurrent Systems*, Springer-Verlag, N.Y., 1992.

[18] Milner, R., *A Calculus of Communicating Systems, Volume 92 of Lecture Notes in Computer Science*, Springer-Verlag, 1980.

[19] Ostroff, J.S., *Temporal Logic for Real-Time Systems.* Research Studies Press, 1989.

[20] Paige, R. and R.E. Tarjan, "Three Partition Refinement Algorithms," *SIAM Journal of Computing*, 16(6):973-989, Dec. 1987.

[21] Seong, Y.R., T.G. Kim and K.H. Park, "Mapping Modular, Hierarchical Discrete Event Models in a Hypercube Multicomputer," *Simulation Practice and Theory*, vol. 2, no. 6, pp. 257-275, 1995.

[22] Zeigler, B.P., *Multifaceted Modelling and Discrete-Event Simulation.* Academic Press, 1984.

[23] Zeigler, B.P., *Object-oriented Simulation with Hierarchical Modular Models*, Academic Press, 1990.

[24] Zeigler, B.P., H. Praehofer, and T.G. Kim, *Theory of Modeling and Simulation* (2nd Ed), Academic Press, 2000.

# Chapter 9

# Representation of Dynamic Structure Discrete Event Models: A Systems Theory Approach

F.J. Barros

*The Parallel Dynamic Structure Discrete Event System Specification (DSDE) can represent systems with a time-varying structure. Changes in structure are broadly defined and include changes in models, components and their interactions. We show that the DSDE is closed under the composition operation. This property allows the construction of hierarchical and modular models. The abstract simulators necessary to execute dynamic structure models are presented. These simulators allow a description of models independently of the actual simulation procedure. The DSDE formalism handles simultaneous events in parallel, and it determines, without ambiguity, the network composition when structural changes occur.*

## 9.1    Introduction

Many real systems have the capability to change their structure. The Parallel Dynamic Structure Discrete Event System Specification (DSDE) can represent systems with such a dynamic structure [4]. Some advantages of dynamic structure models include better and efficient representation and the ability to change model resolution. The DSDE formalism uses three levels of detail to represent models. At the first level models are described by the DEVS formalism [12]. A second level of representation is achieved by the structured DSDE formalism. Changes in model structure can be represented at a third, network level.

The concept of abstract simulators was introduced by [13] to execute simulation models. These simulators provide the separation of the simulation procedure from models and thus promote model reuse. A new type of simulator able to support structural changes at simulation runtime is developed in this work.

Simultaneous events are a major source of static structure model errors [8]. Dynamic structure models poses a new challenge, for it is of fundamental importance to have a well define structure at any time. The DSDE formalism defines, without ambiguity, the network structure when changes in structure occur.

Closure under coupling permits to build models in a hierarchical and modular manner. We show that the DSDE is closed under the operation of composition what permits the use of DSDE models to represent complex systems.

This paper is organized as follow: Section 2 presents the DEVS formalism. Section 3 presents the structured DEVS formalism. Section 4 presents the DSDE formalism and its closure under coupling. Section 5 focuses the DSDE approach to deal with simultaneous events at structural changes. Section 6 describes the simulators necessary to run DSDE models. The conclusions of this research are presented in Section 7.

# 9.2   Discrete Event System Specification

The *Discrete Event System Specification* (DEVS) is a formalism introduced in [12] to describe discrete event systems. In the DEVS formalism a basic model is described by

$$M = (X, S, q_0, Y, \tau, \delta, \lambda)$$

where

$X$ is the set of input values

$S$ is the set of partial states (p-states)

$Q = \{(s,e) \mid s \in S, 0 \le e \le \tau(s)\}$ is the state set

$q_0 = (s_0, e_0) \in Q$, is the initial state, with

   $s_0$ the initial p-state (partial state)

   $e_0$ the time elapsed in p-state $s_0$

$Y$ is the set of output values

$\tau: S \to \mathbf{R}_0^+$ is the time advance function

$\delta: Q \times X^\phi \to S$ is the transition function, where

   $X^\phi = X \cup \{\phi\}$

   $\phi$ is the null value (absence of value)

$\lambda: S \to Y$ is the partial output function

The output function, $\Lambda: Q \to Y^\phi$, is defined by

$$\Lambda(s,e) = \begin{cases} \lambda(s) & \text{if } e = \tau(s) \\ \phi & \text{if } e < \tau(s) \end{cases}$$

We describe briefly the DEVS behavior. If no event arrives to the system it will stay in partial state $s$ for time $\tau(s)$. When $e = \tau(s)$, and under the assumption of no external event arrival, the system changes to the state $(\delta(s,\tau(s),\phi),0)$. If an external event, $x \in X$, arrives when the system is in the state $(s,e)$ it will change to the state $(\delta(s,e,x),0)$. If an external event, $x \in X$, arrives when $e = \tau(s)$, the system changes to the state $(\delta(s,\tau(s),x),0)$. A detailed description of DEVS semantics can be found in [12].

ASSUMPTION 1. *Non instantaneous propagation*
A model receiving an input at time $t$ will only change its state at time $t^+ = t + \Delta t$, $\Delta t > 0$, and $\lim \Delta t \to 0$.

This assumption is based on the causality principle stating that the cause must precede its effect. In other words, if the cause happens at time $t$ then the effect must only exist after time $t$. We denote the causality constraint by saying that the effect exists only at time $t^+$. This time difference can be arbitrarily small and thus can be ignored on most situations. However, we will see that Assumption 1 is of fundamental importance to define structural changes without any ambiguity.

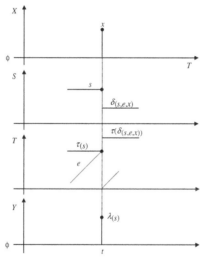

Figure 9.1: Component state trajectories.

In Figure 9.1 is represented a graphical interpretation of the non-instantaneous propagation assumption. At time $t$ when $e = \tau(s)$, an input $x$ is received by the system when it is in p-state $s$. By Assumption 1 the system only changes its p-state at time $t^+$. The p-state of this system is given at time $t^+$ by $\delta(s,e,x)$. The system output at time $t$ is given by $\lambda(s)$. This value is independent of the input value at that time. Thus, Assumption 1 also makes possible to connect an output from a component with itself (self-loop) without any ambiguity for it isolates component output from component input. If Assumption 1 doesn't hold, the input value at time $t$ will be a function of the output value at time $t$. This output value will also depend on the input value at the same time, leading thus, to an non-ended recursive definition.

DEFINITION 1. A model $M = (X,S,q_0,Y,\tau,\delta,\lambda)$ is in a *transitory p-state* $s$ if $\tau(s) = 0$.

Let's consider the situation that occurs when a component receives several inputs when in a transitory p-state, as represented in Figure 9.2. At time $t$ the component receives an input $x_1$ when it is in state $(s,\tau(s))$. It changes to p-state $s' = \delta(s,\tau(s),x_1)$ at time $t^+$. The p-state $s'$ is transitory and thus $\tau(s') = 0$. At time $t^+$ the component receives an input $x_2$ and it changes, at time $t^{++}$, to p-state $s'' = \delta(s',0,x_2)$, another transitory p-state. Input value $x_3$ arrives at time $t^{++}$ and the component changes to the non-transitory p-state $s''' = \delta(s'',0,x_3)$ after time $t^{++}$. The set of output values is the sequence $\lambda(s)$, $\lambda(s')$ and $\lambda(s'')$ at times $t$, $t^+$ and $t^{++}$, respectively.

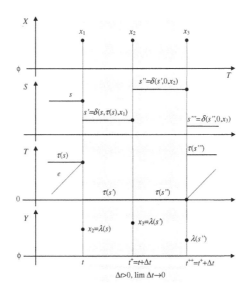

Figure 9.2: Behavior in a partial transitory state.

At time $t$ the system has changed from state $s$ to $s'''$, by sequentially passing through the states $s'$ and $s''$.

## 9.3 Structured Discrete Event System Specification (SDEVS)

The *Structured Discrete Event System Specification* (SDEVS) provides a formalism for obtaining a fine-grained control over models. The transition function, for example, can be decomposed into a set of transitions, where each one is used when certain conditions hold. The same applies to the other functions. In the SDEVS formalism a model is described by [6]

$$S = (X,S,q_0,Y,\kappa,I,\{\tau_i \mid i \in I\},\{\delta_i \mid i \in I\},\{\lambda_i \mid i \in I\})$$

where

$I$ is a set of indexes

$\kappa: S \to I$, is the index function

EQUIVALENCE 1. A SDEVS model $S = (X,S,q_0,Y,\kappa,I,\{\tau_i\},\{\lambda_i\},\{\delta_i\})$, is equivalent to the DEVS model $M = (X,S,q_0,Y,\tau,\delta,\lambda)$, where for all $s \in S$, $\tau(s) = \tau_{\kappa(s)}(s)$, $\delta(s) = \delta_{\kappa(s)}(s)$ and $\lambda(s) = \lambda_{\kappa(s)}(s)$.

EXAMPLE. We consider a buffered server with a constant service time of 5 time units. This server has two phases, idle and busy, that summarize the server state. In the SDEVS formalism we assign a transition function to each one of these phases. The buffered server is represented by

$$B = (X,S,q_0,Y,\kappa,I,\{\tau_i\},\{\delta_i\},\{\lambda_i\})$$

where

$X = \{j_1,j_2,\ldots,j_n,\ldots,\}$ is a set of jobs

$Y = X$

$S = \{idle,busy\} \times \mathbf{R}_0^+ \times X^*$

$q_0 = ((idle,\infty,[]),0)$

   $X^*$ is the set of lists containing zero or more elements from set $X$; the empty list is represented by []; $[h|r]$ represents a list where the first element is $h$ and the remaining elements are represented by list $r$; $[f::l]$ represents a list whose last element is $l$ and the first elements are represented by list $f$;

$I = \{idle,busy\}$

$\kappa(phase,\_,\_) = phase$

$\tau_{busy}(\_,sigma,\_) = \tau_{idle}(\_,sigma,\_) = sigma$

$\delta_{idle}((\_,\infty,[]),e,x) = (busy,5,[x])$

$\delta_{busy}((\_,sigma,buffer),e < sigma,x) = (busy,sigma - e,[buffer::x])$

$\delta_{busy}((\_,sigma,[h|r]),e = sigma,x) = (busy,5,[r::x])$

$\delta_{busy}((\_,sigma,[h]),e = sigma,\phi) = (idle,\infty,[])$

$\delta_{busy}((\_,sigma,[h|r]),e = sigma,\phi) = (busy,5,r)$

$\lambda_{idle}(\_,\_,[h|t]) = \lambda_{busy}(\_,\_,[h|t]) = h$

A structured description can be used in some situations where dynamic models used to be helpful. Replace models or change model functions can, in many situations, be achieved by structured models. For example it is much easier to implement a set of indexed functions than to change a method in run time. These features are only supported in the very few object-oriented languages oriented to instances, like Self [9], and more difficult to implement in class oriented languages like Smalltalk or Java.

## 9.4 Dynamic Structure Discrete Event System Specification

The problem of representing discrete event systems that exhibit structural changes has been subject of research [11,10]. A comparison of approaches can be found in [3]. A rigorous approach was accomplished by the DSDEVS formalism [1,2]. The *Parallel Dynamic Structure Discrete Event System Specification* (DSDE) is a generalization of the original DSDEVS formalism, and allows the specification of basic or dynamic structure networks of discrete event systems [4]. A Parallel Dynamic Structure Discrete Event System Network is defined by a 4-tuple

$$DSDEN_N = (X_N, Y_N, \eta, M_\eta)$$

where

$N$ is the network name

$X_N$ is the set of network input values

$Y_N$ is the set of network output values

$\eta$ is the name of the dynamic network executive

$M_\eta$ is the model of the executive $\eta$

The overall network structure is kept in the state of a special DEVS component, the executive. This component acts like a regular DEVS component and thus it can change its own state and produce output values. Because of the correspondence existing between executive p-states and network structures, changes in the executive p-state can cause changes in the network structure. These changes of p-state can be achieved by the executive transition function that can be triggered by both external values and/or the influence of the time to output function.

The model of the executive, is a modified basic model defined by the 9-tuple

$$M_\eta = (X_\eta, S_\eta, q_{0,\eta}, Y_\eta, \gamma, \Sigma^*, \tau_\eta, \delta_\eta, \lambda_\eta)$$

where

$\gamma: S_\eta \to \Sigma^*$ is the structure function

$\Sigma^*$ is the set of network structures

To obtain a shorter notation, the executive model can be defined explicitly in the network model

$$DSDEN_N = (X_N, Y_N, (X_\eta, S_\eta, q_{0,\eta}, Y_\eta, \gamma, \Sigma^*, \tau_\eta, \delta_\eta, \lambda_\eta))$$

The structure function $\gamma$ establishes the mapping from executive p-states to network structures. A structure $\Sigma_j \in \Sigma^*$ associated with the executive p- state $s_{j,\eta} \in S_\eta$, is given by

$$\Sigma_j = \gamma(s_{j,\eta}) = (D_j, \{M_{i,j}\}, \{I_{i,j}\}, \{Z_{i,j}\})$$

where

$D_j$ is the set of component names associated with the executive partial state $s_{j,\eta}$

for all $i \in D_j$, $M_{i,j}$ is the model of component $i$

for all $i \in D_j \cup \{\eta, N\}$, $I_{i,j}$ is set of components influencers of $i$

for all $i \in D_j \cup \{\eta\}$, $Z_{i,j}$ is the input function of component $i$

$Z_{N,j}$ is the output function of the network $N$

The network structure is defined by four elements: the names of the network components $D$, the model of each component $i \in D$, represented by $\{M_i\}$, the influencers of each component $\{I_i\}$, and the input function of each component $\{Z_i\}$. In the definition, all these sets can have a different value for each p-state $s_{j,\eta}$ of the executive, and thus, the subscript $j$ affects all these sets. Sets $\{I_i\}$ and $\{Z_i\}$ represent the connections among components, and sets $D$ and $\{M_i\}$ represent the components themselves. The model of a component gives its dynamic behavior, and because we are dealing with discrete event entities, we describe components by DEVS models. If models were continuous, the Continuous Flow System Specification formalism (CFSS) could be used instead [7].

Variables are subject to the following constraints for every $s_{j,\eta} \in S_\eta$:

$\eta, N \notin D_j$

$N \notin I_{N,j}$

$M_{i,j} = (X_{i,j}, S_i, q_{0,i}, Y_{i,j}, \underline{\tau}_i, \delta_{i,j}, \lambda_{i,j})$ is an atomic DEVS model, for all $i \in D_j$, with
$\delta_{i,j}: Q_i \times X_{i,j}^\phi \to S_i$

For notational simplicity we constraint the partial state set, the initial state and the time to output function to remain constant.

$$Z_{i,j}: \underset{k \in I_{ij}}{\times} V_{k,j} \to X_{i,j}, \text{ for all } i \in D_j \cup \{\eta\}$$

where

$$V_{k,j} = \begin{cases} Y_{k,j} & \text{if } k \neq N \\ X_N & \text{if } k = N \end{cases}$$

$$Z_{N,j}: \underset{k \in I_{N,j}}{\times} Y_{k,j} \to Y_N$$

$$Z_{i,j}(\phi, \ldots, \phi) = \phi, \text{ for all } i \in D_j \cup \{\eta, N\}$$

This last constraint is commonly accepted for discrete event systems, where a component can only receive a non-null value when at least one of its influencers provides a non-null value.

**DEFINITION 2.** The 4-tuple $(D, \{M_i\}, \{I_i\}, \{Z_i\})$, is referred to as the *network structure*.

**EQUIVALENCE 2.** The DSDE network $M_N = (X_N, Y_N, (X_\eta, S_\eta, q_{0,\eta}, Y_\eta, \gamma, \Sigma^*, \tau_\eta, \delta_\eta, \lambda_\eta))$ is equivalent to the structured model $S = (X, S, q_0, Y, \kappa, I, \{\tau_i\}, \{\delta_i\}, \{\lambda_i\})$. The equivalence between the structured model $S$ and the basic model $M = (X, S, q_0, Y, \tau, \delta, \lambda)$ is guaranteed by Equivalence 1.

Equivalence 2 is fundamental. It allows the definition of hierarchical models for it shows that any network model can be replaced by its atomic equivalent. Because the equivalence we provide is constructive, it also defines rigorously the semantics of DSDE network models.

We show how to construct a structured model from the network $M_N =$

$(X_N,Y_N,(X_\eta,S_\eta,q_{0,\eta},Y_\eta,\chi,\Sigma^*,\tau_\eta,\delta_\eta,\lambda_\eta))$. The input set $X$ of the structured model is given by

$$X = X_N$$

We define $C_\alpha$, the set of components, executive included, associated with a state $s_{\alpha,\eta} \in S_\eta$, by

$$C_\alpha = D_\alpha \cup \{\eta\}$$

The partial state set $S$ is given by

$$S = \bigcup_{s_\alpha \in S_\eta} (\underset{i \in C_\alpha}{\times} Q_i)$$

$$q_0 = ((s_{0,\eta},e_{0,\eta}),(s_{0,a_1},e_{0,a_1}),\ldots,(s_{0,a_n},e_{0,a_n})),e_0)$$

where

$$C_0 = \{\eta,a_1,\ldots,a_n\}$$

and

$$e_0 = \min\{e_{0,i} | i \in C_0\}$$

Let the partial state set of the executive be given by $S_\eta = \{s_{0,\eta}, s_{1,\eta}, s_{2,\eta},\ldots,s_{\alpha,\eta},\ldots\}$, then the set of indexes $I$ is given by

$$I = \{0,1,2,\ldots,\alpha,\ldots\}$$

The index function, $\kappa: S \to I$, is defined by

$$\kappa(s) = \kappa((s_{\alpha,\eta},e_\eta),\ldots) = \alpha$$

The output set is given by

$$Y = Y_N$$

We define $r_i$, the time component $i$ must still remain in the current partial state, by

$$r_i = \underline{\tau}_i(s_i) - e_i$$

The time advance function at every index $\alpha \in I$ is given by

$$\tau_\alpha: S \to \mathbf{R}_0^+$$

and is defined by

$$\tau_\alpha(s) = \min\{r_i | i \in C_\alpha\}$$

Given a set $A = \{a_1,a_2,\ldots,a_n\}$ we define the n-tuple associated with the property $p$ of the elements of $A$ by

$$\underset{i \in A}{\otimes} p_i = (p_{a_1},p_{a_2},\ldots,p_{a_n})$$

The partial output function at index $\alpha$ is defined by

$$\lambda_\alpha(s) = Z_{\alpha,N}(\underset{i \in I_{N,\alpha}}{\otimes} \Lambda_{i,\alpha}(s_i,e_i + \tau_\alpha(s)))$$

The output function at index $\alpha \in I$ is defined by

$$\Lambda_\alpha(s,e) = Z_{N,\alpha}(\underset{i \in I_{N,\alpha}}{\otimes} \Lambda_{i,\alpha}(s_i,e_i + e))$$

The set of states $Q$ is given by

$$Q = \{(s,e) \mid s \in S, 0 \le e \le \tau(s)\}$$

The transition function at index $\alpha \in I$, $\delta_\alpha: Q \times X^\phi \to S$, is given by

$$\delta_\alpha(\underset{i \in C_\alpha}{\otimes} q_i,e,x) = \underset{j \in C_\beta}{\otimes} q_j$$

To define the transition $\delta_\alpha$ we show how to obtain the new partial executive state $s_{\beta,\eta}$ from the previous state $s_{\alpha,\eta}$. The next executive state $q_{\beta,\eta}$ is given by

$$(s_{\beta,\eta}, e_\eta) = \begin{cases} (s_{\alpha,\eta}, e_\eta + e) & \text{if } x_\eta = \phi \wedge r_\eta > e \\[2ex] (\delta_\eta(s_{\alpha,\eta}, e_\eta + e, x_\eta), 0) & \text{if } x_\eta \neq \phi \vee r_\eta = e \end{cases}$$

where

$$x_\eta = Z_{\eta,\alpha}(\underset{i \in I\eta,\alpha}{\otimes} v_i)$$

with

$$v_i = \begin{cases} \Lambda_\eta(s_i, e_i + e) & \text{if } i \neq N \\[2ex] x & \text{if } i = N \end{cases}$$

The new structure associated with the partial state $s_{\beta,\eta}$ is given by

$$\Sigma_\beta = \gamma(s_{\beta,\eta}) = (D_\beta, \{M_{i,\beta}\}, \{I_{i,\beta}\}, \{Z_{i,\beta}\})$$

To finish the definition of the transition function we need to show how the remaining components are changed. The set of new components is given by $A = D_\beta - D_\alpha$, and the set of kept components is given by $K = D_\alpha \cap D_\beta$. The state $q_i \in Q_i$ of each component $i \in D_\beta$ is given by

$$q_i = \begin{cases} (s_i, e_i + e) & \text{if } i \in K \wedge (x_i = \phi \wedge r_i > e) & (1) \\[2ex] (\delta_{i,\alpha}(s_i, e_i + e, x_i), 0) & \text{if } i \in K \wedge (x_i \neq \phi \vee r_i = e) & (2) \\[2ex] q_{0,i} & \text{if } i \in A & (3) \end{cases}$$

where

$$x_i = Z_{i,\alpha}(\underset{j \in I_{i,\alpha}}{\otimes} v_j)$$

with

$$v_j = \begin{cases} \Lambda_{j,\alpha}(s_j, e_j + e) & \text{if } j \neq N \\[2ex] x & \text{if } j = N \end{cases}$$

Line 1 of the definition computes the next state of the unchanged components. These models only update their elapsed time. Line 2 computes the next state of the models that either receive an external input or are scheduled to change.

All the outputs are taken simultaneously and the current network structure $(D_\alpha, \{M_{i,\alpha}\}, \{I_{i,\alpha}\}, \{Z_{i,\alpha}\})$, is used with these values. The new structure $(D_\beta, \{M_{i,\beta}\}, \{I_{i,\beta}\}, \{Z_{i,\beta}\})$, by Assumption 1, will only be used at the time of the next transition. If Assumption 1 doesn' t hold the network will be undefined when structural changes occur, for it will not be defined which structure should be used.

Line 3 describes the state of the added components. By controlling the initial p-state and the elapsed time of the new components, it is possible to model mobile components. The key to mobile agents modeling is the ability to resume components exactly at the same state (not only p-state) when they were removed. Due to the closure property of the DSDE formalism, basic components and network components are all handle in the same manner, and thus a mobile component can have basic or network nature.

EXAMPLE. We consider a change in a production line to modify product routing. This system has three different configurations and the initial layout is represented in Figure 9.3. The first configuration has just one workstation, a different configuration is obtained when a new workstation is added to the flow-shop. The third layout is obtained by the reconfiguration of workstation $B$ that changes its operation and thus is described by a new model. The flow-shop is represented by

$$F = (X_F, Y_F, (X_\eta, S_\eta, q_{0,\eta}, Y_\eta, \gamma, \Sigma^*, \tau_\eta, \delta_\eta))$$

where

$X_F = J^\phi \times \{\textbf{add}, \textbf{remove}, \textbf{change}, \phi\} - \{(\phi, \phi)\}$

$Y_F = J = \{j_1, j_2, \ldots, j_n, \ldots, \}$ is a set of jobs

$X_\eta = \{\textbf{add}, \textbf{remove}, \textbf{change}\}$

$q_{0,\eta} = (s_{0,\eta}, 0)$

$S_\eta = \{s_{0,\eta}, s_{1,\eta}, s_{2,\eta}\}$

$\tau_\eta(s_\eta) = \infty$, for all $s_\eta \in S_\eta$

$\Sigma^* = \{\gamma(s_{0,\eta}), \gamma(s_{1,\eta}), \gamma(s_{2,\eta})\}$

$\delta_\eta(s_{0,\eta}, e, \textbf{add}) = s_{1,\eta}$

$\delta_\eta(s_{1,\eta}, e, \textbf{change}) = s_{2,\eta}$

$\delta_\eta(s_{2,\eta}, e, \textbf{change}) = s_{1,\eta}$

$\delta_\eta(s_{1,\eta}, e, \textbf{remove}) = s_{0,\eta}$

$\delta_\eta(s_{2,\eta}, e, \textbf{remove}) = s_{0,\eta}$

$\delta_\eta(s_{i,\eta}, e, \_) = s_{i,\eta}$

The initial network structure is represented in Figure 9.3 and is given by

$\gamma(s_{0,\eta}) = (D_0, \{M_{i,0}\}, \{I_{i,0}\}, \{Z_{i,0}\})$

with

$D_0 = \{A\}$

$I_{\eta,0} = \{F\}$, $I_{F,0} = \{A\}$

$Z_{\eta,0} \colon X_F \to X_\eta$, $Z_{F,0} \colon Y_{A,0} \to Y_F$

$M_{A,0} = M_A = (X_A, S_A, q_{0,A}, Y_A, \tau_A, \delta_A, \lambda_A)$

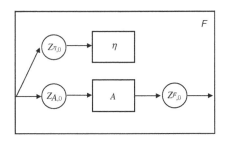

Figure 9.3: Single workstation flow-shop.

When the executive receives an **add** input it changes the structure to the network represented in Figure 9.4, and given by

$$\gamma(s_{1,\eta}) = (D_1, \{M_{i,1}\}, \{I_{i,1}\}, \{Z_{i,1}\})$$

with

$D_1 = \{A,B\}$

$M_{A,1} = M_A$

$M_{B,1} = (X_{B,1}, S_B, q_{0,B}, Y_{B,1}, \tau_B, \delta_{B,1}, \lambda_{B,1})$

$I_{\eta,1} = \{F\}, I_{A,1} = \{F\}, I_{B,1} = \{A\}, I_{F,1} = \{B\}, I_{A,1} = \{F\}$

$Z_{\eta,1}: X_F \to X_\eta, Z_{F,1}: Y_{B,1} \to Y_F$

$Z_{A,1}: X_F \to X_A, Z_{B,1}: Y_{A,1} \to X_{B,1}$

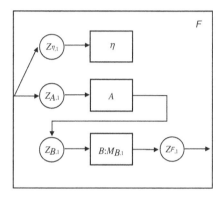

Figure 9.4: Flow-shop with two workstations.

When the executive receives a **change** input it changes the structure to the network represented in Figure 9.5, and defined by

$$\gamma(s_{2,\eta}) = (D_2, \{M_{i,2}\}, \{I_{i,2}\}, \{Z_{i,2}\})$$

with

$D_2 = \{A,B\}$

$M_{A,2} = M_A$

$M_{B,2} = (X_{B,2}, S_B, q_{0,B}, Y_{B,2}, \tau_B, \delta_{B,2}, \lambda_{B,2})$

$I_{\eta,2} = \{F\}, I_{A,2} = \{F\}, I_{B,2} = \{A\}, I_{F,2} = \{B\}, I_{A,2} = \{F\}$

$Z_{\eta,2}: X_F \to X_\eta, Z_{F,2}: Y_{B,2} \to Y_F$

$Z_{A,2}: X_F \to X_A, Z_{B,2}: Y_{A,2} \to X_{B,2}$

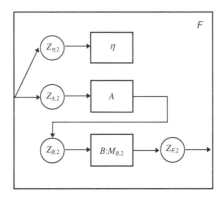

Figure 9.5: Reconfiguration of workstation $B$.

At this state the network switches between $\gamma(s_{2,\eta})$ and $\gamma(s_{1,\eta})$, for every **change** input. The network returns to the initial structure when it receives a **destroy** value. We note that although component $B$ switches between two different models, these changes do not affect directly component state. When the model of a component changes its current state remains the same because only in the next transition this new model will be used to compute the next state.

## 9.5   Simultaneous Events

To understand how structure is defined in the DSDE formalism when simultaneous events occur we consider again the network represented in Figures 9.3-9.5. Both workstations $A$ and $B$ are servers with unlimited buffers described in Section 3. Figure 9.6 describes a possible component behavior over time, where for simplicity we have omitted partial state subscripts. At time $t_1$ a job leaves workstation $A$ when the network changes its structure to a 2 workstation model. This job leaves the network at time $t_1$ when there is a connection between $A$ and the network. At time $t_2$ a job finishes processing at workstation $B$. However, at the same time the network structure changes and $B$ is removed. Using Assumption 1 the structure changes only at time $t_2^+$, and consequently the job leaves the network at time $t_2$ immediately before the structural change.

At time $t_3$ workstation $B$ is finishing a job processing when the executive receives a command to change the component $B$ model. However at time $t_3$ the structure is still given by $\gamma(s_{1,\eta})$ and not by $\gamma(s_{2,\eta})$; thus network output is given by $Z_{F,1}(\lambda_{B,1}(s_B))$ and not by $Z_{F,2}(\lambda_{B,2}(s_B))$ as it would be if Assumption 1 does not hold.

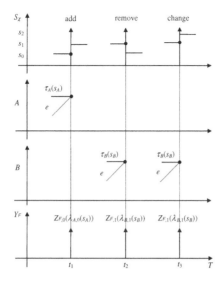

Figure 9.6: Component behavior at simultaneous events.

Assumption 1 also permits the existence self of loops without any type of undefined behavior. Because inputs do not change model state at the time they arrive but only after, outputs from a model do not change the conditions under which they were created. Most of all, if Assumption 1 does not hold, model behavior at structural changes would become unpredictable, for it would not be possible to know what structure should be used at that instant. A more detailed discussion of simultaneous events can be found in [5].

## 9.6   Abstract Simulators

In this section, we describe the abstract simulators necessary to perform the operations implicit in the DSDE models. These simulators allow a description of models independently of the actual simulation procedure, and thus encourages model reuse [6]. The *Simulator* is able to perform simulations using the implicit behavior contained in basic models, and the *NetworkSimulator* can simulate dynamic structure network models. The *Synchronizer* manages the simulation time. The separation between models and the simulation procedure was introduced in [13].

### 9.6.1   The Synchronizer

The *Synchronizer* coordinates the overall simulation. The *child* parameter is the topmost NetworkSimulator (or a Simulator if there is only an atomic model).

The simulation starts when the Synchronizer receives the (SIMULATE,$t$) message represented in Figure 9.7, and stops when its *child* is passive ($t_{Nchild}$ = ∞).

---

when receive (SIMULATE,$t$)
    send (START,$t$) to *child*
    while ($t_{N_{child}} \neq \infty$) do
        "Computes the output of all the models"
        send (OUTPUT,$t_{N_{child}}$) to *child*
        "Makes the transition"
        send (TRANSITION,$t_{N_{child}}$,$\phi$) to *child*
    endWhile
end

---

Figure 9.7: Synchronizer start message.

The message (OUTPUT,$t_{N_{child}}$) ensures that every model keeps a copy of its output just before state change. Thus, transitions can be executed in any order. The message (TRANSITION,$t_{N_{child}}$,$\phi$) is sent to the child and computes component transition.

## 9.6.2 The Simulator

The *Simulator* is necessary to drive basic models. Variables $t_L$ and $t_N$ are used to hold the time of the last transition (time last), and the time for the next transition (time next), respectively. When a component is added to the simulation at time $t$ its initial state his set by the method (START,$t$) represented in Figure 9.8. This method sets the partial state to $s_0$ and the value $e_0$ is interpreted as the time elapsed from the last event to time $t$.

---

when receive (START,$t$)
    if $e_0 \notin [0, \tau(s_0)]$ ERROR endIf
    $t_L \leftarrow t - e_0$
    $s \leftarrow s_0$
    $t_N \leftarrow t_L + \tau(s)$
end

---

Figure 9.8: Simulator start function.

When the simulator receives the (TRANSITION,$x$,$t$) message it performs model transition. Null values sent to a simulator are ignored. Simulator external transition is described in Figure 9.9. The time elapsed since the last transition of any element at time $t$ is computed by $e = t - t_L$.

---

when receive (TRANSITION,$t$,$x$)
    if $t \notin [t_L,t_N]$ ERROR endIf
    if $t < t_N$ and $x = \phi$ then RETURN endIf
    $s \leftarrow \delta(s,t - t_L,x)$
    $t_L \leftarrow t$
    $t_N \leftarrow t + \tau(s)$
end

---

Figure 9.9: Simulator transition.

The output function of a basic component is represented in Figure 9.10. This value must be stored before the change of state caused by the transition function. Storing this value permits to execute the transitions in any order or in the presence of a parallel computer, simultaneously.

---

when receive (OUTPUT,$t$)
    if $t = t_N$ then
        $y \leftarrow \lambda(s)$
    else
        $y \leftarrow \phi$
    endIf
end

---

Figure 9.10: Simulator output function.

Because the (OUTPUT,t) message implements model output function, its value is null if time $t \neq t_N$.

## 9.6.3   The NetworkSimulator

*NetworkSimulators* are attached to network models. A network component when placed in simulation initializes first all its components, and then it computes $t_L$ and $t_N$. The value of $t_L$ is the maximum of the values of $t_{Li}$ of components. The value of $t_N$ is computed as the minimum of $t_{Ni}$. This initialization procedure is described in Figure 9.11, where set $C$ represents the current set of components including the executive. The START message can be called in any order for components are independent.

```
when receive (START,t)
    send (START,t) to C
    t_L ← max{t_{L_i}|i ∈ C}
    t_N ← min{t_{N_i}|i ∈ C}
end
```

Figure 9.11: Network simulator start function.

For convenience we have defined the initial state as $(s_0, e_0')$, where $e_0'$ means the elapsed time from the last transition until the simulation start. The initial time last is defined by $t_{L_0} = \max\{t_{L_{0,i}}| i \in C\} = \max\{t - e_{0,i}'| i \in C\} = t - \min\{e_{0,i}'| i \in C\}$, where $t_{L_{0,i}} = t - e_{0,i}'$. The value of $e_0$ is defined as the time after the last transition, that in general is not equal to $e_0'$ at the simulation start. The value $e_{0,i} = t_{L_0} - t_{L_{0,i}} = t - \min\{e_{0,i}'| i \in C\} - t + e_{0,i}' = e_{0,i}' - \min\{e_{0,i}'| i \in C\}$. Thus the value given at the specification is not the *true* elapsed time. However, the given value of $e_0'$ is easier and intuitive to specify. Actually, as we can see, the value of $e_{0,i}$ depends on the value of the other components and cannot be specified directly. The values $e_0'$ and $e_0$ can only be different at the simulation start. When structural changes occur the value of $t_L$ corresponds to the current time $t$, for these changes can only occur by an executive transition. Because $t_L = \max\{t_{L_i}| i \in C\}$, this gives that $t_L = t$ for at least the executive has its time last equals to $t$, if a structural change has occurred.

To describe simulator transition we define $v_i$ as the value received from component $i$. This value can be the component output, if the component is not the network $N$, or the network input otherwise.

$$v_i = \begin{cases} y_i & \text{if } i \neq N \\ x & \text{if } i = N \end{cases}$$

The simulator transition is handled by the (TRANSITION,$t,x$) method shown in Figure 9.12, where $D$ represents the current set of network components and $C$ represents set $D$ plus the executive. If this message is sent to the executive, the network structure can possibly change.

when receive (TRANSITION,$t$,$x$)
1:   if $t \notin [t_L,t_N]$ then ERROR
2:   if $t < t_N$ and $x = \phi$ then RETURN
3:   $D' \leftarrow D$
4:   send (TRANSITION,$t$,$Z_i(\underset{j \in I_i}{\otimes} v_j)$) to $\{i|i \in D\}$
5:   send (TRANSITION,$t$,$Z_\eta(\underset{j \in I'}{\otimes}_\eta v_j)$) to $\eta$
6:   send (START,$t$) to $D - D'$
7:   $t_L \leftarrow t$
8:   $t_N \leftarrow \min\{t_{N_i}|i \in C\}$
end

Figure 9.12. Network simulator transition.

Line 1 checks for state validity. Line 2 ignores the transition message if the input is null and the component is not scheduled to change. Line 3 keeps the current set of components, just before the structural changes occur. Line 4 computes the transition of all the components excluding the executive. Thus changes in structure will only affect the next transition as required by the formalism. Line 5 computes the executive transition and defines the new network structure. The new components are initialized by line 6. Lines 7 and 8 set the time of the last event and the time of the next event, respectively.

The network transition algorithm supports both sequential and parallel implementations. Because all models are independent, theirs transitions can be triggered in any order, either sequentially or in parallel. The only constraint is that the transition of the executive can only be made after all other transitions occur, for this transition can change the network structure. Thus, making the executive transition be the last transition avoids a copy, in most of the cases very expensive, of the current network structure.

The network output function is defined in Figure 9.13. This function is called before each transition for correct formalism interpretation, ensuring that the output of a component does not depend on the transition order.

when receive (OUTPUT,$t$)
    if $t = t_N$ then
        send (OUTPUT,$t$) to $\{i|i \in C\}$
        $y \leftarrow Z_N(\underset{i \in I_N}{\otimes} y_i)$
    else
        $y \leftarrow \phi$
    endIf
end

Figure 9.13: Network simulator output function.

Because components are independent of each other all the outputs can be computed concurrently.

## 9.7  Conclusions

We have presented the DSDE formalism and we have shown that the formalism is closed under coupling. The DSDE formalism can model any type of structural change. Changes of structure include add/delete operations over connections and components, and the modification of components' models. The abstract simulators necessary to run DSDE models were also described. These simulators permit to describe models independently from the actual procedure to run the models. Abstract simulators can be implemented in both sequential and parallel processors.

## Acknowledgements

This work was partially founded by project PRAXIS/14152/1998

## References

[1]  Barros, F.J. [1995], "Dynamic Structure Discrete Event System Specification: A New Formalism for Dynamic Structure Modeling and Simulation." *Proceedings of the 1995 Winter Simulation Conference*, Arlington(VA), pp. 781-785.

[2]  Barros, F. J. [1996], "Dynamic Structure Discrete Event System Specification: Formalism, Abstract Simulators and Applications." *Transactions of the Society for Computer Simulation*. **13**, pp. 35-46.

[3]  Barros, F. J. [1997], "Dynamic Structure Discrete Event Systems: A Comparison of Methodologies and Environments." In *Proceedings of SPIE 11th Annual International Symposium on Aerospace/Defense Sensing, Simulation and Controls: Enabling Technology for Simulation Science* **3083**, pp. 268-277.

[4]  Barros, F. J. [1997], "Modeling Formalisms for Dynamic Structure Systems." *ACM Transactions on Modeling and Computer Simulation*, **7**, pp. 501-515.

[5]  Barros, F. J. [1998], "Handling Simultaneous Events in Dynamic Structure Models." *Proceedings of SPIE 12th Annual International Symposium on Aerospace/ Defense Sensing, Simulation and Controls: Enabling Technology for Simulation Science*, 3083, pp. 355-363.

[6]  Barros, F. J. [1998], "Abstract Simulators for the DSDE Formalism." *Proceedings of the 1998 Winter Simulation Conference*, Washington DC, pp. 407-412.

[7]  Barros, F. J. [2000], "A Framework for Representing Numerical Multirate Integration Methods." In *Proceedings of the Sixth Annual Conference on AI, Simulation and Planning in High Autonomy Systems*, Tucson (AZ), pp. 149-154.

[8]  Chow, A. C. and Zeigler, B. P. [1994], "Abstract Simulator for the Parallel DEVS Formalism." In *Proceedings of the Fifth Annual Conference on AI, Simulation and*

*Planning in High Autonomy Systems*, Gainesville (FL), pp. 157-163.

[9]   Unger, D. [1987], "Self: The Power of Simplicity." *SIGPLAN Notices*, **22**, 227-241.

[10] Uhrmacher, A. M. and Arnold, R. [1994], "Distributing and Maintaining Knowledge: Agents in Variable Structure Environment." *Proceedings of the Fifth Annual Conference on AI, Simulation and Planning in High Autonomy Systems* (Gainesville, FL, December 7-9), pp. 178-184.

[11] Vasconcelos, M. J. [1993], *Modeling Spatial Dynamic Ecological Processes with DEVS-Scheme and Geographic Information Systems*. Ph.D. Thesis, School of Renewable and Natural Resources, University of Arizona.

[12] Zeigler, B. P. [1976], *Theory of Modelling and Simulation*. Wiley, New York.

[13] Zeigler, B. P. [1984], *Multifaceted Modelling and Discrete Event Simulation*. Academic Press, London.

# Chapter 10

# Timed Cell-DEVS: Modeling and Simulation of Cell Spaces

## G. Wainer and N. Giambiasi

*DEVS and Cellular Automata formalisms are applied to define a modeling paradigm for cellular models. Different delay functions to specify the timing behavior of each cell, allowing the modeler to represent the timing complex behavior in a simple fashion. Implementation models for the formalism are presented according with the modeler and developer points of view. As a result, efficient and cost-effective development of cellular models simulators could be achieved.*

## 10.1 Introduction

In recent years, a wide number of artificial systems has become commonplace (i.e., computer networks, traffic controllers, flexible manufacturing plants, embedded applications, etc.). The development cost of such systems is crucial for their successful implementation, and their complex analysis has been attacked using simulated models. It is well known that the use of a formal modeling approach can produce important cost reductions. Fortunately, several modeling paradigms have been developed.

As the specified models are analyzed through simulation, their timing information becomes crucial. Hence, it is needed a paradigm allowing *timed models*, representing the event dates in the system. The DEVS formalism (Discrete EVent systems Specification) proposed by Bernard Zeigler [[22], [19]], allows this kind of specifications. Here, the model's timing is described as a lifetime for each state variable. DEVS is a discrete event paradigm that allows a hierarchical and modular description of the models. Each DEVS model can be behavioral (atomic) or structural (coupled), consisting of inputs, outputs, state variables, and functions to compute the next states and outputs. Object Oriented approaches have been incorporated to the basic concepts [[20], [21]]. The paradigm improves the security of the simulations, reducing the testing time and increasing productivity.

We are interested in modeling systems that can be represented as executable cell spaces. The Cellular Automata formalism [[18]] has been widely used to describe complex systems with these characterictics. These automata evolve by executing a global transition function that updates the state of every cell in the space. The behavior of this function depends on the results of a function that executes locally in each cell.

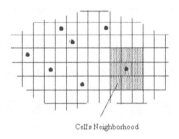

Cell's Neighborhood

Figure 10.1: Sketch of a Cellular Automaton

Conceptually, these local functions are computed synchronously and in parallel, using the state values of the present cell and its neighbors. This discrete time paradigm constrains the precision and efficiency of the simulated models. Furthermore, it is usual that several cells do not need to be updated in every step, wasting computation time. These problems can be solved using a continuous time base, providing instantaneous events that can occur asynchronously at unpredictable times. This approach was considered in [[22], [19]], where discrete event cellular models were presented. Discrete event cellular models were applied in real world applications in later works [[8], [23]].

These ideas served as a basis for the approach presented here, which will be called Timed Cell-DEVS. We present a summary of the efforts done in building this approach, devoted to describe and simulate discrete event cellular models [[16], [17], [9], [11], [13], [14]]. A main contribution of the work consists in adapting delay constructions and defining them as a functional component of the model defining each cell [[7]]. The extensions allow to define explicit timing for each cell, providing a simple mechanism to define it. The specifications of the formalism were used to build a set of tools for modeling and simulation of cell spaces. As a result, the approach allows a modeler to describe complex temporal behavior avoiding the detailed mechanism used for the delays.

The article is organized as follows. First, a description of Timed Cell-DEVS atomic models is introduced. After, coupled cell spaces are considered. Then, several issues related with the implementation models for the formalism are considered. Some examples are used to show implementation issues. Finally, the improvements in the development activities obtained when this approach is used are introduced.

## 10.2   Timed Cell-DEVS Atomic Models

Timed Cell-DEVS models are defined as a space composed of individual cells that can be lately coupled to form a complete cell space. This section presents the specification of each cell in a space as a DEVS model with explicit delays. Each cell is a continuous time model, defined by very simple rules and a few parameters. Complex timing definition is overruled due to the use of delay functions. Two kinds of constructions are employed: *transport* and *inertial*. We introduced two kind of delays with different semantics to allow the construction of models at two levels of accuracy. Transport delay has an anticipatory semantics, that is to say that every input event is just delayed. This is an extension of discrete event models with implicit time representation in which event are only ordered. Inertial delays allows to represent more complex temporal behavior because they have preemtive semantics. An event scheduled for a future time will not neccessary executed. For example, this can of delay allows to analyse frequency responses of systems.

An atomic cell can be formally described as:

$$TDC = < X, Y, I, V, \theta, E, \text{delay}, d, \delta_{int}, \delta_{ext}, \tau, \lambda, D >$$

where for $\#T < \infty \wedge T \in \{ N, Z, R, \{0,1\} \} \cup \{\phi\}$;

$X \subseteq T$ is the set of external input events;
$Y \subseteq T$ is the set of external output events;
$I = < \eta, \mu^X, \mu^Y, P^X, P^Y >$. Here, $\eta \in N, \eta < \infty$ is the neighborhood's size,
  $\mu^X, \mu^Y \in N, \mu^X, \mu^Y < \infty$ is the number of other input/output ports, and
  $\forall j \in [1, \eta], i \in \{X, Y\}, P_j^i$ is a definition of a port
    (input or output respectively), with
      $P_j^i = \{ (N_j^i, T_j^i) / \forall j \in [1, \eta+\mu^i], N_j^i \in [i_1, i_{\eta+\mu}]$ (port name), y $T_j^i \in I_i$
      (port type)}, where $I_i = \{ x / x \in X$ if $X \}$ or $I_i = \{ x / x \in Y$ if $i = Y \}$ ;
$V \subseteq T$ is the set of values that can be used as state variables for the cell;
$\theta$ is the definition of the state variables used in each cell, defined as
  $\theta = \{ (s, \text{phase}, \sigma\text{queue}, \sigma) / s \in V$ is the status value for the cell,
    phase $\in \{\text{active, passive}\}, \sigma\text{queue} = \{ ((v_1, \sigma_1), ..., (v_m, \sigma_m)) / m \in N \wedge$
    $m < \infty) \wedge \forall (i \in N, i \in [1,m]), v_i \in V \wedge \sigma_i \in R_0^+ \cup \infty\};$
      and $\sigma \in R_0^+ \cup \infty \}$ ; for transport delays, or
  $\theta = \{ (s, \text{phase}, f, \sigma) / s \in V, \text{phase} \in \{\text{active, passive}\}, f \in T,$

and $\sigma \in R_0^+ \cup \infty$ }; for inertial delays;
$E \in V^{\eta+\mu}$ is the set of values of input events;
**delay** $\in$ {transport, inertial};
$d \in R_0^+$, $d < \infty$ is the transport delay for the cell;
$\delta_{int}: \theta \to \theta$ is the internal transition function;
$\delta_{ext}: QxX \to \theta$ is the external transition function, where Q is the state values defined as:
$$Q = \{ (s, e) / s \in \theta \ x \ E \ x \ d; e \in [0, D(s)] \};$$
$\tau: E \to V$ is the local computation function;
$\lambda: \theta \to Y$ is the output function; and
$D: \theta \ x \ E \ x \ d \to R_0^+ \cup \infty$, is the state's duration function.

The present definition, based on the work presented in [[6]], is independent of the simulation technique used. Therefore, it allows to specify the system behavior independently of the implementation details.

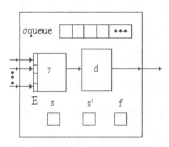

Figure 10.2: Informal description of an atomic cell.

The cell's interface is composed of a fixed number of ports ($P^x$, $P^y$), each connected with a neighbor. A cell can use other inputs and outputs of the interface ($\mu_x$, $\mu_y$) to interchange data with models outside the cell space. Each port in the interface has a name composed by an identifier (**X** for input; **Y** for output) and a natural number (port number). These inputs are stored in the **E** set, whose values are used to compute the future state of the cell. The results obtained when the local function $\tau$ executes, can be deferred by using a delay function. To allow this behavior, the cell's state variables ($\theta$) include the cell's present value, the feasible future value for the cell (**f**), and a queue to keep track of the next events ($\sigma$**queue**), and the model's phase. The state's lifetime function **D** controls the elapsed time of a cell state, and its evolution is defined by the delay functions. Finally, DEVS transition ($\delta_{int}$, $\delta_{ext}$) and output ($\lambda$) functions are included. In previous works [[17], [11],[6]], the definition of the delay functions was presented as DEVS models. Here, the semantics of the delay functions is presented with detail in the Figure 10.3.

Each time the external transition function receives a message, the local computing function uses the **E** inputs to obtain the new cell's value. If it is different from the existing, the new value should be sent to the cell's influencees. Otherwise, the neighbors cannot change and the cell remains quiescent [[22], [19]]. The result is transmitted only after the completion of the delay function associated with the cell.

$\delta_{int:}$        $\sigma = 0;$        $\sigma queue \neq \{\varnothing\};$        $phase = active$

$$\forall\ i \in\ [1, m],\ a_i \in \sigma queue,\ a_i.\sigma = a_i.\sigma - head(\sigma queue.\sigma);$$
$$\sigma queue = tail(\sigma queue);$$
$$s = head(\sigma queue.v);\quad \sigma = head(\sigma queue.\sigma);$$

$\sigma = 0;$        $\sigma queue = \{\varnothing\};$      $phase = active$

$\sigma = \infty$      $\wedge\ phase = passive$

$\lambda:$        $\sigma = 0;$

$$out = s;$$

$\delta_{ext:}$    $(s', transport) = \tau(N_c);$     $\sigma \neq 0;$   $e = D(\theta \times E \times d);$   $phase=active;$

$$s \neq s' \Rightarrow (s=s' \wedge \forall i \in [1,m]\ a_i \in \sigma queue,\ a_i.\sigma = a_i.\sigma-e \wedge \sigma=\sigma - e;$$
$$add(\sigma queue,<s', d>) \wedge f = s\ )$$

$(s', transport) = \tau(N_c);$   $\sigma \neq 0;$    $e = D(\theta \times E \times d);$      $phase = passive;$

$$s \neq s' \Rightarrow (\ s = s' \wedge \sigma = d\ \wedge\ phase = active\ \wedge\ add(\sigma queue, <s', d>)\ \wedge f = s\ )$$

$(s', inertial) = \tau(N_c);$    $\sigma \neq 0;$         $e = D(\theta \times E \times d);$  $phase = passive;$

$$s \neq s' \Rightarrow\ (\ s = s'\ \wedge\ phase = active \wedge\ \sigma = d \wedge\ f = s\ )$$

$(s', inertial) = \tau(N_c);$    $\sigma \neq 0;$   $e = D(\theta \times E \times d);$  $phase = active;$

$$s \neq s' \Rightarrow\ s = s'\ \wedge\ (f \neq s'\ \Rightarrow\ \sigma queue = \{\varnothing\} \wedge \sigma = d\ \wedge\ f = s)$$

Figure 10.3: Definition of $\delta_{int}$, $\delta_{ext}$ and $\lambda$ for TDC models.

The next events to be transmitted should be queued, because several external events can arrive during a **transport** delay. If the changing cell is passive, it is activated. Instead, if it is active, the values of σ stored in the queue must be updated to reflect the elapsed time since the last event. In both cases, the external transition function schedules an internal event after the time defined by the delay. When the time of an internal event arrives, the first value in the queue is sent to the output ports. The internal transition function removes the first member of the queue recently transmitted. If the queue is not empty, the first element will be used to schedule the internal event. Otherwise, the cell is passivated.

When **inertial** delays are used, the last arrived event can be preempted if a new input arrives before the scheduled time. This only happens if the new external value is different of that one previously stored. If both values are the same, the new external event occurred has the same value than the previous one.

The following figure presents the behavior of both kinds of delay functions. Let us consider a transport delay of 5 time units for a given cell. The Figure 10.4(a), shows the results delayed for 5 time units. Here, the cell remains active while there are queued values waiting to be transmitted. Oppositely, the behavior of inertial delays can be studied by analyzing the input/output trajectories in the Figure 10.4(b). In this case, an inertial delay function of 5 time units is used. The input values are delayed as in the previous case, but in the simulated time 19, the input of the delay function changes. As this change occurs before the consumption of the delay, the previous event is preempted. The input-output trajectories are piecewise constant for this illustration, in the model, trajectories are transformed in discrete event trajectories.

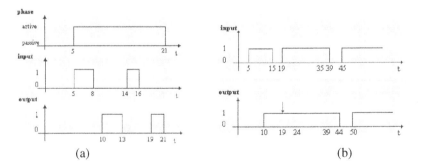

(a)                               (b)

Figure 10.4: (a) Transport delay behavior; (b) Inertial delay behavior.

## 10.3   Coupled Cell-DEVS

The atomic cell models presented previously can be coupled with others, forming a multicomponent model. These are defined as a space consisting of atomic cells connected by the neighborhood relationship. After, they can be integrated with other Cell-DEVS or DEVS models.

When modeling a coupled cell space, two different couplings have to be considered. First, the internal coupling defines the connection of a cell with the neighborhood. Then, the external coupling is used to connect certain components in a Cell-DEVS with components in other models. Therefore, we can build complex models consisting of several submodels with different behavior using different paradigms or abstraction levels. These models can be represented as:

$$GCTD = \; < X, \, Y, \, Xlist, \, Ylist, \, I, \, \eta, \, N, \, \{m, n\}, \, C, \, B, \, Z, \, select >$$

where for $\#T < \infty \; \wedge \; T \in \{ N, Z, \boldsymbol{R}, \{0,1\} \} \cup \{\phi\}$;

$X \subseteq T$ is the set of external input events;
$Y \subseteq T$ is the set of external output events;
**Ylist** = { $(k,l) \, / \, k \in [0,m], \, l \in [0,n]$} is the list of output coupling;
**Xlist** = { $(k,l) \, / \, k \in [0,m], \, l \in [0,n]$} is the list of input coupling; and
$I = \; < P^x, P^y >$ represents the definition of the modular model interface. Here,
for $i = X \mid Y$, $P^i$ is a port definition (input or output respectively), where
$P^i = \{ \, (N(f,g)^i, \, T(f,g)^i) \, / \, \forall \, (f,g) \in Xlist, \, N(f,g)^i = i(f,g)_k$ (port name), and
$T(f,g)^i \in T$ (port type)};

$\eta \in N$ is the neighborhood size and **N** is the neighborhood set, defined as
$$N = \{ \, (i_p, j_p) \, / \, \forall \, p \in N, \, p \in [1,\eta] \Rightarrow i_p, j_p \in Z \wedge \, i_p, j_p \in [-1, 1] \, \};$$
$\{m, n\} \in N$ is the size of the cell space;
**C** defines the cell space, where $C = \{C_{ij} \, / \, i \in [1,m], j \in [1,n]\}$, with
$$C_{ij} = \; < I_{ij}, \, X_{ij}, \, Y_{ij}, \, S_{ij}, \, N_{ij}, \, d_{ij}, \, \delta_{intij}, \, \delta_{extij}, \, \tau_{ij}, \, \lambda_{ij}, \, D_{ij} >$$
is a Cell-DEVS component such as those defined in section 3;
**B** is the set of border cells, where
  - $B = \{\varnothing\}$ if the cell space is wrapped; or
  - $B = \{C_{ij} \, / \, \forall \, (i = 1 \vee i = m \vee j = 1 \vee j = n) \wedge C_{ij} \in C\}$ , where
    $$C_{ij} = \; < I_{ij}, \, X_{ij}, \, Y_{ij}, \, S_{ij}, \, N_{ij}, \, d_{ij}, \, \delta_{intij}, \, \delta_{extij}, \, \tau_{ij}, \, \lambda_{ij}, \, D_{ij} >$$
is a Cell-DEVS component, such as those defined in section 3, if the atomic border cells have different behavior than the rest of the cell space.
**Z** is the translation function, defined by:
$$Z: P_{kl}Y_q \to P_{ij}X_q, \text{ where } P_{kl}Y_q \in I_{kl}, \, P_{ij}X_q \in I_{ij}, \, q \in [0,\eta] \text{ and } \forall (f,g) \in N,$$
$$k = (i+f) \bmod m; \; l = (j+g) \bmod n;$$
$$P_{ij}Y_q \to P_{kl}X_q, \text{ where } P_{ij}Y_q \in I_{ij}, \, P_{kl}X_q \in I_{kl}, \, q \in [0,\eta] \text{ and } \forall (f,g) \in N,$$
$$k = (i-f) \bmod m; \; l = (j-g) \bmod n;$$

**select** is the tie-breaking selector function, with select ⊆ mxn → mxn.

The present definition only allows bidimensional cell spaces. The formal specification for n-dimensional spaces can be found in [[11]]. The coupled model includes an interface **I**, built using two lists. **Xlist** is the group of cells where the model's external events are received. **Ylist** includes the cells whose outputs will be collected to be sent to other models. The cell space **C** is a coupled model defined as a fixed size (**m x n**) array of atomic cells with η neighbors each. The neighborhood set (**N**) is represented by a list defining relative position between the neighbor and the origin cell . The present definition only allows regular neighborhoods in adjacent cells (other kinds of neighborhoods can be found in [[11]]).

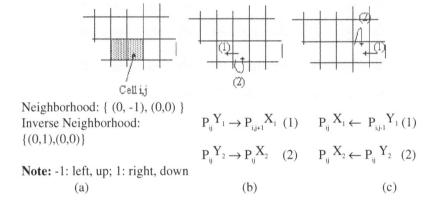

Neighborhood: { (0, -1), (0,0) }
Inverse Neighborhood:
{(0,1),(0,0)}

$P_{ij}Y_1 \rightarrow P_{i,j+1}X_1$ (1)    $P_{ij}X_1 \leftarrow P_{i,j-1}Y_1$ (1)

$P_{ij}Y_2 \rightarrow P_{ij}X_2$ (2)    $P_{ij}X_2 \leftarrow P_{ij}Y_2$ (2)

**Note:** -1: left, up; 1: right, down

(a)                              (b)                              (c)

Figure 10.5: (a) Neighborhood definition; (b) Output ports; (c) Input ports.

The B set defines the cell's space border. If it is empty, every cell in the space has the same behavior. The space is "wrapped", meaning that the cells in one border are connected with those in the opposite one using the neighborhood relationship. Otherwise, the border cells will have different behavior than those of the rest of the model.

Finally, the Z function allows to define the coupling of cells in the model. This function translates the outputs of the m-eth output port in cell $C_{ij}$ into values for the m-eth input port of cell $C_{kl}$. Each output port will correspond to one neighbor and each input port will be associated with one cell in the inverse neighborhood [[22], [19]]. The ports' names are generated using the following notation: $P_{ij}X_q$ refers to the q-eth input port of cell $C_{ij}$, and $P_{ij}Y_q$ to the q-eth output port. The cell to be coupled with is obtained by adding the cell's position with the values of the N set.

The definition for DEVS coupled models was extended to include Cell-DEVS, as follows:

$$CM = < X, Y, D, \{M_i\}, \{I_i\}, \{Z_{ij}\}, \text{select} >$$

$X$ is the set of input events;
$Y$ is the set of output events;
$D$ is an index for the components of the coupled model, and
$\forall i \in D$, $M_i$ is a basic DEVS model, where
$$M_i = GCC_i = < I_i, X_i, Y_i, \text{Xlist}_i, \text{Ylist}_i, n_i, \{m, n \}_i, N_i, C_i, B_i, Z_i, \text{select}_i>$$
if the coupled model is Cell-DEVS, and
$$M_i = < I_i, X_i, S_i, Y_i, \delta_{inti}, \delta_{exti}, I_i >$$
otherwise.
$I_i$ is the set of influencees of model i, and $\forall\, j \in I_i$, and
$Z_{ij}$ is the i to j translation function, where
$\quad Z_{ij}: Y_i \rightarrow X_j$ if none of the models involved are Cell-DEVS, or
$\quad Z_{ij}: Y(f,g)_i \rightarrow X(k,l)_j$, with $(f,g) \in \text{Ylist}_i$, and $(k,l) \in \text{Xlist}_j$ if the models i
$\qquad$ and j are Cell-DEVS.
Finally, **select** is the tie-break selector.

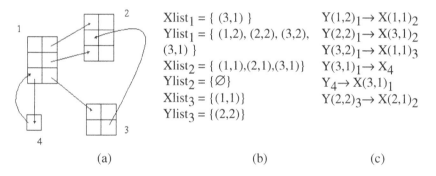

$$\text{Xlist}_1 = \{ (3,1) \} \qquad\qquad Y(1,2)_1 \rightarrow X(1,1)_2$$
$$\text{Ylist}_1 = \{ (1,2), (2,2), (3,2), \quad Y(2,2)_1 \rightarrow X(3,1)_2$$
$$(3,1) \} \qquad\qquad\qquad\quad Y(3,2)_1 \rightarrow X(1,1)_3$$
$$\text{Xlist}_2 = \{ (1,1),(2,1),(3,1)\} \quad Y(3,1)_1 \rightarrow X_4$$
$$\text{Ylist}_2 = \{\varnothing\} \qquad\qquad\quad Y_4 \rightarrow X(3,1)_1$$
$$\text{Xlist}_3 = \{(1,1)\} \qquad\qquad Y(2,2)_3 \rightarrow X(2,1)_2$$
$$\text{Ylist}_3 = \{(2,2)\}$$

(a)                                    (b)                                    (c)

Figure 10.6: Model interconnection (a) Basic models; (b) Xi and Yi lists for each model; (c) Zij coupling.

The specifications defined in this section allows to define complete cell spaces in a parametric fashion. A modeler only has to define the behavior for the local computing function and the duration and kind of the delay. After, a complete cell space is specified by defining the neighborhood shape, the size of the space, and the cells chosen as inputs/outputs for the cellular model. Finally, the connection with other models is defined using the translation lists. This approach reduces the development efforts for this kind of models, thus providing a simple framework to develop complex cellular spaces.

# 10.4  Implementation Models for DEVS-Cells

This section is devoted to analyze several issues related with the development of implementation models following the conceptual framework recently introduced. A tool that allows the definition of those aspects was defined in [[16], [1]]. This environment was built using the conceptual definitions previously studied, and has been extended to execute n-dimensional Cell-DEVS [[9]].

This section presents two points of view related with the implementation models that can be built using the tools. First, a modeler should be able to define a conceptual model using the formal specifications previously defined. This specification should be executable, improving model's validation and verification. Besides, the point of view of the designer of a modeling environment is presented. Previous existing definitions for DEVS models' simulation have been used to define a Cell-DEVS environment.

## 10.4.1 Definition of Cell-DEVS implementation models

The previous Cell-DEVS specifications shows that a modeler should be able to represent three basic aspects: **dimension** (size and shape of the cell space), **influencees** and **behavior**.

The **influencees** are specified by defining the cell's neighborhood. Input/output ports for each cell are created following the formal definitions. The cells are coupled applying the procedure presented earlier. When the cell space is to be coupled with other DEVS models, the external connections are specified using the contents of the $X_i$list and the $Y_i$list sets. The specification for the influencees is completed by defining the border cells (otherwise, the cell space is wrapped).

These aspects are defined using the following syntax:

- **Components**: it describes the DEVS and Cell-DEVS models integrating the coupled model. The format is **model_name@class_name**. The model name is used to allow more than one instance of the same atomic model, defined as an existing base model.
- **Out**: It describes the output ports names.
- **In**: It describes the input ports' names.
- **Link**: It describes the internal and external (input and output) coupling scheme. The format is: **origin_port[@model] destination_port[@model]**. The model name is optional and, if not included, it is considered as corresponding to the coupled model being specified.

Cell-DEVS specifications are completed by adding the following parameters:

- *type*: [cell | flat].
- *width*: INTEGER.
- *height*: INTEGER.
- *link*: in this case it must use the name of the cell space and the corresponding input/output cell (Model(x,y)).
- *border*: [ WRAPPED | NOWRAPPED ].
- *delay*: [ TRASPORT | INERTIAL ].
- *neighbors*: Cell-DEVS_name($x_1$, $y_1$), ..., Cell-DEVS_name($x_n$, $y_n$).
- *localTransition*: It defines the description for the behavior specification used for the local computation function.
- *zone*: transitionName {$range_1$..$range_n$}. It associates a behavior specification with the cells included into the rage defined by the sentence. In this way, different ranges can provide different behavior.

The remaining parameters of the specification are related with the cell's **behavior**. The local computing function is defined using a simple specification language (presented in [[11]]), and it is translated into an internal behavior representation for the space. The functions are built as a set of logical expressions, providing results from the present state of the cell and its neighborhood. As explained earlier, the timing behavior is specified by the duration and kind of the delay for the cell. The following figure presents a part of the specification language used to define the local transition functions. Further details will be presented in several examples in the following section.

```
rule : result delay { condition }
result: Float
delay: Float
condition:  The  condition  is  a  boolean  expression  using  the
following BNF grammar:
BoolExp := Relexp | NOT BoolExp | BoolExp AND BoolExp | BoolExp OR
BoolExp
Relexp := IdRef | Exp OpRel Exp
Exp := IdRef | Exp Oper Exp
IdRef := CellRef | '(' BoolExp ')'  | Constant  | Function
Constant := Float | Int | Bool
Function := TRUECOUNT | FALSECOUNT | UNDEFCOUNT
CellRef := '(' Exp ',' Exp ')'
OpRel := = | != | > | < | >= | <=
Oper := + | - | * | /
Int := [Sign] Digit {Digit}
Float := [Sign] Digit {Digit} [. Digit {Digit} [E [Sign] Digit
{Digit} ] ]
Bool := 0 | 1 | t | f | ?
Sign := [+] | -
Digit ::= 0 | 1 | ... | 9
```

Figure 10.7: Basic syntax of the implemented specification language.

The specification of a cellular model is translated into an executable model. The local computing function scans the specification, verifying the logical expressions included and computing the new state value for the cell. Several errors of the specification can be found at runtime, allowing the detection of inconsistencies in the model definition:

- Ambiguous models: a cell with the same precondition can produce different results;
- Incomplete models: no result exists for a certain precondition;
- Non-deterministic models: different preconditions are satisfied simultaneously. If they produce the same result, the simulation can continue, but the modeler is notified. Instead, if different results are found, the simulation should stop because the future state of the cell cannot be determined.

## 10.4.2 Implementation of a Cell-DEVS simulation framework

This section includes several aspects that should be considered by the developer of a Cell-DEVS simulation framework. This point of view will be exemplified considering our development experiences. A generic DEVS environment was first released [[1]], and it was extended to allow the simulation of timed cell spaces (using the ideas defined in [[17]] and [[14]]). As a final step, the tool was extended to include n-dimensional Cell-DEVS [[9]].

### 10.4.2.1 Basic Structure of the Tool

The tool (called CD++) consists of a set of basic classes extending those defined in [[20]]. The two base classes, *Models* and *Processors* provide the constructors for DEVS models. The *Models* base class provides the basic methods to manage DEVS models. The *Atomic-Model* class is used to represent the behavior of atomic models, by using the *internalFunction, externalFunction*, and *output-Function* methods. The *CoupledModel* class implements the hierarchical constructions. It is responsible to add and manage components, recording the dependencies between them.

The *Processors* implement the abstract simulation mechanisms. These classes should manage the connection between a *processor* with its corresponding *model* and its *parent* processor. *Simulators* and *Coordinators* are specializations that manage the activation of atomic and coupled models respectively. *Root Coordinator* represents the root of the processor's tree, and it is used to start and finish the simulation. It also should manage its global aspects including the maintenance of an *ExternalEvents* list and the global time (*clock*).

The tools follow the basic simulation mechanisms defined in [[14]], extending the basic classes presented. *AtomicCell* is a specialization of *Atomic* that represents the behavior of a cell and its delay function (transport or inertial). It must execute the local computing function (*localFunction*) depending on the *neighborhood* values. It also defines the interconnection with other models (*outport, NeighborPort*), and keeps the *value* and *delay* for the cell.

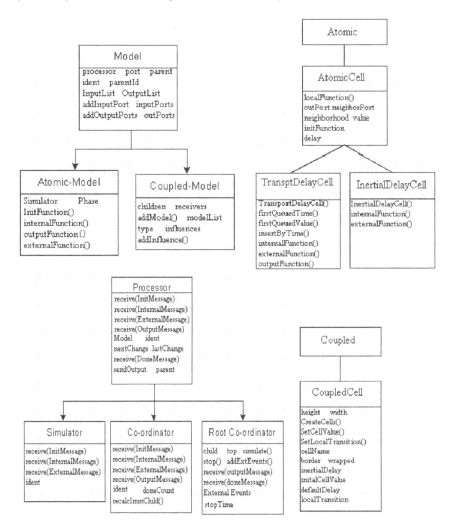

Figure 10.8: Basic classes defined by the tool [[1]].

The *CoupledCell* class is in charge of managing all the cells as children models. In a cell space, all the children of a coupled model are alike. Therefore, when the cells are created, the specified behavior is assigned to allow them and they are linked with the models defined by the neighborhood relationship.

A *CellCoordinator* class, specialized in the management of cell spaces has been defined. It is in charge of creating the set of processors associated with the cell space. As the coupled model consists of several atomic ones (the cells), one simulator is associated with each cell. The simulators are created and their names defined using the parameters defined earlier. The definitions of the input/output lists are used to couple the output ports in the interface of a Cell-DEVS with the input ports in the other. The internal coupling is set up as presented earlier, and a coordinator is associated with each coupled model.

## 10.4.2.2 CD++ Message Interaction

Inter-process interaction is carried out through message passing. Each message includes information of the source (or destination), the event simulated time, and a content (consisting of a port and a value). *Message* is the base class that defines the different messages. There are four different messages: * (internal event), X (external event), Y (model's output), and done (a model has finished with its task).

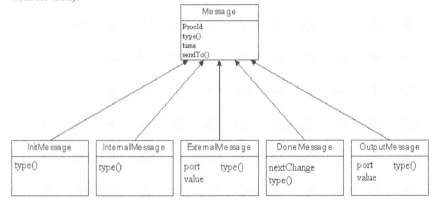

Figure 10.9: Message class hierarchy.

The basic ideas of message interaction defined in [[19], [20]] have been extended to allow the simulation of Cell-DEVS models. When an external message arrives, a X-message is consumed and the external transition function executed. The local computing function is activated, and its output is delayed, scheduling and internal transition. In this case, the imminent model will be a cell in the space. When a *-message is received by the cell space coordinator, the imminent cell is selected. Then, the simulator associated with that cell activates the model's output and internal transition functions, executing the procedures presented earlier.

The simulators return done-messages and Y-messages that are converted to new *-messages and X-messages, respectively. These messages are translated using the coupling mechanisms previously defined. The main task of the cell space coordinator is to translate the outputs in inputs by using the internal coupling and the external lists.

### 10.4.2.3 Support for N-Dimensional Models

The real systems that can be studied using cellular models are usually represented by using models in two or three dimensions. Several theoretical problems can be defined as cellular models with four or more dimensions. The original version of the tool only allowed to define two-dimensional cell spaces, constraining its use in more general problems. An extension, following the formal specification of [[11]], allowed the definition of n-dimensional models.

CD++ was implemented by storing the cell states in a two-dimensional array of $d_1 \cdot d_2$, where the element $(x_1, x_2)$, $x_i \in [0, d_i-1]$, is in the position $x_1 + x_2 \cdot d_1$. In an analogous fashion, N-CD++ uses an array of $\Pi_{i=1..n} d_i$ to store the states for the cellular automata with dimension $(d_1, d_2, ..., d_n)$, and in this case $(x_1, x_2, ..., x_n)$ occupies the position $\Sigma_{i=1..n} x_i \cdot ( \Pi_{k=1..i-1} d_k )$.

The specification language was adapted to include references to cells in n-dimensional cell spaces. The definition of *zones* in the cell space was extended. Each zone now is defined by a set of cells determined by the cell range $\{(x_1, x_2, ..., x_n)...(y_1, y_2, ..., y_n)\}$. Using this capability, different zones into the same cellular model can present different behavior.

### 10.4.2.4 Flat Simulation of the Cell Spaces.

DEVS allows hierarchical module definition, and the proposed simulation mechanism has hierarchical nature. Therefore, intermodule communication produces a high degree of overhead, moreover in Cell-DEVS simulations consisting of a large number of cells. One way to avoid this interaction (reducing the related overhead) is by flattening the Processor's hierarchy. This is the goal of the *Flat_Coordinator* class.

Here, the message passing overhead is avoided by creating a unique processor including the values for the cell space, and executing a specialized simulation method [[14]]. Therefore, the *FlatCoupledCell* creates a set of cells and records the local computing function for each one.

The *FlatCoordinator* is in charge of the flat execution of the cell spaces. This coordinator is implemented as a bidimensional array of records associated with the cell space. Each record includes information of the state, delay, and a neighborhood list for the cell. When this approach is used, multiple intermediate processors are eliminated, as it can be seen in the Figure 10.11. Each cell in theflat simulation mechanism can use inertial or transport delays.

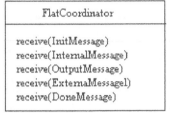

| FlatCoupled |
| --- |
| createCells() |
| setCellValue() |
| selLocalTransition() |
| initFunction() |
| externalFunction() |
| internalFunction() |
| NextEvents |
| eventsList |
| Xlist    Ylist |
| FlatCoupledCell() |
| ExternalList() |
| nextEventList() |
| insertByTime() |

| FlatCoordinator |
| --- |
| receive(InitMessage) |
| receive(InternalMessage) |
| receive(OutputMessage) |
| receive(ExternalMessagel) |
| receive(DoneMessage) |

Figure 10.10: Flat models definition.

A Next-Events list records the cells scheduled to execute their transition functions. A cells' array is used to record the present cell's space state and to detect changes in the model. When a change is detected, the Next-Events list is updated. The results produced by the imminent cells are stored in a New-States list. In this way, the flow of the global transition function of the cell space can be reproduced.

A flat coordinator starts the simulation by detecting quiescent states for the initial state of the cell space. Non-quiescent cells (v.g., those whose state can change) are added in the Next-Events list. When an instance of the *FlatCoordinator* class receives a X-message, it is also inserted in this list. After, the coordinator removes the first element of the Next-Events list, and it invokes the *externalFunction* method.

The coupled models still compute the local transition function for the desired position, and apply the delay algorithm, changing the Next-Events list. If the cell is in the Ylist, the coordinator will create a Y-message containing the cell state value, and will transmit it to the upper level coordinator. When it is finished, it sends a *DoneMessage* to the parent coordinator with the event date of the next imminent child. When an *internalMessage* is received, the *FlatCoordinator* invokes to the *internalFunction* method of the coupled model. If the cell state has changed, its value is returned and the next event time for the cell is computed. This one iterates through all the imminent cells, and generates their output, adding all the influenced cells in the next-events list. Then, the *external-Function* method is executed for all the virtual cells in this list.

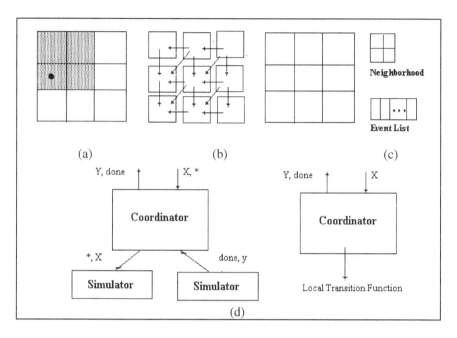

(a)                    (b)                    (c)

(d)

Figure 10.11: Cell space structures. (a) Basic cell space and its neighborhood. (b) Coupling using hierarchical coordinators. (c) Definition using flat models. (d) Coordinator's reaction to messages.

## 10.5  Development Experiences With Cellular Models

This section will focus on some development experiences done with Cell-DEVS. The first one, presented in the following figure, shows one specification for the Life game [[5]] using the tool CD++. Here, the coupled model consists only of one Cell-DEVS, called "Life". The parameters of the specification defined earlier are included here: model's dimension, kind and length of the delay, shape of the neighborhood, and the local transition function. The local function says that a cell can have a live/dead (1/0) state. A living cell remains alive only if it has three or four living neighbors. Otherwise, it dies. Instead, a new born cell appears when there are exactly three living neighbors of a dead cell.

```
[top]
components : life

[life]
width : 10                          height : 10
delay : inertial                    defaultDelayTime : 100
border : wrapped                    localtransition : life-rule
neighbors : life(-1,-1) life(-1,0) life(-1,1) life(0,-1) life(0,0)
neighbors : life(0,1) life(1,-1)  life(1,0) life(1,1)

[life-rule]
rule : 1 100 { (0,0) = 1 and (truecount = 3 or truecount = 4) }
rule : 1 100 { (0,0) = 0 and truecount = 3 }
rule : 0 100 { t }
```

Figure 10.12: Life game specification using CD++.

The following figure shows the model's execution using inertial delays. The first row of the figure presents the execution of the model given an initial configuration. Instead, the second row shows the influence of inputs to certain cells using inertial delays. It can be seen that, for instance, a new value is inserted in the position (8,7) in simulated time 15. Therefore, the internal events scheduled for 20 in the cells (7, 7) and (8, 6) are preempted, and these cells die. This happens because these cells have now five living neighboring cells. Therefore, as an inertial delay is being used, the state changes are preempted.

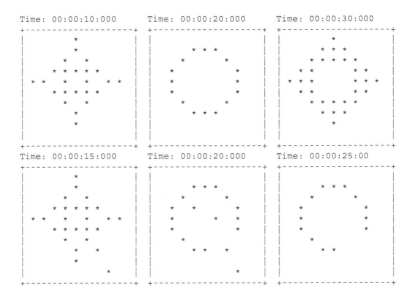

Figure 10.13: Life game execution with inertial delays.

The following figure shows that extensions to three dimensional models can be easily implemented. This example is an extension of the previous one, using a population of active cells distributed in an area of 7x7x3. Likewise, extensions to models of higher dimensions can be defined. We can see that the coupled model is specified by the dimension, kind of delay and neighborhood (3x3x3 adjacent cells). The local function defines a new born being when the cell has more than 9 living neighbors. A cell remains alive when the neighborhood contains 8 or 10 living neighbors. Otherwise, the cell dies.

```
[3d-life]
type : cell              dim : (7,7,3)              border : wrapped
delay : transport        defaultDelayTime : 100
neighbors: (-1,-1,-1) (-1,0,-1) (-1,1,-1) (0,-1,-1) (0,0,-1) ...
neighbors: (1,-1,1) (1,0,1) (1,1,1)

[3d-life-rule]
rule : 1 100 { (0,0,0) = 1 and (truecount = 8 or truecount = 10) }
rule : 1 100 { (0,0,0) = 0 and truecount >= 10 }
rule : 0 100 { t }
```

Figure 10.14: Description of a variation of the Life game.

The following figure shows the results obtained when this model is executed (each plane separately). The execution starts with a high number of living cells, but the execution result is not stable. The number of living cells turns to be reduced, and, finally, in the instant 00:00:01:000, the population is extinguished.

```
Time: 00:00:00:000                          Time: 00:00:00:100
   0123456      0123456      0123456           0123456      0123456      0123456
  +-------+    +-------+    +-------+          +-------+    +-------+    +-------+
0 |*      |  0 |       |  0 |*      |        0 | *    *|  0 |**    *|  0 | *    *|
1 |* *  **|  1 |**   **|  1 |   *** |        1 |* *   *|  1 |*     *|  1 |* **  *|
2 |*    * |  2 |   ** *|  2 |* **   |        2 |**   * |  2 |*     *|  2 |**    *|
3 |       |  3 | *  **|   3 |     **|        3 |   *** |  3 | *  * *|  3 |    * *|
4 | *   **|  4 | *  * |   4 |*    **|        4 |       |  4 |    ** |  4 |       |
5 | **  * |  5 |  *  * |  5 |**   * |        5 |*  *** |  5 |* *** *|  5 |*  ** *|
6 |*  *  *|  6 | *   * |  6 | * ** *|        6 |       |  6 |*      |  6 |* *   |
  +-------+    +-------+    +-------+          +-------+    +-------+    +-------+
Time: 00:00:00:200                          Time: 00:00:00:900
   0123456      0123456      0123456           0123456      0123456      0123456
  +-------+    +-------+    +-------+          +-------+    +-------+    +-------+
0 |*     *|  0 |      *|  0 |*     *|        0 |       |  0 |       |  0 |       |
1 | **  * |  1 | *   * |  1 | **  * |        1 |       |  1 |       |  1 |       |
2 |    ** |  2 | *    *|  2 |       |        2 |       |  2 |       |  2 |       |
3 |*      |  3 |*   **|   3 |*    **|        3 |       |  3 |       |  3 |       |
4 |  **** |  4 |    ** |  4 |   ****|        4 |*    * |  4 |*   **|   4 |*    * |
5 |*    * |  5 |* *  * |  5 |*  *  *|        5 |       |  5 |       |  5 |       |
6 |**   **|  6 |**   **|  6 |** ***|         6 |       |  6 |       |  6 |       |
  +-------+    +-------+    +-------+          +-------+    +-------+    +-------+
```

Figure 10.15: Execution results for the modified Life game.

The next example represents a three dimensional heat diffusion model. Each cell contains a temperature value, computed as the average of the values of the neighborhood. In addition, a heater is connected to the cells (2,2,1) and (3,3,0). On the other hand, a cooler is connected to the cells (1,3,3) and (3,3,2).

```
[top]
components : room Heater@Generator Cooler@Generator
link : out@Heater HeatInput@room
link : out@Cooler ColdInput@room

[Heater] [Cooler]
distribution : exponential            mean : 10

[room]
type : cell           dim : (4, 4, 4)           border : wrapped
delay : transport     defaultDelayTime : 100
neighbors : room(-1,0,-1) room(0,-1,-1)
neighbors : room(0,0,-1) room(0,1,-1)
...
neighbors : room(0,0,-2)  room(0,0,2) room(0,2,0)
neighbors : room(0,-2,0)  room(2,0,0) room(-2,0,0)
initialvalue : 24
in : HeatInput ColdInput
link : HeatInput in@room(3,3,0) in@room(2,2,1)
link : ColdInput in@room(3,3,2)
link : ColdInput in@room(1,3,3)
localtransition : heat-rule
portInTransition : in@room(3,3,0) in@room(2,2,1) setHeat
portInTransition : in@room(3,3,2) in@room(1,3,3) setCold

[heat-rule]
Rule: {( (-1,0,-1)+(0,-1,-1)+(0,0,-1)+ (0,1,-1) + (1,0,-1) +
       (-1,-1,0) + (-1,0,0) + (-1,1,0)  + (0,-1,0) +(0,0,0)+
       (0,1,0)+(1,-1,0)+(1,0,0) + (1,1,0) + (-1,0,1) + (0,-1,1) +
       (0,0,1)+(0,1,1)+(1,0,1)+(0,0,-2)+(0,0,2)+(0,2,0)+
       (0,-2,0)+(2,0,0) + (-2,0,0) ) / 25 } 1000 { t }

[setHeat]
rule : { uniform(24,80) } 1000 { t }

[setCold]
rule : { uniform(-45,10) } 1000 { t }
```

Figure 10.16: Definition of the heat diffusion model.

Here, the upper level model is composed by three basic components: the room, a heater and a cooler. The last two models are DEVS, defined as random generators. The heater simulator generates a flow of temperatures between 24° C and 80° C with uniform distribution. The cooler creates random values with uniform distribution in the range [-45, 10]. Both generators create values every $x$ time units, where $x$ has exponential distribution with mean of 10 time units. The model representing the room is composed by a Cell-DEVS of 10x10x4 cells. The function computes the present value for the cell as an average of the neighbors. The model has two input ports (HeatInput, ColdInput) connected to the input ports of the corresponding cells. Whenever a value is received through these ports, the *portInTransition* rules are activated. Here, *setHeat* generates a temperature value in the range [24, 80]. Likewise, *setCold* generates temperatures in the range [-45, 10]. The values of the corresponding cells will be updated using these functions.

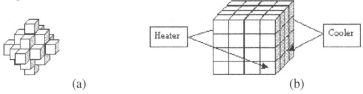

(a)                                                      (b)

Figure 10.17: Heat diffusion model. (a) Neighborhood shape. (b) Coupling scheme.

These examples show the implementation of the formalism: the models are specified following a formal description, and the implementation models executes them. The hierarchical and flat simulation mechanisms produced different execution performance for these examples. The number of messages involved in the flat simulation is reduced because interaction only occurs between the higher level coordinator and the Root coordinator. The following figures show the differences for both cases. Those results were obtained for the Life game, and a one-way traffic model, but similar behavior was obtained for most implemented models. The test starts with more than 75% of active cells. The first test shows the influence of increasing the size of the cell space. The second test used a fixed size space (2500 cells), and the duration of the simulation was increased.

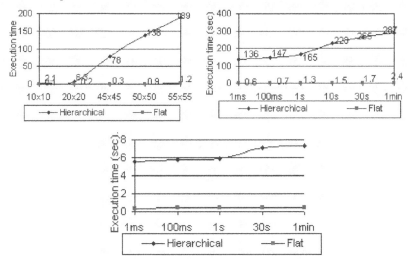

Figure 10.18: Life game and traffic model, increasing the size and simulation length.

A main goal of the new formalism was to reduce the development times for the simulators. The results obtained were promising though the developed experiences were simple prototypes used to check the use of the tools and the formalism. Several data were recorded relating the development times for the different solutions, classifying the different users and their development activities. These results are presented following.

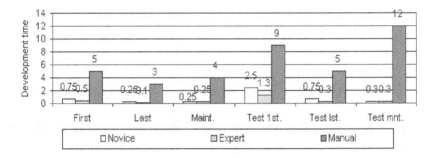

Figure 10.19: Comparison of development times for the Life game.

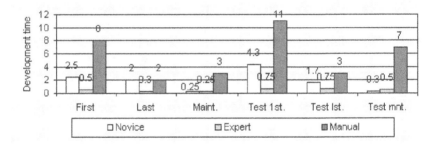

Figure 10.20: Comparison of development times for the traffic simulation.

The development activities were classified according with the experience of the modelers, and the kinds of activities being considered. The use of the tool was compared to the development of the same problems by hand. Several groups of developers were analyzed, and their first and last developed applications were recorded. The maintenance times for the applications was also registered, considering development times and testing times sepparately.

It can be seen that the results obtained highly improved the development times of the simulations. The main gains have been reported in the testing and maintenance phases, the most expensive for these systems. It also showed performance improvements for the flat models, providing speedups from 2 to 7 times in the execution for the cellular models. Ten-fold improvements could be achieved for expert users although the tested models were simple prototypes of simple cellular models.

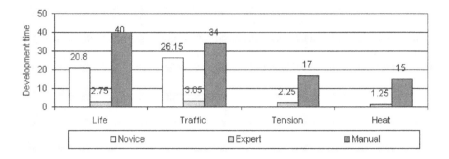

Figure 10.21: Comparison between total development times for different applications.

## 10.6   Present Work

This section briefly presents a set of the results derived from the initial specifications of Cell-DEVS models.

### 10.6.1  Parallel Cell-DEVS

As stated in [[2]], if we call **e** to the elapsed time since the occurrence of an event, a model can exist in the DEVS structure at either e=0 or e=D(s). A modeler can use the *select* function to solve the conflicts of simultaneous scheduled events in coupled models. In these cases, ambiguity arises when a model scheduled for an internal transition receives an event. The problem here is how to determine which of both elapsed times should be used. The *select* function solves the ambiguity by choosing only one of the imminent models. This is a source of potential errors, because the serialization may not reflect the simultaneous occurrence of events. Moreover, the serialization reduces the possible exploitation of parallelism among concurrent events.

These problems were solved defining the Parallel DEVS [[2]]. Cell-DEVS models could be coupled with these traditional DEVS submodels. Also, it was proved that a bag is needed for the Cell-DEVS with zero-time transitions [[12]]. Considering these factors, the Cell-DEVS models were redefined to include parallel behavior [[15]].

A general environment for parallel simulations was built, considering the use of optimist/pessimist synchronization approaches. A mapping between the Cell-DEVS simulators and these algorithms were defined, and at present, they are being used to build a parallel extension of the tools. After, an extension to the HLA standard will be faced. This approach will enhance the production of results. By introducing a parallel coordinator, execution speedups of several orders of magnitude can be achieved without touching the specifications. Furthermore, a parallel implementation of each problem hand-coded could produce ten-fold delays in the development.

## 10.6.2 Extensions to the Cell's Specification Language

At present, several modifications were done to the specification language used to define the cell's behavior. The first one is related with the topology of the cellular models. At present, the defined models include rectangular meshes. Nevertheless, several existing cellular models have triangular or hexagonal patterns. Therefore, the tool is being extended to run these approaches. In a first stage, a translator is being used to define rectangular rules derived from the triangular and hexagonal ones. Then, the extended topologies will be included in the tool.

A set of new delay constructions has been defined [[12]]. These ones allow to define complex timing behavior for inertial delays, improving the definition of timing behavior for cellular models. These constructions are being combined with the new definitions of parallel Cell-DEVS. The new local confluent functions should be included in the specification language, allowing the modeler to define the cell's behavior under simultaneous events. The simulation mechanisms are being extended to include a theory of quantized DEVS models [[23]].

The specification of cellular models can be impoved using a specialized graphical interface. The models will be defined using a graphical extension of the specification language, and a graphical output will be defined. These tools will be integrated in a web-based simulation framework, providing a Cell-DEVS simulation server.

## 10.6.3 Applications

Several applications are being considered to apply Cell-DEVS models. A first group of models are related with the definition of physical problems. The first ones include surface tension analysis, lattice gases and studies of echological systems. Some of the results obtained can be seen in the following figure. A second group of applications include the analysis of crystal growth [[10]]. In the latter case, different isotropies will be studied, including triangular, rectangular and hexagonal meshes. Cellular models has also been used to create chaotic patterns to be used in one-time-pad applications in cryptography. The kind of pattern obtained can be seen in the following figure. The cellular models are also being considered as fields of neurons, to be applied as a workbench to build artificial neural networks.

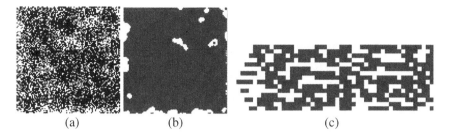

Figure 10.22: Surface tension models (a: initial; b: final); chaotic pattern for crypto-graphic application (c).

Several multimodel applications are being faced. First, a detailed study of development times is being extended to consider the integration of mixed DEVS and Cell-DEVS models. The goal is to characterize the development activities and the cost reductions in more complex applications. Also, multidimensional models are being studied. They are being used to represent different aspects of the same three-dimensional system as a cubic zone of a higher dimensional space.

A final group of applications include a specification language used to define traffic simulations as cell spaces. The streets can be defined, analyzing the traffic direction, number of tracks, etc. Once the urban section is defined, the traffic flow is automatically set up. Therefore, a modeler can concentrate in the problem to solve, instead of being in charge of defining a complex simulation system.

A city section is specified by a set of streets connecting two crossings. The vehicles advance in a right line (surpassing slower vehicles), up to their arrival to a crossing. The speed of each vehicle is represented through a random transport delay. Each street is represented as a sequence of segments. These represent a section of one block of length, where every track has the same traffic direction (one way). Consequently, to build a two-way street is necessary to define one segment for each direction. Several models were defined, depending on the number of lanes, their direction, and maximum speeds in the streets.

Once defined the basic behavior for a city section, different components can be defined. These are also part of the specification language, and include definitions for traffic lights, railways, men at work, street holes, transit signals, parked cars, and so on. Finally, special behavior has been defined for special vehicles: trucks, vans and high priority cars (ambulances, policemen, firefighters) [[4], [3]].

## 10.7  Conclusions

The present work presented a description for cell spaces modeling and simulation. The paradigm is based on the DEVS and Asynchronous Cellular Automata formalisms, using transport or inertial delays. These concepts allows to specify complex behavior in a simple fashion, independently of the quantitative complexity of the models.

Cell-DEVS models were described formally, considering specifications for one cell and for general Cell-DEVS coupled models. The methods presented allow automatic definition of cell spaces using the DEVS formalism. Integration of multiple views for each submodel is possible, letting to combine different models in an efficient fashion. The use of a formal approach allowed to prove properties regarding the cellular models. It also provided a sound basis to build simulation tools related with the formal specifications.

One of the main contributions is related with the definition of complex timing behavior for the cells in the space using very simple constructions. Transport and inertial delays allow the modeler to make easier the timing representation of each cell in the space.

An implementation of the paradigms was presented. The modeler and the developer point of view were considered, allowing efficient and cost-effective development of simulators. Two descriptions for the simulation mechanisms were included. The first one considered a hierarchical simulation mechanism. Subsequently, a method to flatten the hierarchical description of the cell spaces was given.

The approach here presented also permits including a parallel coordinator, achieving execution speedups of several orders of magnitude without changes in the specifications. Therefore, this approach can provide important reduction in the implementation of parallel applications for cellular models.

Finally, the formalism allow to improve the security and cost in the development of the simulations. As shown by the experimental application results, the formalism showed ten-fold improvements for expert developers.

## Acknowledgements

This work was partially funded by ANPCYT Project 11-04460 and UBACYT Projects TX04 and JW10.

# References

[1]   Barylko, A.; Beyoglonian, J.; Wainer, G. "GAD: a General Application DEVS environment". *Proceedings of IASTED Applied Modelling and Simulation 1998.* Hawaii, U.S.A.

[2]   Chow, A.; Zeigler, B. "Revised DEVS: a parallel, hierarchical, modular modeling formalism". *Proceedings of the SCS Winter Simulation Conference.* 1994.

[3]   Davidson, A.; Wainer, G. "Specifying control signals in traffic models". *Proceedings of AIS'2000.* Tucson, Arizona. U.S.A. 2000.

[4]   Davidson, A.; Wainer, G. "Specifying truck movement in traffic models using Cell-DEVS". *Proceedings of the $33^{rd}$ Annual Conference on Computer Simulation.* Washington, D.C. U.S.A. 2000.

[5]   Gardner, M. "The fantastic combinations of John Conway's New Solitaire Game 'Life'.". *Scientific American.* 23 (4). pp. 120-123. April 1970.

[6]   Ghosh, S.; Giambiasi, N. "On the need for consistency between the VHDL language constructions and the underlying hardware design". *Proceedings of the 8th. European Simulation Symposium.* Genoa, Italy. Vol. I. pp. 562-567. 1996.

[7]   Giambiasi, N.; Miara, A. "SILOG: A practical tool for digital logic circuit simulation". *Proceedings of the 16th. D.A.C.*, San Diego, U.S.A. 1976.

[8]   Moon, Y.; Zeigler, B.; Ball, G.; Guertin, D. P. "DEVS representation of spatially distributed systems: validity, complexity reduction". *IEEE Transactions on Systems, Man and Cybernetics.* pp. 288-296. 1996.

[9]   Rodriguez, D.; Wainer, G. "New Extensions to the CD++ tool". *Proceedings of SCS Summer Multiconference on Computer Simulation.* 1999.

[10]  Toffoli, T.; Margolus, N. "Cellular Automata Machines". *The MIT Press*, Cambridge, MA. 1987.

[11]  Wainer, G.  "Discrete-events cellular models with explicit delays". Ph.D. Thesis, Université d'Aix-Marseille III. 1998.

[12]  Wainer, G. "Improved cellular models with parallel Cell-DEVS". To appear in *Transactions of the Society for Computer Simulation.* 2000.

[13]  Wainer, G.; Barylko, A.; Beyoglonian, J.; Giambiasi, N. "Application of the Cell-DEVS paradigm for cell spaces modelling and simulation.". *Internal Report. Departamento de Computación. Facultad de Ciencias Exactas y Naturales. Universidad de Buenos Aires.* Submitted for publication. 1998.

[14]  Wainer, G.; Giambiasi, N. "Specification, modeling and simulation of timed Cell-DEVS spaces". *Technical Report n.: 98-007. Departamento de Computación. Facultad de Ciencias Exactas y Naturales. Universidad de Buenos Aires.* 1998.

[15]  Wainer, G.; Giambiasi, N. "Specification of timing delays in parallel Cell-DEVS models". *Proceedings of SCS Summer Multiconference on Computer Simulation.* 1999.

[16]  Wainer,G.; Frydman, C.; Giambiasi, N. "An environment to simulate cellular DEVS models". *Proceedings of the SCS European Multiconference on Simulation.* Istanbul, Turkey. 1997.

[17]  Wainer,G.; Giambiasi, N.; Frydman, C. "Cell-DEVS models with transport and inertial delays". *Proceedings of the 9th. European Simulation Symposium and Exhibition.* Passau, Germany. 1997.

[18]  Wolfram, S. "Theory and applications of cellular automata". Vol. 1, Advances Series on Complex Systems. World Scientific, Singapore, 1986.

[19] Zeigler, B. "Multifaceted Modeling and discrete event simulation". Academic Press, 1984.

[20] Zeigler, B. "Object-oriented simulation with hierarchical modular models". Academic Press, 1990.

[21] Zeigler, B. "Object-oriented simulation with hierarchical modular models. Revised to include source code for DEVS-C++." *Department of Electrical and Computer Engineering. University of Arizona.* 1995.

[22] Zeigler, B. "Theory of modeling and simulation". Wiley, 1976.

[23] Zeigler, B. P., Cho, H.; Lee, J.; Sarjoughian, H. *The DEVS/HLA Distributed Simulation Environment And Its Support for Predictive Filtering.* DARPA Contract N6133997K-0007: ECE Dept., UA, Tucson, AZ. 1998.

# Chapter 11

# DEVS-Based Modeling and Simulation for Intelligent Transportation Systems

S-D Chi and J-K Lee

*This paper presents the DEVS-based traffic simulation methodology for intelligent transportation systems. To do this, we have proposed the four-layered approach on the basis of object-oriented programming environment; (i) hierarchical, modular, and distributed modeling & simulation layer, (ii) model abstraction layer, (iii) microscopic and macroscopic traffic modeling layer, and (iv) ITS simulation system layer. It supports an intelligent, interacted, and integrated transportation simulation environment based on the distributed DEVS formalism. So that it can provide a convenient means for evaluating the alternative signal control strategies at the operation level of advanced traffic management systems and for generating the simulation-based forecasting information for advanced traveler information systems. The $I^3D^2$ Transportation Simulation System, which has been developed to address the proposed methodology, is briefly introduced.*

## 11.1   Introduction

The growth of urban automobile traffic has led to serious and worsening traffic congestion problems in most cities around the world. Since travel demand increases at a rate often greater than the addition of road capacity, the situation will continue to deteriorate unless better traffic management strategies are implemented. One of the most attractive remedial measures for addressing the congestion problem is the development of Intelligent Transportation Systems (ITS) [13]. In recent years simulation has become a tool commonly used to understand the characteristics of a traffic system and to select an appropriate design for ITS. Thus, the modeling and simulation techniques provide a convenient means for evaluating the alternative signal control strategies at the operation level of Advanced Traffic Management Systems (ATMS) and for generating the simulation-based forecasting information for Advanced Traveler

Information Systems (ATIS) [8, 12]. Traffic simulation models can be classified as being either microscopic or macroscopic models. In microscopic simulation models the individual vehicle is studied, and the attention is focused on their performance in the context of the whole traffic network system. This approach has usually been adopted for the simulation of relatively small or simple systems. On the other hand, the macroscopic approach can be used to simulate the large network or complex traffic system. This approach uses simplified models of roads and intersections [11]. Discrete event modeling technique can be basically employed to describe macroscopic models. However, by allowing the level of abstraction that is only possible in the hierarchical modeling and simulation environment, the microscopic level of modeling can be also accomplished.

This paper presents the traffic simulation methodology for ITS based on the distributed DEVS (Discrete Event System Specification) formalism. To do this, we have proposed the four-layered approach on the basis of object-oriented programming environment; (i) hierarchical, modular, and distributed modeling & simulation layer, (ii) model abstraction layer, (iii) microscopic and macroscopic traffic modeling layer, and (iv) ITS simulation system layer. It supports an intelligent, interacted, and integrated transportation simulation environment based on the distributed DEVS formalism. The $I^3D^2$ Transportation Simulation System has been also developed to address the proposed methodology.

The remainder of this paper is organized as follows. We first briefly review a background on conventional traffic simulation systems. Then, we propose a DEVS-based design methodology for the transportation modeling and simulation system. This is followed by the case study: $I^3D^2$ Transportation Simulation System.

## 11.2 Background on Traffic Simulation Systems

Traditionally, traffic simulation models were developed independently for different facilities (e.g. freeways, urban streets, etc.). A wide variety of simulation models exist for various applications. Most of these models were developed for evaluation and few for real-time support of ATIS operation and traffic prediction (e.g. DYNASMART, DYNAMIT). Most of the old generation models (for example, NETSIM, and earlier versions of AIMSUN2), however, do not represent vehicle paths [13]. Analytic flow models such as FREFLOW, TRANSYT-7F or HCS do not track individual vehicle movements and do not have sufficient detail for analyzing ATMS and ATIS studies. Although NETSIM and FRESIM do provide microscopic performance models, these microscopic models cannot effectively meet the requirements of evaluating integrated ATIS and ATMS application at an operational level, because they have limited representation of travel behavior or are inflexible in modeling more advanced surveillance and control systems [7].

A new generation of traffic simulation models has been developed for ITS applications. Examples are AUTOS and THOREAU. AUTOS is a macroscopic traffic model developed for ATMS application at traffic management centers such as testing signal optimization, emergency vehicle response management, and human factors. THOREAU is a microscopic model developed for ITS evaluation. However, it has a very long running time [13]. PARAMICS is also a recently developed microscopic traffic simulation and visualization tool for ITS analysis which a suit of high performance software tools for microscopic traffic simulation [1, 9]. Other microscopic simulation models are also under development for modeling Automated Highway Systems.

While these models have all been successfully applied in particular studies, a common shortcoming is the relatively limited range of applications. Some of them are designed for particular applications and useful only for specific purposes, while others do not support advance surveillance and control systems or integrated networks. No model has the integrated componentry and functionality required for evaluation of dynamic control and route guidance strategies on general networks [13].

Recently, Deshpande et al. [4] have developed a hybrid traffic modeling s/w environment, called SHIFT, which allows specifications of both continuous-time and discrete-event dynamics. This research proposed the formal semantics of the model and successfully applied to automated highway systems, however, it is not clear that it could support advanced modeling features, such as a hierarchical & modular modeling, distributed simulation, and model abstraction capabilities. The advantages of these capabilities, such as reduction in model development time, support for reuse of a database of models, and aid in model verification and validation, are becoming well accepted [10, 5]. In ITS study especially, these capabilities provides convenient means to construct and analyze complex traffic network systems. By employing these adventages, we have proposed the layered design methodology for ITS simulation.

## 11.3    Design Methodology for ITS Simulation

Based on the object-oriented programming environment, we have been proposed the four-layered methodology as shown in Figure 11.1. The features of ITS Simulation system can be better understood by organizing them within a set of layers that characterizes its software design structure. Layer I provides a hierarchical, modular, and distributed modeling & simulation environment on which the system is built. The properties of this lowest layer make it possible to realize similar properties at the higher layers. The next layer, model abstraction, can be framed in terms of their ability to reduce the complexity of a model. The microscopic and macroscopic traffic modeling can be accomplished within the Layer III. ITS simulation environment can be finally achieved in the layer IV.

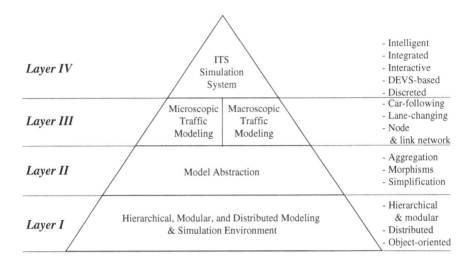

Figure 11.1: Layered approach for designing transportation simulation systems

## 11.3.1 Layer I: Hierarchical, Modular and Distributed Modeling & Simulation Environment

The System Entity Structure / Model Base (SES/MB) framework was proposed by Zeigler as a step toward interfacing the dynamic-based formalism of simulation with the symbolic formalisms of AI [17]. The framework has an advantage of facility of hierarchical design for system and reusability according to modularity and hierarchical design [14]. Furthermore, fostered by the promulgation of the HLA (High Level Architecture) [16, 3] distributed simulation, the use of multiple computers for model execution is fast becoming the predominant form of simulation, especially, the urban traffic simulation. To deal with these capabilites, D-Sim/HLA (DEVS-based distributed simulation environment) has been developed in the Visual-C$^{++}$ on the basis of the HLA-compliant DEVS formalism [15, 3].

## 11.3.2  Layer II: Model Abstraction

Abstraction, as a process, refers to a method or algorithm applied to a model to simplify its complexity while preserving its validity. The amount of detail in a model can be taken as the "product" of its scope and resolution. Scope refers to how much of the real world is represented; resolution refers to the number of variables in the model and their precision or granularity. Given a fixed amount of resources (time, area, # of cars, etc.), and a model complexity that exceeds this limit, there is a tradeoff relation between scope and resolution. We may be able to represent some aspects of a system very accurately but then only a few components will be presentable. Or we may be able to provide a comprehensive view of the system but only to a relatively low resolution. Such abstraction process is especially important for the flexible traffic analysis based on both microscopic and macroscopic models as shown in Figure 11.2. Aggregation is an abstraction process that works at the coupled model level and involves three steps [15]: (1) grouping components into blocks (i.e., the number of individual cars on each road represented by the microscopic model is accumulated), (2) abstracting the blocks into a simplified forms (i.e., build a macroscopic model, ROAD), and (3) coupling of the lumped components to form the overall lumped model (complete the macroscopic traffic network model with CROSS, GENR, and TRANSD) so as to constitute a valid simplification of the original base microscopic model.

## 11.3.3  Layer III: Microscopic and Macroscopic Traffic Modeling

Traffic simulation models can be classified as being either microscopic or macroscopic models. In microscopic simulation models the individual vehicle is studied, and the attention is focused on their performance in the context of the whole traffic network system. This approach has usually been adopted for the simulation of relatively small or simple systems. On the other hand, the macroscopic approach can be used to simulate the large network or complex system. This approach uses simplified models of roads and intersections [11].

### *11.3.3.1     Microscopic Traffic Modeling*

Microscopic model is based on the discrete-time approach that is generally applied and analyzed by the car-following model and the lane-changing model, so as to trace the behavior of each vehicle at every time period.

*Car-following models:* Car-following is the study of how the driver of a following vehicle try to conform with the behavior of the lead vehicle with acceleration and/or deceleration activities [6, 11]. In this model, the first vehicle on the road decides its acceleration/deceleration rate according to the speed limits of the occupied road, the speed capacity of vehicle, and the characteristics of the driver. On the other hand, if the vehicle is not the first one on the occupied road, the acceleration/deceleration rate is decided by the car-following model that provides this rate according to the distance and speed of the front vehicle.

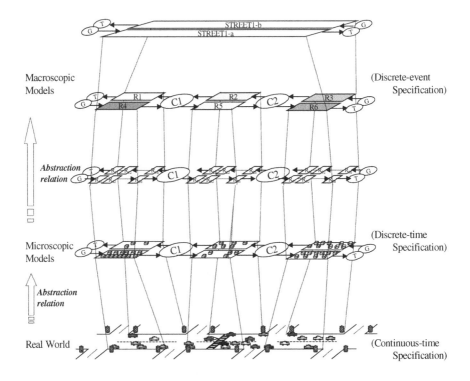

Figure 11.2: Abstraction hierarchy for the traffic modeling

*Lane-changing model:* The lane-changing model is the core of multi-lane microscopic traffic model in company with the car-following model, which is relatively complex because of the intervention of driver's characteristics and decision making [13]. In general, the lane-changing model is classified into two types: mandatory and discretionary. Mandatory lane-changing model occurs when the driver has to change his/her lane in order to avoid a restricted lane, bottleneck area, etc. On the other hand, the discretionary lane-changing model refers to cases in which the driver changes his/her lane in order to increase speed, bypass slower or heavy vehicles, and connect to the next link on their path, etc.

## *11.3.3.2        Macroscopic Traffic Modeling*

The macroscopic traffic model, which can be abstracted from the microscopic model, consists of nodes and links as shown in Figure 11.3. A node represents either an intersection (CROSS: cross), an external sink (TRANSD: transducer), or a source (GENR: generator); a link (ROAD: road) denotes a uni-directional pathway for vehicles between nodes.

*CROSS*: a signal light model. It sends a light signal to its neighboring ROADs depending on the signal switching control strategy, which can be characterized by cycle, split, and offset.

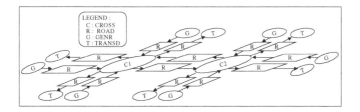

Figure 11.3: Macroscopic modeling example

*ROAD*: an uni-directional road model between nodes, i.e., CROSS, GENR, and TRANSD.  It receives a group of vehicles from the rear nodes. When it receives a green signal from the front node, it starts to send a group of vehicles to its neighboring nodes. The number of vehicles to be sent to next roads can be computed on the basis of the duration of green signal, available number of vehicles, probabilistic route choice, etc. of the ROAD.  The occurrence of traffic incidents and/or other blocking events can be specified within this model.

*GENR*: an external source model. It injects a group of vehicles to its front ROAD depending on the control strategy so that it behaves like a mixed model of CROSS and ROADs that is external to the given traffic network.

*TRANSD:* an external sink model. It first generates a light signal to its rear ROAD and then receives a group of vehicles form the ROAD so that it behaves like a mixed model of CROSS and ROADs that is external to the given traffic network.

## *11.3.3.3        Layer IV: ITS Simulation System*

The overall methodology for ITS simulation is described in Figure 11.4.  The simulation scope, objectives, requirements, and constraints -- for example, the light signal control policy and road condition, etc. -- are specified in PHASE I. In PHASE II, the system entity structure (SES) that represents all possible traffic network configurations is automatically pruned to generate a pruned entity structure (PES), i.e., a specific configuration to be tested, based on the modeling scope and objectives. This PES can be saved for later use. Then each microscopic and/or macroscopic component model and possible traffic event model, such as traffic incidences and other blocking events, are initialized according to the transportation database and finally transformed along with the PES to construct the simulation model. In PHASE III, the discrete event simulation model proceeds by injecting the start message into the simulation model. The traffic flow analysis and display of the simulation result can be performed in PHASE IV. This result maybe directly utilized for the ATIS and/or ATMS in PHASE V, however, this will affect the driver's behavior and/or signal control policy at the operational level so that the state variables of each simulation model should be changed again during the simulation. This integrated, intelligent, and interacted simulation environment provides convenient means for the traffic flow analysis as well as ITS evaluation.

## 11.4   Case Study: I3D2 Transportation Simulation System

Based on the DEVS-based modeling and simulation methodology for ITS, we have been developed the $I^3D^2$ Transportation Simulation System, in which the $I^3D^2$ means "Intelligent", "Interactive", "Integrated", "DEVS-based", and "Distributed". The "intelligent" means that it provides a knowledge-based modeling environment for considering the human factor i.e., driver's behavior, upon receiving the ATIS information. The "interactive" means that it supports the run-time interaction to modify the simulation condition and/or generate the simulation reports during the simulation. The "integrated" means that it allows an integrated modeling environment by combining the traffic dynamics with other transportation components such as driver's behavior, signal control policy, sensory readings, and the transportation database. The "DEVS-based" means that it is developed on the basis of the advanced hierarchical modular object-oriented techniques and the "distributed" represents that it supports a HLA-compliant distributed simulation environment.

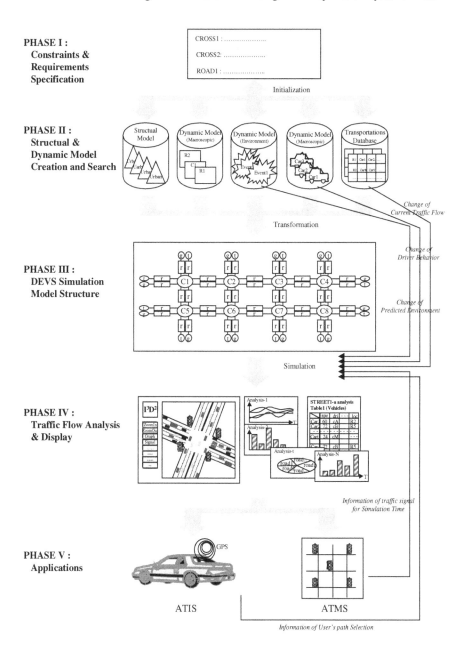

Figure 11.4: Simulation analysis methodology for ITS

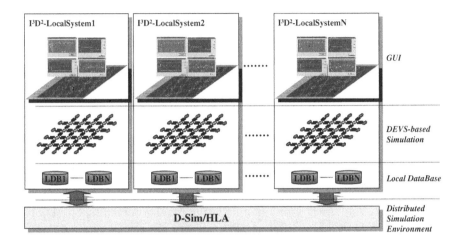

Figure 11.5: $I^3D^2$ system overview

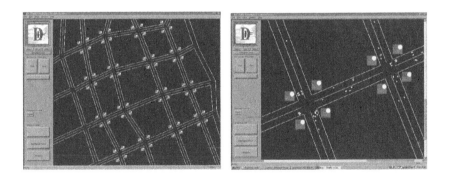

Figure 11.6: User Interface

Figure 11.5 illustrates the whole concept of $I^3D^2$ system, in which the simulation is proceeded as follows; first the simulation model of each $I^3D^2$ Local system is first initialized according to the current traffic monitoring information of the local database and than the local simulation is started to generate traffic behavior of specified area. The incomming/outgoing vehicles from/to neighboring areas can be handled by other $I^3D^2$ via distributed environment either by on-line or off-line(using the local database). $I^3D^2$ system is currently being developed and tested under the stand-alone environment. Figure 11.6 shows several screen shots of the user interface. Figure 11.7 illustrates several simulation results represented by the measure of effectiveness (MOE) example such as total throughput, stop time and number, etc. Detail descriptions on MOEs are available in [13].

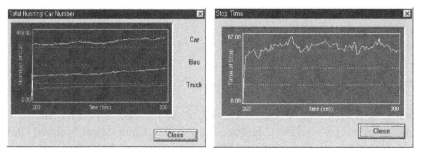

(a) Throughput of entire network          (b) Stop-time

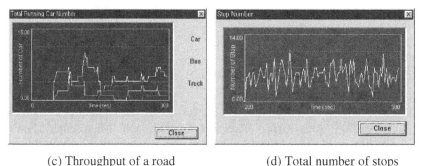

(c) Throughput of a road                  (d) Total number of stops

Figure 11.7: Simulation Results.

## 11.5  Conclusions

DEVS-based design methodology of the traffic simulation system for the ITS has been discussed. Basically, the discrete event modeling technique can be employed to describe macroscopic models. However, by allowing the level of abstraction that is only possible in the hierarchical modeling and simulation environment, the microscopic level of modeling can be also accomplished. To do this, four-layered approach based on the object-oriented programming environment is proposed; (i) hierarchical, modular, and distributed modeling & simulation layer, (ii) model abstraction layer, (iii) microscopic and macroscopic layer, and (iv) ITS simulation system layer. It supports an intelligent, interacted, and integrated transportation simulation environment based on the distributed DEVS formalism. Therefore, it provides a convenient means for evaluating the alternative signal control strategies at the operation level of advanced traffic management systems and for generating the simulation-based forecasting information for advanced traveler information systems. The $I^3D^2$ transportation simulation system based on the proposed methodology has been successfully implemented and tested. Research needs to be continued to validate the proposed methodology and S/W tools.

# Acknowledgments

The authors would like to thanks Dr. B.J. Kim, J.S. Lee, Y.H. Lim, and K. C. Jung, Hangkong Univ., Dr. C.H. Park and Dr. K.S. Chun, Seoul National Univ. This research was supported by Ministry of Science & Technology under contract 98-N10-03-01-A-02, "Development of Simulation System Architecture and Application Systems".

# References

[1] Abdulhai, B., J.B., Sheu, and W. Recker, 1999. "Simulation of ITS on the Irvine FOT Area Using 'Paramics 1.5' Scalable Microscopic Traffic Simulation: Phase I: Model Calibration and Validation." Research Report, UCB-ITS-PRR-99-12. California PATH, UC. Berkeley.

[2] Chi, S.D., J.O., Lee, and Y.K. Kim, 1997. "Using the SES/MB Framework to Analyze Traffic Flow", Trans. of Computer Simulation International, Vol. 14, No. 4(Dec.): 211~221.

[3] Cho, H.J., 1999. Discrete Event System homomorphisms: Design and Implementation of Quantization-based Distributed Simulation Environment. Ph.D. dissertation, Dept. Elec. Comput. Eng., Univ. of Arizona, Tucson.

[4] Deshpande, A.R. et al., 1996. SHIFT Reference Manual, California PATH.

[5] Eskafi, F. and A. Göllü, 1997. "Simulation Framework Requirements and Methodologies in Automated Highway Planning." Trans. of Computer Simulation International, Vol. 14, No. 4(Dec.): 169~180.

[6] Han, L.D. 1992. Traffic Flow Characteristics of Signalized Arterials Under Disturbance Situations. Ph.D. dissertation, Univ. UC. Berkely.

[7] Niedringhaus, W.P. and Wang, P. 1993. "IVHS Traffic Modeling Using Parallel Computing" In Proceedings of the IEEE-IEE Vehicle Navigation and Informations Systems Conf.(Ottawa, Canada, Oct. 12-15), 157-162.

[8] Nelson, J.R., et al. 1993. "Experiences gained in implementing an economical, universal motorist information system." In Proceedings of the

IEEE-IEE Vehicle Navigation and Informations Systems Conf.(Ottawa, Canada, Oct. 12-15), 67-71.

[9]  Paramic traffic simulation Ltd., 1997. Paramic v1.5 manuals.

[10]Sargent, R., 1993. "Hierarchical modeling for discrete event simulation." In Proceedings of the Winter Simulation Conference (Los Angeles, California), p569.

[11]Simonsson, S.O., 1993. "Car-following as a Tool in Road Traffic Simulation." In Proceedings of the IEEE-IEE Vehicle Navigation and Informations Systems Conf.(Ottawa, Canada, Oct. 12-15), 150-156.

[12]Tritter, D.B. and J. Zietlow, 1993. "Designing a traffic management communication system to accommodate intelligent vehicle highway systems." In Proceedings of the IEEE-IEE Vehicle Navigation and Informations Systems Conf.(Ottawa, Canada, Oct. 12-15), 182-185.

[13]Yang, Q., 1997. A Simulation Laboratory for Evaluation of Dynamic Traffic Management Systems. Ph.D. Dissertation, Dept. of Civil and Environmental Engineering, M.I.T.

[14]Zeigler, B.P., 1990. Object-oriented Simulation with Hierarchical, Modular Models: Intelligent Agents and Endomorphic systems, Academic Press, San Diego, CA.

[15]Zeigler, B.P., G., Ball, H.J., Cho, J.S., Lee, H.S., Sarjoughian, 1999. "Implementation of the DEVS Formalism over the HLA/RTI: Problems and Solutions." Simulation Interoperation Workshop (SIW), Orlando, FL. June.

[16]Zeigler, B.P. and J.S. Lee, 1998. "Theory of Quantized Systems: Formal Basis for DEVS/HLA Distributed Simulation Environment." In Enabling Technology for Simulation Science(II), SPIE AeoroSense 98. Orlando, FL.

[17]Zeigler, B.P., H., Praehofer, and T.G., Kim, 2000. Theory of Modeling and Simulation. 2 ed. Academic Press, New York, NY.

# Chapter 12
# Dynamic Neuronal Ensembles: Neurobiologically Inspired Discrete Event Neural Networks

S. Vahie

*The past decade has seen a resurgence in the research, development and application of artificial neural networks. This is due, in part, to the adaptive and autonomous nature of these computational mechanisms that lend themselves to real-world application. Although the early motivation for the development of artificial neural networks was inspired by biological neural networks, today's artificial neural networks have little or nothing in common with their biological counterparts. However, recent advances in neuroscience have uncovered some of the mechanisms responsible for the adaptive, communicative, and computational power of biological neural networks. Such neurobiological theories, though not always supported by mathematical formalisms, provide new insights and solutions to some of the problems facing today's neural network formalisms. This paper highlights some of the benefits of incorporating biological mechanisms in traditional and current state-of-the-art neural networks. We employ the discrete event abstractions using the DEVS formalism to incorporate such mechanisms. Due to their dynamic topology and their analogy to biology, we call them dynamic neuronal ensembles. An application to biological defensive response demonstrates the validity of the simulation model. Potential applications to flexible control systems are discussed.*

## 12.1 Introduction

This paper proposes a new class of artificial neural networks that complements existing neural network algorithms and paradigms. Our proposal emerges from a neurobiological perspective and is implemented within a discrete event modeling formalism to greatly increase the computational power, adaptability and dynamic response of artificial neural networks. We call these networks *dynamic neuronal ensembles (DNE)*. Formulated in the DEVS formalism (see e.g., Chapter x of this book)), a DNE is a coupled model of components that are themselves coupled models called *dynamic neurons (DN)*. The formulation exploits unique properties of the DEVS formalism such as hierarchical, modular construction and ability to support dynamic structural change.

## 12.1.1 Terms & Definitions

Before proceeding, a few definitions and explanations of terms are needed to avoid confusion in our subsequent presentation.

A neural network is *a non-algorithmic, non-digital information processing system that is intensely parallel.*. Although there are exceptions, such networks for engineering, business and science applications, have been modeled as networks composed of elements called *neurodes* that are interconnected by *links*. In such *artificial neural networks* (ANN), each link has a *weight* associated with it that affects the value of the signal being transmitted. The number and geometry of the links in a network determine the network's *topology*.

Each node in an ANN has a **transfer function** that determines the transition of an input signal to an output signal. Transfer functions commonly have three stages in their computation process:

- Computing Net-Weighted input: by multiplying all incoming signals with their link weight before summing them.

- Computing Activation level: by applying the input to an activation function.

- Computing Output level: by applying the activation level to the output function.

The behavior of an ANN is characterized by its **topology** and the **transfer functions** used by its nodes. An important feature of ANNs is that practical forms of learning have been implemented. Typically, *learning* is accomplished through *training* and the result of one or more training sessions. *Training* (in typical ANNs) is the process of modifying connection weights of neurodes in a network. Training can be supervised, graded or reinforced, and unsupervised or self-organized [4].

## 12.1.2  Objective of the Chapter

Artificial neural networks, as just formulated, are mathematical abstractions of biological neural networks found in nature. Neuroscientists have uncovered many aspects of real biological neurons and networks that are not captured in such ANNs. This chapter is concerned with identifying some of these aspects and how they might be captured in more refined neural network models. Particularly, as already indicated, a new class of dynamic neuron ensembles (DNN) is discussed which has the potential to increase the computational power, adaptability and dynamic response of ANNs by incorporating representations of some of the known features of biological neural networks. Formulated in DEVS, DNNs have much greater sophistication in their temporal behavior, including the ability to dynamically alter their structure, while still retaining computational feasibility. This dynamism opens up the potential to solve new classes of problems. However, giving up the relatively simple structures of conventional ANNs also incurs a cost both in execution time and more critically, in ability to develop a DNN to achieve a given task. Indeed, the straightforward training paradigms of ANNs just mentioned no longer apply. Therefore, the objective of this chapter is to discuss both the potential capabilities that DNNs open up as well as the obstacles that must be overcome to realize these potentials. DNNs must be considered a work in progress – a paradigm that offers promise for overcoming the limitations of current ANNs but offers considerable challenges to its realization.

## 12.1.3  Structure of the Presentation

We start with a short introduction to artificial neural networks (their definition, history and resurgence in research). We go on to identify some of the neurobiological characteristics that can complement the behavior of conventional ANNs. This is followed by an introduction to the dynamic neurons and DNEs. A DNE simulation of a biological snail's defensive response to varying levels of input stimuli shows the validity of the model. The paper concludes with a brief account of possible applications for the new models to control of chemical processes.

## 12.2  Background

### 12.2.1  History of Neural Networks

The history of neural networks can be traced back to the 1940s. In 1943, McCulloch (a neuroanatomist and psychiatrist) along with Pitts (a mathematics protégé) attempted to represent the events in the human nervous system. In doing so, they described the logical calculus of neural networks [20]. A few years later Donald O. Hebb (the father of modern Neuroscience) published *The Organization of Behavior* [8] which presented a physiologically based theory for learning through **synaptic modification**, thus laying the foundation for *plasticity*. The *Hebbian theory* provided a basis for the development of computational models of biological neuron ensembles. It helped identify the network topology (along with the neuron's transfer function) as a key determinant of network behavior. Rochester, Holland, Habit and Duda in 1956 [4] were the the first to attempt to develop a model that emulates the Hebbian learning. The model demonstrated the use of simulation in analyzing and validating physiological and mathematical theories of learning.

In 1954, Marvin Minsky completed and defended the first doctoral thesis on neural networks at Princeton University entitled *Theory of Neural-Analog Reinforcement Systems & Its Applications to the Brain-Model Problem* [20]. This helped established the study of neural networks as a formal discipline. A few years later Taylor and Steinbuch started the development of neural models of associative memory [1]. VonNeumann introduced the idea of redundancy into neural networks to enhance reliability in 1956 [20].

The origin of artificial neural networks as we know them today is traceable to the *Perceptron*. [16] introduced by Rosenblat, in 1958. Since then the number of types and forms of neural networks have greatly proliferated but the basic structure has not been substantially altered

Military funding and research interest in ANNs evaporated with a mathematical proof by Minsky and Papert [12] demonstrating the inability of perceptrons to classify non-linearly separable input patterns. In particular, learning of the exclusive-or function and common arithmetic and geometrical patterns was shown to be impossible. After several decades of neglect, it was eventually realized that the Minsky/Papert proof actually applied only to networks with only two layers, for input and output, respectively. The breakthrough came with the addition of a third layer, or hidden middle layer (Figure 12.1), that supplied the ability to group the input data into problem-dependent features before recombination into final outputs as well as a practical learning algorithm, called backpropagation for supervised training [18].

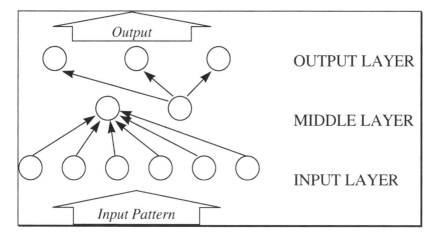

Figure 12.1: Structure of an Artificial Neural Network

The 1970s and 1980s were dominated by the development and successful application of networks with three or more layers using backpropagation as the most widely used neural network algorithm. A full account of the variety of ANNs that have been developed is available in many books (e.g., [4]).

## 12.2.2 Resurgence in ANNs

In the last decade or so, we have seen a resurgence in interest for artificial neural networks. This rekindling of interest in ANNs can be attributed to the infiltration of digital electronics into every aspect of modern living. The industrial successes that have accompanied this infiltration have only helped fuel its growth.

Today's industries and markets demand more from these digital systems. While these digital systems were forgiven for being rigid and procedural only a few years ago; markets and consequently industry demands real-time, apparently intelligent systems today. Artificial neural networks, with their ability to learn one or more patterns, appear to adapt to their users' needs and provide the much needed flexibility to the rigid digital systems.

ANNs have recorded successes in a number of sensory and simple pattern recognition domains becoming the "eyes and ears" to the traditionally "blind and deaf" digital systems. Current efforts focus on making neural networks more efficient at learning patterns and adapting to changes in their environment.

# 12.3   Requirements for Dynamic Neuron Ensembles

This section discusses some of the primary requirements that motivated the design and implementation of DNEs. There are three basic characteristics that should complement the capabilities of traditional neural networks:

1. DNEs should enable the modeler to *embed domain-based information* into the design of the DNE using network topology.

2. *Hebbian learning* should be implemented using dynamic connections and dynamic weight changes. Learning should be accomplished through the addition and deletion of axon-to-dendrite connections based on temporal integration of correlated activity as suggested by biological counterparts.

3. Unlike traditional neural networks, DNEs should not have a training phase independent from the execution phase. They should learn while they perform in *real-time*.

We now discuss each requirement in greater depth.

## 12.3.1  Embedding Knowledge (Domain Dependent Design)

Communications between entities in any system seem to have an overwhelming influence on the behavior of that system. This communication is determined by the lines or "channels" of communication available, also referred to as its *topology*. It has been suggested [10], that the topology of a network system is the primary determinant of the network's behavior. Traditional ANNs make little, if any, use of the net's topology. Using the idea of topology as a behavioral parameter, DNNs should provide the network designer with a more conceptual means of defining behavior.

Biological systems use cells in different, malleable configurations to elicit special behavioral responses and start from birth with many patterns of connections that are genetically determined. This capability is completely lacking in most traditional ANNs which always start from a *random* state and have no procedures to embed *apriori* information into the network. However, in many applications some information about the problem domain is usually available. Such pre-existing connectivity may help reduce the overall training time or increase performance. Procedures for representing causal and logical information in networks (or circuits) have already been developed and are actively used in VLSI and controller design. However, these representations are fixed in silicon and are not malleable. By developing similar circuits a non-physical, intangible medium we can provide them a *virtual malleability*. Thus we can enable the designer to embed information or knowledge into the system without committing to its absolute validity for all time[1].

To better illustrate how knowledge (from non-biological domains) is embedded into DNEs, a few examples of simple digital circuits (AND, OR, NOT gates) will be presented. Our building blocks, following those of McCulloch and Pitts, are the following (see Figure 12.2):

- An element that produces a positive (or excitatory) output in response to input.

- An element that produces a negative (or inhibitory) output in response to input.

- Weighted, unidirectional links used to connect elements to one another.

- Thresholds, determine if an element becomes active.

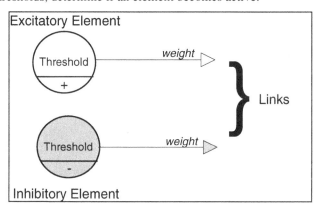

Figure 12.2: Network Development Toolset

Given these elements, we can build basic digital logic nodes (Figure 12.3). Using simple, double and single input nodes, more complex circuits exhibiting sophisticated behavior may be developed. By adding Hebbian learning and capabilities for nodal plasticity complex virtual circuits capable of learning and evolving in a dynamic environment may be developed. From a neural network perspective, this provides a methodology for the development of knowledge-based ANNs.

---

[1] In more abstract yet familiar terms, this is analogous to the notion of *beliefs* which help shape our behavior and decision-making process as long as there is no evidence to the contrary. Over time, these beliefs gain strength and become harder to challenge. However, since beliefs are defeasible they can be modified without affecting other beliefs [13].

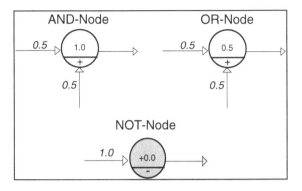

Figure 12.3: Digital Logic Nodes

Braitenberg [2] illustrates the development of complex behavior using simple elements and topologies. However, he to does not explicitly propose a theory for enabling the development of virtual malleability in behavioral networks. Given the ability to embed knowledge into a malleable network, our next task is to provide it with a means for modifying initially given connections.

## 12.3.2 Implementing Hebbian Learning

Let us recall the *classical conditioning paradigm* introduced by Pavlov [ref]. Animals usually salivate at the sight of food, but rarely at the sound of a bell. Pavlov rang a bell every time food was placed for the dog. After a number of trials he noticed that the dogs produced a conditioned response (i.e., they began to salivate at the sound of the bell). The dogs learnt to associate the bell with food, consequently producing the same response for both stimuli. Hebbian learning was the first attempt at providing a cellular level explanation for classical conditioning [3]. His statement, paraphrased, is commonly referred to as *Hebb's Rule*:

> When a neuron activates another neuron, causing it to fire, and consistently takes part in firing it, the connections between the neurons are strengthened.

Hebb proposed that percepts, concepts, ideas and images could all be realized in the brain as reentrant ensembles of nerve cells and phase sequences. Learning could occur at the synapses between cells in an assembly whenever conditions of sufficient correlated activity existed; reverberation increased the likelihood that these threshold conditions would be achieved.

Although, Hebb's rule suggests an explanation of learning, at a cellular level, the information it provides is inadequate to build a computational model of learning. The following information is necessary to develop a complete computational model of Hebbian learning:

- By how much should the connection between neurons change?

- How does one measure the individual, and correlated, activities of two neurons?

- What are the quantitative conditions under which the connection strengths should be increased?

- If connections are not increased should the connection strengths decrease? If yes, how?

- Are their any upper or lower bounds for the connection strengths?

A number of attempts have been made to address these questions and to mathematically represent Hebbian learning. We'll briefly review some of these theories.

*Neo-Hebbian Learning Theory,* introduced by Stephen Grossberg in 1960, is one of the first restatements of Hebb's Rule into a mathematical form,. This mathematical restatement was later supported by Grossberg and Cohen's stability proofs [7]. Neo-Hebbian Learning Theory consists of two dynamical differential equations governing the *activity* changes, and the *weight* changes, in the network at any instant of time, respectively.

Computer simulations of Neo-Hebbian Learning are implemented as **difference equations** rather than **differential equations**. Difference equations help exploit the trade-off between *accuracy* and *simulation time*. The output or activity and weight-change equations are represented as:

**Activity equation**:
$$Y_j(t+1) - Y_j(t) = DY_j(t) = -AY_j(t) + I_j(t) + \Sigma\, w_{ij}(t)[Y_i(t-\tau)-T]$$
where:

| | |
|---|---|
| $\Delta Y_j(t)$: | change in activity from $t$ to $t+1$ |
| $-AY_j(t)$: | decay of activity (decay constant A) |
| $I_j(t)$: | external input |
| $[Y_i(t-\tau)-T]$: | input received from $i$ (transmission time $\tau$, threshold T) |

**Weight-change equation**:
$$w_{ij}(t+1) - w_{ij}(t) = \Delta w_{ij}(t) = -Fw_{ij}(t) + GY_j(t)[Y_i(t-\tau)-T]$$
where:

-Fw$_{ij}$(t):                                transmission attenuation (decay constant F)

GY$_j$(t)[Y$_i$(t-τ) -T]:                Hebbian Rule (correlation constant G)

This representation of the Hebbian Learning Rule implies that a weight is strengthened only when neurode-j is active as a direct or partial consequence of activity in neurode-i. The transaction decay term (also known as the "forgetting" term) is designed to emulate the loss of signals during synaptic transfer, and tends to control the growth of weights.

Hebbian learning provides us with only a theory of synaptic weight modification. It provides no concrete data on its implementation. The Neo-Hebbian hypotheses suggest the use of a biologically unrealistic attenuation factor (F). Sutton and his colleagues [4] proposed a variation of Hebb's rule to incorporate both positive and negative weight changes

**Differential Learning Theory:**

$$\Delta w_{ij} = \beta \Delta Y_i \Delta Y_j \; (\beta \text{ is the learning constant in the range } [0,1]$$

However, differential learning theory has its own problems. Firstly, it does not correctly model classical conditioning because it considers stimuli (e.g., the food and bell) as being related even when they were not temporally related. Secondly, it presented a linear rather than a (biologically realistic) sigmoidal learning curve.

Harry Klopf, further modified Differential Hebbian Learning to model classical conditioning. *Drive Reinforcement Theory* [4] offers one of the best mathematical representations of classical conditioning and learning.

**Activity equation:**     $Y_j(t) = \Sigma \; w_{ij}(t)[Y_i(t) - T]$

The activity of the j[th.] node is the weighted sum of activity from all the i[th.] nodes.

The weight change is sensitive to a change in the activity of the receiving neurode, multiplied by a weighted sum of the change in activity of the sending neurode

**Weight-change equation:** $\Delta w_{ij} = \beta \Delta Y_j(t-k) \sum_{k=1}^{\tau} \beta |w_{ij}(t-k)| \Delta Y_i(t-k)$

## 12.3.3  Limitations of Differential Equation / Advantages of Discrete Event Models

While drive reinforcement theory provides a good representation of Hebbian learning and a viable model for classical conditioning, it does not represent the physiology of the connections and synaptic weight modifications, namely, the physical factors that affect the behavior of the cell. *In addition, the time-indexing behavioral capabilities afforded by discrete-event models are not exploited. For example, by keeping track of past inputs received, an accurate aggregation of temporally decayed weights is possible.*

Dynamic connections provide us with the tools necessary to make and break connections using the Hebbian paradigm. It also provides a means for dynamic weight modification through reinforcement learning.

While the learning theories presented here have their merit, our approach supplements them by providing a means for topological variability, dynamic weight change and temporal integration; characteristics lacking in traditional neural networks.

## 12.3.4  Real-time Execution and Learning

The following issues need to be addressed for real-time processing:

1.  Training or Learning: Does the network require training before execution? Can the network be trained in the environment? Is training or learning independent from execution, i.e., is it a discrete or ongoing process?

2.  Environmental Characteristics: Is the environment static or dynamic, i.e., does it change over time? For dynamic environments, do they grow in complexity? If so, *load-balancing* may have to be addressed.

3.  Execution Time: Is execution time constant for the network? If not, on what it depend?

4.  Deadlock Avoidance: Are their circular pathways? If so, can the network deadlock by entering any of these paths? What facilities are provided for deadlock avoidance?

In most traditional ANNs, training takes place before execution and no learning is done at run-time. This severely cripples the network. Once trained, any modifications in the environment render it useless.

Most real-world environments are dynamic in nature and require systems to adapt to moderate changes in the environment. DNEs should learn in an unsupervised or self-organizing way, based on Hebbian principles. Each input should be evaluated with respect to the knowledge in the network and changes are propagated. This would integrate learning and execution, where mistakes are made part of the learning experience. Although an optimal response cannot always be guaranteed, a good response based on the information and experience of the DNE can be expected.

The environment for which the network is designed plays a crucial role in determining the feasibility of a specific network. If the environment is highly volatile, the network must have the ability to adapt and correct errors quickly. However, traditional ANNs have been used in relatively constrained environments- where environmental variability is minimized.

For environments that *grow in complexity*, the network may need to grow in size and robustness. DNEs should provide structural variability through the addition and deletion of connections and components (neurodes). Conversely, complex environments may become more deterministic (less volatile and complex). In such cases, being able to remove neurodes and connections and load-balance can significantly improve performance. DNEs should autonomously remove connections and components when their contributions to the network diminish below a user-defined activity level. This can be done by incorporating a rule that *reverses the effects of Hebbian learning*.

Recurrent or circular topologies, always run the danger of **deadlocking** in an infinite loop. Biological systems have provided a number of mechanisms to prevent deadlocking a network or sub-net. *Refractory periods* prevent a cell from firing continuously for an extended period of time. A cell <u>must</u> rest for a fixed period before being able to fire again. This period is referred to as the **absolute refractory period**. For a period following the absolute refractory period, the threshold level exponentially decays from an *infinite value* (during the absolute refractory period) to the *normal threshold value*. This period is referred to as the **relative refractory period**. Inputs received during this period are evaluated against heightened threshold values. DNEs should incorporate both absolute and relative refractory periods.

Inter-neuron communication is accomplished through the release of **neurotransmitters**. Neurotransmitters are chemical substances that are released from the axons or output ports of neurons. The quantity of neurotransmitter in an axon is fixed. As the neurotransmitter decreases (with activation), the output from that axon diminishes. Rapid or continuous firing would cause *depletion* and eventual lack of neurotransmitter in the cell-- preventing it from communicating with other cells. This prevents a cell from firing at its maximum frequency for an extended period of time. Neurotransmitters are replenished by the cells periodically. By modeling this replenishment process in DNEs we can incorporate this mechanism for deadlock avoidance.

Negative or inhibitory inputs provide another mechanism for the deadlock avoidance. Recurrent biological circuits often have inhibitory cells to prevent deadlock. DNEs should also provide the capacity to develop inhibitory nodes.

In real-time systems, an important consideration in network design and development is a means for the transmission of **critical inputs**. An input is deemed *critical* if it has a potentially damaging effect on the environment or system that is being monitored. The relatively slow process of weight modification is not be efficient enough for the emergency on hand. However, critical inputs can be handled through the transmission of multiple output levels. For example, a node may fire at different levels (frequency, neurotransmitter discharge) for different types of inputs where the largest level is reserved for system critical inputs.

## 12.4    Dynamic Neuronal Ensembles

Dynamic Neuronal Ensembles represent a new paradigm for learning, based on biological neural networks. A prototype definition of DNEs was developed using the Discrete Event System Specification (DEVS) formalism [23,26] and implemented in the DEVS-C++ simulation environment [24]. To implement the dynamically changing collections of components we used container classes that support the DEVS-C++ environment [25]. Alternative realizations of dynamic structure DEVS are discussed in [1,22]. The definition, implementation, and examples of application of DNEs are thoroughly presented in a [19]. In this section we review the design of DNEs and discuss their structure and behavior.

### 12.4.1  The Dynamic Neuron

The proposed neuron model is composed of three basic components: the *dendrite*, the *cellbody* and the *axon*.[2] The *dendrite* receives the inputs, adjusts each according to its weighting requirements and requests connection alterations. The cellbody adds the input signals received from its attached dendrites to its decayed potential level. A **fire** signal is sent to the cellbody's attached axons if the potential level meets or exceeds the thresholds. The cellbody makes decisions about the addition or deletion of connections and implements its decisions. Upon receiving a fire signal the *axon* produces an output. This output is weighted with respect to the available neurotransmitter and input values.

The neuron coupled model consists of three kinds of components (Figure 12.4) the dendrites, the cellbody and the axons. Each cellbody can connect with multiple dendrites and axons. The dendrites are the input devices, the cellbody is the controlling device and the axons are the output devices for the neuron model. The following sub-sections discuss, in detail, the functionality of the three classes of components.

---

[2] Background in neurobiology is available in references [17-19]

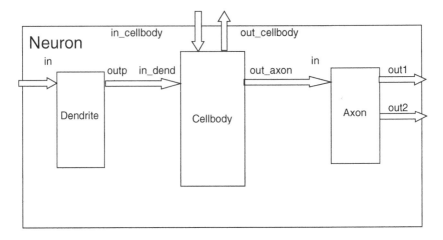

Figure 12.4: The Dynamic Neuron

## 12.4.1.1    The Dendrite Model

The dendrite is as an atomic model (Figure 12.4). Each dendrite receives its inputs from some other neuron's axonal output connections (Figure 12.5). Each dendrite can handle up to three input connections and each connection has its own weighting factor.

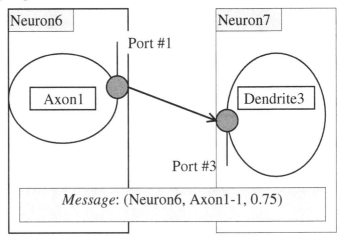

Figure 12.5: Dendrite's input signal.

The input potential can be modified by its connection's weighting factor. A new weighting factor is calculated each time the connection receives an input value. This new weighting factor causes a modification in the strength of the connection. The weighting factor is calculated by first summing all the cumulated weighted inputs that are within a given time period (Eq. 1) and subtracting the last cumulated weighted input from it.

$$present\_cumulative\_weighted\_input == \eta_{i_{(t)}} = \sum_{l=0}^{t-1} \gamma_{il}$$

Eq. 1:
$$where:$$
$$\gamma_i = weighted\_input(connection\_i)$$

The difference between the present and previous cumulative weighted inputs $\left(\eta_{i_{(t)}} - \eta_{i_{(t-1)}}\right)$, is then multiplied by a constant, to scale the impact of the value. To slow the rate of change of the weight values, the constant is set to a value between 0 and 1. The last weight value is then added to the scaled value to reach a new weight factor (Eq. 2).

$$new\_weight == \omega_i = \delta_i + .1*\left(\eta_{i_{(t)}} - \eta_{i_{(t-1)}}\right)$$

Eq. 2:
$$where:$$
$$\delta_i = last\_weight(connection\_i)$$
$$\eta_{i_{(t-1)}} = last\_cumulative\_weighted\_input(connection\_i)$$

The input is then multiplied by the new weight value to reach a new weighted input value (Eq. 3).

$$weighted\_input(connection\_i) == \gamma_i = X_i * \omega_i$$
$$\gamma_i = X_i * \delta_i + .1*\left(\eta_{i_{(t)}} - \eta_{i_{(t-1)}}\right)$$

Eq: 3:
$$where:$$
$$X_i = input\_value(connection\_i)$$
$$\delta_i = last\_weight(connection\_i)$$
$$\eta\eta_{i_{(t-1)}} = last\_cumulative\_weighted\_input(connection\_i)$$
$$\gamma_i = weighted\_input(connection\_i)$$

The weights are updated and the weighted input value is added to the dendrite's potential for each input connection.

After a weight value is calculated, it is tested to ensure that it does not exceed the preset **maximum weight value**. If the new weight value is greater than maximum weight the dendrite will make a request for a **new connection**. After two "add" requests have been received *from the same axon within the predefined* *time period*, the "add a connection" message is emitted when the third "add" message is received. At this time, the present weight of the axon connection is halved.

The stored weighted input values for each connection name will have its *history cleaned* before evaluating its input potentials. The *clean history* function was designed to incorporate recent memory about past events into each cell. To improve the dendrite's ability to modify it weights, i.e., its reaction to external inputs, the removal of past weighting information causes the weights to reflect the latest activity at the input. If the number of weighted input values remaining, after executing "clean history" is equal to zero, the dendrite will request the connection's removal. This indicates that the dendrite has not received any significant input for a fixed period of time. After three "remove" requests from the same axon connection have been received within a preset time period, the connection is removed and this information is sent to the cellbody. All traces of the connection are removed from state variables.

When all the inputs to the dendrite have been received and evaluated the dendrite will be activated and the output signal is sent to its cellbody. The output function can have three possible keys *sum*, *add*, and *remove*. The "sum" key has a float for its value, the "add" key has a set of connections for its value and the "remove" key also has a set of connections for a value. The request from the dendrite to the cellbody to **add** or **remove** connections sets the stage for dynamic modification.

The dendrite's setup method is accessed directly by the cellbody when a new connection to the dendrite is made. This setup method will add the axon identifier and an initial weight value to its weight data function. The setup method also stores the axon identifier (axon name) and time the connection is made. This is useful for tracking modifications to the topology.

## 12.4.1.2    The Cellbody Model

The cellbody is an atomic model. All of the attached dendrites and axons' names and pointers are stored by the cellbody. It therefore acts as the central repository for information within the cell. The cellbody will add and remove connections to its dendrites and from its axons when required. When a new axon or dendrite is added, the cellbody will make an instance of it and add it to the parent digraph model. Messages are passed among the cellbodies for connection modifications.

The cellbody receives an input message from its attached dendrites (Figure 12.6). This message is a function containing three keys, "sum", "add" and "remove". The "sum" key's value is the weighted input received from connected axons, which is summed with all the other input values from other active dendrites in the neuron. The "add" key's value is the set of requested connections to be added to the dendrite. The "remove" key's value is the set of connections to be removed from the dendrite.

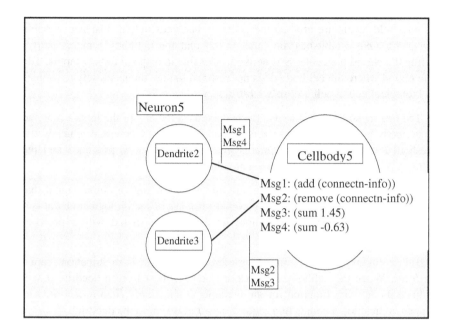

Figure 12.6: A cellbody's input signal "in_dend"

The cellbody also receives an input message on port "in_cellbody" from all the other cellbodies in the network. The message is a function containing three keys, "add", "request" and "remove". The "add" key's value is the set of connections to be added. The "request" key's value is the set of connections requiring a new axon connection. The "remove" key's value is the set of axon connections to be removed.

Instance variable, *decay factor* will influence the duration that the cellbody's potential will be maintained between inputs (Eq. 4). The cellbody will decay its potential level over the elapsed time between inputs before adding the summed input value to its potential level. Mathematically:

$$vv_t = v_{t-1} * e^{-(\tau * \beta)}$$

$$where:$$

Eq. 4:    $$vv_t = cellbody\_potential$$

$$\tau = elasped\_time\_between\_inputs$$

$$\beta = decay\_cons \tan t$$

The updated cellbody potential is tested against the threshold levels, if any of the threshold levels are crossed the cellbody becomes **active**. Instance variable *processing time* establishes the time period that the cellbody remains active. During the period the cellbody is active it is unable to respond to new inputs. The time period where the cellbody does not respond to new inputs closely resembles the biological neural cell's *absolute refractory period* [7].

The *fire* message is sent to its attached axons at the end of the input cycle and the cellbody potential returns to zero. When the cellbody potential is below the threshold levels the cellbody remains **passive**, no output is produced and the cellbody potential remains at its present value.

The output response will vary in amplitude, producing an output signal that approximates the variable frequency output response of the biological neural cell [23]. There are three preset threshold levels each associated with a prefixed firing level.

The cellbody has its connecting dendrites stored in a function called *dendrites*. When the cellbody receives an "add" request from a dendrite it will evaluate its dendrite function for an available connection. When a dendrite has an open connection a connection request message is sent to the dendrite.

With no existing dendrite connections available, the cellbody will check if the number of its dendrites is less then the maximum number of possible dendrites. When the number of dendrites is less then the maximum number of dendrites the cellbody will make a new dendrite and add its pointer to the parent model. The connecting cellbody receives the "request" message and tests if an axon connection is available.

When the cellbody receives a "remove" request from a dendrite it will remove the dendrite from its dendrite function and remove the connection between the dendrite and axon.

The axons function records information about the attached axons. Keys for axons are the axon names and the values are the axon identifiers for the active outputs.

When the cellbody receives a request for a new connection a *recharge* message is sent to the axon with the corresponding connection identifier, in the original connection. This feedback will allow an axon to *increase its neurotransmitter percentage due to a successful triggering at its input destination.*

When a connection is available on an existing axon, the axon name and identifier are returned to the cellbody requesting a connection. When no existing axon connection is available, the cellbody will check to see if its number of connecting axons is less then its maximum number of possible axons. In this case a new axon is created, and this information is returned.

When the cellbody receives a remove message, it will remove the axon from the "axons" function and send a message to the corresponding axon.

Upon receiving the "add" message from another cellbody, a connection is added to the "dendrites" function. The dendrite that the connection is being added to will have its setup executed. A dendrite's setup method prepares the dendrite to receive messages on a new connection. Coupling required from the new connection's axon to the dendrite and from the axon to the transducer is added here.

The cellbody can add and remove the connections upon receiving the request from the dendrite. *Increasing and decreasing connections between neurons demonstrates its ability to grow.* This growth is similar to the biological neural cell's ability to make alterations in the synaptic connections.

All outputs are stored in the output functions "output axon" (for output to the axon) and "output cellbody" (for output to the cellbody). These functions will be executed at the end of each active cycle and then cleared.

## 12.4.1.3    The Axon Model

This subsection provides a detailed description of the axon's functionality. The axon receives an input from its cellbody. Figure 12.7 shows the messages received by the axons. The input message, a function, can consist of up to four keys "fire", "recharge", "add", and "remove". The key "fire" has a value that indicates the fire level. The remaining keys "recharge," "add" and "remove" have a set of axon identifiers for their values. This input message is broadcast to all the axons connected to the cellbody. An axon has only two output ports. At any time both, one or none of the output ports can be active. Which of the ports are active is controlled by the cellbody and depends on the requirement for connections.

On receiving the *fire* signal from its cellbody the axon will produce an output signal. The axon's output signal is computed using the input fire signal level, the type of axon, the percentage of neurotransmitters and the preset axon output value. The key "fire" tells the axon to prepare an output signal according to the equation below (Eq. 5).

$$axon\_potential = \alpha = c * \rho * \zeta * \kappa$$

$$where:$$

Eq. 5:
$$c = constant, \pm 1$$

$$\rho = percent\_neurotransmitter$$

$$\zeta = standard\_output\_level$$

$$\kappa = input\_threshold\_level$$

The axon's potential is the product of a **constant** (that determines the *polarity of the cell*), the **level of neurotransmitter** in stock (as a percentage), **a**

**standard output level** and an **input threshold level**. When the constant is set to a negative one at setup time, the axon output is negative and causes the neuron to be an *inhibitor*. The constant will default to a positive one to provide an *excitatory* neuron. The percentage of neurotransmitters originally equals 100% (1.0) and is decreased by 5% each time an output signal is sent with the value never going below 50%. The standard output level is a constant used to adjust the level of axon's output potential. The decreasing value of neurotransmitter and standard output level value can be redefined at setup. Input threshold levels can range from 1 to 3. Level 3 being the highest. Each level has its own characteristic output and frequency.

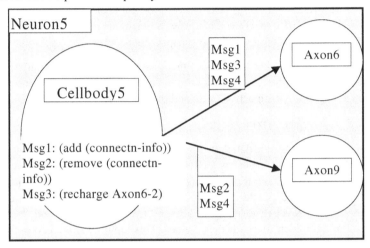

Figure 12.7: Axon Input Signal "in".

The axon tests to ensure that the message belongs to itself by testing if the message's axon name is matches its own before executing actions from keys "recharge", "add" and "remove". If the identification test is satisfied the following actions are executed.

If the axon has not received any input from the cellbody for the predetermined time period specified by instance variable "recharge time", the neurotransmitter level will be reset to 80% (0.80). Each port has its own neurotransmitter value. Upon receiving the key "recharge", the axon will test which port is to receive the recharge and then add to its percentage of neurotransmitters an amount of fifteen points, never going above 150%. When key "add" is received, the axon will check the axon identifier and activate the port specified by the axon identifier. The axon will initially be setup with port one active and port two inactive. When the key "remove" is received, the axon will get the axon identifier name and deactivate the specified port.

### *12.4.1.4      Component Naming Convention*

Cellbodies are named with single capital letters such as A, B or C. Dendrites are named with the capital letter of their attached cellbody and a lower case letter indicating which dendrite. For example, the first, second and third attached dendrites to cellbody A are Aa, Ab and Ac, respectively. An Axon's name starts with a lower case 'a', a capital letter of its attached cellbody, a lower case letter indicating which axon and a the number 0 or 1 indicating the output port. For example, the first, second and third attached axons to cellbody B are aBa1, aBb1 and aBc0, respectively

## 12.4.2 Ensembles of Dynamic Neurons

DNE are ensembles or inter-connected collections of *dynamic neurons*. Each neuron represents a node in the network of interconnections. Using the principles discussed in Section 3.1 (Embedding Knowledge), *dynamic neurons* may be interconnected through their components (axons and dendrites). This is done by connecting axonal ports to available ports on dendrites. Each *dynamic neuron* is given a unique identifier (see **Component Naming Convention** in Section 4.1) to distinguish it from other nodes in the environment. The process of connecting is used to develop the desired network topology. *Connection weights* and *cell thresholds* are initialized using the **setup methods** provided by the component classes.

## 12.5   Example: A DNE Model to Distinguish Threats from Annoyances in the Environment

A system has only limited resources at its disposal and can't afford to waste them on non-threatening stimuli, however annoying they may be. On the other hand, if stimuli appear that signal major threats to survival then the tuning out has to be reversed and attention paid to these stimuli. Snails exhibit this kind of behavior. They quickly tune out low level repetitive inputs that could be normal sea waves so that they rest quietly in place. However, if their shells start taking a pounding, their reaction quickly grows more sensitive to the same stimuli. Modeling of this kind of habituation (tuning out) / hypersensitization (tuning in) behavior seems ideally suited to the DNE concept. Habituation develops naturally from using up synaptic resources while hypersensitivity can be explained by increasing weights and eventually adding connections – a particular feature of DNEs not found in most other neural network models.

An *Aplysia* is a large marine snail whose nervous system was first studied in 1803.

The *Aplysia* has distinct neural responses to different levels of external stimuli. One of these distinct responses is the *gill-withdrawal reflex*. The strength of this reflex will decrease from a recurrent mild external stimulus. However, a potentially dangerous level of stimuli will increase the sensitivity to a mild stimulus. The **defensive** gill-withdrawal reflex is caused by a strong or potentially dangerous stimulus to the *Aplysia* body. After such a stimulus the gill-withdrawal reflex *reacts more vigorously to mild or weak stimulus* [9] A single electrical shock to the tail of the *Aplysia* increases the gill-withdrawal response for up to an hour. Repeated shocks increase the duration of the heightened response to mild stimulus. These habituation/hypersensitization behaviors were demonstrated in laboratory experiments by Kandel, Castellucci and Byrne [3].

Based on these experiments, DNEs were used to model the neural circuit and behavior of the snail Aplysia. Using the same DNE model two behavioral tests were performed, the first tested the response of the gill-withdrawal reflex, while the other was designed to capture the defensive gill-withdrawal which is a result of hypersensitization.

## 12.5.1 The Gill-Withdrawal Reflex of the *Aplysia*

Figure 12.8 shows the gill-withdrawal reflex model configuration. Approximately 24 sensory neuron cells participate in the gill-withdrawal reflex. Each time the siphon (skin) is given a point stimulus only about eight sensory neurons are excited [3]. The sensory neurons make *direct connections* to at least one inhibitor interneuron (L16) and two excitatory interneurons (L22, L23). Neurons (L16, L22, L23) supply input stimulus to the motor neurons (L7, LDG1, LDG2, RDG, L9G1, L9G2). The three major motor neurons (L7, LDG1, LDG2) make direct connections with the gill. The three minor motor neurons (RDG, L9G1, L9G2) are assumed to make direct connections. Removing either major motor neurons (L7 or LDG1) from the network will result in a reduction of the reflex response by 30-40 percent [9].

## 12.5.2  DNE Model of Aplysia

One model was developed to demonstrate both the gill-withdrawal reflexes. This model involves three layers with the first layer including eight sensory neurons (S1, through S8). The second layer includes the interneurons (Int.2 ensemble, L16, L22, L23) and the third layer the motor neurons (L7, LDG1, LDG2, RDG, L9G1, L9G2). A generator supplied the input stimulus to the sensory neurons and the transducer will receive the motor neurons' responses.

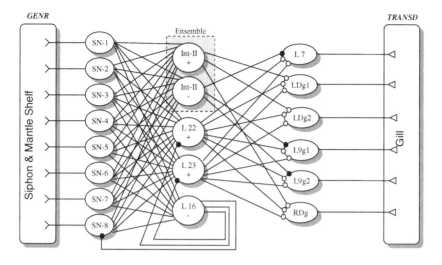

Figure 12.8: Circuit/Network Diagram for Gill Withdrawal

## 12.5.3  Response of DNE Model to Mild Stimuli

The generator provides a low level input every 30 time units for 10 cycles (Figure 12.9) then no input for one 100 time units cycle to allow the neurons to recharge themselves. After the recharge time period the low level input is repeated every 30 time units for another 10 cycles. This cycle is repeated three times and the output results are shown in Figure 12.10. The clean history method is set to 500 time units.

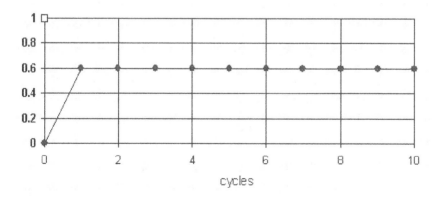

Figure 12.9: Repeated Mild Input Stimulus

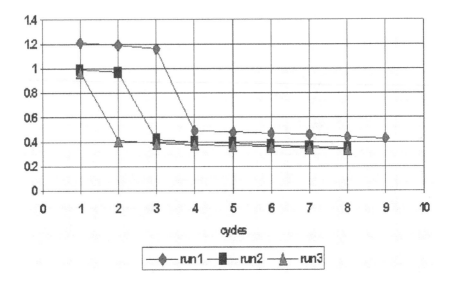

Figure 12.10: Motor Neurons Output Response

The motor neurons output decrease in response by approximately 60 percent after three cycles during the first simulation run. After each rest period the decrease in the response occurred in fewer cycles. The peak output amplitude of the second and third simulation runs were lower than the maximum amplitude by approximately 18 percent. The motor neurons internal potential is below minimum threshold level during the ninth or tenth cycle.

## 12.5.4 Response of DNE Model to Strong Stimuli

The generator provides a series of inputs during the simulations. In the first simulation run the first two inputs are weak, the next two inputs are strong, the following inputs again are weak and the clean history time period is set to 250. During the second simulation run the first three inputs are weak, the next four inputs are strong, the following inputs again are weak and the clean history time period is set to 500. The third simulation run has the first two inputs are weak, the next seven inputs are strong, the following inputs again are weak and the clean history time period is set to 550. Figure 12.11 shows the sensory neurons input stimulus and Figure 12.12 shows the motor neuron's output results.

During the first simulation run the motor neurons maintain an increased output response level, to mild stimuli, for one cycle after the two strong input pulses. The motor neurons then display a decrease in output response seen in the previous simulation. In the second simulation run the motor neurons maintain an elevated output level response, to mild stimuli, for three cycles after the four strong input pulses.

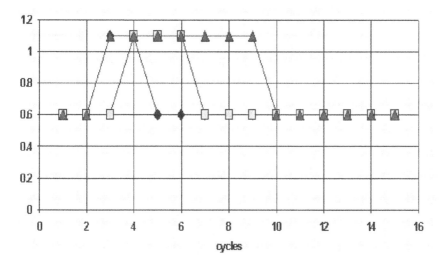

Figure 12.11: Stimulus for Strong Input

The third simulation produces a much stronger response after the seven strong inputs. In the 12 cycle the sensory neurons request new connections to the interneurons. The new connections cause an increase in the input drive to the interneuron from the sensory neurons resulting in an extended duration of increased response to mild stimuli in the motor neuron's output.

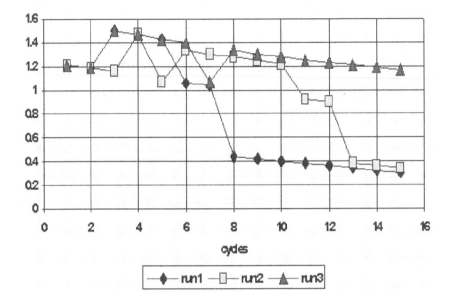

Figure 12.12: Output Response to Strong Input Stimulus

## 12.5.5 Results of DNE Aplysia modeling

The Aplysia model displayed habituation through a decrease in the strength of the gill-withdrawal reflex from a recurrent mild external stimulus. The neurotransmitter depletion and recharge provided the dynamic neuron ensemble with the ability to exhibit this response. An increase in sensitivity to a mild external stimulus after a potentially dangerous stimulus was also successfully modeled. The case study demonstrates the dynamic neural ensemble's ability to learn similarly to the biological neural network of the *Aplysia's* gill-withdrawal reflex.

Experience with using the DEVS-C++ implementation of DNEs showed that there are many parameters (e.g., depletion rate, recharge level, etc.) that need to be set to make a model behave in the desired fashion. Moreover, values are often interdependent, so that a sequential search approach will not work. Although it was a non-trivial task to determine combinations values, we found that it could be managed with some effort in the fairly small net we used to the results demonstrated above. The combinatorial problem is a definitely a barrier to overcome as networks of interest grow larger. However, experience with smaller nets, and the values for parameters that work with them, may carry over to greatly reduce the calibration problem for larger nets.

In this chapter two examples of engineering applications are discussed. The first is a design for a controller for a chemical plant. The second is an application of the DNE model of habituation and hyper-sensitization, developed for the snail Aplysia, incorporated into a spatial decision making.

## 12.6   DNE Control Application: Dynamic Control in a Chemical Plant

The advent of sophisticated sensors of different types (temperature, pressure, light etc.) has laid the basis for development of more autonomous production lines. Control, however is still done with some human intervention. The primary reason for humans in the process control loop is the uncertainty and unreliability of production parameters with respect to time and quality.

Controllers that have been designed to function for fixed time/quality processes have had little success in the real-world. Expert systems and AI based fuzzy systems have enjoyed some success [13]. Controllers capable of mapping domain/control information and changing with the environment are needed. DNEs provide the support for dynamic control and enable domain-based control information to be mapped into the network topology and weights.

The example presented here is one for a chemical production company (Figure 12.13). The chemical or fluid produced at this plant contains essential, insoluble salts and minerals. The fluid density and viscosity must be constantly checked to maintain the concentrations needed. The motor is turned on in the storage tank to maintain optimal fluid concentrations. This fluid is pumped into trucks for delivery to a customer. There is a cost associated with keeping a truck waiting for more than the time needed to fill the truck. The *objective function* uses a cost optimization algorithm to minimize this cost.

Control is accomplished through the **sensors** and **actuators** provided in the assembly to track states and initiate actions, respectively. The state of the system is defined as follows:

$S = \{Vi, Vo, Fl, T, TL, Fd, M\}$
where:

| | |
|---|---|
| $Vi$ : | Input Valve (open=1) |
| $Vo$: | Output Valve (open=1) |
| $Fl$: | Level of Fluid in the tank. (high=1) |
| $T$: | Truck Weight Sensor (truck-in=1) |
| $TL$: | Level of fluid in Truck (full=1) |
| $Fd$: | Fluid density or viscosity (normal=1) |
| $M$: | Motor (on=1) |

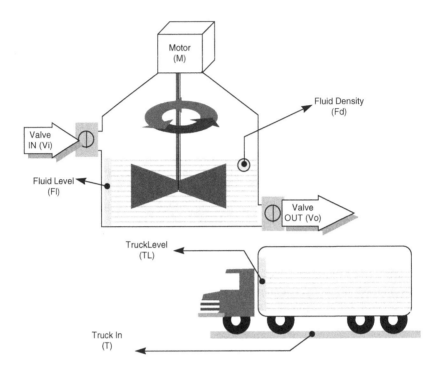

Figure 12.13: Graphical Representation of Chemical Plant

There are four (4) sensors in the system: the $Fl$ (tank fluid level), $Fd$ (fluid density or viscosity), $T$ (truck weight) and $TL$ (truck fluid level) sensors. The three actuators control the input and output valves ($Vi$ and $Vo$) and the motor in the tank ($M$).

The system's state transition diagram is given below (Figure 12.14). The dark lines indicate sensory inputs into the system, while the lighter lines are actuator inputs. The objective function is used to evaluate a conflicting scenario, where a cost-based decision needs to be made. In the event that a truck arrives when the fluid level or density is not optimal, the motor needs to be turned on to mix the fluid in the tank and get the correct texture or an even density. However, the truck may have to wait while the fluid is being mixed- this will cost the production unit. On the other hand, supplying un-mixed or non-optimal fluid will also incur a cost through loss in sales. Using quantitative data, available from the sensors, the objective function will determine the course of action that should to pursued to minimize cost.

Using domain information, available from the state transition diagram (Figure 12.14) we develop a DNE with the sensor modeled as sensory Dn.s and the actuators models as motor Dn.s (Figure 12.15).

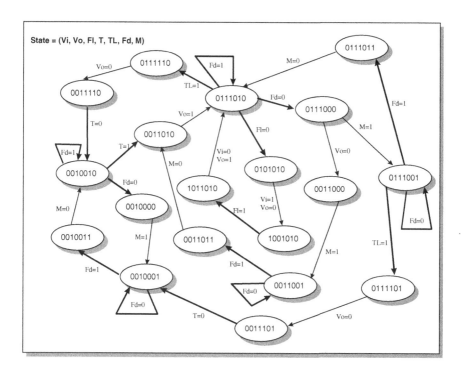

Figure 12.14: State Transition Diagram

In the DNE model all thresholds for the interneurons are equal to one (1), as shown by the number in the right half circle. Connections that terminate in a small white circle, are **excitatory** or positive connections. Likewise, the connections that terminate in a black circle are **inhibitory** connections. All connection weights are equal to one (1.0) unless explicitly shown.

In addition to the sensory, inter and motor (or output) neurons, an attention unit is provided to activate the DNE. If any system parameter changes, an input is provided to the attention component and signals are sent to the interneurons in the DNE (Figure 12.15).

Vi :      Input Valve (open=1)
Vo:      Output Valve (open=1)
Fl:      Level of Fluid in the tank. (high=1)
T:      Truck Weight Sensor (truck-in=1)
TL:      Level of fluid in Truck (full=1)
Fd:      Fluid density or viscosity (normal=1)
M:      Motor (on=1)

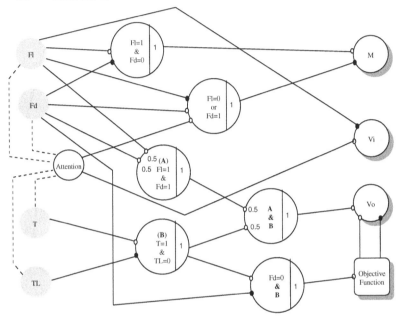

Figure 12.15: DNE Model of Controller

A positive input to a motor neuron activates (turns on/opens) that component, while a negative input to a motor neuron will deactivate (shutdown/close) the component. For example a positive input to the motor will start the motor, and the same input to the input valve will open the valve. Conversely, if negative inputs are received by the motor and the input valve, the motor will be turned off and the valve will be closed. However, if both positive and negative inputs are received by the motor neurons concurrently, no action is taken by the actuator.

The topology provides an intuitive representation of system states and their transitions. We expect that over time the network will become more efficient at responding to system changes because of changes made to connections and weights. Although it has not been implemented, the example illustrates how domain knowledge may be initially installed into a DNE and later modified on-line.

# 12.7    Conclusions and Future Work

In this paper we have presented a new paradigm for the development of artificial neural networks. The uniqueness of the paradigm stems from the approach underlying their design and development. While most developments in ANN come from mathematical manipulations and enhancements to algorithms, DNEs approach the problem from a neurobiological perspective. Current and traditional network paradigms seem to have lost touch with the seed that bore them – the neurobiological networks found in animate systems.

## 12.7.1 Dynamic Neuronal Ensembles: Complementing Current ANNs

We believe that the neurosciences have a great deal to offer the intelligent systems and dynamic control systems communities, and DNEs attempt to scratch this surface. The DNE paradigm provides a tool for the conceptual development of dynamic learning and control systems.

The Dynamic Neural Ensemble (DNE) paradigm, although capable of performing in traditional neural network domains, provides additional features that make it especially useful in dynamic, real-time environment.

The ability to **embed domain-dependent knowledge** into a network radically simplifies the training process for learning and control type problems.

A **dynamic implementation** of **Hebbian learning** provides classical conditioning type learning in uncertain environments.

**Learning during execution** provides a paradigm capable of performing in real time. The incorporation of safety features such as **deadlock avoidance** and **critical input handling** strengthen the case for the use of DNEs in real-time learning and control.

We do not claim that DNEs are the best paradigm for learning and control. We do, however, suggest that the DNE paradigm has a lot to offer traditional neural network paradigms, from a conceptual and implementational point of view.

## 12.7.2 How DNEs Exploit the DEVS Formalism and Object-Orientation

By developing the DNE in an object-oriented environment (C++), within the DEVS formalism, we provide modularity, reusability and information hiding.

*Modularity* provides *closure under coupling*. Each component is treated as an independent entity, free from functional dependencies. The only constants required by a component are its input andoutput ports and message structures. We could therefore modify a component's internal behavior (its algorithm and internal structure) without having to modify other components in the environment. This proves to be extremely helpful in keeping up with advances made in the neurosciences, for this application.

*Reusability*, enables the creation of multiple copies or instances of a single component or structure without having to start with unconnected nodes. For example, we could develop a controller for a sub-system and reuse its design to expand applicability to the entire system. For DNEs, we therefore have the ability to save entire ensembles and edit them or incorporate them into other larger (or more robust) ensembles when the need arises. This characteristic is also true at the component or *dynamic neuron* level.

*Information hiding*, protects the initialization setup for components, nodes and ensembles. Component or model parameters are accessible through pre-defined methods and cannot be modifies accidentally during setup, initialization or a rerun. This is necessary to maintain component and ensemble validity during execution.

The object-oriented paradigm provides the implementation with the flexibility and maintenance required for usability and robustness. The DEVS formalism provides us with an environment to design, develop and simulate the dynamic neuronal ensembles.

## 12.7.3  Relation to Other Discrete Event Biologically Relevant Neuron Models

Work on alternative neuron architectures has recently yielded a strong argument for "one spike per neuron" processing in natural neural systems [6] "One-spike-per-neuron" refers to information transmission from neuron to neuron by single pulses (spikes) rather than pulse trains or firing frequencies. A face recognition multi-layered neural architecture based on the one-spike principles has been demonstrated to better conform to the known time response constraints of human processing and also to execute computationally much faster than a comparable conventional artificial neural net [17]. The distinguishing feature of the one-spike neural architecture is that it relies on a temporal, rather than firing rate, code for propagating information through neural processing layers. This means that an interneuron fires as soon as it has accumulated sufficient "evidence" and therefore the latency to the first spike codes the strength of this input. Single spike information pulses are thus able to traverse a multi-layered hierarchy asynchronously and as fast as the evidential support allows.

The one-spike neurons offer a second example of the utility of discrete event abstractions of biological neurons. These neurons can be formulated as order-of-arrival processors in that they are sensitive to the order of arrival of stimuli from different sources [6]. Nets of these neurons are much faster and more efficient in terms of use of neurons than conventional counterparts. Use of discrete pulses and information transmission based on their timing is a unique feature of discrete event models. Formal properties of the DEVS formalism, such reactivity to input pulses and hierarchical construction are well-matched to formulating such models. Thus dynamic neuron ensembles and order-of-arrival neuron nets provide two examples of the applicability of discrete event principles to express interesting and useful dynamical systems properties.

Work Needed to Render DNEs as a Practical Control System Technology

Although we have demonstrated the applicability of the Dynamic Neuron Ensemble, and its parent, the DEVS formalism, to models of biological and technical systems, there is still much to do to achieve this potential and gain wide spread acceptance in the research and applications communities. As mentioned, the calibration process must be simplified for user convenience either through guidelines developed from experience or automation of parameter space search. For example, we could use of a DNA-like genetic representation of DNE structure and its parameters for network optimization and system definition. It should be noted as well, that conventional neural nets also have troublesome training methods and long training times and their success often depends on the expertise of the human user to set up the proper training regime. Thus, the expressiveness and ability of DNEs to support initial knowledge embedding, may afford an attractive alternative to conventional neural net designs.

# Acknowledgements

I would like to thank Dr. Bernard Zeigler for his help in revising this paper for publication in this book. Thanks also to Dr. Hessam Sarjoughian for his efforts to assure the high quality of this paper and this book.

# References

[1]    Barros, F. (1996). *Dynamic Structure DSDEVS:Structural Inheritance in the DELTA Environment*. AI, Simulation and Planning in High Autonomy Systems, San Diego, Web: www-ais.arizona.edu.

[2]    Braitenberg, V. *Vehicles: Experiments in Synthetic Psychology*. The MIT Press, Cambridge, Ma. (1987).

[3]    Byrne, C., V. Castellucci, and E. Kandel, *Contribution of Individual Mechanoreceptor Sensory Neurons to Defensive Gill Withdrawal Reflex in Aplysia*. J. Neurophysiology, 1978. 41(1): p. 413-431.

[4] Caudill, Maureen and Butler, Charles. *Understanding Neural Networks Volume 1: Basic Networks*. The MIT Press, Massachusetts Institute of Technology, Cambridge, MA. (1994).

[5] Eccles, S.J. and e. al., Synapse, in *The Biological Bases of Behavior*, N. Chalmers, R. Crawley, and S.P.R. Rose, Editors. 1971, Open University Press: London.

[6] Gautrais, J. and S. Thorpe (1998). *"Rate Coding Versus Temporal Coding: A Theoretical Approach."* BioSystems 48(1-3): 57-65.

[7] Grossberg, S. and M. Kuperstein, *Neural Dynamics of Adaptive Sensory-Motor Control*. Expanded ed. ed. Neural networks, research and applications. 1989, New York: Pergamon Pub.

[8] Hebb, Donald O. *The Organization of Behavior: A Neurophysiological Theory*, Wiley Pub. New York, NY (1949).

[9] Kandel, E.R., *Behavioral Biology of Aplysia. Books in Psychology*, ed. R.e.a. Atkinson. 1979, San Francisco, Ca.: W. H. Freeman & Co.

[10] Koestler, A. *Janus: The Summing Up*. Hutchinson Pub., London, UK. (1978).

[11] Levitan, I.B. and L.K. Kaczmarek, *The Neuron: Cellular & Molecular Biology*. 1991, New York: Oxford University Press.

[12] Minsky, M. and Papert, S. *Perceptrons: An introduction to Computational Geometry*. The MIT Press, Cambridge MA. (1969).

[13] Passino, K. and P. J. Antsaklis, Modeling &Analysis of Artificially Intelligent Planning Systems, in An Introduction to Intelligent and Automonous Control, P.J. Antsaklis and K. M. Passino, Editors. 1992, Kluwer Academic Pub.: Boston, MA. P. 191-214

[14] Pollock, John L. *Contemporary Theories of Knowledge*. Rowman & Littlefield Pub., Inc. Savage, ML (1986).

[15] Reichert, H., *Introduction to Neurobiology*. 1992, New York: Oxford U. Press.

[16] Rosenblatt, F. *Principles of neurodynamics; perceptrons and the theory of brain mechanisms*. Washington, Spartan Books,1962

[17] Rullen, R. V., J. Gautrais, et al. (1998). *"Face Processing Using One Spike Per Neurone."* BioSystems 48(1-3): 229-239.

[18] Rumelhart, D.E. and the PDP Research group, *"Parallel Distributed Processing: Explorations in the microstructure of cognition"*, Cambridge, MA MIT Press.

[19] Sankait, V. *"Dynamic neuronal ensembles : a new paradigm for learning"*, Doctoral Dissertation, Tucson, Arizona : University of Arizona, 1996

[20] Shannon, C.E. and J. McCarthy: *Theory of Neural-Analog Reinforcement Systems & Its Applications to the Brain-Model Problem*. Automata Studies, Princeton, NJ., Princeton Univ. Press.

[21] Shepherd, G. and C. Koch, *Introduction to Synaptic Circuits, in The Synaptic Organization of the Brain*, G. Shepherd, Editor. 1990, O.U.P.: New York. p. 3-31.

[22] Uhrmacher, A. M. and B. P. Zeigler (1996).*Variable Structure Models in Object-Oriented Simulation*. Int. J. Gen. Systems 24(4): 359-375.

[23] Zeigler, B.P. *Object-Oriented Simulation with Hierarchical Modular Models*. Academic Press (1990).

[24] Zeigler, B. P., Y. Moon, et al. (1997). *"The DEVS Environment for High-Performance Modeling and Simulation."* IEEE Comp. Sci. & E ng, 4(3): 61-71.

[25] Zeigler, B. P. *Objects and Systems*. Springer-Verlag Pub., New York, NY (1997).

[26] Zeigler, B. P., Praehofer, H., and T.G. Kim, *Theory of Modeling and Simulation*, Academic Press (2000).

# Chapter 13

# Simulation for Meaning Generation: Multiscale Coalitions of Autonomous Agents

A.M. Meystel

*This paper is inspired by B. Zeigler's book [33]. The paper is just trying to emphasize the semiotic essence of B. Zeigler's results. There is more to these results than further development of the theory of computer software, object oriented programming, and associated application engineering. The book is permeated by the underlying connections to intelligence and intelligent systems within the scope of their multidisciplinary semiotic associations. The paper should make this streak more explicit.*

## 13.1  Global Semiotics of Virtual Agents: Simulating Complex Systems

*Encyclopedia Britannica* defines *simulation* in "industry, science, and education, as a research or teaching techniques that reproduce actual events and processes under test conditions." Certainly, the term "reproduce" is a stretch: most of the simulation techniques do not aspire to achieve more than just approximate this actual event/process. Says Britannica: "Developing a simulation is often a highly complex mathematical process. Initially a set of rules, relationships, and operating procedures are specified, along with other variables." That's true: simulation starts with developing a model as a combination of diversified tools. Undoubtedly, this process is not bound by just "mathematics." Anything goes – just make the system of these tools approximate well. Once the contrivance of the model is here, we can do with it much more than we intended. As Britannica promises: "The interaction of these phenomena create new situations, even new rules, which further evolve as the simulation proceeds."

The description of simulation with goal, its tools, and its promise is amazingly similar to the description of *intelligence*. It has been developed in living creatures as a mechanism of simulation. It is intended to reproduce and anticipate events and processes with maximum similarity, it requires a model which usually employs a system of knowledge representation. Once emerged it helps us to create images of possible worlds, simulate unexpected situations in these worlds and derive new rules, theories and laws. It is a commonplace that it uses signs and symbols to model, it develop possible worlds that are quicker and cheaper than the real world, thus it can help to learn the future before it happens, it allows to anticipate, it warns, alerts and tempts with all consequences of these unsettled verbs. Of course, this requires more than mathematics: it requires all ammunition of Semiotics (including mathematics). So, it looks like Semiotics (including mathematics) is the proper toolbox applied by our intelligence).

More people are interested in semiotics than in mechanisms of intelligence. If you have doubts, check the cyberspace. However, only a small fraction of these people links semiotics with *what semiotics really is: the science of intelligence*. Before XIX$^{th}$ Century, Intelligence was a non-constructive subject, it was an introspective issue. XX$^{th}$ Century has demonstrated that Intelligence is the core of all issues, while Semiotics is a tool of understanding and constructing Intelligence. This role of semiotics generally follows from its definitions: we just should read them properly.

The ubiquitous Encyclopaedia Britannica says also that semiotics "is a study of signs and sign-using behavior, including the use of words, of tone of voice, tempo, or drawl, of body motions and gestures and animal communication." Although, this definition appeals to and is understood by laymen, it contains the spirit of semiotic essence: semiotics is a science of signs. Why signs? The signs transmit compressed information, or messages; the messages contain meanings concerning the events and processes; the meanings are constructed and produced by intelligence from signs and the inner knowledge; now, we are equipped for further simulating activities. So, *Signs and their processing (the body of semiotics) embody Intelligence (the machinery for simulation)*. Some would even say, they embody "Life and Intelligence" since the manifestations of these phenomena are very similar as far as signs are concerned. In Figure 13.1, the types of semiotics are shown that depend on the general strata of human activities where semiotic is used., then the descriptive domains within these areas are shown. Finally it boils down to the five major groups of methodological tools employed within semiotics.

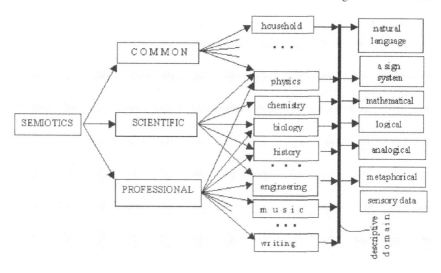

Figure 13.1: Types of semiotics

Yet, I would like to be fair to the rest of Nature. Inanimate objects produce signs, too. They even can be considered signs of themselves. The process of communication between two atoms of hydrogen and one atom of oxygen leads to a formation of the molecule of water. Looks like a stretch? I would not say so: the laws of forming and communicating the messages in this example are similar to the corresponding laws typical for living creatures. These atoms behave as "semiotic agents." We can talk about semiotic agents without specifying whether we mean animate or inanimate Nature.

In addition, when we, the living creatures are talking about the matters of Life and Intelligence, it is natural and productive to use metaphors: they help us to simulate things known only generally, i.e. with the level of detail insufficient for the thorough simulation. But make no mistake: metaphors are a legitimate mechanism of simulation at a particular level of generalization. So, let us allow the inanimate world to talk about us, too; and let it use its cold and lifeless metaphors. We will escape this confrontation between animate and inanimate phenomena by attaching *semiotics* to an *agent*. We will talk about *semiotic agents*. We will construct systems for simulation based upon semiotic agents. The role of semiotics will be to describe and predict these agents' behavior, to explicate meaning of these agents, to interpret them and the situations related to them. The role of simulation will be to create the imaginary worlds and processes within these worlds by using semiotic agents and subject the results for the subsequent semiotic interpretation.

## 13.2  The Worlds Are Multimodal

As we can see from Figure 13.1, the descriptive domain is irrelevant: as soon as we apply semiotic methodology for simulating the World, we should be proficient in formal techniques that semiotics employs: natural language, mathematics, logic, the skill of finding analogies, and the skill (art) of constructing metaphors.

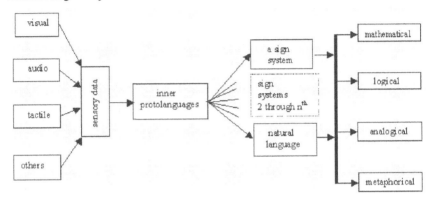

Figure 13.2: Transformation of sensory modalities into semiotic representations

However, there is one additional important distinction between the information units and their semiotic carriers. This distinction is related to *sensory modality* of communication associated with all information units represented via semiotic entities. Obviously, the Worlds are encoded by using a combination of sensory modalities (see Figure 13.2). Indeed, information units can be communicated in natural language by using various modalities of it: oral (the source of the message is talking, the recipient is listening), written (the source is writing, the recipient is reading), visual (the source of language moves lips, the recipient reads the lip movements; both the source and recipient use a sign system based upon natural language), tactile (natural language statements are transmitted via system of tactile signs).

## 13.3  The World is Meaningful if the Property of Closure Holds

Semiotic systems for understanding the Worlds are shown in the right side of Figure 13.2. Protolanguages encode the diversity of sensory information so that the unity could be achieved in the World representation. Obviously, using only protolanguages for understanding and communicating this understanding is insufficient, and a variety of sign systems emerges: mathematical, logical, analogical and metaphorical languages. All of them offer their tools of generalization and inference. All of them allow for representing the World's closure as thetemplate for registering consistency of the World, as the initial source of causal explanations of the empirical reality.

Closure in a space of tasks such that this occurs is an objective property of real systems [22, 16]. It is shown

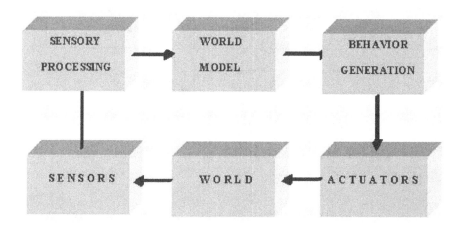

Figure 13.3: Semiotic Closure

In Figure 13.3, The closure emerges because the World is sensed (SENSORS), encoded and perceived (SENSORY PROCESSING), represented and reasoned (WORLD MODEL) not only for communication but in order to generate behavior (BEHAVIOR GENERATION) and enable actions (ACTUATORS) that eventually change the WORLD. If closure would not hold, the goal-oriented activity would not be possible. The phenomenon of closure reflects the thesis of rationality underlying the very thesis of the need for simulation. It is not a matter of having inputs and outputs specified properly; it is a matter of having a loop *necessarily*. The diagram in Figure 13.3 is called Elementary Loop of Functioning (ELF). If ELF cannot be demonstrated, then information of the system, its components, its variables, its goals, etc., must be incomplete. Semioticians call this loop: the loop of *semiosis*. In this loop the process of learning and interpretation is run, and the convergence of it should be achieved.

Thus, as we reason about the World and its processes, the property of closure should be satisfied. Thus, as we construct a simulation system, the property of closure should be satisfied with the help of this simulation system. In Figure 13.4, a structure of closure is shown as an Elementary Loop of Functioning for the case of intelligent controller simulated functioning.

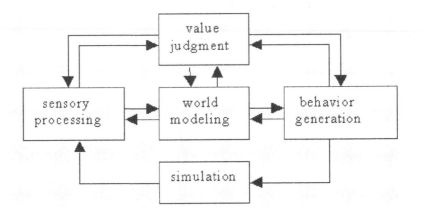

Figure 13.4: ELF for a Simulation of an Intelligent Control System

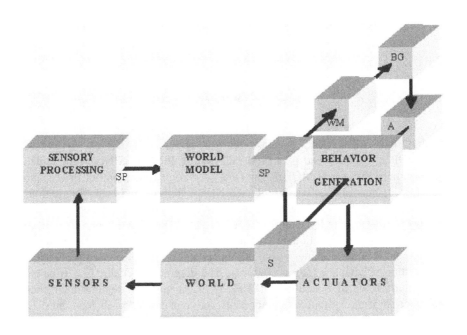

Figure 13.5: ELF for a system shown with ELF of one of its modules.

An ELF within an ELF is shown in Figure 13.5 for behavior generation module. The modules ACTUATORS-WORLD-SENSORS are to be substituted by a simulation system that receives control commands from the intelligent controller and generate simulated sensor inputs for it. For a simulation system, the components of the system functioning associated with value judgment should be explicated and made available for observation. Certainly, functioning of ELF's modules can be described adequately only if ELFs can be constructed for its modules, too.

## 13.4   The Meaning is Multiresolutional!

Through millenia people use the phenomena of larger and smaller pictures, bird's eye vie, etc. However, only recently we have arrived at the scientific awareness of the following: we see the same things and recognize different objects and phenomena depending on spatial and temporal resolution of our interest. B. Mandelbrot's fractals came as a surprise [15] because suddenly we realized that at different scales there is always more than the eye can see. All signs pertain to some particular scale of consideration. Semiotic offers its views also in scales: it is a multiscale, or multiresolutional phenomenon, too. (See more about this in [16]).

Therefore, no matter whether you are a follower of Frege's analysis of dual correspondence between the sign and the object, or you consider Peirce's triangles scientifically adequate, do not forget that each triangle pertains to its own resolution. Each scale encompasses a particular World with its vocabularies, grammars, goals and pursuit of happiness pertaining to this particular scale.

Each scale has its system of signs and is related to the adjacent scales by the set of rules that represent relationships of generalization (bottom-up) and instantiation (top-down) that exist between the scales. In Figure 13.6, an example with two scales of resolution is demonstrated. It is equivalent to the simultaneous existence of two ELFs, one at high resolution and one at low resolution (two loops of semiosis).

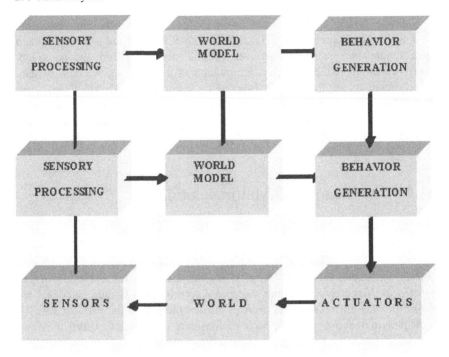

Figure 13.6: ELF with two levels of resolution (two scales of representation)

It is possible to demonstrate that all paradoxes emerge because of squeezing together different scales of the world, different levels of resolution into a unified flat crowd of things that actually do not belong to each other. The great Kant's double-sided table of antinomies has the scale-related interpretation deeply ingrained in it [7] although it might take a semiotician to recognize this. The logical inference should always appreciate the fact of multiscale character of the World: slowly we are approaching understanding of the Godel Theorem of Incompleteness but the phenomena emerging in self-referential systems [27] boil down to the multiscale world representations.

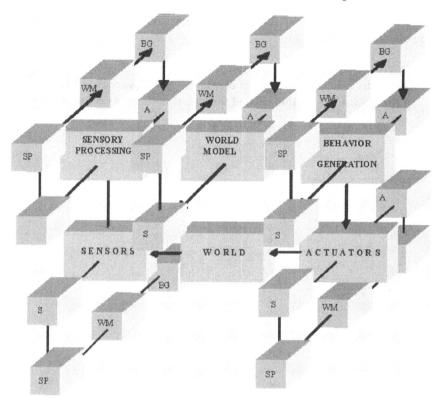

Figure 13.7: ELF of a particular level with the full set of its ELFs of the corresponding modules

What is logical and consistent at one level of resolution might be totally intolerable at another. The loop of semiosis can be constructed only separately at each level. Yet, to fully understand the *meaning* we should bear in mind and consider all scales simultaneously (more precisely: at least three of them: the one of immediate interest, the one above and the one below).

It is imperative not to confuse multiple resolutions for the ELF of interest (the process to be simulated) and the set of all ELFs for the modules of the main ELF (similar the one shown in Figure 13.5). In Figure 13.7, all ELFs for the modules are shown: $ELF_S$, $ELF_{SP}$, $ELF_{WM}$, $ELF_{BG}$, and $ELF_A$. The meaning of these ELFs is determined by practical purposes. For example, the main process has 4 levels of resolution. Each of the levels of resolution is represented and simulated as an ELF. Thus, we can consider it a separate agent. Now, the process of BG is supposed to be run in each single agent. Under particular conditions of horizon of planning and its accuracy the problem of BG might be computationally prohibitive and require a multiresolutional solving of this problem *for a single agent*. This multiresolutional BG for multiagent system is demonstrated in Figure 13.7.

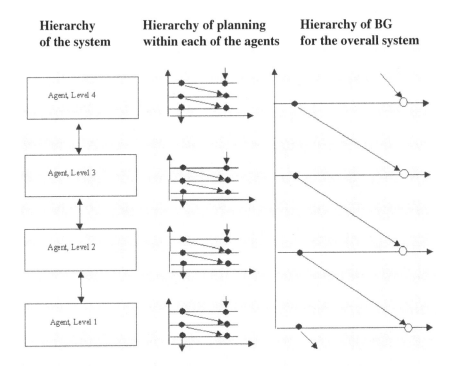

Figure 13.8: A four-level (four-agent) multiresolutional system is shown.

At each level of it, its own multiresolutional decomposition and processing is performed. By constructing signs and systems of signs, by creating and maintaining laws of symbols formation and interpretation, by arranging them into a multiresolutional (multiscale) system, by discovering rules of transformation between levels of resolution and between the symbolic system and the reality (re: symbol grounding), semiotics works as a tool of constructing the system of world representation for the subsequent simulation, running the simulation and analyzing its results, their interpretation and meaning extraction. As soon as this representation is ready, semiotics teaches us how to simulate possible worlds and alternative processes in them, how to make decisions upon simulations with this representation, create plans and generate activities. Sounds like a decent *science*.

At this point, a number of questions emerge: Is this approach limited just to Science and Scientific Phenomena? Can it be applied to social systems? Is it applicable to analysis of Education? Can it be valid for analysis of Psychological and Cognitive processes? Is it possible to use it for analysis of Natural Language processing? How is it related to the Literary activities? Can we use it for simulating Art? Can we expect that Journalism, TV and Cinema would follow the same recommendations? Why only Science?

This is an important set of questions to answer. Especially, if one believes Britannica's definition of science:

> "any system of knowledge that is concerned with the physical world and its phenomena and that entails unbiased observations and systematic experimentation. In general, a science involves a pursuit of knowledge covering general truths or the operations of fundamental laws."

This definition is narrowed down to the physical world and its phenomena and would not be applicable neither to the stock market, nor to the mechanisms of metaphor generation in text. It stringently demands for unbiased observations (as if such a thing exists) and systematic experimentation (as if such a thing as "systematic experimentation" is possible in realistic cases). Even an attempt to define "unbiased observations" and "systematic experimentations" meets unovercomable difficulties.

## 13.5   Meaning in Biophysics Is Conveyed Via Semiotic Agents

In his set of lectures [8], S. Kauffman talks about autonomous agents in a system-theoretical way having in mind to establish the biophysical fundamental of life. His autonomous agents are living semiotic creatures as simple as cells, maybe groups of cells, and as complex as animals, maybe even as populations of animals. He defines agents that develop in an evolutionary way, and determines some general laws of their possible functioning as a part of constructing "a system." He discusses a theory of the origin of life and demonstrates the emergence of *collectively self-reproducing systems.* He introduces the principle of "adjacent possible" that can serve as a valid justification of some of the practically applied *algorithms of search* that do not test all nodes in the graph, just adjacent nodes.

In fact, the paradigm turns out to be characteristic of the theory of *self-organizing symbolic representation,* i.e. it overlaps with semiotics significantly. S. Kauffman defines the autonomous agent using an analogy with a bacterium swimming upstream in a glucose gradient; a bacterium which is acting on its own behalf, seeking dinner. By his definition, an ***autonomous agent is a collectively autocatalytic system that performs one or more thermodynamic***

**work cycles**. A *catalyst* does not affect the position of equilibrium of a chemical reaction; it affects only the rate at which equilibrium is attained. *Autocatalytic* reaction is the one that produces a *catalyst* as one of its outputs. Actually, the concept of "catalyst" plays a role of sheer metaphor; the whole discourse is much broader in its purpose than its chemistry aspect. I am not sure that its chemistry aspect can be convincingly presented solely within the domain of Chemistry. The concept of collectively self-reproducing symbolic systems is native to the overlapping areas of cybernetics and semiotics. If contains substantial explanatory power as far as intelligent simulation systems are concerned at least in the domains of science and engineering.

It can serve also a fruitful basis for unifying the domains of Science and Engineering with the domains of Life and Intelligence, Literature, Art, Journalism and Cinema is about systems of knowledge that are concerned of *collectively self-organizing symbolic representation*, i.e. of semiotics. Moreover: this is semiotics for the sake of simulation.

# 13.6  The Inner Meaning of Semiotic Agents

Life and Intelligence, Science and Engineering, Literature and Art, Journalism and Cinema, Physics and Chemistry, Computers and Internet, Stock Market and Politics – these are just domains that serve as metaphor generators. They pursue the Truths by the virtue of metaphors generation if no regular formal theory is in sight. As one can see from Figure 13.1, metaphors are legitimate for constructing a semiotic model for the subsequent simulation of the system.

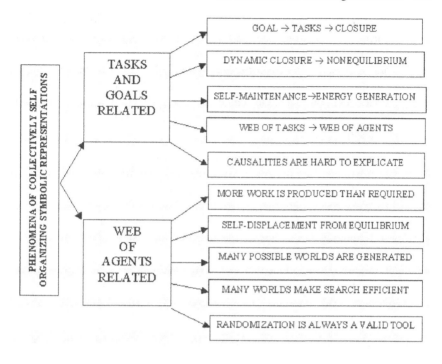

Figure 13.9: The derivative concepts of the collectively self-organizing symbolic representation

Let us concentrate on special particular tools of metaphor generation: the metaphor of a special type of process with autocatalytic properties. The latter leads to several concepts that are either overlapping, or compatible with concepts that are used in the areas of intelligent systems and semiotics (see Figure 13.9).

1.  **A concept of Task Space** which produces the concept of Task Closure for an Autonomous Agent. Thus, the Autonomous Agent is driven by its *task* that allows for determining what is the *goal*. An Autonomous Agent achieves a new kind of "closure" in a space of catalytic and work tasks such that the components of the Agent are amplified or reproduced and all the tasks are accomplished. Living cells are collectively autocatalytic systems. The Author and the Reader with a new novel are an autocatalytic system generating the Truth. *This closure means that an Autonomous Agent is a functionally coherent self sustaining system with a goal.*

2. **Autonomous Agents must be displaced from equilibrium** in a particular direction, and perform their work cycles in a particular direction to achieve the task closure. Therefore, Autonomous Agents are, necessarily, *non-equilibrium systems*. Notice, that the intention to construct and analyze *equilibrium systems* is a little bit outdated, or at least overemphasized. One can demand a satisfaction of the condition of closure at any particular moment of time (we can call it a *dynamic closure*).

3. **Autonomous coordinate "propagating work"** - linked sequences of events many or all of which require that *external energy* be used to drive the process. Autonomous agents themselves do work to construct the very constraints that channel the release of energy and allow it to constitute work. Part of the collectively self-consistent coherence of an Autonomous Agent lies in the fact that each such constraint and the related work carries out a "task." Autonomous Agent maintains or reproduces itself. One can even anticipate that systems of signs might not only control flows of energy but can serve as *energy generators* (for non-physical systems the concept of energy can be treated metaphorically as well; see [29]).

4. **The emergence of collectively self-consistent linked webs of work and tasks increases efficiency of a system**. It is similar to the emergence of collectively autocatalytic reactions networks where the number of reactions increases faster than the number of molecular species. As this variety and diversity of causal consequences increases, it is easier to achieve collective coherence. Actually, this is well applicable to an architecture of literary pieces, musical, artistic, journalistic and other phenomena associated with "humanities."

5. **Only some, not all, of the causal consequences of any part or work constitutes the "task" carried out**. Once the self-consistent coherently linked web of propagating work is in place, the "task" carried out by each bit of work among its many causal consequences is definable in the context of the whole Autonomous Agent. It might be not easy to start thinking of everything in the terms of autonomous agents. But this organization of thought should be productive and explanatory for functioning of intelligence.

6. **Autonomous Agents produce more work than required for their sustainability**. In order to act on their worlds, Autonomous Agents must not use all the propagating work merely to construct the constraints that allow work to propagate. Some of the work must be done on the outside the world, including other agents. In other words, this paradigm promises to be extremely creative, generating useful byproducts and

becoming a cornucopia of ideas. (Compare this with Derrida's deconstruction).

7.  **Autonomous agents displace themselves further from equilibrium** which can be seen from the fact that Autonomous Agents perform work cycles in a non-equilibrium state. It is possible to prove that non-equilibrium offers more speedy and productive results. Lots of opportunity for active and impatient minds! This is related both to the technological and artistic areas. This is related to the area of analysis of our mental endeavors, to the models of mind, and models of life. A non-equilibrium at one scale might be an equilibrium at another scale.

8.  **As displacement from equilibrium increases, the number of possible alternative accessible microstates of the system increases,** thereby increasing the need to apply the "adjacent possible." This is an appeal to congregation of similarities. New metaphors of matter and of mind emerge by the virtue of clustering and generalization. The latter are exercised at any scale. The result of this generalization is always generation of the world of a new scale (resolution).

9.  **The increase in the need of adjacent possible means that autonomous agents can more readily incorporate novel means to coordinate the activities** and work cycles and constraint construction that correspond to their evolving organization and reproduction. In different disciplines, we talk about this phenomenon in different words. But the phenomenon is broadly entertained and explored.

10. **Autonomous Agents use random and/or randomized search algorithms**. On the average, evolution by mutation and selection might be no better than random search. Everybody uses randomization of search as a tool for increasing the productivity and inventiveness of planning and control processes in Control Theory and Artificial Intelligence. Great Russian poets Mayakovsky and Yesenin were used (sometimes) to initiate the process of writing a new poem by drawing a random combination of words from a set of little pieces of papers with words written in each of them. So, Art and Literature are still methodologically similar to other domains!

In addition to the strong line of the goal-dependence, S. Kauffman emphasizes the issues of consistency, self-consistency, collective self-consistency and coherence. This means that the issue of efficiency, or otherwise, some measure of performance quality is critical for Autocatalytic Autonomous Agents sustainability. This coincides with our evaluation of the role of Value Judgment. S. Kauffman attempts to interpret such agents as non-equilibrium Maxwell Demons. This esoteric creature symbolizes the need to represent something which is not very clear for us: the phenomenon of choice (why does it happen, indeed?) This connection of goal-orientedness and fighting with the Second Law of Thermodynamics is looming in many multiple-agent intelligent architectures. We want to emphasize this as a feature to be broadly applied in semiotics, and as well, in most of the presently existing disciplines hiding in their comfortable ivory towers.

## 13.7   The Meaning of Knowledge Representation Regulated by Maxwell Demons

The need in building up the system of World Representation is fundamental in Kauffman's theory although he never talks about this explicitly. He does not call it "representation", or "knowledge base", he calls it *propagatable records* which seems to be more appropriate term for a biologically inclined group (coalition, community). For engineering professionals, one might prefer using the term *world representation*. To extract work from their environments Maxwell Demons must make records of their environments, transform these records, then pay a cost of this transformation. Agents perform work to create the constraints on the release of energy which itself constitutes work. Work creating constraints (the autocatalytic property) is itself requisite for the occurrence of work. Work and constraints, therefore, must jointly and self consistently arise in Agents and must be parts of their ongoing coherent organization, which cannot be understood otherwise than *architecture*. "Organization" is that arrangement of matter and flows which creates constraints that allow work - the constrained release of energy - to propagate. Records as correlated, coherent macroscopic states usable to extract work, and Propagatable Records (or World Representation). This biological lingo can be considered for us a metaphorical and/or analogical representation which allows for confirm a part of what we are doing now, anyway.

Given a physical definition of an Autonomous Agent, semantics acquires a physical meaning. Here, S. Kauffman alludes to the semiotic concept among relations between the physical object, the sign, and the way it is interpreted: *"Pierce's triad of signs is present once there are Agents."* Its self consistent structure and dynamical logic constitute the embodied "record" of its environment, its reproduction and proliferation carries out linked work cycles and simultaneously, via mutation and selection, updates its record. A growing microbial population constitutes something like "propagating co-constructing organization of propagating constraints - work - record."

This leads to a more general concept that "organization" is fundamentally related to that coordination of matter and energy which enables and controls the constrained release of energy - work - to be propagated. Such coordination is achieved, fundamentally, by doing work to create structures that alter the potential barriers involved in the release of energy from components in the system. Work is done to construct the agents that then self-organize into a membrane that is, actually, a decision making mechanism of applying constraints for making choices. Organization, so defined includes constructing constraints, the resultant structure, and its dynamical logic. Entropy is itself an equilibrium concept concerned with ergodic flow to macrostates having the largest number of microstates.

Surprisingly enough, communities cannot exist without some demon making choices for them. In this case, we are talking about Maxwell Demon. Once Autonomous Agents exist, a genuine semantics, with a physical interpretation, appears to arise. A co-evolving community of non-equilibrium Maxwell Demons is a union of matter-energy-information into an organization that proliferates and constructs hierarchical complexity which is illustrated by S. Kauffman as follows:

- An Agent is a single cell organism.

  In technology, it should be interpreted as any goal oriented unit: a bolt, a carburetor, a car, a robot, a multinational corporation. In Art and Literature it is a brush stroke, a metaphor, a subset of a painting, a novel, a movement like "impressionism."

From this "existential statement" the other elementary statements follow:

- Each cell internally processes its molecular inputs.

  So, how does it work? The "closure" of its independent functioning is of interest.

- Each cell mounts a response to some of its molecular inputs and combinations of inputs.

  So, the external attachments are getting of concern.

- Each cell sends its outputs to its specific types of "output" eco-neighbors.

  Formation of coalitions should be analyzed (G. Saridis' concept of coordination seems to be an analogy for the communication with eco-neighbors).

- An ecosystem is a WEB of single cell organisms.

  This is the machinery behind the linkage between two adjacent levels of resolution (scales). Like a painting which emerges as a result of the web of strokes, like "impressionism" which emerges out of congregating units of "adjacent possible" like in Salon of Rejected (Salon des Refusés, 1863).

- Each cell in the WEB receives molecular input signals from certain other types of cells, its "input" eco-neighbors.

  This is presumed in the previous statement, As a separate issue this appeals to properly reflecting this phenomenon in the overall model.

- Then a community of cells is itself a parallel processing dynamical system. Each cell may itself be within the ordered regime, at the edge of chaos, or the chaotic regime.

  Simultaneously, the community, considered as a parallel processing dynamical system, may itself be within the ordered regime, the chaotic regime, or at the edge of chaos.

- The state space of an Agent is partitioned into "conical" volumes, each leading to a specific response.

  We would not aspire to introduce the concept of state space in this editorial. Let us just say that this partitioning into discrete response volumes constitutes both the categorization carried out by the agent, and the coarse graining of its world.

After this, introduction of the **Coalitions of Agents** is inevitable. These are S. Kauffman's arguments:

1. As parallel processing systems, such Agents will lie within the ordered regime or at a phase transition between dynamical order and chaos. ... Autonomous agent Maxwell Demons endogenously create their own relevant coarse graining of their worlds.

   This statement is especially interesting: it confirms our hypotheses that multiresolutional representation is the tool of entropy reduction, and is an incarnation of Maxwell's demons within the context of large complex systems.

2. As the members of the community tune their positions on their internal order-chaos axis and their couplings to one another, these evolutionary adaptations simultaneously tune the ruggedness of fitness landscapes the web structure of the ecosystem. On the other hand, any Agent's landscape is deformed by the mutational alterations of other agents.

3. As parallel processing systems, Autonomous Agents will tune their internal molecular diversity and the species diversity of coalitions of Agents, such that each Agent is subcritical (i. e. is on the verge of a fork

in its possible behavior that can drastically differ because of the small difference in a particular factor.

Certainly, an indefinite hierarchy of Agents can be introduced, since Agents can be comprised of Agents. This hierarchy reflects a hierarchy of combinatorially complex entities, and each entity can be considered an agent. The possibility of considering life cycles for agents consisting of multiple agents depends on the level of granularity (resolution, scale). Obviously, lower resolution formation of agents (communities, societies, populations) will have a longer life cycle. This seems to be consistent with other experimental results and theoretical models. Higher order autonomous agents (lower resolution agents) such as multi-celled and colonial organisms, social insects colonies, economic entities such as firms, epistemological entities such as laws of nature as opposed to high resolution experimental data testify for better sustainability of the system.

The model we discussed here, seems to be motivated by thinking about biological issues. But notice, how staunchly it is related to all possible domains of semiotic analysis: Literature and Art, Science and Technology, and all others. This happens because all of them depend on and are determined by our mechanisms of mind and intelligence, especially by one of the most powerful one: the mechanism of *generalization*.

# 13.8    Generalization by Coarsening Produced by GFS-triplet

GFS is described in [16] as a tool for agent clustering. This is a triplet of *computational* (or *mental* which is the same) operators: **grouping, focusing attention**, and **combinatorial search**. (This is why sometimes it is called GFACS). For simplicity, we will use abbreviation GFS (grouping, filtering, search). It does not allude to any specific computational algorithm: the latter can be chosen depending on the availability or habits in a particular system and/or environment. More important is that the G-operator clusters, or otherwise groups units of information (units of signs) depending on the criterion of similarity chosen, F-operator bounds limits from above and below to the subset of attention within the G-operator will be applied. Focusing attention is about confining the world of attention for a semiotic agent at hand. Finally, the appropriate groups should be searched for – and this is what the S-operator is for.

One would not be able to find living systems, or intellectual processes that would not depend on and determined by a particular GFS-triplet. All phenomena of emergence happen because some GFS-operator is functioning there. Sometimes, it is not easy to recognize it. But, otherwise, no process of emergence, gestalt, generalization can happen. This statement is related to domains both of Life and Intelligence. It is equally applicable to Biology, Computation, Technology, Literature, Art, Economics, and other disciplines demonstrating some attachment to Life and Intelligence (which many of them have).

This triplet of elementary operators performs clustering of all units of information available, or performs clustering of all real systems available as information units in a system of representation. Not only clustering is being performed: the chosen clusters are assigned names and they become new entities. These new entities do not belong to the initial level of resolution anymore: the new level of scale emerges. Certainly, this operator has autocatalytic properties: it tends to apply to everything it produces, it develops new entities, e.g. new agents, new levels of resolution, etc.

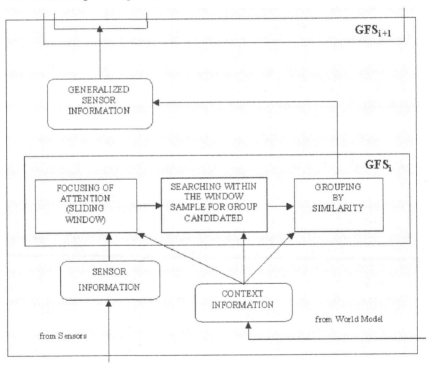

Figure 13.10: GFS: a computational mechanism of coarsening (1 level process is shown)

It is not important what is the concrete algorithm of GFS: the structure of GFS determines its functioning while the concrete algorithm might be induced by the individual properties of the elementary functioning loop, the protocol of encoding, the computational platform, and/or a concrete architecture of the accepted computer system. No matter whether the activities of SP, WM, or BG are involved, coarsening is the first operation that is imposed upon information: coarsening for generalization.

Generalization is the key algorithm of Life and Intelligence. The simplest argument: people generalize all the time for the sake of decision making no matter how actively some elementary and middle schools are trying to extinguish this habit. The abundance of generalization tools we have is unquestionable. Yet, each and all of them are doing the same: GFS!

This approach allows for interpreting the GFS-triplet as an autonomous meta-agent that persistently performs coarsening: grouping, focusing of attention, and combinatorial search upon the available information until the multiscale system of representation (of agents) is constructed. After GFS is admitted, the rapid growth of multiresolutional (multiscale) systems of representation and decision making is inevitable.

# 13.9   Propagation of Meaning Run by Symbols ⟺ Agents

From the very beginning of our discussion about Life and Intelligence, they were treated as properties (or rather a faculties) of some individual unit of reality (or rather an individual system, or individual information system). Yet, we must emphasize that the mechanisms of intelligence are always described and explained as the ability to process and manipulate the multiplicities of symbols including:

- grouping them together based upon their properties and relations among them

- focusing the attention upon subsets of symbols

- searching among symbols, or groups of symbols

- considering some of the emerging groups of symbols to be new symbols belonging to the next  level of consideration (level of lower resolution symbols).

This is how the ***multiscale hierarchies of symbols*** are presumably derived.

Now, let us consider each of these symbols to be a notation for a separate system (an agent, or even an intelligent agent). Indeed, we are walked around and are being invited to give a label and/or notation to what surrounds us, and behind each label is a subset of reality, a unity of some system, an agent. Then, our considerations related to the multiplicity of symbols and our search for grouping them, if possible, will be actually related to the multiplicities of *agents*, Grouping of these agents leads to an interesting result: each group behaves as a unit and can be considered an agent belonging to the lower level of resolution. This is how the ***Multiscale Hierarchies of Agents*** emerge.

These agents tend to interact, form relationships, refer to each other, refer to themselves and develop self-organizing activities. Somehow, it stimulates and generates emergence of new energies (realistically and/or metaphorically – does not matter). As the intelligence of the agents gets more advanced, the agents at a level cannot be considered just a relational network, it becomes a *coalition of agents* On the other hand, each of the agents can be considered a symbol. The concepts of symbols and agents become interchangeable: everything developed for *symbols* is applicable for the *agents* and vice versa. All systems are presumed to include, or to be composed of "agents" that unlike many other subsystems are active and can produce changes by the virtue of creating "outputs" as a response to arriving "inputs". Sentences are agents, stories are agents, movies are agents, even robots are agents.

Therefore, from the mathematical point of view, agent is nothing more than an "automaton." Yet, the concept of "agent" is given tremendous attention: this concept is ascribed multiple properties which can be interpreted with no difficulty if one remembers this equivalence "agent ⟺ automaton." This is how some authors interject a teleological flavor into the concept of an "agent":

> Here is how it works: first you decide to treat the object whose behavior is to be predicted as a rational agent; then you figure out what beliefs that agent ought to have, given its place in the world and its purpose. Then you figure out what desires it ought to have, on the same considerations, and finally you predict that this rational agent will act to further its goals in the light of its beliefs. A little practical reasoning from the chosen set of beliefs and desires will in most instances yield a decision about what the agent ought to do; that is what you predict the agent will do. (Dennett, *The Intentional Stance*, p. 17).

The chain of ideas that lead to the imaginary hidden properties of the concept of the "agent" can be traced as follows:

Agent's behavior → Rational agent *(Implication 1)*

Rationality → Agent's beliefs, functions of its state and purpose *(Implication 2)*

Beliefs → Desires *(Implication 3)*

Desires + Purpose + State → Prediction of Agent's behavior (Implication 4)

(Please, notice that these statements are equally applicable to agent-systems and to agent-symbols).

Similar four implications can be made about any automaton. All of it is a result of the fact that the "Rationality, beliefs, purpose," ascribed to the agent (a non-intelligent one), are a result of the agent's design process. The designer has endowed the agent with all these properties by filling in the look-up tables of transition and output functions.

Therefore, the automata (including all simple agents) act on behalf of the designer, and since the designer does is not required to be around during the automaton functioning, the automated device, or a software unit is called sometimes "autonomous" which creates an enormous confusion.

Analysis of semiotic agents should help us to bring to the state of creative autonomy not only entities of Science and Engineering but the pieces of Art, Literatures, Journalism, Music and Cinema.

# 13.10 Emergence of the Multiscale Communities of Agents

We will demonstrate the evolution of a set of concepts from simple agents through autonomous agents to intelligent agents, and from single agents to coalitions of agents. We will discuss both intellectual, or computational agents and realistically existing agents of the physical world. It is our intention to arrive at the architectures of intelligence constructed as interrelated communities of semiotic agents.

The term "Agents" is ubiquitous in the literature on large and complex systems, intelligent systems, robotics, software engineering, and internet. Yet it is rarely defined, and its existing interpretations are very vague. At the present time, we have three salient groups of agents reflected in the literature.

## 13.10.1    Simple Rational Agents

Agents were formally introduced in the discipline of Artificial Intelligence [9]. The concept of "rationality" is associated with following the existing laws of thinking, e.g. laws of logic. "A rational agent is the one that does the right thing" (page 31). This alludes indirectly to the concept of success, and the latter invokes the idea of performance measure. Agent is a system that is immersed into some environment, has "percepts" as its inputs and actions as its outputs. Percepts enter through sensors, actions are produced by "effectors". Sequences of percepts are mapped into sequences of output actions, and this is no different from a normal automaton. Russell and Norwig [25] distinguish the following types of agents:

- Simple reflex agents

- Agents that keep track of the World

- Goal-based Agents

- Utility based Agents

Rational Agents are like automated machines, or pre-programmed robots. One also can interpret them as a couple "The Textbook and A Diligent Student." They can be equipped by simple devices for choosing one out of few preplanned solutions. They can have rudimentary World Representation and simple learning capabilities (like recognition of single repeated moves or their strings). The intelligence of rational agents is limited, although they have their field of application. In many areas, rational agents are called *automated devices*, or *automated systems*.

## 13.10.2    Autonomous Agents

Automated systems work with no human operator involvement, i.e. autonomously, although it is known in advance what and when will happen. The term *autonomous* is used when the upcoming situations are not pre-scheduled and the agent has some freedom to decide what, when and how to act. There is a broad variety of autonomous functioning starting with the case of limited and known input vocabulary and ending with total unawareness of the situations that the system might encounter.

The term "autonomous agents" was introduced and characterized somewhat more in-depth by the organizers of the 2nd International Conference on Autonomous Agents in 1998 sponsored by AAAI, ACM SigArt and Microsoft Research:

"Autonomous agents are computer systems that are capable of independent action in dynamic, unpredictable environments." (It was not clear whether any goal is being pursued by these agents...) "Agents are also one of the most important and exciting areas of research and development in computer science today. Agents are currently being applied in domains as diverse as computer games and interactive cinema, information retrieval and filtering, user interface design, and industrial process control."

At this conference, the set of problems to be solved was outlined (in the keynote lecture by L. Gasser, NSF):

- High autonomy
- Managed complexity
- Long lived, robust sustainable
- Principled rationality
- Knowledge Rich
- Physically capable
- Organizable/organized
- Seamless integration through multimodal

- Sociable and socially conforming
- Evolution
- Learning/forgetting
- High level programming
- Team level interventions and policies
- Emerging agent and behaviors
- Adaptation to heterogeneity and dynamics
- Long term reliability, interactivity and sociability

Taken together, these properties require technologies that can be developed only in the future, none of the existing or attempted intelligent systems can demonstrate all these properties. The mechanisms of possible achieving these properties are not specified, however, from the subsequent materials we can discover that building up the communities of elementary agents is a possible way to achieve these properties (maybe the only way).

The usage of the term "autonomous agent" in the literature is very multifaceted one. P. Maes (Media lab, MIT) describes the area of Agent-research as follows: I am mostly interested these days in so-called "communityware," software which allows large decentralized groups of people to perform activities which previously required centralized organizations. I am interested in developing powerful technology for communityware as well studying its social implications" [28]. The statements of other researchers from this laboratory are informative, too:

- "My interests include Agent-mediated Electronic Commerce (with a focus on knowledge marketplaces), Adaptive / Distributed Multiagent Systems and Artificial Life" (A. G. Moukas).

- "I'm studying how to build decentralized Internet systems. Some of the themes I am researching include mobile agents, distributed objects, metadescriptions of agent capabilities, and emergent phenomena in general," (N. Minar).

- "I am interested in Agent-mediated Electronic Commerce and distributed/multiagent systems. I am currently focusing on Reputation Mechanisms for online communities," (G. Zacharia).

- "I'm working on issues of the sociology, politics, and security of distributed agents; my test case, Yenta, forms coalitions of people interested in similar topics," (L. Foner)

- "I am working on agents for wearable computers," (Tuan Q. Phan)

- "I helped lead the Agent-mediated Electronic Commerce Initiative at the Media Lab and developed a variety of decision support, negotiation, and user interface technologies to help to facilitate online transactions," (R. H. Guttman).

Most of the papers in this area treat agents collectively as an entity that allows for interaction and/or can conduct some rational activities with a definite degree of independence.

## 13.10.3   Software Agents, or Mobile Agents

Software agents are computational units including, or not including the subsystem of Simulation. The best characterization of computational agents was given by M. Minsky: "...each mind is made of many smaller processes. These we'll call *agents*. Each mental agent by itself can only do some simple thing that needs no mind or thought at all" [20]. Software agents that can change their location in the system are called mobile agents. These are slightly different since they are, kind of, internet related:

"Mobile agents are agents that can physically travel across a network, and perform tasks on machines that provide agent hosting capability. This allows processes to migrate from computer to computer, for processes to split into multiple instances that execute on different machines, and to return to their point of origin. Unlike remote procedure calls, where a process invokes procedures of a remote host, process migration allows executable code to travel and interact with databases, file systems, information services and other agents.

Mobile agents have been the focus of much speculation and hype in recent years. The appeal of mobile agents is quite alluring -mobile agents roaming the Internet could search for information, find us great deals on goods and services, and interact with other agents that also roam networks (and meet in a gathering place) or remain bound to a particular machine. Significant research and development into mobile agency has been conducted in recent years, and there are many mobile agent architectures available today. However, mobile agency has failed to become a sweeping force of change, and now faces competition in the form of message passing and remote procedure call (RPC) technologies," [30].

Mobile Agents can be illustrated by the system of views from Tutorial: Mobile Software Agents for Dynamic Routing [9]. As portable digital devices of all kinds proliferate, wireless networks that allow for flexible, timely and efficient data communication become more and more important. Networks for mobile devices are quite difficult to design for several reasons, chief among them the problem of routing packets across networks characterized by constantly changing topology. In this article we describe ways to address the routing problem using a new technique for distributed programming, mobile software agents. Mobile agents are actively promulgated to make the contemporary manufacturing systems, especially CORBA-oriented [3]. (For more on mobile agents see [4]).

It does not take too much of imagination to find that mobile software agents and the books, movies, TV-shows and other artifacts of the world presently belonging to the class of humanities can be described as and behave similar to software autonomous agents. One can expect that semiotics of agents should focus upon all of them.

## 13.10.4    Individual Agents vs Coalitions of Agents

We will introduce here a fundamental concept, that is, a core concept for the whole issue of intelligent systems:

*groups of agents behave as agents, too.*

Clearly, this is a fundamental concept of multiresolutional (multiscale) representation. These groups can be considered generalized agents. Moreover, groups of groups of agents can be also lumped together into even more generalized agent. Let us make it clear that in order for this to happen, an operator of **generalization** (GFS) should be applied to the set of individual agents [17, 18]. It consists of three sub-operators working in parallel and/or sequentially: grouping, filtering (or focusing of attention), and searching (or combinatorial searching). The operator of generalization is applied externally, or is one of the computational tools that the agents are equipped with (one of the operators of self-organization).

## 13.10.5    Hierarchies of Processing Within Coalitions of Agents at Each Level of Resolution

At the level of lower resolution we are interested in the relations between "group of groups". One relation represents all interwoven relationships between single agents that are shown in the imaginary busy picture. At the level of lowest resolution we have one agent (the group of groups of groups) that embodies the set of formations under consideration. So, we have an example that can be interpreted as merger of multiple agents into groups (one level), groups into coalitions (second level), coalitions into a society (third level). In such a multiscale hierarchy of the communities of agents, each next grouping makes the discussion simpler but the resolution gets lower.

A coalition of agents is considered to be an agent of the lower level of resolution (Figure 13.11). It is described by a set of generalized properties, therefore instead of considering a space with a very high number of dimensions equal to the sum of variables for all agent members of the coalition, we are dealing with a substantially smaller number of generalized coordinates. For example, instead of considering a sum of variables for the steering and propulsion system of a vehicle together with the coordinates of the outstanding points of the vehicle body (e.g. all four corners of the vehicle), at the lower level of resolution, the vehicle is considered as a material point, the center of a fuzzy zone representing the vehicle and its X-Y motion is analyzed.

The lower resolution agent has an "office" that takes care of its activities. This office has its own agenda (it should plan the motion of the object), and to follow this agenda, a substantial amount of work should be performed. The job of the "office" should be performed with minimum complexity, and therefore, an inner schedule of multiresolutional activities can be expected to be produced.

Within the "plan" computed by the level above, a task (with a particular subgoal) is assigned for the level under consideration. New plan should be computed (how to achieve this subgoal). Sometimes, this problem requires search in the state space at the resolution higher than at the level above, and the complexity can be reduced by considering it in a multiresolutional (multiscale) manner at one level of the main system hierarchy. Multiple examples of this multiresolutional job organization within the level of a multiresolutional system can be given from the area of computer vision systems, or manufacturing scheduling.

In conclusion, we would like to present a metaphor that makes these concepts better understandable: the metaphor of bees, merging into swarms, swarms gathering into swarms of swarms. This is how the organism of an animal can be visualized in the light of this metaphor (from J. Hoffmeyer's book *Signs of Meaning in the Universe*):

"One quadrillion of bacteria, in the form of ten trillion cells, collaborate on the job of being a human. Like an astronomical swarm of swarms all of these cells stream together through one single solitary brain-body as it makes its way along the path of life toward all those unknown futures that will eventually become just one single life story" [5].

A coalition of agents is considered to be an agent of the lower level of resolution. It is described by a set of generalized properties, therefore instead of considering a space with a very high number of dimensions equal to the sum of variables for all agent members of the coalition, we deal with a substantially smaller number of generalized coordinates. For example, instead of considering a sum of variables for the steering and propulsion system of a vehicle together with the coordinates of the outstanding points of the vehicle body (e.g. all four corners of the vehicle), at the lower level of resolution, the vehicle is considered as a material point, the center of a fuzzy zone representing the vehicle and its X-Y motion is analyzed. Another example: instead of describing the sum of individual behavior of a multiplicity of people, we can introduce a new agent a "crowd." The behavior might turn out to be simpler than the sum of behavior of its components-individual. Sometimes, it might be simpler than a behavior of a single member of this crowd.

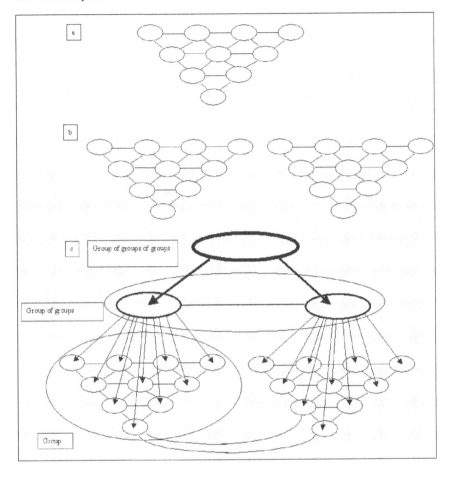

Figure 13.11: Formation of the coalition of agents (a- a single coalition that can be treated as a single agent, b- two coalitions that can be treated as two single agents: a potential coalition, c- a multiscale coalition of agents)

The lower resolution agent has an "office" that takes care of its activities. This office has its own agenda (it should plan the motion of the object), and to follow this agenda, a substantial amount of work should be performed. The job of the "office" should be performed with minimum complexity, and therefore, a need can be expected for producing the inner schedule of multiresolutional activities. This interplay of the inner and outer scales is a matter of further analysis.

## 13.10.6   Integrating the Sources of Meaning: Toward Semiotic Tools of Simulation

However, the body of knowledge for the subsequent engineering problems is always taken from the stories told in natural language. But where is the Natural Language in our discourse? where is Literature? where is the Art and Music? where is Multimedia? why only Science? Somehow, I have a feeling that we are slipping again into the morass of "scientific" discourse that narrows down substantially the *pursuit of meaning*. No doubt, this is the peculiarity of our habits to look for an equilibrium in a constructive way. It will take an immense effort to develop from the scholarly habits of two cultures to the unified semiotic culture.

Who told you that *semiotics* is for the science only? As planning activities emerged (on the dawn of our existence), imagination became a working tool of human multimodal activity. In fact, planning is creation of imaginary worlds. The main tool for doing this is semiotics: what else can explore dealing with symbolic representation. I hope nobody doubts that imagination is about representation, thus is working with signs and symbols. Moreover, imagination is an active part of the process of learning, and it is not difficult to demonstrate [1,10,2] that learning is the semiosis as C. Peirce, C. Morris and J. Uexkull visualized it [23,21,31].

Art, Literature, and Multimedia Simulation Systems are the disciplines of creation of imaginary worlds for the sake of simulation, too. Their imaginary worlds are allowed to be less probable, maybe even impossible at all. But still, they are mechanisms of the semiotic analysis of reality, and their purpose is the same as the purpose of planning: they are for learning. They are using the same tools of signs and symbols manipulation that are used for planning. More frequently that we can realize, they allow us not to get involved in the devastating and senseless trials and tribulations of natural evolution. The difference is in the fact that Art and Literature are capable of doing things that simple rational agents (rational people?) are not always familiar with. Imagination of Art and Literature is driven by motivations that are not clearly understood by rational agents. *(This might be the case for the Multimedia Simulation Systems, too)*. However, rational agents develop and grow. Gradually they become aware of the powerful tools that can be utilized for performing their job. If one knows that, one cannot bypass the famous rift between the "two cultures."

Yu Lotman was the one who did not have problems with a merger between science-oriented and humanities-oriented kinds of semiotics. I believe that his powerful "Culture and Explosion" is a roadmap for the upcoming theoretical merger between them [32]. We are still to discover plenty of exciting surprises on our way to unity. I believe that very soon semioticists will study works of A.

Losev [12,13,14], semiotic works of J. S. Mill [19] and W. Stanley Jevons [6], and many others.

Semioticists live in diaspora within a multiplicity of sciences, and when they meet occasionally, they barely understand each other because they talk different languages. Watch what happens to the logicians serving different sciences. As a result we have almost as many logical approaches as we have scholarly domains!

The movement for using unified semiotic approaches as a Simulation Methodology will be difficult but it becomes stronger every year. There are scholarly communities that consider this drive one of the most important in the contemporary world noosphere, or at least human intellectual culture. A strong example: the semiotic school of D. A. Pospelov that can be judged upon by multiple collections of scholarly papers in semiotics, the founder and source of energies behind many semiotic activities in Russia. One can judge upon the nature of such activities, for example by [26]. Such enclaves exist in many countries of the world, based upon sheer scholarly enthusiasm of participants and mild curiosity of the rest of academic community.

On the other hand, the difficulty of this process cannot be overestimated. The powerful desire to talk about definite things is different language is tempting. The most contentious topic is related to the issue of generalization. The habit to see engineering design outside of the framework of cognitive models of brain has generated multiple peculiar terms. C. Landauer and K. Bellman gave an example of this in their paper [11]. Software engineers have many pseudonyms for "generalization" and for the need in it. The situation of "getting stuck" is the clear example of the situation when the density of information exceed the ability to process it without prior generalization. Authors emphasize the importance of semiotic tools for escaping the "getting stuck" situations. However, there is no hope that they would be properly understood in the near future, and that the need in generalization would be admitted by the users that need it the most. The situation is grim: authors understand what software engineers are talking about. But they are pessimistic about building up a paradigm with a different view upon systems simulation in general. Yet, multiple band-aids on the body of an engineering discipline is not a good solution. The watershed between two (and probably even more) cultures is frightening.

...After all, maybe there was some reason (if not merit) in having Babel tower not finished? [24]

# References

[1]  Albus, J, A. Lacaze, A. Meystel, "Evolution of Knowledge Structures During the Process of Learning", in *Architectures for Semiotic Modeling and Situation Analysis in Large Complex Systems*, Proc. of the 1995 10ᵗʰ IEEE Int'l Symposium on Intelligent Control Workshop on Architectures for Intelligent Systems, CA, 1995, pp. 329-335

[2]  Albus, J, A. Lacaze, A. Meystel, "Theory and Experimental Analysis of Cognitive Processes in Early Learning", Proc. of the 1995 International Conference on Systems, Man and Cybernetics "Intelligent Systems for the 21st Century", Vancouver, BC Canada, 1995, pp. 4404-4409

[3]  Ben-Natan, R: *CORBA: A Guide to Common Object Request Broker Architecture*, McGraw-Hill, New York, 1995

[4]  Bradshaw, J.M. *An Introduction to Software Agents. In: Software Agents*, J.M. Bradshaw (Ed.), Menlo Park, Calif., AAAI Press, 1997, pages 3-46

[5]  Hoffmeyer, J: *Signs of Meaning in the Universe*, Indiana University Press, Bloomington, IN 1996

[6]  Jevons, W. S: *The Principles of Science*: The Treatise on Logic and Scientific Method, Dover, New York, 1958 (originally published in 1873)

[7]  Kant, I: *Critique of Pure Reason* [1982, originally published in German, 4th ed., 1794]

[8]  Kauffman, S: "The World of Autonomous Agents and the Worlds They Mutually Create", Lectures, 1996, (http://www.santafe.edu/sfi/People/kauffman/Investigations.html)

[9]  Kramer, K. H, N. Minar, and P. Maes, "Tutorial: Mobile Software Agents for Dynamic Routing", see URL http://nelson.www.media.mit.edu/people/nelson/research/routes-sigmobile/

[10] Lacaze, A, M. Meystel, A. Meystel, "Multiresolutional Schemata for Unsupervised Learning of Autonomous Robots for 3D Space Application", Proc. of the 1994 Goddard Conference on Space Applications of AI, Greenbelt, MD, 1993, pp. 103-112

[11] Landauer, C, K. Bellman, "Symbol Systems in Constructed Complex Systems", Proc. of the 1999 IEEE Int'l Symposium on Intelligent Control, Intelligent Systems, and Semiotics, Cambridge, MA 1999

[12] Losev, A. F: *Existence, Name, Cosmos*, Publ. "Thought", Moscow, 1993 (in Russian)

[13] Losev, A. F: *Myth, Number, Essence*, Publ. "Thought", Moscow, 1994 (in Russian)

[14] Losev, A. F: *Form, Style, Expression*, Publ. "Thought", Moscow, 1995 (in Russian)

[15] Mandelbrot, B: *The Fractal Geometry of Nature*, Freeman and Co., New York, 1982

[16] Meystel, A: *Semiotic Modeling and Situation Analysis: An Introduction*, Publ. AdRem, 158 p., 1995

[17] Meystel, A: "Intelligent Systems: A Semiotic Perspective", *International Journal of Intelligent Control and Systems"*, Vol.1, No. 1, 1996, pp. 31-58

[18] Meystel, A: "Learning Algorithms Generating Multigranular Hierarchies", in *Mathematical Hierarchies and Biology*, Eds.: B. Mirkin, F. R. McMorris, F. S. Roberts, A. Rzhetsky, DIMACS Series in Discrete Mathematics, Vol. 37, American Mathematical Society, 1997, pp. 357-384

[19] Mill, J. S: *A System of Logic: Ratiosinative, and Inductive*, Longmanns, 1930

[20] Minsky, M: *The Society of Mind*, Simon and Schuster, New York, 1985

[21] Morris, C: In the *International Encyclopedia of Unified Science*, Eds. O. Neurath, R. Carnap, C. Morris, University of Chicago Press, Chicago, 1955

[22] Pattee, H: "Physical basis and origin of control, in *Hierarchy Theory*, ed., Braziler, NY, [see p. 94]

[23] Peirce, C: *Collected Papers*, Vol. 5, Harvard University Press, Cambridge, MA, 1931, p. 488

[24] Pieter Bruegel the Elder "The Tower of Babel," oil painting,1563; in the Kunsthistorisches Museum, Vienna

[25] Russell, S., P. Norvig, *Artificial Intelligence: A Modern Approach*, Prentice Hall, Upper Saddle River, NJ 1995

[26] *Semiotics and Informatics*, Collections of papers, Published by VINITI since 1971

[27] Smullyan, R. M: *Godel's Incompleteness Theorem*, Oxford University Press, New York, 1992 [see Ch. 11, "Self-Referential Systems"]

[28] Software Agent Group, http://agents.www.media.mit.edu/groups/agents/people/

[29] Taborsky, E: "Emotions as Forms of Consciousness", Proceedings of the 1999 IEEE Int'l Symposium on Intelligent Control/Intelligent Systems and Semiotics, Cambridge, MA, 1999, pp. 58-63

[30] URL http://www.davidreilly.com/topics/software_agents/mobile_agents/.

[31] Von Uexkull (ed), T, J. Von Uexkull's Theory of Meaning, Special issue of *Semiotica*, Vol. 42(1), 1982, pp. 1-87 (originally was published in 1940)

[32] Yu. M. Lotman, *Culture and Explosion*, Publ. "Gnosis", Moscow, 1992 (in Russian)

[33] Zeigler, B: *Object-Oriented Simulation with Hierarchical, Modular Models*, Academic Press, Boston, 1990

# Chapter 14

# Evolutionary Learning in Agent-Based Modeling

## S. Takahashi

*This paper develops a general model for evolutionary learning in agent-based modeling. The central concepts of the general model lie in internal model principle and mutual learning of agent's internal models in an evolutionary way. This paper particularly presents network-type dynamic hypergame as a model to describe an evolutionary learning process in multi-agent situation and a simulation method by genetic algorithm to perform a network-type dynamic hypergame. The experimental results given in this paper show some requisite conditions to progress the learning process effectively.*

## 14.1  Introduction

Agent-based modeling is basically a modeling method to reveal the nature of complex systems especially including complex social systems. The primal way of agent-based modeling is based on simulation of agents and their interactions involved in a complex system. One essential goal of agent-based modeling is to enrich our understanding of fundamental processes that may appear in a variety of applications for decision making.

Axelrod [1] insists that agent-based modeling is a third way of doing science, when it is contrasted with the two standard methods of induction and deduction. It is, at least, sure that agent-based modeling is becoming a powerful methodological tool of simulation to aid our intuition and decision making capability.

The aspects stated above give only a general notion of agent-based modeling. How each agent should be modeled depends on what we use as a specific formalism to describe the situation and agents.

"Evolutionary learning," appearing in the title, mainly includes a comprehensive way of "evolutionary approach to learning process" by which we can understand the process that each agent involved in a complex situation learns in an evolutionary manner the situation and its relevant features. The term evolutionary approach indicates essential use of research methods originated from Darwin's theory of evolution and its derived forms [9]. As an evolutionary learning method in simulation this paper will employ genetic algorithm developed by J.H.Holland [10].

The purposes of this paper are (1) to develop a general framework for evolutionary learning in agent-based modeling, (2) to introduce network-type dynamic hypergame to describe an evolutionary learning process based on game situation, and (3) to perform basic experiments of evolutionary learning by using genetic algorithm.

Recently, the concept and methodology of multiagent systems are playing one of central roles in many fields such as distributed artificial intelligence, organization theory, game theory or economics.

As an approach to distributed artificial intelligence, the area of learning in multiagent systems receives broad and steadily increasing attention [18]. Agents behave in intelligent or autonomous manners. We can distinguish various learning techniques provided in artificial intelligence and machine learning such as reinforcement learning or classifier systems based on genetic algorithms. They deal with learning models that basically maintain each agent's policy or the rule of actions [27].

The characteristics of agents modeled in this paper share mostly with the notion of agents formulated mainly in distributed artificial intelligence. Each agent in a complex system makes a decision autonomously according to the "rule" for agent's behavior. Furthermore this paper adds a more essential feature to agents: "internal model principle." The internal model principle requires each agent to have his own "internal model" of the situation. Each agent selects his action as a result of his decision based on both his internal model and the rule of behavior. Originally the internal model principle was introduced in the context of control theory [5]. In this paper we will extend and apply it to agent-based modeling, and clarify the relationship between internal model and the situation.

The internal model of an agent can be regarded as a model of "situation" in which the agent is involved or of "environment" with which the agent interacts. Hence evolutionary approach developed in this paper deals with the learning of the situation itself, while major learning techniques in distributed artificial intelligence focus on the learning of the rule of agent's actions.

On the other hand, economics also deals with adaptation process of bounded rationality, the rationality which assumes agents has insufficient ability to calculate optimal solutions. Several mathematical learning models have been provided such as least square learning [11] and Bayesian learning [3]. These models mostly assume a representative agent who represents a whole group of agents, improves his belief and react to his expectation based on some learning rule [6].

In this paper we formulate network-type dynamic hypergame to describe complex situations and internal models of agents to realize the general framework for evolutionary learning. Then we perform simulation of evolutionary learning process of the individual perceptions of the complex situation by applying genetic algorithm to a specific model of network-type dynamic hypergame.

The situation described in the network-type dynamic hypergame basically shows a game situation. In this paper such a situation is called a "hypergame situation." It, however, has intrinsically different aspects from the "traditional" game situation [12,17] in the sense that each agent involved in the hypergame situation makes his decision based on the result from his "own" internal model of the situation.

The game situation is a framework for dealing with interactions of decision making of autonomous agents in social or economic system. The basic components of the framework of game are players, strategies, payoffs and preferences, in terms of which the situation is described. In a game situation each player has a set of strategies as options of actions, expects results when the strategies are selected, and gets some payoffs given by a payoff function assigning real numbers to strategies. According to the payoffs, the preference orderings are given. Each player plays a game by "rationally" selecting a strategy, which means he selects an optimal solution that maximized his payoffs.

A game can be formally defined by

$$< N, \{S_i, f_i\}_{i \in N} >$$

where $N$ is a set of players, $S_i$ is a set of strategies of player $i$ and $f_i$ is a payoff function of player $i$, which assigns each strategy a real number. Nash solution is usually used as an optimal solution concept. The set of strategies $(s_1,...,s_n)$ is said to be a Nash solution if for any $i$ in $N$ and any $t_i$ in $S_i$,

$$f_i(s_1,...,s_{i-1}, s_i, s_{i+1},...,s_n) \geq f_i(s_1,...,s_{i-1}, t_i, s_{i+1},...,s_n).$$

The Nash solution can be interpreted as the strategies from which every player has no motivation to move.

Hypergame [2,19] also describes the situation with the notions of players, strategies, payoffs and preference. In this sense, the hypergame situation can be said to be a kind of the game situation. However, in the hypergame situation no payoff functions are shared as common knowledge of the agents. This means that "the bounded rationality" is clearly and partly expressed in the hypergame situation.

On the other hand, the traditional game situation assumes a single description of the situation that is represented as a common payoff matrix, while in the hypergame situation each agent can have his own payoff matrix. From this point of view, evolutionary game theory [9,25] is based on "traditional" game theory and our evolutionary approach based on hypergame situation can be considered as another framework for learning of mutual perceptions.

In game theory [12,17] imperfect information game is also concerned with the situation where a player does not have exact knowledge about other player's payoff functions. However in game theory the imperfect information game is transformed into a Bayesian game, which is assumed as "equivalent" to the imperfect information game. Bayesian game is a "usual" game, in which any rules of game are provided as common knowledge among the players. In this sense, usual game theory does not primarily describe the hypergame situation.

This paper also presents a simulation model by genetic algorithm to perform network-type dynamic hypergame. The experiments in this paper specifically perform the learning of the payoff matrices as agent's perception of the situation.

## 14.2  Internal Model Principle for Agent-based Modeling

Given a complex situation in which agents are involved, internal model is a representation of the situation created by an agent himself. Internal model is constructed "inside" the model describing agent's behavior.

The notion of internal model was originally introduced in control theory. The main result about internal model is known as the internal model principle [5]: a control system should include a regulator isomorphic to the system to be controlled. Even when the environmental system for a control system should be controlled, the internal model principle is applicable and commutativity and faithfulness of dynamic properties of the control system should hold.

Complex social system comprises multiple agents who interact one another in making decisions. It is indispensable for each agent to "recognize" the characteristics of other agents about how they make their decisions and select their actions. This recognition of each agent can be represented as his internal model of the situation. The characteristics of agents in a particular decision making situation in agent-based modeling can be composed of, for example, alternatives the agents create, preferences among the alternatives, and so on. Hence an internal model in agent-based modeling should describe such characteristics as the rules of game in a game situation. Then an internal model works as a principle for each agent to make his decision. We should notice that an agent's internal model is possibly different from other agent's ones, whereas in usual game theory every agent has the same rule of game.

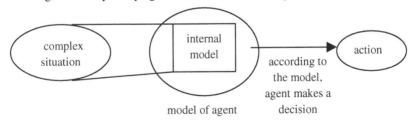

Figure 14.1: Internal Model

Each agent makes his decision according to his internal model. For example, when agent A prefers alternative y to x and believes that agent B prefers x to y, then agent A takes y based on his belief. If, however, agent B prefers y to x, then there must arise a conflict between agents A and B.

Internal model principle for agent-based modeling can be given as the phrase: an agent should construct his internal model isomorphic to the complex situation to make a "good" decision. This is our conjecture.

There are two aspects from which the homomorphism concept for validation in modeling methodology [8,22,23,28,29,30] is applicable to agent-based modeling. One is a homomorphism between an internal model of each agent and the situation. The other is a homomorphism between the model of agents and the reality. The usual concept of validation is concerned with the latter case. We should point out that the former case of "validation" of an internal model can be given by the "agent" based on only his "internal" criterion of decision principle, not by "us" as observers. An agent himself should examine the validity of his internal model, and build a valid internal model based on his decision and its response from the situation. In this sense learning process of internal models of agents would inevitably include the process of validation of each agent.

Based on the concept of internal model we need develop an effective way of actually constructing a "good" model isomorphic to the complex situation. One of the primary purposes of our research in agent-based modeling is to find a mechanism to evolve the internal models of agents. As a hopeful one this paper proposes an evolutionary way for such a mechanism.

# 14.3   Basic Steps and Method for Evolutionary Learning in Agent-based Modeling

This section clarifies the basic steps to be realized in simulation for evolutionary learning in agent-based modeling and provides belief sketch of genetic algorithm as a simulation tool.

## 14.3.1 Basic Steps

The framework for evolutionary learning in agent-based modeling consists of the following four steps.
  (1) Each agent makes a decision and takes an action based on his decision independently.
  (2) Each agent exchanges the results as responses from the complex situation with other agents.
  (3) Each agent improves his "internal model" of the situation in some evolutionary manner.

(4) Each agent makes a new decision and takes an action based on the improved internal model.

Since we assume hypergame situation, each of the above steps can be interpreted in term of game. In step (1) each agent selects a "strategy" so that the equilibrium can be achieved. In step (2) the only direct response from the situation is "opponents' strategies" actually taken. Each agent also knows his own strategy taken and the payoff returned from the situation. We should notice that an agent never knows a priori what payoffs his opponents actually obtained. In step (3) an agent's internal model can be represented by the components of a game; e.g. opponents' strategy sets and opponents' payoff functions. Then each agent improves his payoff matrix.

## 14.3.2 Genetic Algorithm

Genetic algorithm is a simulation tool originated from an evolutionary mechanism in biology [10]. Some essential concepts and words are borrowed from evolution theory: e.g. "chromosome," "gene," "selection," "fitness," "crossover," "mutation," and so on. The steps of simple genetic algorithm are

(1) generation of initial population,

(2) calculation of fitness value of individuals,

(3) selection based on the fitness values,

(4) crossover,

(5) mutation, and

(6) repeat from the step 2.

It is quite natural and important from several reasons that the genetic algorithm is applied directly to evolutionary learning in agent-based modeling.

First genetic algorithm can provide an effective computational way to perform the process of the improvement of internal models by distributive share and exchange of cognitive information of the complex situation. Furthermore genetic algorithm itself can be considered as a specific model of this process.

Second an actual learning process in genetic algorithm can be seen as a process of learning an internal model. Hence, in a sense, we can "observe" how the perception of the complex situation is improved, and an internal model adapts the situation.

# 14.4   Hypergame Model for Evolutionary Learning

A hypergame situation is basically described as a game situation in terms of the basic notions of "game," such as player, strategy and payoff. However the hypergame situation has essentially different features from the game situation.

In a hypergame situation each player behaves as an autonomous agent who makes a decision based on his own "internal model" that describes individually and independently the complex situation where he is involved.

This means that the rule of the game is not shared as the common knowledge among the players in a hypergame situation. Each component of the game is constructed individually based on each player's perception of the situation.

For example, let us describe a hypergame in international relations [11]. A and B are rulers of two nations, each desiring peace but suspicious of the other. They both want mutual disarmament, but a search for security prompts an arms race as reacting to the threat of the other's weapons. They do not trust each other. We can model such a situation as a rather artificially simple one. We suppose that each player has the same strategies: arm or disarm. Figure 14.2 depicts the perceived strategies and their outcomes. A is supposed to love peace and have the following preference order:

Mutual disarmament > Arms lead for A (A arms, B disarms)
> Arms race
> Arms lead for B (A disarms, B arms).

This is not the situation B sees. He believes that A would most prefer an arms lead. Hence A's preferences "as perceived by B" are different from A's actual ones. Similarly A perceives B. Then the hypergame is described as in Figure 14.3.

|  |  | Nation B | |
|  |  | Disarm | Arm |
|---|---|---|---|
| Nation A | Disarm | Mutual disarmament | Arms lead for B |
|  | Arm | Arms lead for A | Arms race |

Figure 14.2: Strategies and Outcomes

| A | | B | | | | B | | | |
|  |  | Disarm | Arm | |  | Disarm | Arm | |  |
|---|---|---|---|---|---|---|---|---|---|
| A | Disarm | 4, 3 | 1, 4 | |  | 3, 4 | 1, 3 | Disarm | A |
|  | Arm | 3, 1 | 2, 2 | |  | 4, 1 | 2, 2 | Arm |  |

game perceived by A      game perceived by B

Figure 14.3: Hypergame: Example of "Mutual Suspicion"

If they both make their decisions and take their behavior according to their belief, then an arms race would be unfortunately selected, although the mutual armament should be realized as the most preferable alternative for both.

The hypergame above would help explain what was going on in the real situation. The problem we are concerned with is how both the nations could learn the situation or improve their belief to make a desirable decision. We should notice that the concept of hypergame situation does not properly include the learning process, but describe a complex situation to explain what was/is going on. To develop the learning process in hypergame situation we will define network-type dynamic hypergame after clarifying the problem of learning in hypergame situation.

A primitive description of hypergame situation is usually formalized as a simple hypergame. Here we call this model one-shot two-person hypergame since by essentially enhancing it we formulate an evolutionary model below as network-type dynamical hypergame.

**Definition 4.1 (One-shot Two-person Hypergame)** A one-shot two-person hypergame is defined by

$$(S_1, S_{12}, S_2, S_{21}, f_1, f_{12}, f_2, f_{21})$$

where

$S_i$ is the set of strategies of player $i$,

$S_{ij}$ is the set of strategies of player $i$ perceived by player $j$,

$f_1$ is the payoff function of player $1$ from $S_1 * S_{21}$ to the set of real numbers,

$f_{12}$ is the payoff function of player $1$ perceived by player $2$
from $S_{12} * S_2$ to the set of real numbers,

$f_2$ is the payoff function of player $2$ from $S_{12} * S_2$ to the set of real numbers,

$f_{21}$ is the payoff function of player $2$ perceived by player $1$
from $S_1 * S_{21}$ to the set of real numbers.

In usual (traditional) game theory, non-cooperative two-person game is considered to be defined by $S_i = S_{ij}$, $f_i = f_{ij}$. This means that in hypergame the recognition by player 1 is possibly different from the actual elements of the game of player 2. Then $S_{ji}$ and $f_{ji}$ represent the internal model of player $i$.

The problem concerning the learning process in agent-based modeling is to understand the process how each player can learn the rule of the game.

For example, in two-person hypergame given in Definition 4.1 the elements of the game, i.e. players, strategy sets, payoff functions, define the "situation" for players. In this situation we can say that player 1 completely "learns" the situation for him, if $S_{21} = S_1$ and $f_{21} = f_1$ are achieved.

We should notice that no player can know that the above conditions are actually achieved since player 1 can only perceive $S_{21}$ and $f_{21}$. Hence such "correct" elements, i.e. $S_{21}$ and $f_{21}$, cannot be used as the criteria of the player for the "learning" process in hypergame situation. The criteria of the player should be "internally" made from the actually perceived information and response from the situation.

There are two essential aspects to give an answer to the above learning problem in agent-based modeling.

One aspect is that the game should be repeatedly played, as the term "learning" implies "repeating." Each game in one period of the repetition should be more improved than in the former period. In this sense this should not be called a "repeated game" that is performed with the same game in every period. We need to extend "one-shot" hypergame to more dynamic one.

The other essential aspect for learning in hypergame situation is "network." The players in the situation should form a network with other players such as organization. As described above, a single player can have only a restricted section of information of the complex situation. To produce effective information for learning the situation the players need to aggregate by "network" various sections of information gained from multifaceted aspects of them.

This shows a way of decision making by forming network. Autonomous decision makers form a network to exchange their sections of information and aggregate them. Then each decision maker improves his perception of the situation based on the result of the aggregation and makes the next step of decision. This type of decision making can be called "network-type decision making."

Hence we extend one-shot hypergame to network-type dynamic one. First we define the network-type two-person hypergame.

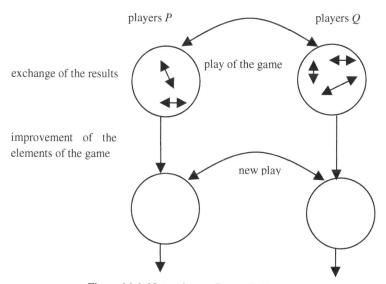

Figure 14.4: Network-type Dynamic Hypergame

**Definition 4.2 (Network-type Two-person Hypergame)** A network-type two-person hypergame is defined by

$$< \{P,Q\}, \{S_P, S_{Qpi}, G_{pi}, G_{Qpi}\}_{pi \in P}, \{S_Q, S_{Pqj}, G_{qj}, G_{Pqj}\}_{qj \in Q} >$$

where
$P$ and $Q$ are respectively the sets of players, $P=\{p_1,...,p_m\}$ and $Q=\{q_1,...,q_n\}$,
$S_P$ is the common strategy set of the players $P$,
$S_{Qpi}$ is the perceived strategy set of the players $Q$ by player $p_i$,
$G_{pi}$ is $p_i$'s payoff function from $S_P*S_{Qpi}$ to the set of real numbers,
$G_{Qpi}$ is the perceived payoff function of $Q$ by $p_i$ from $S_P*S_{Qpi}$
to the set of real numbers, $S_Q$, $S_{Pqj}$, $G_{qj}$, $G_{Pqj}$ are similarly given for $Q$.

The players in the same player set form a network to exchange the information. $S_{Qpi}$, $G_{Qpi,}$ $S_{Pqj,}$ and $G_{Pqj}$ represent the internal models of player $p_i$ or $q_j$.
The above network-type two-person hypergame expresses a one-shot game, in which only one play is performed. Based on this definition of network-type hypergame, we define the network-type dynamic hypergame to represent the learning process in hypergame situation.

**Definition 4.3 (Network-type Dynamic Hypergame)**   A network-type dynamic hypergame is composed of a network-type two-person hypergame and the following steps.

1. **Play.** Each player in the player set plays with some player in the other player set and obtains the outcome and payoff.   ⁄
2. **Exchange of the results.** Each player exchanges his results of the play with the players in the same player set.
3. **Improvement of the elements of the game.** Improvement of the perceived strategy set or the perceived payoff function. Each player changes and improves his perceived strategy set or payoff function so as that it is most plausible to interpret the exchanged results of the play.
4. **New play.** Then each player again plays with another player based on the newly perceived game.

A network-type dynamic game is evolutionarily repeated in the above way.

# 14.5   Simulation of Evolutionary Learning based on Network type Dynamic Hypergame

We demonstrate evolutionary learning process by some experiments based on the framework of network-type dynamic hypergame. First we put some assumptions to perform simulation.

## 14.5.1   Assumptions

This paper deals with the case where each player of $P$ perceives a possibly different payoff function, but correctly perceives the strategy set of the opponent players. The player $Q$ is supposed as the "nature" so that $Q$ correctly perceives the situation.

We assume that $S_P = S_Q = \{a,b,c\} = S_{Qpi} = S_{Pqj}$ and the payoffs of each player are either 0,1 or 2. Hence each payoff function, $G_{pi}$, $G_{qj}$, is a function from $\{a,b,c\}^2$ to $\{0,1,2\}$, which might be different from the targets of the learning, i.e. it might be that $G_{Qpi}$ is not equal to $G_{qj}$. These are parts of the common knowledge among the players.

In the current experiment, the payoff functions are given as follows.

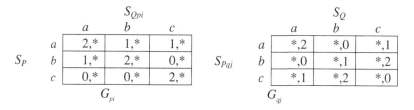

Figure 14.5: Payoff Functions

The values of the asterisks (*) in Figure 14.5 are given by $G_{Qpi}$ and $G_{Pqj}$ that are interpreted as "internal models" of the players.

Some specific interpretations of the above model are possible. For example, let us consider a marketing group that wants to know the behavior of consumers. Then the marketing group corresponds to the player set $P$ and the consumers to $Q$ as "nature."

## 14.5.2  Steps of the Simulation

The basic steps of the current evolutionary simulation by genetic algorithm are as follows.

1.  The simulator generates the player set, $P$, with the size of 30 populations. Each individual is expressed by

    $$(x_1, x_2, x_3, x_4, x_5, x_6, x_7, x_8, x_9), x_i \in \{0,1,2\},$$

    which are the elements of the perceived payoff functions, $G_{Qpi}$ (see Figure 14.6).

$$S_{Qpi}$$

|       | a       | b       | c       |
|-------|---------|---------|---------|
| a     | 2,$x_1$ | 1,$x_2$ | 1,$x_3$ |
| b     | 1,$x_4$ | 2,$x_5$ | 0,$x_6$ |
| c     | 0,$x_7$ | 0,$x_8$ | 2,$x_9$ |

$S_P$ (left label), $G_{pi}$

Figure 14.6: The game player P perceives

2.  The strategy sets are specified. In the current simulation, $S_p = S_Q = \{a,b,c\}$ is assumed to be correctly perceived by each player.
3.  Each player of $P$ plays with $Q$. Based on the individually perceived payoff function that is expressed as in the first step, one of the Nash solutions is performed in each play. To make Nash solution meaningful, we assume that each player "believes" that his internal model is correct and the opponent player also see the same payoff matrix. If the payoff functions have no Nash solution, then a strategy is randomly chosen. We should notice that any player cannot know which payoff his opponent has obtained. Each player can see only the strategy his opponent took, his own strategy and the payoff obtained.
4.  The simulator calculates the fitness value of each player from the results of the play. The fitness, as stated later, is essential for the learning. It represents the characteristics of the exchange of information in the player set
5.  Some players are selected as good parents using the proportional strategy of the fitness.
6.  The one-point crossover is done. Then the perceived payoff functions are improved.
7.  The next generation set of players are generated, and repeated from the 3rd step.

In the current experiments we did not use mutation, since it would not play any essential role in the results.

## 14.5.3 Fitness

In this section we describe the fitness used in the current experiments. From the result of a play in one period, each player can know directly the strategy what his opponent player took and his own payoff he got. The fitness is basically calculated from two values: opportunity loss and cost for changing the representation. The fitness $f$ is defined as follows:

$$f = \frac{1}{1 + w * (\text{opportunity loss}) * (\text{cost for changing the representation})}$$

where $w$ is a weight parameter.

The opportunity loss expresses the difference between the actually obtained payoff and the payoff that would have been obtained if the perceived payoff function were correct. In our case since each player plays a Nash solution, he could obtain the maximum payoff 2 if the perceived payoff function is correct. Then the opportunity loss can be calculated by 2-(the actually obtained payoff).

The cost for changing the representation (payoff function) indicates a kind of penalty that should be paid in improving the payoff function from the results of the play. It is calculated basically by

$ABS((\#existing\ Nash\ solutions) - (\#expected\ Nash\ solutions)),$

where $ABS(*)$ stands for the absolute value of $*$, $(\#existing\ Nash\ solutions)$ is the number of the Nash solutions existing in the payoff function and $(\#expected\ Nash\ solutions)$ is the number of the Nash solutions that are expected with some subjective probability. Here the probability is given according to the combinatorial structure of the payoff function: the probability that there is no Nash solution is $0.296(=8/3^3)$, the probability that there is one Nash solution is $0.444(=4/9)$, the probability that there are two Nash solutions is $0.222(=2/9)$ and the probability that there are three Nash solutions is $0.037(=1/3^3)$.

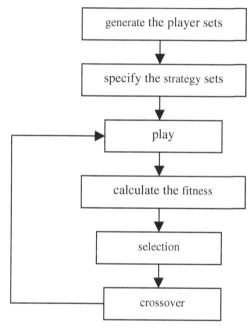

Figure 14.7: Steps of the Simulation

The following cases are separately calculated.

Case 1. The opportunity loss is zero and $(\#existing\ Nash\ solutions) = (\#expected\ Nash\ solutions) = 2$.

Then the cost for changing the representation takes 0 or 2 randomly.

Case 2. The opportunity loss is not zero, and

Case 2-1: $(\#existing\ Nash\ solutions) = (\#expected\ Nash\ solutions) = 1$,

then the cost for changing the representation is given by 2, since we think that a Nash solution is not in the expected pair of strategies but in the unexpected one;

Case 2-2: $(\#existing\ Nash\ solutions) = 1$ and $(\#expected\ Nash\ solutions) = 2$,

then the cost for changing the representation takes 1 or 3 randomly;

Case 2-3: *(#existing Nash solutions)* = 2 and *(#expected Nash solutions)* = 1, then the cost for changing the representation is given by 3;
Case 2-4: *(#existing Nash solutions)* = *(#expected Nash solutions)* = 2, then the cost for changing the representation takes 0 or 2 randomly.

## 14.5.4 Selection and Crossover

In the 4th step of the simulation, we use the proportional strategy of the fitness to select two parents for the crossover. The probability $Pi$ that an individual $i$ is selected is given by

$$Pi = \frac{f_i}{\sum_{j=1}^{n} f_j},$$

where $f_i$ is the fitness of $i$.

The crossover used in the 5th step is performed at one point chosen randomly. The children inherit the "genes" of one of the parents that have better payoff in the then play.

# 14.6  Results

The results of the experiments shown in this section are obtained by setting the□ parameters as follows. At first 30 sets of population are randomly generated. The probability of crossover is 0.6. The weight $w$ varies from 0.1 to 10 by 0.1 step. These parameters were chosen based on the results of preparatory experiments done before the experiments. Under the same parameter conditions we repeated 3 times of simulation. Then in total we have 900 sets of players to be learned (30 sets of population*10 weights*3 repeats).

The results of learning fall into three categories as follows.

1. Learning the positions of Nash solutions in the payoff function (category 1).
2. Learning the positions of the maximum payoff 2 (category 2).
3. Learning the payoff function completely (category 3).

It seems impossible to achieve the learning of category 3 since in hypergame situation no player can obtain other information about the opponents than their taking strategies. Indeed from the results it is hard to distinguish the learning of category 3 from random search.

The learning of category 1 is weaker than that of category 2 in the sense that if the positions of payoff 2 are correctly perceived, then every Nash solution can be found. Our current experiment includes the case that there is no Nash solution in the payoff functions. Then category 2 is more suitable for the concept of learning in our case.

The following figures indicate the experimental results.

Successful sets in number
Category 2              328/900
Category 3               47/900

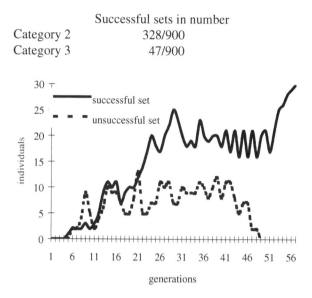

Figure 14.8: Typical Learning Process

When the weight is 0.1, the individuals succeeded most in category 2. Successful individuals in number decreased as the weight increased. In category 3 there was no remarkable difference among the weights. Though the successful learning processes depended on the patterns of the initial population sets generated in the first step, we did not see any specific one in the population sets. In particular, the experimental results did not depend on if the initial population set included the individuals having the same payoff with player $Q$. A typical learning process is shown in Figure 14.8.

The positions for the crossover used in this experiment were determined randomly. This caused fatal chromosomes, which had to be taken care separately. If the crossover is done so as not to cause fatal chromosomes, the result would be improved.

## 14.7   Conclusions

In this paper we developed a general framework for evolutionary learning in agent-based modeling. The framework consists of the four basic steps, in which the internal model and its improvement process are essential for the evolutionary learning. The internal model of an agent can be validated only by the agent's "internal" criterion of decision principle.

Then we formulated network-type dynamic hypergame to describe an evolutionary learning process based on game situation. A hypergame model is simple but very powerful to describe internal model of agent involved in the complex situation.

Based on network-type dynamic hypergame, we performed basic experiments of evolutionary learning by using genetic algorithm. The experiments given in this paper should be considered to provide a "basis" for further development of hypergame situation. There are a lot of directions to extend the current experiments based on the framework of evolutionary learning. A game situation can be recognized as a hypergame situation, when more than one element of the rules of the game are not shared with players. The elements of the rules of the game include strategies, payoffs, players and outcomes. Then we can have many possibilities of problems: how agents learn about what strategies other agents have or how many agents are involved in the situation, and so on. So far some of extensions have been studied. They include the cases that two player sets learn "simultaneously" the other player's payoff matrix [20], or that three player sets are involved in the situation [21], or that a player set learns the strategies of the nature under some restricted conditions on strategy [15,16].

Finally we should point out that organizational learning would be an important application field of evolutionary learning in agent-based modeling [4,7]. Organizational learning generally consists of two phases: learning by individuals and learning in organizational decision making by aggregation of individual capabilities. The concept of internal model can play an essential role in the both phases. In particular we expect that evolutionary approach would provide an effective method for the aggregation of internal models to extend the capability of organizational decision making.

# References

[1] R.Axelrod, "The Complexity of Cooperation," Princeton University Press, 1997.

[2] P.G.Bennet, "Hypergames: Developing a Model of Conflict," Futures, Vol.12, pp.489-507, 1980.

[3] L.E.Blume and D.Easley, "Learning to be Rational," J. of Economic Theory, 26, 340-351, 1982.

[4] K.M.Carley and L.Gasser, "Computational Organization Theory," in G.Weiss (Ed.), Multiagent Systems – A Modern Approach to Distributed Artificial Intelligence, MIT Press, 1999.

[5] R.C.Connant and W.R.Ashby, "Every good regulator of a system must be a model of that system," Int.J.Systems Sc., 1(2), pp.89-97, 1970.

[6] H.Dawid, "Adaptive Learning by Genetic Algorithms – Analytical Results and Applications to Economic Models," 2nd Ed., Springer, 1999.

[7] R.Espejo, W.Schuhmann, M.Schwaninger, and Bilello,U.,"Organizational Transformation and Learning,"Wiley, 1996.

[8] R.L.Flood and E.R.Carson, "Dealing with Complexity," Plenum, 1988.

[9] H.Hanappi, "Evolutionary Economics," Avebury, 1994.

[10] J.H.Holland, "Adaptation in Natural and Artificial Systems," Ann Arbor: University of Michigan Press, 1975, (2nd ed) MIT Press, 1992.

[11] A.Marcet and T.J.Sargent, "Convergence of Least Squares learning Mechanisms in Self Referential Linear Stochastic Models," J. of Economic Theory, 48, 337-368, 1989.

[12] A.Okada, "Game Theory," Yuhikaku Press, 1996 (in Japanese).

[13] C.Patterson, "Evolution," British Museum (Natural History), 1978.

[14] U.S.Putro,K.Kijima and S.Takahashi, "Simulation of Adaptation Process in Hypergame Situation by Genetic Algorithm," SAMS, (to appear).

[15] U.S.Putro,K.Kijima and S.Takahashi, "Simulation Approach to Learning Problem in Hypergame Situation by Genetic Algorithm," Proceedings of IEEE International Conference on Systems, Man, and Cybernetics, Vol.IV, pp.260-265, 1999.

[16] U.S.Putro,K.Kijima and S.Takahashi, "Adaptive Learning of Hypergame Situations by Using Genetic Algorithm," IEEE Trans. of Systems, Man and Cybernetics (to appear).

[17] E.Rasmusen, "Games and Information," Basil Blackwell, 1989.

[18] S.Sen and Gerhard Weiss, "Learning in Multiagent Systems," in G.Weiss (Ed.), Multiagent Systems – A Modern Approach to Distributed Artificial Intelligence, MIT Press, 1999.

[19] J.Rosenhead (ed.), "Rational Analysis for a Problematic World - Problem Structuring Methods for Complexity, Uncertainty and Conflict," Wiley, 1990.

[20] S.Takahashi, "Evolutionary Approach to Hypergame Situation," IEEE Trans. of Systems, Man and Cybernetics (submitted).

[21] S.Takahashi, "Evolutionary Approach to Three-person Hypergame Situation," Proceedings of IEEE International Conference on Systems, Man, and Cybernetics, Vol.IV, pp.254-259, 1999.

[22] S.Takahashi, "General Morphism for Modeling Relations in Multimodeling," Transactions of the Society for Computer Simulation International, Vol.13, No.4, pp.169-178, 1997.

[23] S.Takahashi and Y.Takahara, "Logical Approach to Systems Theory," Springer-Verlag, 1995.

[24] S.Takahashi,B.Nakano and M.Arase, "Application of Genetic Algorithm to Analysis of Adaptation Processes of Individual Perceptions in Hypergame Situation," J.of Japan Association of Management Information, Vol.4, No.1, 1995 (in Japanese).

[25] F.Vega-Redondo, "Evolution, Games, and Economic Behaviour," Oxford University Press, 1996.

[26] J.W.Weibull, "Evolutionary Game Theory," MIT Press, 1996.

[27] M.Wooldridge, "Intelligent Agents," in G.Weiss (Ed.), Multiagent Systems – A Modern Approach to Distributed Artificial Intelligence, MIT Press, 1999.

[28] B.P.Zeigler, "Theory of Modelling and Simulation," Wiley, 1976.

[29] B.P.Zeigler, "Multi-Faceted Modelling and Discrete Event Simulation," Academic Press, 1984.

[30] B.P.Zeigler, "Object Oriented Simulation with Hierarchical, Modular Models: Intelligent Agents and Endomorphic Systems, Academic Press," 1990.

# Chapter 15

# A System Theoretic Approach to Constructing Test Beds for Multi-Agent Systems

## A.M. Uhrmacher

*As the number of multi-agent systems grows so does the need for testing agents in virtual dynamic environments. A system theoretic approach to constructing test beds for multi-agent systems is presented. The formalism is rooted in DEVS and describes agents and their environments as reflective time triggered automata. The hierarchical compositional model design is complemented by an abstract simulator to support the parallel, discrete event execution of the reflective automata.*

*This theoretical exploration has brought into being the simulation system JAMES, a Java-Based Agent Modeling Environment for Simulation. It constitutes a framework for constructing test beds, in which the effects of different agent strategies, e.g. referring to deliberation, mobility, and interaction, can be experimentally analyzed. The model design allows describing and embedding agents that deliberately change the overall systems' interaction and composition structure, e.g. by moving from one interaction context to another. The execution layer realizes the abstract simulator in a distributed environment. To reduce communications over the net, a move at the model level from one interaction context to another is answered by migrating processes at the execution layer. Thus in JAMES, modeling and simulation layer are coined equally by an agent-based perspective.*

## 15.1 Introduction

As the number of agent-oriented software systems is increasing, so does the need for tools which support the testing of multi-agent systems. Testing of agents means not necessarily testing within predefined, arbitrary, dynamic or static scenarios, which, as Hanks points out [7], bears the danger to become an end in itself, but ultimately should be aimed at analyzing how agents will perform in the environment they are constructed for. With agents, Artificial Intelligence methods have moved towards embedded applications, "the ultimate interest being not simplified systems and environments but rather real world systems deployed in complex environments." [p.18] [7]. This ultimate goal is the very reason why Steve Hanks doubts the effectiveness of small world experimentation and Martha Pollack interprets them as the only possible approach to begin with. If we assume that testing in the small and testing in the large complement each other in constructing agents, we have to ask what a test environment has to look like to nurture both approaches.

A modular, compositional construction of experimental frames facilitates reuse and the testing of agents in different environments. It allows also one to build more realistic environments from simpler ones. To characterize "the agent, the world, and their relationship" [p.37] [7], which is essential in interpreting and communicating the results gained in experimentation, a declarative, sound description of the experimental frame is mandatory. This extends to the integration of agents, the modeling of interaction, and the temporal dimension of the overall system.

This argumentation line leads us to the formal approaches of discrete event simulation and the question which among those to choose. Petri Nets, DEVS, Event-Oriented Graphical Techniques [10], to name only a few, all offer a specific view in modeling dynamic systems. Whereas most discrete event simulations pertain to events and processes as the elementary units, DEVS [20,23] describes dynamic systems as time and event triggered state automata, a perception which coincides with an acknowledged interpretation of agents.

State automata are used as a unifying abstract perception throughout the literature on agents and multi-agent systems. Rosenschein and Kaelbling introduce a situated automaton whose interaction with its environment is characterized as a stream of inputs and a stream of outputs [13]. The automaton transforms inputs into outputs to control its environment. Within situated automata knowledge is compiled into transition rules. Therefore, they are typically associated with reactive agent architectures, or "reflex agents with state". Reflex agents with state represent one stage in the evolution of agents as proposed by Russell and Norvig within their textbook on Artificial Intelligence [14]. An agent updates its state according to the percepts that are interpreted with respect to its current state, chooses its action and updates its state to report its selection. Finally, it executes the action. Whereas strategies to select the best action vary and the state is structured differently, the sketched scheme resurfaces as a unifying frame to describe agents that *reason logically*, that *act logically*, or that *act under uncertainty*.

State automata are not only used as a frame to construct agents, but to specify agents and their behavior. E.g. based on state automata d'Inverno and his colleagues specify protocols that are used within the agent system AGENTIS to control the registration, provision, and negotiation of services between agents [5]. Automata form an abstraction to specify the behavior of agents, this type of abstraction can also be employed by agents themselves. Agents might perceive other agents as state automata. In this case, learning the behavior pattern of another agent means deriving a state automaton which mimics the "opponent's" behavior and allows the agent to choose the most rational action, e.g. in a repeated two player game [3].

Thus, state automata play a central role in bringing together "the different strands of research and development in multi-agent systems" as d'Inverno and his colleagues demonstrated "by taking a commercially developed system (Agentis) and providing it with a firm, formal foundation that lends itself to further analysis and investigation" [p.14][5].

Our exploration starts with merging the automaton based view of agents with the model design in DEVS. To capture the phenomenon of adaptation in multi-agent systems a reflective mechanism is called for. In the introduced formalism a model is perceived as a minimal set of state automata each of which might create depending on its state a new automata which again belongs to the overall model. Each of these represents an incarnation of the model, a phase within the life of a model which is characterized by homogeneous structure and behavior pattern. The adaptation refers not only to an agent's own behavior and properties but to the composition of and interaction with its environment. As in DEVS, network models are introduced to group atomic models. In network models, the set of components and interactions might vary from one network incarnation to the next initiated by the changes at the atomic level. An abstract simulator produces the intended behavior of the proposed modeling formalism. The implementation of the formalism and its application in simulating multi-agent systems are illuminated by JAMES. JAMES, a Java-Based Agent Modeling Environment for Simulation, constitutes a framework for constructing test beds, in which the effects of different agent strategies, e.g. referring to deliberation, mobility, and interaction, can be experimentally analyzed. The model design which allows describing and embedding agents that deliberately change the overall systems' interaction and composition structure is illustrated by a small application example. The execution layer realizes the abstract simulator in a distributed environment. To reduce communications over the net, a move at the model level from one interaction context to another is answered by migrating processes at the execution layer. The description of the distributed and concurrent execution concludes the paper.

# 15.2  DEVS

Whereas other formal approaches to discrete event simulation emphasize the concept of event, or activity, or process, DEVS (Discrete Event Systems

Specification), a system theoretical approach to discrete event simulation emphasizes state [20,23].

DEVS distinguishes between atomic and coupled models. Since we are interested in describing concurrently active agents, we will focus on a DEVS dialect that allows the processing of simultaneous internal and external events [4]. An atomic model is a time triggered state automaton. It is described by a set of input events, a state set, a set of output events, an internal, external, and confluent transition function, an output and time advance function. The internal transition function dictates state transitions due to internal events, the time of which is determined by the time advance function. The external transition function is triggered by external inputs which are defined as bags over simultaneously arriving input events. If an external and internal event coincide, the behavior of a model is defined by the confluent transition function. Often the confluent transition function is realized by applying the external transition function to the result of the internal transition function. Each model communicates with the external "world" through its input and output events, the latter of which it produces given an internal event (Figure 15.1).

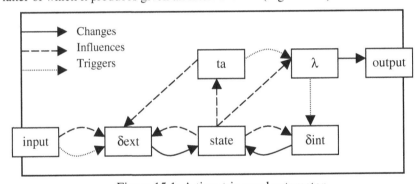

Figure 15.1: A time triggered automaton

An atomic model can easily be interpreted as an agent. The state space of an atomic model can be structured to describe and link modules of deliberative agents, e.g. desires, intentions, and beliefs. The transition functions can be employed to describe stimulus response pattern but can embrace deliberative processes as well, e.g. for planning and learning. With each state, the time advance function associates the time this state will persist "per se". It determines the time of the next internal event and output, e.g. the time an agent needs for reacting. Besides describing the time needed for reaction or deliberation, the time-advance function allows also a pro-active behavior of an agent, since outputs depend on an agent's current state and are triggered by the flow of time. Thus, an agent does not require any external event to stay active.

Besides atomic models, DEVS supports the definition of coupled models. A coupled model is a model consisting of different components and specifying the coupling of its components. Its interface to its environment is given by a set of external input and output events, a set of component models, that may be atomic or coupled and the coupling which exists among the components and between the components and its own input and output. Coupled models support a modular and hierarchical modeling. According to the coupling, coupled models forward messages which have been produced by components to other components or to their own output. Thus, the coupling restricts the possible interaction between agents and their environment.

The modeling layer is complemented by a separate simulation layer: the abstract simulator which is comprised of a set of simulators and coordinators. Each simulator is associated with an atomic model and each coordinator is associated with a coupled model [20,23].

## 15.3   A formalism to Describe Reflective Dynamic Systems

From a system theoretic perception multi-agent systems form a specific type of dynamic system. An agent's deliberation and activity is based on its internal knowledge, i.e. internal model [22,15], of its environment. This knowledge enables agents e.g. to control continuous processes in the model's environment [12] and to manipulate the model's and its environment's structure [15]. Whereas the DEVS formalism is sufficient general to embrace deliberation processes, internal models, and controlling the environment by output generation, an agent that changes its interaction structure and the composition of its environment cannot easily be expressed. As do other formal approaches to discrete event simulation, DEVS presupposes a static structure of the overall model. The activities of a DEVS model are restricted to changing the values of its state variables and to charging the output ports with messages to be sent to other models. To describe models whose description contains the possibility to change their own structure and consequently their behavior, Zeigler emphasizes the necessity to "introduce a higher level of system specification, corresponding to Klir's [9] meta system level" [p.196][21].

Structural changes can be found in many domains. However, the appearance and disappearance of models and interaction structures are a characteristic and salient feature of multi-agent systems. Agents are constructed to work in environments, whose composition and interaction might vary due to the environment's inherent dynamics or due to an agent's deliberative manipulation, including its own migration. Thus, mechanisms that empower the atomic model to reflect about its own performance and to initiate structural changes are required, e.g. to launch new agents, commit suicide, and access its own interaction structure.

To be applicable to multi-agent systems the original DEVS formalism has to be changed to capture reflectivity by a recursive definition of models [19]. In *Dynamic DEVS* a model might change its behavioral and structural pattern depending on the current state. Whereas in traditional DEVS, transitions result in a changed state of a model only, in Dynamic DEVS transitions possibly give rise to "new" models [19].

**Definition 1 (dynDEVS)** *A Dynamic DEVS is a structure*
$dynDEVS =_{df} < X, Y, m_{init}, M(m_{init})>$ *with*

| | |
|---|---|
| $X, Y$ | *structured set of inputs and outputs* |
| $m_{init} \in M$ | *the initial model* |
| $M(m_{init})$ | *the least set\* with the following structure* |

$\{ < S, s_{init}, \delta_{ext}, \delta_{int}, \delta_{con}, \rho_\alpha, \lambda, t_a > |$

| | |
|---|---|
| $S$ | *structured set of sequential states* |
| $s_{init} \in S$ | *the initial state* |
| $\delta_{ext}: Q \times X \to S$ | *external transition* |
| | *with $Q = \{(s, e) : s \in S, 0 \le e \le ta(s)\}$* |
| $\delta_{int}: S \to S$ | *internal transition* |
| $\delta_{con}: S \times X \to S$ | *confluent transition* |
| $\rho_\alpha: S \setminus s_{init} \to M(m_{init})$ | *model transition* |
| $\lambda: S \to Y$ | *output function* |
| $t_a: S \to R_0^+ \cup \{\infty\}$ | *time advance function g }* |

*\*$M(m_{init})$ is the least set for which the following property holds*
$\forall n \in M(m_{init}). (\exists m \in M(m_{init}). n = \rho_\alpha(s^m)$ *with* $s^m \in S^m) \lor n = m_{init}$

*In addition, a dynDEVS satisfies the following constraint: The model transition $\rho_\alpha$ does not interfere with other transitions, it preserves the values of variables which are common to two successive models in dynDEVS and assigns initial values to the "new" variables.*

$i(S^m) = s^m \land \rho_\alpha(s^m) = n \land i(S^n) = s^n \to$
$\qquad \forall d \in D^m \cap D^n . s_d^m = s_d^n \land \forall d \in D^n \setminus D^m . s_d^n = s_{initd}$

*$S^m$ and $S^n$ are the set of states of $m \in M(m_{init})$ and $n \in M(m_{init})$. As does DEVS, Dynamic DEVS defines states as structured sets with $D^m$ and $D^n$ sets of variable names and i the assignment function, which assigns values to the variables. $s_d^n$ denotes the state, i.e. current value, of the variable d in n.*

In structured sets, variables play the role of a co-ordinate, they have a name and a range set, within which one element is tagged as the initial value. To maintain values of variables while applying the model transition $\rho_\alpha$, means are required to identify variables that occur in successive incarnations of a *dynDEVS* model and to discern them from those that are new, i.e. that occur in the later but not in the former incarnation.

Models might differ referring to state space, internal, external transition, output, time advance, and model transition function. Whereas internal and external transition functions are responsible for changing state values the model transition $\rho_\alpha$ produces, given a state, a new incarnation of the model which adheres to the above constraint (Figure 15.2). Since each application of $\rho_\alpha$ depends only on the current state of the model the produced set of models beginning with the new incarnation constitutes a subset of the set of models produced by the initial incarnation $m_{init}$.

**Proposition 1** *Each of the temporary incarnations of a Dynamic DEVS model, m* ∈ *M( $m_{init}$), gives rise to a Dynamic DEVS model itself, i.e.:*

$$< X, Y, m, M(m)> \text{ with } M(m) \subseteq M(m_{init})$$

All successive models produced by the model transition will be contained in the set $M(m_{init})$. Whereas the internal structure of a model might change during simulation, its interface will stay the "same". Structural changes are kept transparent for an external observer, even if the output produced by a model might vary due to internal structural changes.

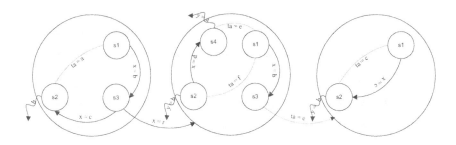

Figure 15.2: Structural and non-structural transitions in Dynamic DEVS [19]

A Dynamic DEVS can obviously simulate the behavior of a DEVS model. But also a DEVS model can be constructed which simulates a Dynamic DEVS model. It can be shown that both formalisms are bisimilar [19].

In Dynamic DEVS, the reflective nature of varying state spaces and behavior pattern is emphasized by a recursive definition of Dynamic DEVS models based on a set of models. Model transitions map the current state of a model into a set of models the former belongs to. A model's structure is a result of the model's dynamics and evolves dynamically. In contrast, regular DEVS requires to have a global idea of what might happen from the very beginning, the state space, transition and output function have to foresee all eventualities (cp. [1]).

Like coupled models structure the organizational plane and support a modular construction by composition, reflectivity structures the temporal plane into chunks of homogeneous state and behavior pattern. Variable structures support a modular and space efficient model design by substitution.

## 15.3.1 Dynamic DEVS Networks

Networks (alias coupled models) do not add functionality to atomic models since each network can be expressed as an atomic model (due to the closure under coupling property inherited from DEVS) [20], however they enable the compositional construction of models.

**Definition 2 ( dynNDEVS)** *A Dynamic network, a dynNDEVS, is the structure* $dynNDEVS =_{df} < X, Y, N_{init}, N(n_{init})>$ *with*

| | |
|---|---|
| $X$ | *set of inputs* |
| $Y$ | *set of outputs* |
| $n_{init} \in N(n_{init})$ | *the start configuration* |
| $N( n_{init} )$ | *the least set * with the following structure* |
| $\{ < D, \rho_N, \{ dynDEVS_i\}, \{I_i\} >\|$ | |
| $D$ | *set of component names* |
| $\rho_N$ | $S^n \to N( n_{init} )$ |
| | $( S^n = \times_{d \in D} \oplus_{m \in dynDEVS\ d} S^m \setminus$ |
| | $\times_{d \in D} \oplus_{m \in dynDEVS\ d} \{ s_{init}^m \} )$ |
| $dynDEVS_i$ | *set of Dynamic DEVS components with* $i \in D$ |
| $I_i$ | *set of influencers of i with* $I_i \subset D \cup d_N$ |
| | *( $d_N$ name of the network )* |

*$N(n_{init})$ is the least set for which the following property holds*
$$\forall n \in N(n_{init}). (\exists m \in N(n_{init}). n = \rho_N ( s^m) \wedge s^m \in S^m )\vee n = n_{init}$$

*In addition, the dynNDEVS satisfies the following constraint: The application of $\rho_N$ preserves the state and structure of models which belong to the composition of the "old" network and the "new" one. D is the set of component names, each name denotes one Dynamic DEVS model uniquely. Components which are newly created are initialized. Since components represent Dynamic DEVS, their initial state is given by the model $m_{init}$ being in its initial state $s_{init}$.*

$$\forall d \in D^m \cap D^n . m_d^{\ n} = m_d^m$$
$$\forall d\in D^{\ n} \setminus D^m . m_d^{\ n} = m_{initd}$$

The role of the network transition is to answer to external and internal events and their implied structural changes at the component level [19]. The description of a network entails the names of its components $D$ and the domains of these components $dynDEVS_d$. At a time $t$ the network's composition will be given by the current incarnations of the components $dynDEVS_d$. The function $\rho_N$ associates with the state of the network, in terms of the states of its components, a possibly new network with new components, new couplings, new domains of these components, and a new $\rho_N$ function. The domain of each $\rho_N$ function is constructed as the crossproduct over the state space of its components. Since the internal state of a component might vary within the boundary of $dynDEVS_d$ we define the state space of each component as a disjoint sum of the state spaces of its incarnations $m_d$. Even if the internal structure of the components varies, as long as their interface stays the same, the influencers and the output input translation stays valid and with them the network structure which only changes via the network transition.

***Proposition 2 (Elements of a Dynamic Network)*** *Each of the temporary incarnations of a Dynamic DEVS network model, $n \in N( n_{init})$, produces a Dynamic DEVS network itself, i.e.:*

$$< X, Y, n, N(n)> \text{ with } N(n) \subseteq N(n_{init})$$

Network definitions are aimed at structuring the organizational plane, they do not add new functionality. As expected a Dynamic DEVS network can be simulated by a Dynamic DEVS: the introduced formalism is closed under coupling and consequently, bisimilar to original DEVS [19].

## 15.3.2   An abstract simulator for Dynamic DEVS

To produce the behavior of a Dynamic DEVS model is the task of the abstract simulator [23, 5, 26]. With a Dynamic DEVS model a *simulator* is connected.

The simulator holds the incarnation of the model, i.e. $m$, and its state $s_m$, its time of last event $t_{last}$, the time of next event $t_{next}$ and the elapsed time $e$ since the last event. The * message indicates that an event is due, the # message indicates the arrival of an input, the *done* message indicates the completion of an execution.

Whereas the description of the model is time invariant, the simulator is synchronized by external events which are sent to it and which are indexed with a global time measured on an absolute scale. At each simulation step * messages are propagated top down. If the time of next event is due and no inputs are expected the internal transition function is applied, if the time of next event is due and inputs are expected, the confluent transition is invoked, otherwise the external transition will fire. If inputs are expected, i.e. $xCount > 0$ the simulator will wait until all inputs have arrived, i.e. *inpCount* becomes zero.

After the new state is calculated, the model transition $\rho_\alpha$ determines the new model and its state, e.g. the new variables are initialized. After the completion of the transition functions a simulator will inform its parent that the transition has been completed, and will send it the current state of the associated model $m$, the time of next event, and the number of outputs that will be produced at the time of next event.

> when an input ( $*$, $xCount$, $t$) has been received
> $\quad$ $m$ is the associated dynDEVS model and
> $\quad$ $s^m$ the state of the model $m$
> $\quad$ $inpCount = xCount$
> $\quad$ if $t = t_{next}$ then
> $\quad\quad$ send ( $\lambda( s^m )$ ) to parent
> $\quad\quad$ if $xCount = 0$ then
> $\quad\quad\quad$ $s = \delta_{int} (s^m)$
> $\quad\quad$ else
> $\quad\quad\quad$ block until $inpCount = 0$
> $\quad\quad\quad$ $s = \delta_{con}(s^m, x^b)$
> $\quad\quad$ endif
> $\quad$ else
> $\quad\quad$ block until $inpCount = 0$
> $\quad\quad$ $s = \delta_{ext}(s^m, t - t_{last}, x^b)$
> $\quad$ endif
> $\quad$ $m = \rho_\alpha (s^m)$
> $\quad$ $t_{last} = t$
> $\quad$ $t_{next} = t_{last} + ta( s^m )$
> $\quad$ $outCount = 1$
> $\quad$ $x^b = \phi$
> $\quad$ send ($done$, $s^m$, $t_{next}$, $outCount$) to parent
> end

If a simulator receives an input, it decrements $inpCount$ within a separate thread.

> when an input ($\#$; $y$, $t$) has been received
> $\quad$ block until $inpCount > 0$
> $\quad$ $xb = xb + y$
> $\quad$ $inpCount = inpCount - 1$
> end

A simulator's parent, called coordinator, is associated with the coupled model the atomic model belongs to. A simulator receives messages sent by its parent and sends messages to it. The coordinator records the time of last and the time of next event, it calculates the components whose next event is due: $IMM$, components which will receive inputs: $INF$, and the number of their inputs: $iCount$- $r$. It activates its components via $*$ message and waits for the completion of their transitions. To apply the network transition function the coordinator needs some information about the current state of its atomic components. In concrete implementations, neither the simulator nor the coordinator will send the entire state of a model to its parents. Instead it will forward an extraction or abstraction of the state which indicates whether and what kind of structural changes are due to its parent coordinator. To prevent the arrival of inconsistent requests, different implementations employ different constraints on the type of requests each model can induce or the type of model, which can initiate a structural change [19].

when an input $( \ast, xCount; t)$ has been received
    $n$ is the associated Dynamic DEVS network
    imminent children $IMM = \{d \in D \mid t_{nextd} = t \}$
    imminents with output $OM = \{d \mid d \in IMM \wedge outCount > 0\}$
    influencees $INF = \{d \in D \mid \exists i \in OM.i \in I_d \vee ( xCount > 0 \wedge d_N \in I_d)\}$
    for each receiver $r \in INF \cup IMM$
        influencer count $iCount_r = \sum_{d \in Ir \cap OM} outCount_d$
        if $d_N \in I_r$ then
            $iCount_r = iCount_r + xCount$
        send $( \ast, iCount, t)$ to r's processor
        $actCount := actCount + 1$
    end
    block until $actCount = 0$
    $n = \rho_N( s^n )$
    $t_{last} = t$
    $t_{next} = minimum\{ t_{nextd} \}$
    $outCount = \sum_{\{d \in D \mid d \in IdN \wedge tnextd = tnext \}} outCount_d$
    $xb = \phi$
    send $(done, s^n, t_{next}, outCount)$ to parent
end


when $(done, s, t_{next}, outputInfo)$ has been received
    block until $actCount > 0$
    update number of $done$ messages still to be expected
    $actCount = actCount - 1$
    update $s^n$ according to $s$
end


when an input $(\#; y, t)$ has been received
    forward outputs $(x_i, t)$ produced by $i$ according to $Z_{i,j}$
        if $j = d_N$ then to parent coordinator else to component $j$
end

Based on this information the coordinator applies the network transition after all internal, external, and confluent transitions of its components have been completed. Executing the network transition after all other transitions are completed ensures that the network transition does not interfere with non structural transitions.

## 15.4  JAMES

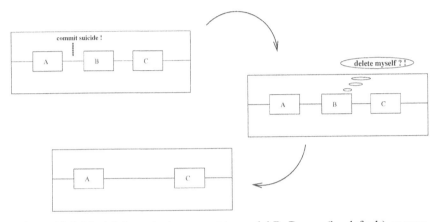

Figure 15.3: Model A sends the request to model B, B may (by default) or may not grant the request

Based on the proposed formalism, JAMES has been developed. In JAMES, each agent has a knowledge base, i.e. a collection of facts about itself and its environment the agent assumes to be true. Based on this knowledge an agent is able to deliberate, e.g. to develop action plans. An action typically has some effect on the internal state of the agent, in addition it might affect an agent's environment. The latter takes shape in charging the output ports and thus, influencing other components via their input ports, or in initiating structural changes, e.g. the change of a behavior pattern, the creation and adding of models, the deletion or removal of itself, and accessing its interaction structure.

Whereas structural changes are initiated by the atomic models, many of them, e.g. the creation of new models, are actually executed at the level of the coupled model. An explicit network transition function does not exist at the level of the coupled model. Instead each component purveys implicitly one part of the network transition which is composed at the coupled model level. Since structural changes can be initiated concurrently, conflicts might arise. To prevent these conflicts and to emphasize the perception of autonomous, yet knowledge and resource restricted agents, the range to initiate structural changes has been restrained. Models can create and add models in the coupled model they belong too, they can delete and remove themselves, and they can access their interaction structure. To initiate structural changes outside their boundary, agents have to turn to communication and negotiation in JAMES. Thus, a movement from one coupled model to another implies that another atomic model complies with the request to add the moving model into the new interaction context. To facilitate modeling, all atomic models are equipped with default methods that allow them to react to those requests. However, these default reactions can be suppressed to decide deliberately what requests shall be executed. The freedom to decide whether to follow a certain request, e.g. to commit suicide (Figure 15.3), and its knowledge, i.e. beliefs, about itself and its environment, distinguish active agents from more "reactive" entities [8].

## 15.4.1   Deliberative agents in JAMES

The "simple planning agent" which Russell and Norvig developed [p.338ff][14] inspired by the beliefs, desires, and intention (BDI) model of agent architectures [6] shall illustrate how an agent can be modeled in JAMES (cp. [16]).

Whereas the original agent does not take deliberation time into account, and does not consider whether the current action is executable as planned, our agent represents a refined version (Figure 15.4). The "still simple planning agent" tests, whether the current planning step is executable according to its beliefs, otherwise it re-plans. The time for deliberation determines when the agent will be able to start with plan execution. It describes the time needed for planning. The longer the agent needs for plan generation, the more likely a re-planning is required in a dynamic environment.

The attitudes, beliefs, desires, and intentions, comprise an agent's internal state. Updating attitudes and the selection of suitable actions are transferred to the external, internal transition (the confluent transition function is defined by applying the external after the internal transition function [4]), and output function (Figure 15.4):

- The external transition function encodes the reaction of the agent to incoming events in terms of state changes. First, its beliefs are updated. Updating the intentions means to develop a plan to achieve the newly selected goals. The time advance function determines the reaction time, the time an agent needs to produce its output.

- Part of the agent's activities is communicating actions to other models. The output function takes the "first" of the intentions and charges its output ports with effects directed to the environment.

- The internal transition completes the activity by updating the agent's state. E.g. the expected effects of the action are added to its beliefs, and the time of next internal event is determined. Sometimes an agent's activity might also refer to structural changes. In this case, the internal or external transition function will execute one of a set of predefined methods which are responsible for e.g. creating, adding a model, removing itself, or changing an interaction with another model.

```
class StillSimplePlanningAgent extends AtomicModel {
    State deltaExt (State state, double elapsedTime) {
        state.beliefs.update(input, elapsedTime);
        if ( intentions.plan == "noOp") {
            state.goals.update( );
            state.intentions.update( beliefs, goals, operators);
            state.setTimeAdvance( intentions.deliberationTime);
        } else {
            state.setTimeAdvance(REACTION);
        }
        return state;
    }

    void lambda ( State state) {
        Action action = state.intentions.getAction( );
        if ( state.beliefs.entail( action.pre))
            outPortPut( "out" , action.outputEffect( state ));
        else outPortPut("out", noOp);
    }

    State deltaInt(State state) {
        Action action = state.intentions.getAction( );
        if (state.beliefs.entail( action.pre )) {
            action.transitionEffect( state);
            state.intentions.popAction( );
            state.setTimeAdvance( INFINITY); }
        else { \\ re-planning ...
            state.intentions.update( beliefs, goals, operators);
            state.setTimeAdvance( intentions.deliberationTime);
        }
        return state;
    }
}
```

Figure 15.4. Extract of the "still simple planning agent" in JAMES [16]

Actions have two layers. The symbolic layer is comprised by beliefs, goals and intentions, which are interpreted by the planning system. On the lower layer, the actual execution of the intended symbolic activity in JAMES has to be specified, i.e. **action.outputEffect** and **action.transitionEffect**. It has to be determined with what kind of information which output port is charged, what effect the action has on the agent's state and its environment in terms of structural changes. In the latter case the transition precipitates a change of the overall structure of the model.

The agent works well if the completion or failure of a plan step is the only thing to be observed in the environment. However, it does not refer to the problem that some plan step might take some time to be completed, and in the meantime other things might happen in the environment. Interrupted while executing its current plan step, the agent will notice that the preconditions for the next plan steps are not achieved and will start re-planning. The moment the agent is triggered by an incoming event, it is not able to distinguish between a failure in execution and a still ongoing execution of a plan step. This requires differentiating between inputs that refer to the current plan step and inputs that do not. A "fail" requires a re-planning. If the desired effect of the current plan step is confirmed, the agent continues executing the plan after the reaction time. If the environment does not inform the agent about a failure, the agent needs some other means to proceed. The time an action will likely take to complete helps in designing a less irritable agent (Figure 15.5). Whereas the first step of a plan is executed after generating the plan, to proceed executing the plan steps the agent waits for inputs as does their blueprint.

```
class PatientPlanningAgent extends AtomicModel {
    State deltaExt (State state, double elapsedTime) {
        state.beliefs.update(input, elapsedTime);
        if ( intentions.plan == noOp) || ( state.beliefs.planFailed( )) ||
            ( elapsedTime > state.timeForAction) {
            state.goals.update( );
            state.intentions.update( beliefs, goals, operators);
            state.setTimeAdvance(intentions.deliberationTime);
        } else {
            if ( state.beliefs.entail( action.pre)) {
                state.setTimeAdvance( REACTION);
            } else {
                state.setTimeAdvance( INFINITY );
            }
        }
        return state;
    }
}
```

Figure 15.5: External transition of a "less irritable agent" in JAMES

We will illustrate the integration of a planning agent in JAMES, with a small example. The structure of the entire model is given in Figure 15.6. The agent is at home (**H**) and believes, that the hardware store (**HWS**) sells drills, and the supermarket (**SM**) sells milk. All these facts are stored in its beliefs. The hardware store and the supermarket are both located at the mall (**M**). Between the agent's home and the mall a transportation system (**T**) is offered.

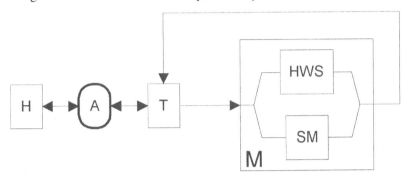

Figure 15.6: The environment of the agent **A** modeled in JAMES

The agent hears that the supermarket has bananas on sale. Thereupon, the agent wants to have milk, banana and a drill. The possible actions to achieve its goals are **goTo(x)** and **buy(x)** with the intuitive preconditions and effects. The reasoning mechanism of the agent follows the pattern depicted in Figure 15.4.

Figure 15.7 illustrates its execution. First, the agent generates a plan (Figure 15.7, time = $t_1$ ). The generated plan includes a **goTo** to the hardware store and to the supermarket, both located in the mall. Therefore, the agent has to move from one interaction context to another. Agents disappear in one interaction context, travel as do other messages through the net, until they appear in another interaction context with unaltered identity and internal state.

In our scenario, the agent will launch itself into the transportation system by charging its output ports with a message directed to the model **HWS**, in which it asks **HWS** to add it as a client. It also specifies the desired interaction in the new location. Within the internal transition function it completes the activity of moving by updating its beliefs and intentions. After executing **goTo(HWS)**, the agent will believe it is at the hardware store (unless contradictory inputs are received) and it will no longer have the intention to go there. Since the agent cannot guess how long the trip to the hardware store will actually take, the time advance is set to **INFINITY**. Finally, the agent will remove itself from the current location. The agent ceases to exist in the former context the moment the internal transition finishes. The activity **goTo(HWS)** is completed, at least from the point of view of the agent (Figure 15.7, time = $t_2$ ).

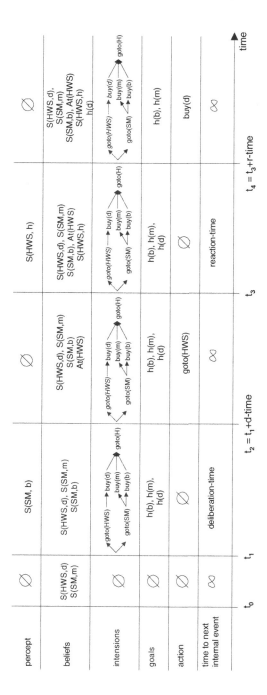

Figure 15.7: Behavior of the "still simple planning agent" [16]

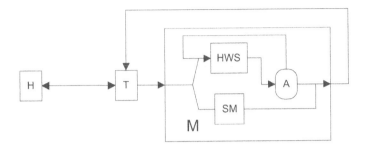

Figure 15.8: The model structure after moving to the hardware store

The moment it has entered the transportation system, the agent is neither able to influence the time of its arrival, nor where the journey will actually lead it. The traveling time depends on the transportation model **T**, which forwards one message after the other with randomized delay according to some routing table. The stations of the journey depend on the structure of the overall model. Messages are sent according to the couplings. Each model checks whether it is the addressee of incoming events. Whereas the supermarket will disregard a request sent to the hardware store, the addressee hardware store **HWS** will acknowledge the request by adding the agent **A** in the context of the coupled model **M** (Figure 15.8). The compliance of the hardware store is a default behavior in JAMES. The hardware store sends all new customers a welcome advertising the products currently on sale (Figure 15.7, time = $t_3$). After some reaction time, the agent proceeds executing its plan by buying the drill (Figure 15.7, time = $t_4$).

The example demonstrates how agents are integrated in JAMES and how plan generation and plan execution intertwine in a simulated environment. To test planning systems and strategies, more complex test beds, e.g. the TILEWORLD scenario, have been realized in JAMES [16].

## 15.4.2 Concurrent simulation of agents

The purpose of JAMES is to support experiments with multi-agent systems, which might be composed of several concurrently acting and deliberating, e.g. planning or learning, agents. Deliberation processes are usually very expensive with respect to calculation time and space. To support an efficient execution, and to avoid the serialization of concurrently active agents by time breaking functions, models in JAMES are executed concurrently in a distributed environment [18].

```
while ( starHandler != null) {
    ...
    // { block until semaphore_count = 0 }
    semaphore_count.blockUntilZero( );
    // update time of last event
    timeOfLastEvent = t;
    // in case of structural requests from atomic childs
    if ( !coordinator.strucInfos.isEmpty( )) {
        // perform changes; this may result in a new time of next event
        timeOfNextInternalEvent = performStructuralChanges( timeOfLastEvent);
    } // endif
    // set flag necessary to estimate the number of incoming events
    // for the influencees of the coupled model
    calculateNoOfOutputsWhenImminent( );
    // send done message
    sendMessage( new DoneMessage(coordinator, parentProcessor,
                                  timeOfNextInternalEvent) );
} // end
```

Figure 15.9: Extract of the coordinator

The simulation adopts the abstract simulator introduced in the earlier section. The employed algorithm ensures that transitions do only take place when all necessary information has arrived. This strategy avoids costly anti-messages that undo the effects of previous messages. The disadvantage of the presented conservative strategy is that a distributed execution of deliberative agents only increases the performance if agents start reasoning at the same simulation time, which is rather unlikely. Ongoing research is directed to equip the current execution with some optimistic elements [17].

Since many structural changes, e.g. creating and removing models and interactions, concern the coupled model, they are completed at the level of the coordinator, which however, stays transparent for the user. Only after the components have completed the transitions, the coordinator, i.e. the **starHandler**, executes the required structural changes by updating components and coupling of the associated coupled model (Figure 15.9). Thus, structural changes are delayed to avoid conflicts with non-structural changes, which take place at the same simulation time. Afterwards it determines the number of outputs the coupled model will produce at its time of next event. Finally, it sends a **done** message to its superior coordinator. A structural change is completed when the coordinator has updated the information in the associated coupled model. Only thereafter does a created model exist and a model is truly removed.

Compared to the creation or deletion of models, the realization of mobility is slightly more complex. To start moving, a model sends a request

**addMovedModelRequest** via its outputs followed by an optional **remove( )** in its internal or confluent transition function. At the moment a model charges its output ports with a message of the type **addMovedModelRequest**, the simulator becomes aware of the intention of the model to move and makes this known to the coordinator. After the completion of the transition the coordinator removes the model from its current interaction context. The arrival of a model depends on the cooperation of an on-site model. In the example it is the model **HWS** which has to grant the requested change, i.e. to add the agent. In this case, the coordinator of the coupled model **M** will receive a **struc2do** message sent by the simulator of the model **HWS**. This message specifies that a model with name **A** shall be added, and that an interaction with the model **HWS** should be realized. The coordinator responds by updating the component and coupling list. It adds the model **A**, sends the current time to the associated simulator of **A**, makes itself known as the simulator's new coordinator, and receives the time of the next internal event of **A**.

From the point of view of the modeler, the model **HWS** adds and embeds the moving model **A** into its new interaction context. However, the actual embedding is done by the coordinator associated with the coupled model the model **HWS** belongs to, i.e. **M**. This happens transparent for the user, as does the distribution of the execution, which we will describe in the following section.

### 15.4.3  Distributed simulation of agents

Specific JAVA libraries provide the functionality for modeling and simulation in JAMES. As do other JAVA-based distributed simulation systems [11], JAMES employs the remote method invocation function of JAVA for a distributed execution of the simulation [18].

Simulators and coordinators, which are located on one node are implemented as parallel threads. Each simulator consists of threads for handling *, # and **done** messages. Simulators and coordinators located on one node communicate by direct message passing. The communication between simulators and coordinators that are located on different nodes is realized as synchronous notification-oriented message passing via the servers which are associated with each node.

Within the abstract simulator concept, each coordinator "knows" how to reach its components and its "super" coordinator. Agent name and register services are structured according to the hierarchical message flow from and to coupled models. They are kept locally at the coordinators, e.g., a coordinator will typically need only the addresses of its component and its superior coordinator. However, in the rare moments of structural change, e.g. a model moves from one location to another, a broker is known to all coordinators where the names of models and their addresses are registered.

The initialization of the simulation run includes the distribution of models with their associated simulators or coordinators, among the involved nodes. All nodes that participate in a simulation are running the program JAMES. One special node contains the master server. Simulation servers register with the master server to make their service public. The master server stores the address of the simulation servers and documents their current work load. It asks each simulation server in a certain frequency by polling to estimate the work load and to check whether a server is still alive. If a client wishes to start a simulation, the only information it has to know is the address of the master server, to whom it sends the model and its address.

According to the registered simulation servers and their current load, the master server determines a partitioning of the model which equally distributes work load in terms of atomic models among the simulation servers. To determine the likely calculation effort, the number of atomic models plays the major role. One type of atomic models are particularly suspicious of being calculation expensive: those executing external commands, e.g. to start a planning system.

The role of the client is to submit the model to the master server for distribution. The client receives as an answer the reference to the simulation server which holds the top model. It initiates the creation of the abstract simulator and finally creates the root coordinator, which stays at the client.

Part of the client is the agent broker, which plays a central role in simulating mobile agents. If models are moving through the modeled network, they do not move physically. Instead an **addMovedModelRequest** moves through the network together with the name of the model and the desired coupling. The concrete model is stored temporarily at the agent broker which is located at the client and whose address is known to all simulator servers.

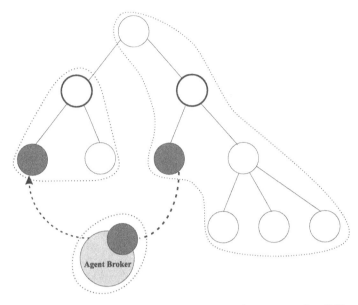

Figure 15.10. Moving models - the execution perspective [18]

After the internal or confluent transition is completed, the simulator informs the coordinator by the message **struc2do** about the move and the coordinator will confirm the prior message of the simulator by sending the moved agent's name and the object including its current state to the agent broker. Afterwards the coordinator will destroy the simulator. The agent broker knows now that this particular agent is moving and expects that in the future another model will ask to receive this model in order to execute the required **addMovedModelRequest**. It will send the model to the requiring simulator, whose coordinator will finally be responsible for creating the simulator for the moved agent and to embed it in its final destination. Figure 15.10 shows a situation where the models (including coordinators and simulators) are distributed among two nodes, the agent broker resides on an additional node.

Whereas from the perspective of the user, the model seems to move through the modeled network actually only its name moves. By sending the model to and requesting it from the agent broker it might move however through the actual, physical network from one simulation server to another simulation server. Thus, the model does not move peer to peer between nodes which are involved in the move of a model, but through a centralized server.

The actual movement of models is not that of "ideal" mobile agents in open environments. The movement happens in a closed world which is limited by the simulation servers participating in the simulation run. Models do not decide when or where to move, since the distribution is not known to the models nor to the user. Agents do not move themselves through the actual network as they move themselves through the modeled one. It forms more a type of process migration since it happens transparently for the user and is motivated by the desire to balance load and to reduce communications over the physical network [2]. We could equally let the model stick to its old place and let the new coordinator communicate with a remote model and its simulator. However this would likely decrease the efficiency of the simulation, since in JAMES like in DEVS a simulator is forced to communicate with and though its coordinator.

## 15.5 Conclusions

Based on DEVS, an implementation independent modeling and simulation formalism has been developed for describing and executing concurrently agents whose description entails the possibility to change their own and their environment's state and behavior pattern. Agents and the environment they shall be tested in are described as composite, reflective time triggered state automaton. A model is perceived as a set of state automata each of which might create depending on its state a new automata which again belongs to the overall model. Each of these represents a phase within the life of a model which is characterized by homogeneous structure and behavior pattern. As coupled models support a modular design of models by composition, the proposed reflective formalism emphasizes the role of variable structure models to structure the temporal plane. It captures agents as reflective dynamic systems that adapt their own structure, their behavior pattern, and that of their environment to their current needs.

JAMES (A Java Based Agent Modeling Environment for Simulation) represents a realization of this formalism. It supports a compositional construction of test scenarios for multi-agent systems, embedding agents, and their execution in a distributed environment. Variable structure models including mobility are described from the perspective of single autonomous agents. With each model a simulation object is associated which is responsible for executing the model. In a distributed execution environment, a move of a model from one interaction context to another is answered by moving models through the physical network to reduce the inter-node communication. The chosen architecture ensures that this migration like the entire distributed execution happens transparently to the user.

The presented parallel execution requires no rollback. However, only at the moment agents start deliberating at the same simulation time, they are executed in parallel. The execution layer of JAMES is currently refined to implement a moderately optimistic simulation strategy which allows a more efficient exploitation of parallelism while keeping the cost of a rollback at bay [17].

# Acknowledgments

Many of the ideas presented in this paper originate in my research stay at the Artificial Intelligence and Simulation Group in Tucson in 1993. I would like to thank Bernard Zeigler for the many thought-provoking discussions we have had during and after my visit to Tucson.

# References

[1] Barros, F.J. Modeling Formalism for Dynamic Structure Systems. ACM Transactions on Modeling and Computer Simulation, 7(4): 501-514, 1997.

[2] Bishop, M. M. Valence, and L.F. Wisniewski. Process Migration for Heterogeneous Distributed Systems. Technical Report PCSTR95-264, Dept. of Computer Science, Dartmouth College, 1995.

[3] Carmel, D. and S. Markovitch. Learning Models of Intelligent Agents. In International Joint Conference on Artificial Intelligence - IJCAI'97, 1997.

[4] Chow, A.C. Parallel DEVS: A Parallel Hierarchical, Modular Modeling Formalism. SCS - Transactions on Computer Simulation, 13(2): 55-67, 1996.

[5] d'Inverno, M. D. Kinny, and M. Luck. Interaction Protocols in Agentis. In International Conference on Multi-Agent Systems ICMAS, 1998.

[6] Georgeff, M.P. and A.L. Lansky. Reactive Reasoning and Planning. In Proceeding of the Sixth Annual Conference on Artificial Intelligence AAAI-87, pages 677-682, 1987.

[7] Hanks, S. M. E. Pollack, and P. R. Cohen. Benchmarks, Test Beds, Controlled Experimentation and the Design of Agent Architectures. AAAI, (Winter): 17-42, 1993.

[8] Jennings, N. R. K. Sycara, and M. Wooldridge. A Roadmap of Agent Research and Development. Autonomous Agents and Multi-Agent Systems, 1(1): 275-306, 1998.

[9] Klir, G. Architecture of Systems Problem Solving. Plenum Press, New York, 1985.

[10] Page, E.H. Simulation Modeling Methodology: Principles and Etiology of Decision Support. PhD thesis, Virginia Polytechnic Institute and State University, 1994.

[11] Page, E.H. B.S. Canova, and J.A. Tufarolo. Web-Based Simulation in SimJava using Remote Method Invocation. In Winter Simulation Conference, Atlanta, 1997.

[12] Praehofer, H. P. Bichler, and B. P. Zeigler. Synthesis of Endomorphic Models for Event-Based Intelligent Control Employing Combined Discrete/Continuous Simulation. In Proc. on the Fourth Annual Conference on Artificial Intelligence, Simulation, and Planning in High Autonomy Systems, pages 120-127, San Diego, 1993. IEEE.

[13] Rosenschein, J.S. and L.P. Kaelbling. A Situated View of Representation and Control. Artificial Intelligence, 73, 1995.

[14] Russell, S. and P. Norvig. Artificial Intelligence - A Modern Approach. Prentice Hall, New Jersey, 1995.

[15] Uhrmacher, A.M. and Zeigler, B.P. Variable Structure Models in Object-Oriented Simulation. International Journal on General Systems, 24(4): 359-375, 1996.

[16] Uhrmacher, A.M. and B. Schattenberg. Agents in Discrete Event Simulation. In European Simulation Symposium - ESS'98, Nottingham, October 1998. SCS.

[17] Uhrmacher, A.M. and K. Gugler. Distributed, Parallel Simulation of Multiple, Deliberative Agents. In Parallel and Distributed Conference PADS'2000, Bologna, 2000.

[18] Uhrmacher, A.M. P. Tyschler, and D. Tyschler. Modeling and Simulation of Mobile Agents. Future Generation Computer Systems, (to appear).

[19] Uhrmacher, A.M. Dynamic Structures in Modeling and Simulation – A Reflective Approach. ACM Transaction on Modeling and Computer Simulation, (to appear).

[20] Zeigler, B.P. Multifaceted Modelling and Discrete Event Simulation. Academic Press, London, 1984.

[21] Zeigler, B.P. Toward A Simulation Methodology for Variable Structure Modeling. In M.S. Elzas, B.P. Zeigler, and T.I. Ören, editors, Modelling and Simulation Methodology in the Artificial Intelligence Era, pages 195-210. North Holland, Amsterdam, 1986.

[22] Zeigler, B.P. Object-Oriented Simulation with Hierarchical, Modular Models - Intelligent Agents and Endomorphic Systems. Academic Press, San Diego, 1990.

[23] Zeigler, B.P. H. Praehofer, and T.G Kim. Theory of Modeling and Simulation. Academic Press, 1999.

# Chapter 16

# A Methodology for the Translation of Knowledge Between Heterogeneous Planners

S. Ramchandran and M.M. Marefat

*Knowledge sharing between planners allows planning systems to collaborate when they encounter a task that cannot be solved by a single problem solver. This paper presents a formal methodology to translate knowledge so that the plans produced in one planner can be utilized and learned from in another. The methodology presented allows entire plans consisting of predicates, actions and the orderings between them to be converted from one representation to another by the use of translators defined in the formalism.*

## 16.1 Introduction

Knowledge sharing between planners allows planning systems to collaborate when they encounter a task that cannot be solved by a single problem solver. The main obstacle to knowledge sharing is communication as each planner has its own representation for queries and plans. Each solution to a query is a plan consisting of actions that are executed within a set of ordering constraints. When a planner receives a solution it must be translated to the local representation before it can be used. What makes this problem interesting is the structure of plans. Plans cannot be translated using techniques that simply map knowledge from one representation to another. Mapping the actions alone does not guarantee a correct and equivalent plan after translation. When actions are translated, they may be broken down into several actions or combined to form compound actions. If this occurs, the orderings between the actions are not identical to those in the original plan. Therefore the translation mechanism must also generate new orderings in the translated plan.

If a planner cannot solve a problem it is because it lacks the knowledge necessary to achieve some of the goals. When a planner receives a solution for such a problem, the solution contains this missing knowledge. To be able to utilize the solution the planner needs a learning mechanism that will add the new information in the solution to its own domain theory.

Most of the research in knowledge translation has been focused on sharing knowledge between databases. Communication among planners has been addressed in [13, 4]. The former lays out a comprehensive framework to achieve knowledge sharing but issues such as multiple translations and knowledge abstraction levels are not addressed. In the latter, a context-based approach to translation is proposed. The objective is to show that plans produced by different planners, using different languages can be combined together. Plans are represented as logical sentences composed of propositions and terms. However the method does not show us how to use the formalism to represent plans containing actions and orderings. Hierarchical planning also contains actions at various levels of abstraction. A planner generates a solution by putting together actions at the highest level of abstraction and then replacing them with the lower level actions. The difference is that one planner will look at the solution plan at various levels of abstraction during plan generation. In this work, we are allow planners that individually contain knowledge at different abstraction levels to exchange information.

A similar line of research is followed in the areas of modeling and simulation. In order to simulate a real system, it is necessary to formalize its inputs, outputs and behavior characteristics. Real systems are normally very complex and cannot be simulated without simplification thus models are abstractions of the system that capture all its salient features. The more abstract a model, the easier it is to simulate, but the less accurate it can be. A trade-off that is made in all models is the sacrifice of accuracy for ease in simulation. When modeling a real world system, the states of the model should correspond to states of the system such that examining the model at a particular time provides the same information as exam examining the system at that time. This correspondence between the states of one object and another is termed homomorphism. In modeling this is achieved if for every real world action that changes the system, there is a corresponding transition that changes the state of the model. Any model, no matter how simple, should have this correspondence with the real world system for accurate simulation.

A system may be modeled at various abstractions depending on the requirements [16]. One method of model abstraction is aggregation where several components of a system are combined together and modeled as a single component [5, 9]. The characteristics of this aggregate component are the same as those of the individual components as seen by the rest of the system. Often during simulation it is necessary to be able to switch form one level of abstraction to another [14]. To transition between models at different abstraction levels, a mapping is required that relates the components and states in one model to those in the other. This concept is similar to that used in the translation of plans from one representation to another. A plan is analogous to a system whose inputs and outputs are the preconditions and postconditions of the plan. Each action can be considered as a component of the system. The preconditions and postconditions of the action are the inputs and outputs of the components respectively. The translation of plans from one level of abstraction to another also involves mappings which relates one action to several others or vice versa. A plan after translation is equivalent to the original, but due to the transformation of the actions, every state in the original plan may not be present among the world states in the translated plan. Thus in translating a plan, homomorphism is not preserved. The states in one plan will be equivalent to a subset of the states in the other. The overall plan however remains equivalent, analogous to two different systems proving the same output for a given input. The methods for knowledge translation that have been presented in this paper can be extended for use with modeling systems. If every model has a fixed format for its representation but different levels of abstraction and ways to express the same information, then by extending the mechanism that we present, models can be exchanged between different parts of the system.

A second issue in modeling is that models at different levels of abstraction may use different formalizations to represent information (examples are Finite State Machines, Petri Nets, equations etc.). To integrate models which use heterogeneous representations, it is necessary to design mechanisms that allow the parameters of one model to be correctly transmitted to and understood by another model [6, 12]. Planners too may use different representations for queries and plans. These require further transformations, other than translation alone, before they can be understood by other planners. Although this is not a topic that is explored in this work, it has been addressed to some extent in [13] which forms the basis for this research. Although the work presented in this paper cannot be directly applied to model abstractions, the concepts are related and much can be gained by exploring them as such.

The contribution that this paper makes is a formal methodology to translate knowledge so that the plans produced in one representation can be utilized and learned from in another. The methodology presented allows entire plans consisting of predicates, actions and the orderings between them to be converted from one representation to another by the use of translators defined in the formalism. We also introduce a learning mechanism to complement the translation process. Learning allows a planner to update its knowledge base with new information that is contained in the solution plans that it receives.

## 16.2  Problem Formulation

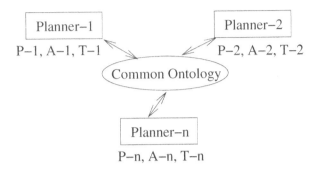

Figure 16.1: A network of planners which communicate using a common ontology. (P-n, A-n, T-n correspond to *Pred_n*, *Actions_n* and *Trans_n* in *Planner_n* respectively.)

Each planner, *Planner_i* in a network of planners, contains a knowledge base, $KB_i$. The knowledge base of *Planner_i* is a 3-tuple, $KB_i$ = < *Pred_i*, *Actions_i*, *Trans_i* >. *Pred_i* is the set of predicates which are used to describe the state of the world at any given time. *Actions_i* contains every action in *Planner_i*. Each action consists of a preconditions list, an add list and a delete list. The first contains predicates that must be true before the action can be executed. The second and third are predicates that are added to and deleted from the state during which the action is executed, resulting in a new state. For an action $a_i^k$ these lists are obtained using the functions Pre($a_i^k$), Add($a_i^k$) and Del($a_i^k$) respectively (For examples, see Table 16.1). *Trans_i* is the set of translators that is used to convert knowledge between *Planner_i* and the common ontology.

|  | Pickup(?x) | Putdown(?x) |
|---|---|---|
| Pre | Clear(?x)  Handempty  Ontable(?x) | Holding(?x) |
| Add | Holding(?x) | Clear(?x)  Ontable(?x)  Handempty |
| Del | Clear(?x)  Handempty  Ontable(?x) | Holding(?x) |

|  | Unstack(?x  ?y) | Stack(?x  ?y) |
|---|---|---|
| Pre | Clear(?x)  Handempty  On(?x  ?y) | Holding(?x)  Clear(?y) |
| Add | Holding(?x)  Clear(?y) | Clear(?x)  On(?x  ?y)  Handempty |
| Del | Clear(?x)  Handempty  On(?x  ?y) | Holding(?x)  Clear(?y) |

Table 16.1: Action Descriptions

The common ontology is the medium of communication between the planners. All information that is sent from one planner to another is translated into the common ontology. The introduction of a common ontology means that each planner needs just one set of translators.

The predicates and actions in a planner's knowledge base are used to form queries and plans. A query consists of two parts, $Query_i = <I_i, G_i>$. $I_i$ is the set of initial conditions of the problem and $G_i$ is the set of predicates which describes the goal state of the problem. An example of a query is

$Query_i$
$I_i$ = On(A,B), Clear(A), Handempty
$G_i$ = Ontable(A)

A plan is represented as $Plan_i = <A_i, O_i>$ where $A_i$ are the actions contained within the plan and $O_i$ are the ordering constraints between the actions. Each plan has a set of conditions that must be true before it is executed and a set that is true after execution. These are provided by the functions $\text{Pre}(Plan_i)$ and $\text{Add}(Plan_i)$ respectively. The set of conditions that is no longer true once the plan has been completed is given by $\text{Del}(Plan_i)$.

$\text{Pre}(Plan_i)$ = The set of predicates that are in $\text{Pre}(a_i^p)$, $\forall a_i^p \in A_i$ and such that they are not achieved by the $\text{Add}(a_i^q)$, $a_i^q \in A_i$, $p \neq q \wedge nec\_before(a_i^q, a_i^p)$.

$\text{Add}(Plan_i)$ = The set of predicates that are in $\text{Add}(a_i^p)$, $\forall a_i^p \in A_i$ and such that they are not deleted by the $\text{Del}(a_i^q)$, $a_i^q \in A_i$, $p \neq q \wedge nec\_before(a_i^p, a_i^q)$.

$\text{Del}(Plan_i)$ = The set of predicates that are in $\text{Del}(a_i^p)$, $\forall a_i^p \in A_i$ and such that they are not added by the $\text{Add}(a_i^q)$, $a_i^q \in A_i$, $p \neq q \wedge nec\_before(a_i^p, a_i^q)$.

An action $a^j$ is necessarily before another action $a^k$ if $before(a^j, a^k)$ is true or if $before(a^j, a^l)$ is true and $a^l$ is necessarily before $a^k$.

$nec\_before(a^j, a^k) = before(a^j, a^k) \vee (before(a^j, a^l) \wedge nec\_before(a^l, a^k))$

An example of a plan is

$Plan_i$
$A_i = \{Unstack_i(A, B), Putdown_i(A), Pickup_i(C), Stack_i(C,D)\}$
$O_i = \{before(Unstack_i(A, B), Putdown_i(A)), before(Pickup_i(C), Stack_i(C,D))\}$

Plans can be represented as graphs (Fig 16.2). Each node is an action in $A_i$ and each edge is an ordering in $O_i$. Two extra nodes, Start and End, are special actions. The Start node represents an action with $\text{Pre}(Plan_i)$ as its add list and no preconditions. The End node is an action whose preconditions are $\text{Add}(Plan_i)$. It has an empty add list and delete list. Every action in a plan is ordered after Start and before End. (These orderings are implicit and are not stated in the plans for clarity.)

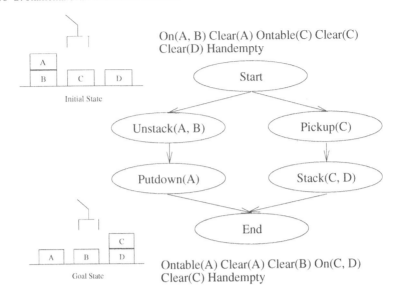

On(A, B) Clear(A) Ontable(C) Clear(C)
Clear(D) Handempty

Initial State

Goal State

Ontable(A) Clear(A) Clear(B) On(C, D)
Clear(C) Handempty

Figure 16.2: An Example Plan

From the information given in a plan, we can construct the state-space graph (SSG) of the plan, Figure 16.3. The nodes of this graph consist of conjunctions of predicates representing all the states that can possibly exist when the plan is executed. The Start and End nodes correspond to Pre($Plan_i$) and Add($Plan_i$) respectively. The edges of the graph represent the actions of the plan. An edge leads away from the state containing the preconditions of the action it represents. It leads towards the state after the action has been executed.

Lastly, each planner contains a predicate truth table. This table (Table 16.2) contains all the predicates that are always true or false in the planner with respect to the common ontology.

| Always True | Always False |
|---|---|
| Handempty | |
| Aligned(?x ?y) | Holding(?x) |

Table 16.2: Predicate Truth Table

We define the correctness of knowledge contained in a planner as follows.

**Definition 1**     *An action $a_i^k$ is correct in Planner$_i$ if*

• *Pre($a_i^k$) does not contain any predicates that are always false in Planner$_i$.*

- $Add(a_i^k)$ does not contain any predicates that are always false in $Planner_i$.

- $Del(a_i^k)$ does not contain any predicates that are always true in $Planner_i$.

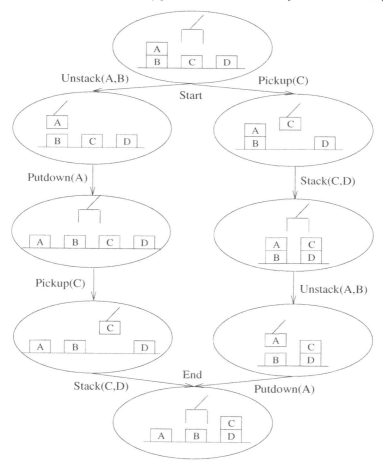

Figure 16.3: State Space Graph

**Definition 2**    $Plan_i = < A_i, O_i>$ produced by the problem solver $Planner_i$ is correct if

- The graph of $Plan_i$ is acyclic.

- All actions in $A_i$ are correct with respect to the domain theory of $Planner_i$.

**Definition 3**    A plan, $Plan_i = < A_i, O_i >$ is a solution to a query $Q_i = < I_i, G_i>$ if

- $Pre(Plan_i)$ is a subset of $I_i$.

- $G_i$ is a subset of Add(Plan_i).

- Beginning with the state $I_i$ and executing the actions in $A_i$ according to the orderings in $O_i$ results in the state $G_i$ (or some superset of this state).

## 16.2.1  The Common Ontology

The common ontology is the medium of communication used by all the planners. It is a knowledge base, $KB_{co} = < Pred_{co}, Actions_{co} >$. $Pred_{co}$ and $Actions_{co}$ are used to represent the queries and replies that are passed between planners. The knowledge contained in each planner is equivalent to a subset of the knowledge in the common ontology. That is, every query and plan in a planner has an equivalent in the common ontology.

Each planner in the network is responsible for translating messages between its own representation and the common ontology.

## 16.2.2  Knowledge Sharing between Planners

When one planner sends a message to another, the message contains either a query or a plan. Let us consider Planner$_a$, which wants to send out $Query_a = < I_a, G_a >$. It is translated to an equivalent query in the common ontology, $Query_{co} = < I_{co}, G_{co} >$ and then sent. Planner$_b$ receives $Query_{co}$, translates it to $Query_b = < I_b, G_b >$ and produces a solution, $Plan_b = < A_b, O_b >$. In order to send a reply, $Plan_b$ is translated to $Plan_{co}$. Planner$_a$ receives $Plan_{co} = < A_{co}, O_{co}>$, translates it to $Plan_a = < A_a, O_a >$ which it uses as the solution.

We can formulate the translation of messages as

1. $Query_i$ is translated to $Query_j$, such that

   - $Query_j \equiv Query_i$.

2. $Plan_i$, the solution to $Query_i$, is translated to $Plan_j$ such that

   - $Plan_j \equiv Plan_i$.

   - $Plan_j$ is a correct plan.

   - $Plan_j$ is a solution to the query $Query_j$.

In the next section, we define what is meant by the equivalence ($\equiv$) of queries and plans.

## 16.2.3   Knowledge Equivalence

We begin by defining the equivalence of predicates which are the building blocks of actions that make up plans.

**Definition 4**   *The subset of predicates $Pred_i^p$ from the domain theory of Planner$_i$ is equivalent to the subset of predicates $Pred_j^q$ in the domain theory of Planner$_j$ if their aggregate semantics are the same. In this case, we write $Pred_i^p \equiv Pred_j^q$.*

Example:

$Pred_i^p$ = Tower(A,B,C), Onblock(D,E), Ontable(E), Cleartop(D)
$Pred_j^q$ = On(A,B), On(B,C), On(C, Table), Clear(A), On(D,E), On(E, Table), Clear(D)
$Pred_i^p \equiv Pred_j^q$

**Definition 5**   *Two queries, $Query_i = <I_i, G_i>$ and $Query_j = <I_j, G_j>$ are equivalent if $I_i \equiv I_j$ and $G_i \equiv G_j$, based on the equivalence in Definition 4.*

Example:

$Query_i$
$I_i = 3\_Tower(A,B,C)$, $2\_Tower(D,E)$
$G_i = 2\_Tower(A,D)$
$Query_j$
$I_j$ = On(A,B), On(B,C), On(C, Table), Clear(A), On(D,E), On(E, Table), Clear(D), Handempty
$G_j$ = On(A,D), On(D, Table)
$Query_i \equiv Query_j$

**Definition 6**   *Two plans, $Plan_i = <A_i, O_i>$ and $Plan_j = <A_j, O_j>$ are equivalent ($Plan_i \equiv Plan_j$) if $Pre(Plan_i) \equiv Pre(Plan_j)$, $Add(Plan_i) \equiv Add(Plan_j)$ and $Del(Plan_i) \equiv Del(Plan_j)$.*

Example:

$Plan_i$
$A_i = a_i^1 = 2\_Tower\_to\_Table(D,E)$, $a_i^2 = 3\_Tower\_to\_Block(A,B,C,D)$
$O_i$ = before $(a_i^1, a_i^2)$
$Plan_j$
$A_j = a_j^1$ = Unstack(D,E), $a_j^2$ = Putdown(D), $a_j^3$ = Unstack(A,B), $a_j^4$ = Stack(A,D)
$O_j$ = before$(a_j^1, a_j^2)$, before$(a_j^2, a_j^3)$, before$(a_j^3, a_j^4)$
$Plan_i \equiv Plan_j$

During the process of translation, we will encounter the need to determine if subsets of actions are equivalent. Every set of actions can be considered as a subplan and so we can apply the above definition to these subplans.

## 16.3   Knowledge Translation

Translation of knowledge is required when information is sent out from a planner as well as when it is received. The knowledge base of each planner contains a set of translators which are used for this purpose. Each planner may have multiple ways to represent the same information. In this case, additional care is required during translation. For example, predicates $On_{co}(A, B)$ and $On_{co}(B, C)$ in the common ontology may translate to the two predicates $On\_block_i(A, B)$ and $On\_block_i(B, C)$ or to the single predicate $Tower_i(A, B, C)$ in $Planner_i$. With multiple mappings, the application of different sets of translators results in different queries and solutions after translation.

*Predicate Mappings in KB$_1$*

| | |
|---|---|
| $On_1(?x\ ?y)$ | $On_{co}(?x\ ?y)$ |
| $Ontable_1(?x)$ | $Ontable_{co}(?x)$ |
| $Cleartop_1(?x)$ | $Clear_{co}(?x)$ |
| $Block_1(?x)$ | $Block_{co}(?x)$ |
| $Big\_block_1(?x)$ | $Big\_block_{co}(?x)$ |
| $Long\_block_1(?x)$ | $Long\_block_{co}(?x)$ |
| $Gripper_1(?x)$ | $Grip_{co}(?x)$ |
| $Bridge_1(?x\ ?y\ ?z)$ | $Long\_on_{co}(?x\ ?y\ ?z)$, $Clear_{co}(?x)$ |

*Action Mappings in KB$_1$*

| | |
|---|---|
| $Block\_to\_table_1(?x\ ?y)$ | $Unstack_{co}(?x\ ?y)> Putdown_{co}(?x)$ |
| $Table\_to\_block_1(?x\ ?y)$ | $Pickup_{co}(?x)> Stack_{co}(?x\ ?y)$ |
| $Block\_to\_block_1(?x\ ?y\ ?z)$ | $Unstack_{co}(?x\ ?y)> Stack_{co}\ (?x\ ?z)$ |
| $Reverse\_block_1(?x\ ?y)$ | $Unstack_{co}(?x\ ?y)> Putdown_{co}(?x) >$<br>$Pickup_{co}(?y) > Stack_{co}(?y\ ?x)$ |
| $Make\_bridge_1(?x\ ?y\ ?z)$ | $Long\_pickup_{co}(?x)> Long\_stack_{co}(?x\ ?y\ ?z)$ |
| $Change\_gripper_1(?x\ ?y)$ | $Replace\_grip_{co}(?x\ ?y)$ |

*Predicate Truth Table of KB$_1$*

| Always Ture | Always False |
|---|---|
| $Handempty_{co}$ | $Holding_{co}(?x)$ |

Table 16.3: Knowledge Mapping and Predicate Truth Table in $Planner_1$

The one restriction that we apply in this paper is that there is only one way to represent information in the common ontology. This means that there is only one mapping for knowledge when it is translated into the common ontology.

In the following sections, the examples show $Planner_1$ which sends out a query describing a problem and $Planner_2$ replies with a solution plan. The knowledge bases $KB_1$ of $Planner_1$ and $KB_2$ of $Planner_2$ are shown in Tables 16.3 and 16.4 respectively. (Orderings are represented using the symbol '>', $a_i^k > a_i^l$ is the same as $before(a_i^k, a_i^l)$.)

## 16.3.1   Translating Queries

*Predicate Mappings in $KB_2$*

| Tower$_2$(?x ?y) | On$_{co}$(?x ?y), Ontable$_{co}$(?y) |
|---|---|
| On$_2$(?xTable) | Ontable$_{co}$(?x) |
| Clear$_2$(?x) | Clear$_{co}$(?x) |
| Block$_2$(?x) | Block$_{co}$(?x) |
| Gripper$_2$(?x) | Grip$_{co}$(?x) |
| Long_on$_2$(?x ?y ?z) | Long_on$_{co}$(?x ?y ?z), Clear$_{co}$(?x) |

*Action Mappings in $KB_2$*

| Block_tower$_2$(?x ?y) | Unstack$_{co}$(?x ?y)> Putdown$_{co}$(?x) |
|---|---|
| Build_two_towers$_2$ (?w ?x ?y ?z) | Pickup$_{co}$(?w)> Stack$_{co}$(?w ?x) Pickup$_{co}$(?y) > Stack$_{co}$(?y ?z) |
| Build_bridge$_2$(?x ?y ?z) | Long_pickup$_{co}$(?x)> Long_stack$_{co}$(?x ?y ?z) |
| Change_gripper$_2$(?x ?y) | Replace_grip$_{co}$(?x ?y) |

*Predicate Truth Table of $KB_2$*

| Always Ture | Always False |
|---|---|
| Handempty$_{co}$ | Holding$_{co}$ |

Table 16.4: Knowledge Mapping and Predicate Truth Table in $Planner_2$

If $Planner_1$ wants to send out $Query_1$ = < $I_1$, $G_1$> it is translated to $Query_{co}$ = < $I_{co}$, $G_{co}$ > in the common ontology. $Planner_2$ receives $Query_{co}$ = < $I_{co}$, $G_{co}$ >. In order to generate a reply, it has to translate it to $Query_2$ in its own representation. Multiple mappings from the common ontology into the local representation mean $Planner_2$ could get more than one query to solve.

The steps to convert a query from one representation to another are shown below. Substitute the appropriate subscript for the translation depending on the direction. For example, when converting $Query_1$ to $Query_{co}$, substitute '1' for 'i' and 'co' for 'j'.

1.   Form all partitions of $Query_i$. For each $Partition_i^k$, every $I_i^{k-l}$ and $G_i^{k-l}$ is an individual element of the partition, which is they are all non-empty, disjoint subsets of $I_i$ and $G_i$ respectively.

$Partition_i^l = \{I_i^{l-1}, I_i^{l-2} \dots I_i^{l-m}\}, \{G_i^{l-1}, G_i^{l-2} \dots G_i^{l-n}\}$

$$Partition_i^2 = \{I_i^{2\text{-}1}, I_i^{2\text{-}2} \ldots I_i^{2\text{-}m}\}, \{G_i^{2\text{-}1}, G_i^{2\text{-}2} \ldots G_i^{2\text{-}n}\}$$

$$\vdots$$

$$Partition_i^n = \{I_i^{n\text{-}1}, I_i^{n\text{-}2} \ldots I_i^{n\text{-}m}\}, \{G_i^{n\text{-}1}, G_i^{n\text{-}2} \ldots G_i^{n\text{-}n}\}$$

such that for all $I_i^{k\text{-}l}$ in $Partition_i^k$, there exists a translator, $T_j^l \in Trans_j$ which represents the mapping $I_i^{k\text{-}l} \rightarrow I_j^{k\text{-}l}$.

Similarly, for all $G_i^{k\text{-}l}$ in $Partition_i^k$, there exists a translator, $T_j^l \in Trans_j$ which represents the mapping $G_i^{k\text{-}l} \rightarrow G_j^{k\text{-}l}$.

2.  Each partition $Partition_i^k$ translates to a different query, $Query_i^k =< I_j^k, G_j^k >$.
    Initialize all $I_j^k$ and $G_j^k$ to be empty sets.

3.  For each partition $Partition_i^k$,

    (a)  To each $I_i^{k\text{-}l}$, apply $T_j^l$ with the appropriate substitutions to get $I_j^{k\text{-}l}$.
         Let $I_j^k = I_j^k \cup I_j^{k\text{-}l}$.

    (b)  Similarly, apply $T_j^l$ to each $G_i^{k\text{-}l}$ and generate $G_j^{k\text{-}l}$.
         Let $G_j^k = G_j^k \cup G_j^{k\text{-}l}$.

4.  Every resulting 2-tuple, $Query_j = < I_j^k, G_j^k >$ is an equivalent of $Query_i$.

$Query_l$ in $Planner_l$ is shown in Figure 16.4.

$Query_l$

$I_l = On_l(B, A)$, $Ontable_l(A)$, $Ontable_l(C)$, $Ontable_l(D)$, $Ontable_l(E)$, $Cleartop_l(B)$, $Cleartop_l(C)$, $Cleartop_l(D)$, $Cleartop_l(E)$, $Block_l(A)$, $Block_l(B)$, $Block_l(C)$, $Block_l(D)$, $Long\_block_l(E)$, $Gripper_l(Reg)$

$G_l = On_l(A,B)$, $Ontable_l(B)$, $On_l(C, D)$, $Ontable_l(C)$, $Bridge_l(E, A, C)$

After partitioning and applying the knowledge mappings in Table 16.3, the following query is obtained in the common ontology.

$Query_{co}$

$I_{co} = On_{co}(B, A)$, $Ontable_{co}(A)$, $Ontable_{co}(C)$, $Ontable_{co}(D)$, $Ontable_{co}(E)$, $Clear_{co}(B)$, $Clear_{co}(C)$, $Clear_{co}(D)$, $Clear_{co}(E)$, $Block_{co}(A)$, $Block_{co}(B)$, $Block_{co}(C)$, $Block_{co}(D)$, $Long\_block_{co}(E)$, $Grip_{co}(Reg)$

$G_l = On_{co}(A,B)$, $Ontable_{co}(B)$, $On_{co}(C, D)$, $Ontable_{co}(C)$, $Long\_on_{co}(E, A, C)$, $Clear_l(E)$

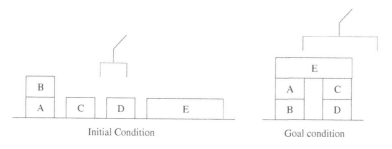

Initial Condition                    Goal condition

Figure 16.4: *Query₁* in *Planner₁*

There is only one set of mappings that is applicable to $Query_{co}$, resulting in $Query_2$ in *Planner₂*.

*Query₂*

> $I_2 = Tower_2(B, A), On_2(C, Table), On_2(D, Table), COn_2(E, Table),$
> $Clear_2(B), Clear_2(C), Clear_2(D), Clear_2(E), Block_2(A), Block_2(B),$
> $Block_2(C), Block_2(D), Long\_block_2(E), Gripper_2(Reg)$
> $G_1 = Tower_2(A, B), Tower_2(C, D), Long\_on_2(E, A, C)$

## 16.3.2    Translating Plans

*Planner₂* generates a solution, $Plan_2 = <A_2, O_2>$ for the query it received. This is translated to $Plan_{co} = <A_{co}, O_{co}>$ and sent out as a reply. *Planner₁* receives the solution and translates it to $Plan_1 = <A_1, O_1>$ in order to use the solution.

When translating a plan, the first step is to partition the actions and orderings in the plan such that one knowledge translator can be applied to each partition. In addition the translated plan must be correct.

## *16.3.2.1    Partitioning Plans for Translation*

Consider the translation of $Plan_i$ from the representation in *Planner₍ᵢ₎* to that of *Planner₍ⱼ₎*.

1. For the plan $Plan_i = <A_i, O_i>$, generate all possible partitions of the actions in $A_i$.

   For each partition of the actions, $\{A_i^{k-1} A_i^{k-2} \ldots A_i^{k-n}\}$, all orderings between the actions contained in an element $A_i^{k-l}$ of the partition are added to $O_i^{k-l}$. All orderings between actions in different elements of the partition are added to $O_i^{k-m}$

   The resulting partitions of the plan are

$$Partition_i^1 = \{<A_i^{1-1}, O_i^{1-1}> <A_i^{1-2}, O_i^{1-2}> \ldots <A_i^{1-n}, O_i^{1-n}> < O_i^{1-m}>\}$$
$$Partition_i^2 = \{<A_i^{2-1}, O_i^{2-1}> <A_i^{2-2}, O_i^{2-2}> \ldots <A_i^{2-n}, O_i^{2-n}> < O_i^{2-m}>\}$$

$$\vdots$$

$$Partition_i^n = \{<A_i^{n-1}, O_i^{n-1}> <A_i^{n-2}, O_i^{n-2}> \ldots <A_i^{n-n}, O_i^{n-n}> < O_i^{n-m}>\}$$

2. Eliminate all partitions, $Partition_i^k$, that will result in plans which are not acyclic.

   $Partition_i^k$ is eliminated if

   $$\exists \, before \, (a_i^p, a_i^q) \in O_i^{k-m} \, and \, \exists \, before(a_i^r, a_i^s) \in O_i^{k-m}, p \neq q \neq r \neq s$$
   $$a_i^p, a_i^s \in A_i^{k-x} \, and \, a_i^q, a_i^r \in A_i^{k-y}, x \neq y$$

3. Eliminate the partitions that will result in plans containing incorrect actions. $Partition_i^k$ is eliminated if for any element $< A_i^{k-l}, O_i^{k-l} >$

   - $Pre(< A_i^{k-l}, O_i^{k-l} >)$ contains predicates that are always false in $Planner_j$, or

   - $Add(<A_i^{k-l}, O_i^{k-l} >)$ contains predicates that are always false in $Planner_j$, or

   - $Del(< A_i^{k-l}, O_i^{k-l} >)$ contains predicates that are always true in $Planner_j$.

4. All the remaining partitions will result in correct plans.

The partitions generated by this process are now considered for translation. $< A_i^{k-l}, O_i^{k-l} >$ are non-empty, disjoint subsets of $<A_i, O_i>$ respectively and each is an element of $Partition_i^k$.

### 16.3.2.2  Plan Translation

The procedure to translate a plan is shown below. As with the translation of queries, the method can be applied in either direction.

1. Generate all partitions (Section 3.2.1) of the actions in $Plan_i$ that will result in correct plans after translation.

   $$Partition_i^1 = \{<A_i^{1-1}, O_i^{1-1}> <A_i^{1-2}, O_i^{1-2}> \ldots <A_i^{1-n}, O_i^{1-n}> < O_i^{1-m}>\}$$
   $$Partition_i^2 = \{<A_i^{2-1}, O_i^{2-1}> <A_i^{2-2}, O_i^{2-2}> \ldots <A_i^{2-n}, O_i^{2-n}> < O_i^{2-m}>\}$$

   $$\vdots$$

   $$Partition_i^n = \{<A_i^{n-1}, O_i^{n-1}> <A_i^{n-2}, O_i^{n-2}> \ldots <A_i^{n-n}, O_i^{n-n}> < O_i^{n-m}>\}$$

2. Check each partition to see if it can be translated into a plan in the common ontology.

A partition $Partition_i^k$ can be translated into the common ontology if for every $< A_i^{k-l}, O_i^{k-l} > \in Partition_i^k$, there is a translator $T_i^l$ such that $< A_i^{k-l}, O_i^{k-l} > \rightarrow < A_j^{k-l}, O_j^{k-l} >$.

If no such partitions exist, then $Planner_j$ does not contain all the required knowledge and learning is required to enhance its domain theory(Section 5).

3.  For each $Partition_i^k$ that can be translated,

    (a)  Apply the translators.

    For each $< A_i^{k-l}, O_i^{k-l} >$, apply $T_i^l$ to get $< A_j^{k-l}, O_j^{k-l} >$.

    $A_j^k = A_j^k \cup A_j^{k-l}$     $O_j^k = O_j^k \cup O_j^{k-l}$

    (b)  Generate new orderings, $O_i^{k-m}$ based on the orderings in $< O_i^{k-m} >$.

    For all orderings $before\ (a_i^p, a_i^q) \in O_i^{k-m}$, if $a_{co}^p \in A_i^{k-j}$ and $a_{co}^q \in A_i^{k-l}$, then $O_i^{k-m} = O_i^{k-m} \cup before(last(< A_i^{k-j}, O_i^{k-j} >), first(< A_i^{k-l}, O_i^{k-l} >))$.

    $first(A_i^k)$ - returns all $a_i^p \in A_i^k$ such that $\neg \exists before\ (a_i^q, a_i^p), a_i^q \in A_i^k$, $p \neq q$.

    $last(A_i^k)$ - returns all $a_i^p \in A_i^k$ such that $\neg \exists before\ (a_i^p, a_i^q), a_i^q \in A_i^k$, $p \neq q$.

    (c)  $O_j^k = O_j^k \cup O_j^{k-m}$

    (d)  The resulting 2-tuple $< A_j^k, O_j^k >$ is one translation of $Plan_i$ in the domain theory of $Planner_j$.

4.  Each plan, $Plan_j^k$ is a translation of $Plan_i$. Every $Plan_j^k$ is checked to determine if it is a solution to $Query_j$. All plans that are not solutions are discarded, leaving the final set of solutions to $Query_j$.

$Planner_2$ generates the following solution for $Query_2$.

$Plan_2$

$A_2 = Break\_tower_2(B, A), Build\_two\_towers_2(A, B, C, D),$
    $Change\_gripper_2(Reg, Long), Build\_bridge_2(E, A, C)$
$O_2 = before(Break\_tower_2(B, A), Build\_two\_towers_2(A, B, C, D)),$
    $before(Break\_tower_2(B, A), Change\_gripper_2(Reg, Long)),$
    $before(Build\_two\_towers_2(A, B, C, D), Change\_gripper_2(Reg, Long)),$
    $before(Change\_gripper_2(Reg, Long), Build\_bridge_2(E, A, C))$

## 16.4  Example and Results

Let us examine the example that has been introduced.

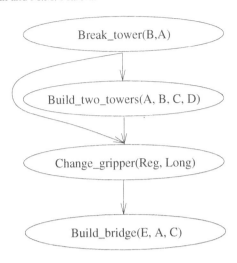

Figure 16.5: *Plan$_2$* generated in *Planner$_2$* as a solution for *Query$_2$*.

The solution produced by *Planner$_2$* (Fig 16.5) is partitioned as below (Steps 1 & 2 of plan translation algorithm) and converted to *Plan$_{co}$* (Fig 16.6) in the common ontology (Step 3 of plan translation algorithm).

*Partition$_2$* = $<$*Break_tower$_2$(B, A)*$>$, $<$*Build_two_towers$_2$(A, B, C, D)*$>$,
$<$*Change_gripper$_2$(Reg, Long)*$>$,$<$ *Build_bridge$_2$(E, A, C)*$>$
$<$*before(Break_tower$_2$(B, A), Build_two_towers$_2$(A, B, C, D)),*
*before(Break_tower$_2$(B, A), Change_gripper$_2$(Reg, Long)),*
*before(Build_two_towers$_2$(A, B, C, D), Change_gripper$_2$(Reg,*
*Long)), before(Change_gripper$_2$(Reg, Long), Build_bridge$_2$(E, A,*
*C))*$>$

*Plan$_{co}$*
    *A$_{co}$* =        *Unstack$_{co}$(B,A), Putdown$_{co}$(B), Pickup$_{co}$(A), Stack$_{co}$(A,B),*
                        *Pickup$_{co}$(C), Stack$_{co}$(C,D), Replace_grip$_{co}$(Reg,Long),*
                        *Long_pickup$_{co}$(E), Long_stack$_{co}$(E,A,C)*
    *O$_{co}$* =        *before(Unstack$_{co}$(B,A), Putdown$_{co}$(B)),*
                        *before(Putdown$_{co}$(B), Pickup$_{co}$(A)),*
                        *before(Putdown$_{co}$(B), Pickup$_{co}$(C)),*
                        *before(Pickup$_{co}$(A), Stack$_{co}$(A,B)),*
                        *before(Pickup$_{co}$(C), Stack$_{co}$(C,D)),*
                        *before(Putdown$_{co}$(B), Replace_grip$_{co}$(Reg,Long)),*
                        *before(Stack$_{co}$(A,B), Replace_grip$_{co}$(Reg,Long)),*
                        *before(Stack$_{co}$(C,D), Replace_grip$_{co}$(Reg,Long)),*
                        *before(Replace_grip$_{co}$(Reg,Long), Long_pickup$_{co}$(E)),*
                        *before(Long_pickup$_{co}$(E), Long_stack$_{co}$(E,A,C))*

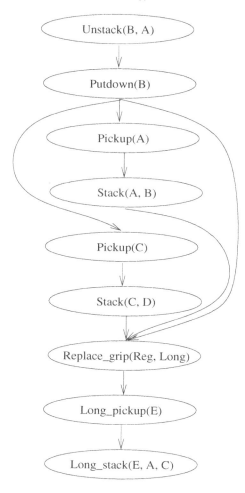

Figure 16.6: *Plan*$_{co}$ - translation of *Plan*$_2$

*Planner*$_1$ receives *Plan*$_{co}$ and finds two partitions (Steps 1 & 2 of plan translation algorithm) that will result in correct plans after translation.

*Partition*$_1^1$ = <{*Unstack*$_{co}$*(B,A)*, *Putdown*$_{co}$*(B)* },
    {*before(Unstack*$_{co}$*(B,A)*, *Putdown*$_{co}$*(B))*})>
    < {*Pickup*$_{co}$*(A)*, *Stack*$_{co}$*(A,B)* }, {*before(Pickup*$_{co}$*(A)*, *Stack*$_{co}$*(A,B))* }>
    < {*Pickup*$_{co}$*(C)*, *Stack*$_{co}$*(C,D)* }, {*before(Pickup*$_{co}$*(C)*, *Stack*$_{co}$*(C,D))* }>
    < {*Replace_grip*$_{co}$*(Reg,Long)* }, { }>
    < {*Long_pickup*$_{co}$*(E)*, *Long_stack*$_{co}$*(E,A,C)* },
    {*before(Long_pickup*$_{co}$*(E)*, *Long_stack*$_{co}$*(E,A,C))*,
    *before(Putdown*$_{co}$*(B)*, *Pickup*$_{co}$*(A))*,

$before(Putdown_{co}(B), Pickup_{co}(C)),$
$before(Putdown_{co}(B), Replace\_grip_{co}(Reg,Long)),$
$before(Stack_{co}(A,B), Replace\_grip_{co}(Reg,Long)),$
$before(Stack_{co}(C,D), Replace\_grip_{co}(Reg,Long)),$
$before(Replace\_grip_{co}(Reg,Long), Long\_pickup_{co}(E)) \}>$

$Partition_1^2 = < \{Unstack_{co}(B,A), Putdown_{co}(B), Pickup_{co}(A), Stack_{co}(A,B)\},$
$\{before(Unstack_{co}(B,A), Putdown_{co}(B))$
$before(Pickup_{co}(A), Stack_{co}(A,B)),$
$before(Putdown_{co}(B), Pickup_{co}(A)) \}>$
$< \{Pickup_{co}(C), Stack_{co}(C,D) \}, \{before(Pickup_{co}(C), Stack_{co}(C,D)) \}>$
$< \{Replace\_grip_{co}(Reg,Long) \}, \{ \}>$
$< \{Long\_pickup_{co}(E), Long\_stack_{co}(E,A,C) \},$
$\{before(Long\_pickup_{co}(E), Long\_stack_{co}(E,A,C)),$
$before(Putdown_{co}(B), Pickup_{co}(C)),$
$before(Putdown_{co}(B), Replace\_grip_{co}(Reg,Long)),$
$before(Stack_{co}(A,B), Replace\_grip_{co}(Reg,Long)),$
$before(Stack_{co}(C,D), Replace\_grip_{co}(Reg,Long)),$
$before(Replace\_grip_{co}(Reg,Long), Long\_pickup_{co}(E)) \}>$

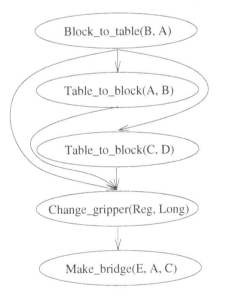

Figure 16.7: $Plan_1^1$ in $Planner_1$ - one translation of $Plan_{co}$.

Applying the mappings in Table 16.3 to the above partitions (Step 3 of plan translation algorithm), we get two plans (Figs 16.7, 16.8) in $Planner_1$ that are solutions to the query.

$Plan_l^1$

$A_l$ = $Block\_to\_table_l(B,A)$, $Table\_to\_block_l(A,B)$, $Table\_to\_block_l(C,D)$, $Change\_gripper_l(Reg, Long)$, $Make\_bridge_l(E,A,C)$

$O_l$ = $before(Block\_to\_table_l(B,A), Table\_to\_block_l(A,B))$, $before(Table\_to\_block_l(A,B), Change\_gripper_l(Reg, Long))$, $before(Table\_to\_block_l(C,D), Change\_gripper_l(Reg, Long))$, $before(Change\_gripper_l(Reg, Long), Make\_bridge_l(E,A,C))$

$Plan_l^2$

$A_l$ = $Reverse\_blocks_l(B,A)$, $Table\_to\_block_l(C,D)$, $Change\_gripper_l(Reg, Long)$, $Make\_bridge_l(E,A,C)$

$O_l$ = $before(Reverse\_blocks_l(B,A), Table\_to\_block_l(C,D))$, $before(Reverse\_blocks_l(B,A), Change\_gripper_l(Reg, Long))$, $before(Table\_to\_block_l(C,D), Change\_gripper_l(Reg, Long))$, $before(Change\_gripper_l(Reg, Long), Make\_bridge_l(E,A,C))$

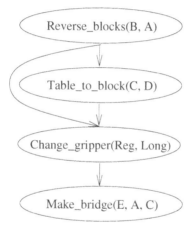

Figure 16.8: $Plan_l^2$ in $Planner_1$ - second translation of $Plan_{co}$.

# 16.5   Learning New Knowledge

On reason problem solver, $Planner_i$ sends out a query is if it does not have the knowledge necessary to solve a certain problem. In this case, the solution will contain actions that cannot be translated to the planners domain theory. Translation using just the translators in $KB_i$ will result in failure. To enable this planner to use the solution, a learning process needs to be developed.

The objective of learning is to add the new information, predicates and actions, contained in the solution plan to the domain theory of the planner.

Translators for these should also be added allowing the translation process to be completed successfully. Updating the knowledge base of a planner in this way allows the planner to utilize the solution and makes this knowledge available for future planning.

There are many ways of learning the new knowledge in a solution. Different combinations of the actions in the common ontology can result in different actions to be added to the domain theory. By learning actions that are similar to those present in the existing domain, we are adding knowledge that is at an optimal level of abstraction. The level of abstraction of knowledge is a measure of the detail that is present in the domain of a planner. A planner that uses a large degree of detail to describe a problem is at a lower abstraction level than one that uses less detail to describe the same problem.

To compare the new knowledge to the existing domain, we define a similarity index that is a measure of the similarity of two actions.

**Definition 7**   *The similarity index of action $a_{co}^q$ when compared to action $a_{co}^p$ is*

*Similarity index$(a_{co}^p, a_{co}^q)$ = no of predicates in common$(a_{co}^p, a_{co}^q)$ - no of predicates not in common$(a_{co}^p, a_{co}^q)$.*
*no of predicates in common$(a_{co}^p, a_{co}^q)$ = $|Add(a_{co}^p) \cap Add(a_{co}^q)| + |Pre(a_{co}^p) \cap Pre(a_{co}^q)|$*
*no of predicates not in common$(a_{co}^p, a_{co}^q)$ = total number of predicates$(a_{co}^p)$ + total number of predicates$(a_{co}^p)$ - 2 * no of predicates in common$(a_{co}^p, a_{co}^q)$.*
*total number of predicates$(a_{co}^p)$ = $|Add(a_{co}^p)| + |Pre(a_{co}^p)|$*

The similarity index is particularly useful when used to decide which of two actions is more similar to a third. We can say that action $a_{co}^q$ is more similar to action $a_{co}^p$ than action $a_{co}^k$ is if

Similarity index$(a_{co}^q, a_{co}^p)$ > Similarity index$(a_{co}^k, a_{co}^p)$

We also compare the similarity of two sets of actions. To compare the similarity of set $\{ a_{co}^q \}$ to $\{ a_{co}^p \}$

1.   For each action $a_{co}^j \in \{ a_{co}^q \}$

    (a)   Find the most similar action $a_{co}^k \in \{ a_{co}^p \}$

    (b)   Calculate Similarity index$(a_{co}^j, a_{co}^k)$

2.   Similarity index$(\{ a_{co}^q \}, \{ a_{co}^p \})$ =

$$\frac{\sum_{\forall a_{co}^j \in \{ a_{co}^q \}, \, a_{co}^k \in \{ a_{co}^p \}} Similarity \quad index \; (a_{co}^j, a_{co}^k)}{no \ of \ action \ in \ \{ a_{co}^q \}}$$

The learning procedure is called when the translation mechanism fails (Step 2 of plan translation). The partitions of the plan that were formed for the translation are examined. Each provides a different way to add new knowledge to the planners domain theory. The learning process chooses one of these partitions and based on its choice a set of actions and translators are learned. The translation process can use this new knowledge and complete the conversion of the plan successfully. The steps involved in learning are:

1. For each partition that is generated (Step 1 of plan translation), find the Similarity Index of the actions formed by each element of the partition when compared to $Actions_i$ in $Planner_i$.

2. Choose the partition, $Partition_{co}{}^k$, that has the highest Similarity Index.

3. For every element, $<A_{co}{}^{k-l}, O_{co}{}^{k-l}>$ in $Partition_{co}{}^k$ that does not have a mapping into the domain theory of $Planner_i$,

   (a) Form a compound action $A_i{}^{k-l}$ in the domain of $Planner_i$ that is equivalent to the subplan represented $<A_{co}{}^{k-l}, O_{co}{}^{k-l}>$.

   (b) Form a translator $T_i{}^{k-l}$ that maps $A_i{}^{k-l}$ to $<A_{co}{}^{k-l}, O_{co}{}^{k-l}>$.

4. Let $Actions_i = Actions_i \cup A_i{}^{k-l}$ and $Trans_i = Trans_i \cup T_i{}^{k-l}$.

Let us consider $Planner_1$, which sends out the following query, $Query_1$ and receives the solution $Plan_{co}$.

$Query_1$
$I_1$ = $Bigon_1(B,A)$, $Bigontable_1(A)$, $Bigontable_1(C)$, $Bigontable_1(D)$, $Bigontable_1(E)$, $Cleartop_1(B)$, $Cleartop_1(C)$, $Cleartop_1(D)$, $Cleartop_1(E)$, $Bigblock_1(A)$, $Bigblock_1(B)$, $Bigblock_1(C)$, $Bigblock_1(D)$, $Long\_block_1(E)$, $Gripper_1(Big)$
$G_1$ = $Bigon_1(A,B)$, $Bigontable_1(B)$, $Bigon_1(C,D)$, $Bigontable_1(C)$, $Bridge_1(E,A,C)$

$Plan_{co}$
$A_{co}$ = $Big\_unstack_{co}(B,A)$, $Big\_putdown_{co}(B)$, $Big\_pickup_{co}(A)$, $Big\_stack_{co}(A,B)$, $Big\_pickup_{co}(C)$, $Big\_stack_{co}(C,D)$, $Replace\_grip_{co}(Big,Long)$, $Long\_pickup_{co}(E)$, $Long\_stack_{co}(E,A,C)$
$O_{co}$ = $before(Big\_unstack_{co}(B,A)$, $Big\_putdown_{co}(B))$,
   $before(Big\_putdown_{co}(B)$, $Big\_pickup_{co}(A))$,
   $before(Big\_putdown_{co}(B)$, $Big\_pickup_{co}(C))$,
   $before(Big\_pickup_{co}(A)$, $Big\_stack_{co}(A,B))$,
   $before(Big\_pickup_{co}(C)$, $Big\_stack_{co}(C,D))$,
   $before(Big\_stack_{co}(A,B)$, $Replace\_grip_{co}(Big,Long))$,
   $before(Big\_stack_{co}(C,D)$, $Replace\_grip_{co}(Big,Long))$,
   $before(Replace\_grip_{co}(Big,Long)$, $Long\_pickup_{co}(E))$,
   $before(Long\_pickup_{co}(E)$, $Long\_stack_{co}(E,A,C))$

Partitioning the solution provides two possible ways to learn. The plan with the higher Similarity Index is chosen and the new knowledge mappings shown in Table 16.5 are added to *Planner₁*. The plan after translation is shown below.

$Plan_1^2$

$A_1$ = *Big_unstack_Big_putdown_Big_pickup_Big_stack₁(B,A),*
   *Big_pickup_Big_stack₁(C,D), Change_gripper₁(Big,Long),*
   *Make_bridge₁(E,A,C)*

$O_1$ = *before(Big_unstack_Big_putdown_Big_pickup_Big_stack₁(B,A),*
   *Big_pickup_Big_stack₁(C,D)),*
   *before(Big_unstack_Big_putdown_Big_pickup_Big_stack₁(B,A),*
   *Change_gripper₁(Big,Long)),*
   *before(Big_pickup_Big_stack₁(C,D), Change_gripper₁(Big,Long)),*
   *before(Change_gripper₁(Big,Long), Make_bridge₁(E,A,C))*

| Big_pickup_Big_stack₁(?x ?y) | Big_pickup$_{co}$(?x)> Big_stack$_{co}$(?x ?y) |
|---|---|
| Big_unstack_Big_putdown_ Big_pickup_Big_stack₁(?x ?y) | Big_unstack$_{co}$(?x ?y)> Big_putdown$_{co}$(?x) > Big_pickup$_{co}$(?y) > Big_Stack$_{co}$(?y ?x) |

Table 16.5:  New Action Mappings in KB₁

# 16.6  Related Work and Discussion

Translation in knowledge sharing has been previously explored in several works. The Tesserae Integeration Engine (TIE) [11], resolves semantic mismatches between a request and information providers. TIE uses metadata consisting of first-order rules to define the semantic relationships between different concepts. A query is posed and the metainformation converts it into simpler requests which are routed to appropriate information sources. The resulting answers are integrated. The process consists of applying the first-order rules to the query and then matching predicates in the information databases. A Name-Space Context Graph [10] is used to resolve the problem of the same term having different semantics in different information sources. It uses contexts to differentiate between name-spaces used by the individual information sources.

The theory of contexts has been formalized in [1, 3, 7, 8]. The basic relationship is *ist (c, p)* which states that proposition *p* is true in context *c*. Knowledge translation using contexts [2] is formalized in terms of truth. A translation rule relates the truth in one context to the truth in another and is an axiom of the form $ist(c_1, p_1) \leftrightarrow ist(c_2, p_2)$. Thus translation is specified as a set of first-order logic sentences each describing a rule which derives a sentence in a target context that is a translation of a sentence in a source context. This formalism is extended to address the issue of translating plans [4]. By combining planning contexts, the objective is to show that plans produced by different planners using different languages can be combined together. The plans are represented as logical sentences composed of propositions and terms. Each subplan is represented as a context and the terms used with each of these contexts may vary greatly. Lifting formulas are used to relate the propositions and terms in a subcontext to propositions and terms in another context.

Another framework, the Knowledge Interchange Interface (KII) framework [13], provides a means for knowledge sharing between heterogeneous planners. All the information that is passed between planners is translated into and out of a common ontology eliminating the need for individual translators between each pair of planners. When a planner is faced with a goal that it cannot achieve, it sends out a query (represented in the common ontology) to another planner in the network. The incoming solution will have actions and predicates that are not a part of the requesting planners knowledge base. These are integrated into the domain theory of the requesting planner along with the appropriate translators. The solution plan is translated into the local knowledge representation for use by the requesting planner.

The work presented in this paper also deals with the communication of knowledge between planners. The basic framework is based on the KII [13]. The two assumptions that the query is passed to a single remote planner and that the solution which this remote planner returns is correct, are removed. Plans consisting of predicates, actions and orderings can be converted from one representation to another by the use of translators defined. A learning mechanism allows a planner to update its knowledge base with new information that is contained in the solution plans that it receives.

# 16.7   Conclusions

The contribution of this paper is a formal methodology to translate knowledge so that plans in one representation can be utilized and learned from in another. In earlier works, both the information and the translation rules were represented using first-order logic. This formalism is not adequate for this purpose because it is unable to correctly map the orderings between actions in plans. If the action translations are not one-to-one mappings, the orderings in the translated plan are different from those in the original and must be regenerated. This has not been taken into account in earlier works. The learning mechanisms that have been developed assume that knowledge contained in a solution will be correct in a planners domain theory. They simply add the new knowledge to the planners domain. The methodology presented in this paper allows entire plans consisting of predicates, actions and orderings to be converted from one representation to another by the use of translators defined in the formalism. The paper also introduces a procedure by which new knowledge in a solution plan can be correctly added to a planners domain theory at an optimal abstraction level. Future work in this area lies in further development of this learning mechanism, a complete definition of abstraction levels and the comparison of knowledge contained in a plan to that in the domain theory of a planner.

# References

[1]  Buvac, S., Mason, I., "Propositional Logic of Context". Proceedings of the Eleventh National Conference on Artificial Intelligence, 1993.

[2]  Buvac, S.,Fikes, R. "A declarative Formalization of Knowledge Translation", Proceedings of the ACM CIKM: The 4th International Conference on Information and Knowledge Management, 1995.

[3]  Buvac, S., Buvac, V., Mason, I., "Metamathematics of Contexts". Fundamenta Informaticae, 23(3), 1995.

[4]  Buvac, S., "Combining Planning Contexts", Advanced Planning Technology - Technological Achievements of the ARPS/Rome Laboratory Planning Initiative. AAAI Press, 1996.

[5]  Davis, P.K. and Hillestad, R., "Families of Models that Cross Levels of Resolution: Issues for Design, Calibration and Management", Winter Simulation Conference, IEEE Press, 1993, pp. 1003-1012.

[6]  Fishwick, P.A., "Abstraction Level Traversal in Heirarchical Modeling", Modeling and Simulation Methodology: Knowledge Systems Paradigms (B.P.Zeigler et al., Eds.), Elsevier North Holland, New York, 1989, pp. 393-429.

[7]  Guha, R.V., "Contexts: A Formalization and Some Applications" PhD. Thesis, Stanford 1991.

[8]  McCarthy, J., Buvac, S., "Formalizing Contexts (expanded notes)", Technical Report STAN-CS-TN-94-13, Stanford University, 1994.

[9]  Moon, Y., and Zeigler, B.P., "Abstraction Methodology based on Parameter Morphisms", Enabling Technology for Simulation Science, SPIE AeoroSence97, Orlando, FL, 1997, pp. 52-63.

[10] Singh, N., Tawakol, O., Geneserath, M., "A Name-Space Context Graph for Multi-Context, Multi-Agent Systems", Proceedings of the 1995 AAAI Fall Symposium Series, Cambridge, MA, Nov 1995, pp. 79-84.

[11] Singh, N., "Unifying Heterogeneous Information Models", Communications of the ACM, May 1998, Vol.41 No.5, pp. 37-44.

[12] Takahashi, S., "General Morphism for Modeling Relations in Multimodeling", Transactions of the Society for Computer Simulation 1996, Vol.13 No.4, pp. 169-178.

[13] Wong, V., Britanik, J., and Marefat, M., "Knowledge Sharing for Planning: The Knowledge Interchange Interface", Proceedings of the 1995 International Symposium on Assembly and Task Planning (ISATP'95). Pittsburgh, PA., August 1995, pp. 28-33.

[14] Zeigler, B.P., "Towards a Formal Theory of Modeling and Simulation: Structure Preserving Morphisms", Journal of the ACM, 1972, Vol.19 No.4, pp. 742-746.

[15] Zeigler, B.P., "Object-Oriented Simualtion with Heirarchical, Modular Models: Intelligent Agents and Endomorphic Systems", Academic Press Inc., 1990.
[16] Zeigler, B.P., "Review of Theory in Model Abstraction", Enabling Simulation Technology for Simulation Science, 13th SPIE, Orlando, FL, 1998.

# Chapter 17

# Towards a Systems Methodology for Object-Oriented Software Analysis

## H. Praehofer

Although the Unified Process for software development is regarded as an important advancement in software engineering practice, it also shows several deficiencies. Especially, for analysis of embedded systems, where the main task is to capture the dynamic behavior of the system, the classical Unified Process does not provide much help. This paper presents several improvements and extensions of the Unified Process which originated from a systems theory background. In particular, it gives guidelines how to define and describe use cases, proposes a general architecture for embedded systems, and shows how to build information models as abstractions of dynamic processes.

## 17.1 Introduction

UML is rapidly establishing itself as a standard for analysis and design of object oriented software. It defines a rich set of modeling formalisms for describing object oriented software and systems [2]. And it defines the Unified Process as a standard software development process [11].

Although the UML modeling language and the Unified Process are considered to be a step into the right direction, they suffer from several severe deficiencies. For example, the Unified Process gets quite vague when the task is to identify use cases, to find an appropriate state set for a model, or to find an abstraction of a real system. With the increasing importance of embedded systems – software systems which are coupled and interact online with a real physical process – those deficiencies become more and more apparent.

System modeling [22, 20, 12] with its affinity to control theory has a long history in developing methods and concepts for complex system design. Many interesting applications have been developed for demanding control problems [7, 8, 19, 20, 9]. Recent developments in robotics [3] embedded software systems

[1, 6], integrated information systems [10], and multi-agent systems [5, 14] show much resemblance to those advanced applications. In this article we show how a rigorous system modeling methodology can help in improving current object oriented analysis and design practice.

First, the UML method is discussed from a system modeling perspective and the deficiencies of the UML development process are pointed out. Then, an improved design process is presented which is based on system modeling concepts. The advantages of the improved design process are demonstrated through the development of an analysis model for an elevator control system.

## 17.2    The Unified Software Development Process

The Unified Process [11] is a software development process which has been defined in continuation of the definition of Unified Modeling Language [2] as a standard for modeling object oriented software. It is supposed to be a generic framework for developing software in many different domains. It has grown out of the Objectory use case driven design process initially defined by Jacobson [10].

The most distinctive characteristic of the Unified Process is that it is requirement-driven. The *use case model* is supposed to define the requirements posed on the system and is intended to drive the whole development process (Figure 17.1). In particular, the functional requirements for the system being developed are stated in the form of *use cases*, which define *interactions* of users with the system in fulfillment of a particular task.

The use case model forms the basis for the further development process as shown in Figure 17.1.

- The analysis model is specified as an initial object structure in the form of UML class and object diagrams which is able to realize the behavior specified in the use cases.
- The design model represents a blueprint of the system to fulfill the requirements. It defines in detail the class and object structures as well as their interactions and dynamic behavior to realize the use cases. It also has to consider all the non-functional requirements posed on the system.
- The implementation model is the realization of the system in form of program code.
- The deployment model represents the architecture of the execution environment to run the software.

- The test model consists of the test cases to verify that the system fulfills all the requirements. The test cases can directly be derived from the use case descriptions.

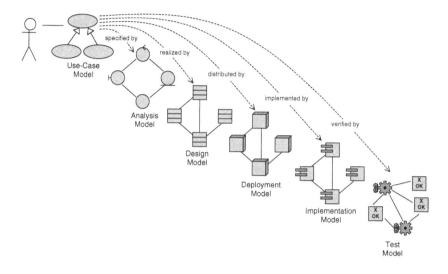

Figure 17.1: Unified Process (from [11])

Besides use cases, architectures play a dominant role in the Unified Process. An architecture embodies the most significant static and dynamic aspects of a the system [11]. Architecture gives the system an initial and overall structure. Architectures represent an important design knowledge orthogonal to use cases. While use cases cast the functions of the system, the architecture gives the system *form*. Both are essential for a system realization. The use cases must be realized within the architecture and the architecture has to provide room for their realization.

The Unified Process is also component-based. The software system is built up of components which have well defined interfaces. Reusable building blocks should be identified during the design process. The building blocks then do not have to be further elaborated but can be reused as is.

## Use case model

The use case model is supposed to capture all the requirements posed on the system from a users/customer perspective. It consists of the definition of the *actors*, i.e., all the components which are outside the system but interact with it in some form, the definition of the *system boundary* through which the actors communicate with the system, and the *use cases*.

Use cases themselves should describe the interaction of the actors with the system in fulfillment of a particular task. They do this by adopting a Black Box view, in that the inputs to and responses from the system are defined, but the interior of the system is concealed. In the Unified Process the input/output behavior captured in the use cases is event-based (Figure 17.2).

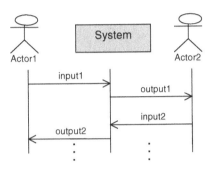

Figure 17.2: Use case as input/output description between actors and the system

## Analysis model

Setting up an analysis model is the first step in the development of the system. The analysis model is intended to define a first structure of the system to be designed in the form of a class and/or an object diagram. The analysis model, therefore, represents an important step in the development process because it gives the system its initial structure which is subject to further refinement in later development steps.

According to the Unified Process, the development of the analysis model has to occur on the basis of the use case specifications. The analysis model has to capable to fulfill the functional requirements stated in the use case descriptions.

The Unified Process gives several guidelines how objects and classes for the analysis model can be found. Domain representation or conceptual modeling [13] is derived from the idea that objects in reality can also be found in the software system. A textual analysis of the problem specification is proposed to be used to filter out objects together with relevant attributes, associations, and operations. Furthermore, the Unified Process suggests to distinguish three types of objects:

- *Interface objects*: are objects to cope with the communication with the actors. They directly correspond to the actor/system interfaces.
- *Entity objects*: are objects to hold information. They often correspond to the objects in reality and can be found by conceptual domain modeling as discussed above.
- *Control objects*: are those objects which coordinate and allocate work between the different objects in fulfillment of a particular use case.

## 17.2.1 Deficiencies of the Unified Process

Although the Unified Process represents a step into the right direction, in everyday practice and also in teaching we have found several severe deficiencies. Those are as follows:

- *How to find use cases*: The Unified Process does not give useful guidelines how to find relevant use cases. It recommends that user sessions are use cases. This however is not practical for embedded systems where actors continually interact with the system.
- *How to find the objects*: We found conceptual modeling inappropriate for complex system analysis and design. First of all, textual problem specifications for complex domains are either not available at all or much too voluminous to lend themselves to textual analysis. A direct derivation of objects types with data structure and behavior from textual descriptions is not practical. The classification of objects into interface objects, entity objects, and control objects can only serve as a crude guideline for modeling.
- *What are useful architectures for analysis*: Although the Unified Process stresses the importance of architectures in the development process, it does not state what useful architecture for analysis models are, nor how such can be found. Software architectures [4, 17], however, either deal with architectures for design, viz. providing useful initial structures to cope with realization issues, or are restricted to very particular application domains, e.g. classical control systems [1].

In the following we will outline ideas how those deficiencies can be overcome. The ideas originate from the systems background [22, 20, 12] which affords a precise methodology for building models and designing systems. Therefore, in the following we review a system modeling methodology and then show how this can be used for object oriented software analysis and design.

# 17.3    A Short Review of the System Modeling Methodology

In this section system modeling methodology is introduced briefly in a rather informal manner. This will provide some background knowledge which will help to clarify the concepts for object oriented analysis introduced in the subsequent sections. For a more detailed exposition and formal treatment of the systems theory modeling methodology the interested reader is referred to [22, 20, 12].

### 17.3.1 Hierarchy of System specifications

Systems theory deals with a hierarchy of system specifications which defines levels at which a system may be known or specified. Table 17.1 shows this hierarchy of system specifications (simplified and adapted from [22].)

| Level | Name | What we know at this level |
|-------|------|----------------------------|
| 0 | I/O Frame | Input and output variables and ports together with allowed values |
| 1 | I/O Behavior | Allowed behavior of the system from an external Black Box view |
| 2 | I/O System | System with state and state transitions to generate the behavior |
| 3 | Coupled Systems | System built up by several component systems which are coupled |

Table 17.1 Levels of System Knowledge.

At level 0 we deal with the input and output interface of a system.

At level 1 we deal with purely observational recordings of the behavior of a system. This is an I/O relation which consists of a set of pairs of input behaviors and associated output behaviors.

At level 2 the system is described by state space and state transition functions. The transition function describes the state-to-state transitions caused by the inputs and the outputs generated thereupon.

At level 3 a system is specified by a set of components and a coupling structure. The components are system on their own with their own state set and state transition functions. A coupling structure defines how those interact. A property of coupled system which is called "closure under coupling" guarantees that a coupled system at level 3 itself specifies a system. This property allows hierarchical construction of systems, i.e., that coupled systems can be used as components in bigger coupled systems.

## 17.3.2 Modeling

The essence of modeling lies in establishing relations between pairs of system descriptions. These relations pertain to the validity of representation of a real system by a model and the validity of a system description at one level of specification relative to a system description at a higher, lower, or equal level of specification.

Based on the arrangement of system levels as shown in Table 17.1, we distinguish between vertical and horizontal relations. A vertical relation is called an *association mapping* and takes a system at one level of specification and generates its counterpart at another level of specification. The downward motion in the structure-to-behavior direction, formally represents the process by which the behavior of a model is generated. This is relevant in simulation and testing when the model generates the behavior which then can be compared with the desired behavior.

The opposite upward mapping relates a system description at a lower level with one at a higher level of specification. While the downward association of specifications is straightforward, the upward association is much less so. This is because in the upward direction information is introduced while in the downward direction information is reduced. Many structures exhibit the same behavior and recovering a unique structure from a given behavior is not possible. The upward direction, however, is fundamental in the design process where a structure (system at level 3) has to be found which is capable to generate the desired behavior (system at level 1).

The horizontal relations relate systems at the same level of specification. We call such a relation a *preservation relation* or *system morphism* because it establishes a correspondence between a pair of systems whereby features of the one system are preserved in the other.

## 17.3.3 System morphisms as a fundamental means for building abstractions

For system morphisms, we take the point of view is illustrated in Figure 17.3, where $S$ represents a detailed model and $S'$ represents a coarse model. Accordingly, the basic orientation is that a part of the behavior of the big system $S$ is mapped on the little system $S'$.

For valid abstractions it is required that the state transitions in the detailed model and the coarse model stay in correspondence with respect to related input behaviors. This is shown in Figure 17.3 (b). Subsets of states of the detailed state space are mapped to states in the coarse state space by function $h$. When one feeds the detailed system with a sequence of inputs and the coarse system with a corresponding input sequence (map $g$), and the systems are in corresponding states $q_0$ and $q_0'$ under $h$ initially, then we require that the resulting system states $q_f$ and $q_f'$ also correspond under $h$.

Abstractions always have to be built with clear objectives in mind. Only with given objectives, which states the purpose the model, it is decidable if a model validly represents a real system. Therefore, in modeling, first the objectives have to be stated. Based on the objectives a valid model can be derived.

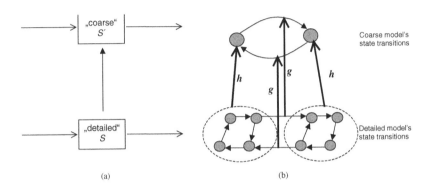

Figure 17.3: Morphisms between a detailed model and a coarse model

## 17.3.4  Use case driven design in the system modeling perspective

The use case driven design process compares to the system methodology as use cases are a special form to record I/O behaviors. And object oriented models with associations and collaborations represent system descriptions at the coupled system level. Object oriented analysis is a process to go from behavior to structure, from use case descriptions to an object oriented class/object diagram.

The main deficit of current object oriented modeling practice compared to the system methodology is its vague concept of building abstractions. In particular in dynamic modeling, concepts for building abstractions are missing. The following is an improved software development process. Although presented in a very informal and pragmatic manner, it finds its background in systems modeling methodology. In particular, the system morphism is taken as a background concept for building software abstractions of real world processes.

# 17.4 Improved Software Development Process

The proposed improvements of the standard Unified Process for software development follow three main lines:

- instead of the usual user-centered approach, a system-centered approach to find and cast use cases
- a general architecture for analysis models of embedded systems which suggests a more fine grained classification of objects
- an approach to model entity objects based on interface descriptions and system morphism concepts.

## 17.4.1 System-centered approach for use case descriptions

Use cases usually describe the interaction of one or more actors with the system in fulfillment of a particular task. This user-centered view, however, often is not very practical when it is not clear when a particular task begins and ends nor is there a clear flow of events in-between. For example, lets assume an elevator control system to be the target of our design (see section 5). Obviously, the task is to transport people between floors. In the usual user-centered view of use case descriptions, one would try to describe a use case from the call of the elevator by a user until the delivery of the passenger at the destination floor. The attempt to do so soon leads to severe problems. After the user's call of the elevator by pressing a button, it is not obvious what happens to the elevator. Too many variations exist dependent on the current status of the elevator, i.e., is the elevator at the floor, parked or busy, approaching or leaving the floor, etc. Normally, there will be no direct reaction of the elevator to this call but the call will be registered only and serviced when it is time to do so.

Much more practical in this case is too adopt a *system-centered* approach for identifying and describing use cases. Such an approach leads to use cases which clearly describe the system's input/output behavior. In a system-centered approach one proceeds as follows:

- First try to get an understanding of the interfaces to the system, in particular, which events are triggered by the actors and which by the system.
- Then look for events which initiate behaviors which will lead to state changes within the software system; such events may come from some actor or come from the system itself (and then are scheduled.)
- Finally, set up the use case for the input/output behavior following the triggering event.

In this way collect a set of input/output specifications to get a clear description of the input/output behavior of the system.

## 17.4.2 Architecture for embedded systems

In distinction and as elaboration to the Unified Process we propose a principal architecture for embedded systems as shown in Figure 17.4. The architecture finds its background in the classical control engineering domain [3, 1]. It tries to generalize these ideas, and transfers them to the object oriented modeling context. It identifies several different object types, which store information and several different control, and interface objects, which are responsible to realize the behavioral aspect of the system, i.e., realize the event flow through the system to update the information structures.

In the architecture information objects of different types are distinguished as follows:

- *State objects*: State objects are similar to entity objects. They have to interpret the inputs and measurements from the real system and store information about the real system behavior.
- *Result objects*: Result objects are objects which store computations. Usually they summarize or filter the state information to report those to the upper level.
- *Task and planning objects*: Those objects are supposed to store tasks and goals received from the upper level. Also planning data may be generated based on the tasks received.
- *Control models*: Control models are used to carry out the control tasks. The planned tasks are broken down into concrete control sequences which contain the sequences of commands which have to be issued to the lower level system. Based on the feedback messages received and the state updates, the control models have to be able to decide on the actions.

Several interface and control objects take over the responsibility to update the information structures accordingly and realize the flow of events through the system in fulfillment of a particular use case. They are as follows:

- *Command interpreter*: Command interpreters receive commands and goals from the superior layer and generate tasks and plans and store them in the planning data base.
- *Task sequencer*: A task sequencer will select tasks or plans from the data base and forward those to the control model which are responsible to execute those.

- *Command generator*: The command generators read the information from the control models and issue commands to the lower level system.
- *Input interpreter*: The input interpreters function as input interface objects to the real system. They encapsulate the transformation of sensor data into higher level information or handle the feedbacks received from the subordinate workers. Based on the information received they update the internal state information. They also supervise the reactions from the real system for errors.
- *Result calculator*: The result calculators observe the state information gathered and compute from those higher level information, i.e., they prepare information for usage at the higher levels. Often this means filtering relevant information out of the magnitude of available state information or computing summary statistics.
- *Report generator*: The report generator reads the results computed and forwards those to the interested upper level components.
- *Coordinator*: Finally, one or more coordinators are employed as central control objects which have the responsibility to coordinate the whole process. In particular, they check if the observed process run is in correspondence with the planned one and, if necessary, update the planning data accordingly.

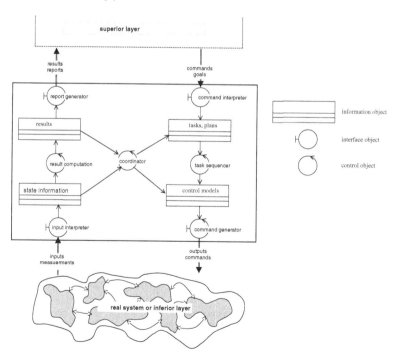

Figure 17.4: Architecture for embedded system

The proposed architecture gives a guideline which objects may be useful and what kind of function they have. Dependent on the application in hand, objects may be missing or one object may take over of role of several object types. The designer's task is to decide upon this individually.

### 17.4.3  System morphisms as a means to build information models

The concrete derivation of the information objects in the architecture follows the principles of building model abstractions based on the system morphism concept as outlined in Section 3. The concrete abstraction level thereby is clearly determined by the input/output interface of the system. Modeling then is guided by the input/output behavior descriptions given in the use cases augmented by knowledge known and assumptions taken about the real system behavior. Let us clarify those principles by looking more closely at the different types of information objects in the architecture.

The state information objects are supposed to store the information about the current status of the real system. This information is based on the inputs and measurements the software receives from the real system. Obviously, there is a direct correspondence between the inputs received and the information the system can have about the status of the real process. The inputs together with the knowledge we have about the real system behavior define the state information objects. Actually, the state information objects should be seen as abstractions of the real system behavior. The state changes in those models are triggered by the inputs and measurements received (Figure 17.5).

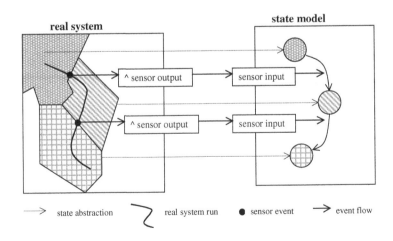

Figure 17.5: real system and state information models

On the other side, the output interface to the upper level will determine the abstractions required for the result objects. The upper level will determine the types of information it is interested in. The real process run has to be abstracted to a level which only gives this relevant information. For example, the upper level might be interested only in some performance indexes, like tasks fulfilled in a particular time, or it might be interested if the system is functioning correctly or not. Any details of the current process status then should be abstracted away. Therefore, knowing the output interface to the upper layer, gives us also the information about the abstraction level and the information to gather (Figure 17.6).

The control output interface to the system gives us the information about the control models. The control models represent the real system in the view of the sequence of operations required to fulfill a particular task. In case of feedback control, control objects are merged with state information objects. Then we obtain models as shown in Figure 17.7. The control models actually are inverse abstract images of the real system [21] where command inputs to the real system are the outputs of the control models. Then the state transitions are triggered by the sensor events coming from the real system.

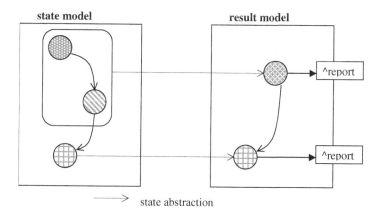

Figure 17.6: State information models and result objects

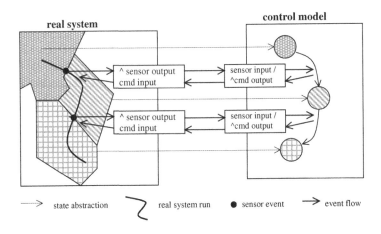

Figure 17.7: Real system and inverse control model

Modeling of the planning data usually is more complex and less obvious (dependent on the sophistication of the planning process planning data may be trivial, e.g., in pure reactive systems, or arbitrary complex, e.g., in deliberative agents.) Planning data has to represent the output commands to issue to fulfill a set of tasks in the assumption that the system will behave in a certain way in the future. Actually, planning data represents the "future" of the system that is supposed to be the best way to perform the tasks.

To set up object structures for planning data therefore has to consider different kinds of interfaces, i.e., the command sequences possible (modeled in the control model objects), the information about the real system behavior (available from the state information objects), and the task received from the upper level. Those different types of information have to be combined to represent the plans for the future operation of the system.

## 17.5   Application Example: Elevator Control System

The software development process outlined in Section 4 is demonstrated by showing the steps in developing a control system for an elevator. Passengers are transported by an elevator between several floors. They call the elevator using call buttons in the floors. When an elevator arrives in a floor, the door is opened and the new passengers determine their destination floors by buttons within the elevator. The task is to develop a control system to control the motor and the door based on the calls from the passengers. Although the application is kept simple, it is capable to demonstrate the process and reflect on the main ideas.

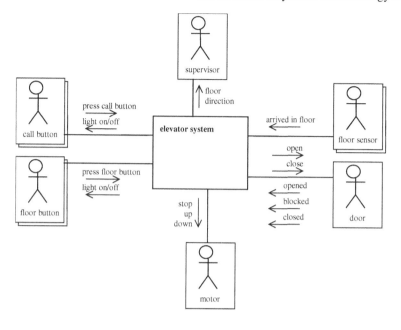

Figure 17.8: Actors and input/output interfaces

## *Defining the system environment and the input/output interactions*

As proposed, initially the system environment and the input/output interface of the system are elaborated. Figure 17.8 shows the interaction events between the various actors and the system. The actors correspond to the hardware components which directly influence or are influenced by the system. Those are:

- the buttons for calling the elevator
- the buttons in the elevator to define the destination floors
- the sensors to signal the arrivals of the elevator in the floors
- the door which contains sensors to signal that the door is open and closed, a light barrier to signal that the door is blocked, as well as a motor to open and close it
- the motor to move the elevator up and down
- a supervisor which gets status reports on the elevator.

Those actors interact with the system with various events as shown in Figure 17.8.

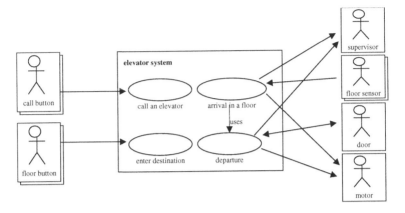

Figure 17.9: Use cases for the elevator control system

## *Identifying and describing use cases*

As a next step, use cases have to be identified by looking for events – external events from the user or internal time scheduled events – which initiate some processes. In this application the following events initiate processes within the elevator control system and directly give indication on use cases:

- *Call an elevator*: Pressing the call button usually will only lead to a registration of the call. Only when the lift is idle and parked, it will be started to service the call immediately.
- *Enter destination*: Pressing the floor button will register the floor as a destination floor.
- *Arrival in a floor*: A signal of an arrival of the elevator in a floor initiates the use case that the elevator eventually stops at the floor, opens the door, and allows people to leave the elevator and new passengers to enter. We assume that this use case is finished with the schedule of a departure event and the "departure" use case follows.
- *Departure*: This use case is initiated by the scheduled departure event within the elevator control system. The door is closed, the direction is determined, and the elevator starts to the next destination floor.

Figure 17.9 shows the resulting use case diagram. Knowing the set of use cases, allows to describe those in detail. Figure 17.10 shows the "arrival in a floor" use case by a sequence diagram.

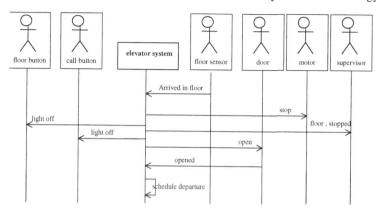

Figure 17.10: Use case "arrival in a floor"

## Finding the information objects

Having a clear understanding of the interfaces to and interactions with the various actors, puts us into the position to easily derive the relevant information objects. Exploiting the information contained in the interactions the following information objects can be derived:

- *Planning objects* (Figure 17.11 (a)): Obviously the calls for elevators as well as the desired destination floors entered by pressing the buttons represent tasks the elevator is supposed to carry out. The call buttons give us the information for which floors open calls exist. This information is stored by object `OpenCalls` which has two sets of floors for which open calls exist up and down. Analogously, an object `DestinationFloors` contains a set of floors where passengers desire to be shipped.

- *State information objects* (Figure 17.11 (b)): The sensor inputs showing the arrivals in the floors and status information about the door provide information about the current behavior of the elevator. Two objects `Elevator` and `DoorStatus` are supposed to store this information. The `Elevator` object has a reference to the floor object which represents the current floor at which the elevator resides. The `DoorStatus` object stores the information about current status of the door using an enumeration attribute.

- *Control model objects* (Figure 17.11 (c)): The outputs to the motor as well as to the door are control commands and therefore have to be handled by control models. The `MotorControl` object shown in Figure 17.11 (c) works without feedback. It is triggered by commands `goUp`, goDown, doStop and forwards those commands to the motor. Note, although this control model is simple, it is useful to filter out forbidden control sequences, e.g., that an up command directly follows a down command. The DoorControl model is a control model with feedback. Therefore, the state information of the DoorStatus object is merged into the DoorControl model. The model receives inputs closeDoor and openDoor from other parts of the elevator control system and forwards those to the door. And it receives feedbacks open, closed and blocked from the door. Note, how the control model reflects the expected behavior of the door, i.e., it is an "inverse model of the door".

- *Result objects* (Figure 17.11 (d)): Finally the outputs to the supervisor as well as the button lights turned on and off report on the current performance of the system. The lights status directly corresponds to the planning objects and therefore no additional result objects are required. The StatusInfo object gathers the information for the supervisor from other objects within the system. The floor last visited is stored as an association to a Floor object. The current direction corresponds to the state of the MotorControl object.

## Putting it together: Realizing the use case behaviors

The final task in the development of an analysis model is to model the behaviors specified in the use cases on the basis of the information structures developed, that is in system terms, deriving the structure to generate the behavior. This incorporates the introduction of interface and control objects, where necessary, or assigning interface and control object responsibilities to information objects. Collaboration diagrams are a useful modeling means to develop the use case realizations.

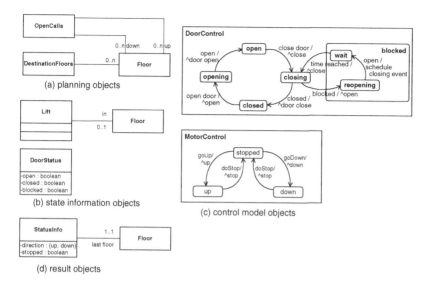

Figure 17.11: Information objects in the elevator system

In Figure 17.12 this is demonstrated for the "arrival in floor" use case. A central Coordinator control object and a FloorSensIO interface object have been introduced. All other interface and control tasks have been assigned to information objects (indicated by respective stereotype symbols in the information objects.)

The use case is handled as follows (compare signal flow in Figure 17.12): The FloorSensIO object receives the signal of an arrival at a floor (1). It updates the state information in the Elevator and StatusInfo objects (2). Then it forwards the event to the central Coordinator object which further handles the arrival (3). The Coordinator initiates deletions of registrations of this floors as open call (4) or destination floor (5). Then the elevator is stopped (6) and the opening of the door is initiated (7). The use case ends with a schedule of a departure event (8).

# 17.6 Summary

In this paper we have presented an extended and improved process for object oriented analysis of embedded systems. This methodology has its background in the systems modeling methodology, in particular, it uses system morphisms as a means for building abstractions of dynamic systems.

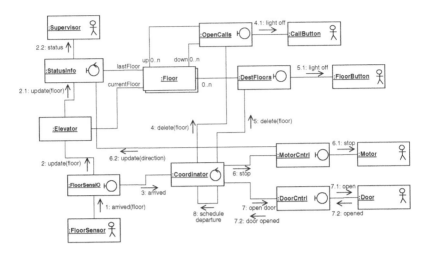

Figure 17.12: Collaboration for "arrival in floor" use case

The main points of the process are a system-centered approach for finding and describing use cases which lead to a clear input/output behavior description of the system, a general architecture for analysis models which takes into account the various types of information flows in and out of the system, and an approach to model information objects based on the system morphisms.

The approach has been demonstrated by the development of a control system for an elevator. The example is kept simple for demonstrative purposes. However, we have found that the approach naturally extends to more complex systems and also to systems which are not of the classical control type. We have studied applications in domains like steal production automation, automated manufacturing, software systems to support business processes, integrated information systems, health care systems, and others. Students who were taught the process with one case study were able to apply it successfully in other application domains.

We regard component based programming, as defined for example in the JavaBeans standard [18], to be an appropriate implementation model which complements the proposed software development approach. The structural principles of the proposed architecture combined with the programming concepts for building reusable components leads to improved software structures with a clear separation of concerns. Furthermore, the relations between objects established during the modeling process – like the information that a state information model has been derived based on some sensor interface or that planning objects are based on certain control models and command interfaces – can be exploited to represent compatibility of components. This allows for the creation of families of software components for a domain. Our future research will go into this direction.

# References

[1] Albus, J. S., *RCS: A Reference Model Architecture Demo III*. National Institute of Standards and Technology, Gaithersburg, MD, NISTIR 5994, 1997.

[2] Booch, G., Rumbaugh, J., and Jacobson, I., *The Unified Modeling Language User's Guide*, Addison Wesley, 1999.

[3] Brooks, R. A., "Intelligence Without Representation," *Artificial Intelligence Journal* (47), 1991, pp. 139--159.

[4] Buschmann, F., Meunier, R., Rohnert, H., Sommerlad, P., and Stal, M., *A System of Patterns*, Wiley, 1996.

[5] *FIPA – Foundations for Intelligent Physical Agents*, FIPA 97 Spacification, Geneva, Switzerland, October 1998.

[6] Hayes-Roth, B., Pfleger, K., Lalanda, P., Morignot, P. and Balabanovic, M., A Domain-Specific Software Architecture for Adaptive Intelligent Systems. IEEE Transactions on Software Engineering, Vol. 21, No. 4, April 1995, pp. 288-301.

[7] Jacak, W. and Rozenblit, J.W., Automatic Simulation of a Task-Oriented Robot Program for a Sequential Technological Process, *Robotica*, 34, 45-56, 1992.

[8] Jacak, W. and Rozenblit, J.W., CAST Tools for Intelligent Control in Manufacturing Automation. In: *Lecture Notes in Computer Science* No. 763, (Eds. F. Pichler and R. Moreno-Diaz), 203-219, Springer-Verlag, 1994.

[9] Jacak, W., *Intelligent Robotic Systems*, Kluwer Academic/Plenum Publisher, 1999.

[10] Jacobson, I., Christenson, M., Jonsson, P. and Övergaard, G., *Object Oriented Software Engineering*, Addison Wesley, 1992.

[11] Jacobson, I., Booch, G., and Rumbaugh, J., *The Unified Software Development Process*, Addison Wesley, 1999.

[12] Klir, G.J., *Architecture of Systems Complexity*, Sauders, NewYork, 1985.

[13] Larman, G., *Applying UML and Patterns*, Prentice Hall, 1998.

[14] O'Hare, G.M.P. and Jennings, N.R. (Eds.), *Foundations of Distributed Artificial Intelligence*. Wiley Interscience, 1996.

[15] Praehofer, H., Jacak, W., Jahn, G., and Haider, G.,"Supervising Manufacturing System Operation by DEVS-based Intelligent Control", *AIS* '94, Gainesville, FL, IEEE/CS Press, Dec. 1994, pp. 221-226.

[16] Rozenblit, J.W. and Zeigler, B.P., Design and Modeling Concepts, In: *International Encyclopedia of Robotics*. (Ed. R. Dorf), 308-322, John Wiley and Sons, New York, 1988.

[17] Shaw, M. and Garlan, D., *Software Architecture - Perspectives of an Emerging Discipline*, Prentice Hall, 1996.

[18] Sun Microsystems: *JavaBeans 1.01 API Specification*. Sun Microsystems, Inc., 1997. see http://java.sun.com/Beans/spec.html

[19] Zeigler, B.P., Cellier, F.E. and Rozenblit, J.W., Design of a Simulation Environment for Laboratory Management by Robot Organizations, *Journal of Intelligent and Robotic Systems*, 1(1), 299-309, 1988.

[20] Zeigler, B.P., *Object Oriented Simulation with Modular Hierarchical Models*. Academic Press, 1990.

[21] Zeigler, B.P, Song, H.S, Kim, T.G, and Praehofer, H. "DEVS Framework for Modeling, Simulation, Analysis, Design of Hybrid Systems," *Lecture Notes in Computer Science: Hybrid Systems II*, pp. 529-551, Springer, 1995.

[22] Zeigler, B.P., Praehofer, H., and Kim, T.G., *Theory of Modeling and Simulation, 2nd Edition*. Academic Press, 2000.

# Index